27.50

Chiao Hung and the Restructuring
of Neo-Confucianism in the Late Ming

Neo-Confucian Studies
sponsored by
The Regional Seminar in Neo-Confucian Studies,
Columbia University

Chiao Hung
and the Restructuring
of Neo-Confucianism
in the Late Ming

Edward T. Ch'ien

New York   Columbia University Press   1986

Columbia University Press
New York   Guildford, Surrey
Copyright © 1986 Columbia University Press
All rights reserved

Printed in the United States of America

The author and publisher gratefully acknowledge the generous
support toward publication given them by the National
Endowment for the Humanities and the Pacific Cultural
Foundation.

The Andrew W. Mellon Foundation, through a special grant, has
also assisted the Press in publishing this volume.

This book is Smyth-sewn and printed on permanent and durable
acid-free paper

Library of Congress Cataloging in Publication Data

Ch'ien, Edward T.
    Chiao Hung and the restructuring of Neo-Confucianism in the
late Ming.

    (Neo-Confucian studies)
    Bibliography: p.
    Includes index.
    1. Neo-Confucianism. 2. Chiao, Hung, 1541–1620.
I. Title. II. Series.
B127.N4C497 1985   181'.09512   85-7693
ISBN 0-231-06022-X (alk. paper)

To Three Teachers
James B. Parsons, Jr.
Donald M. Lowe
Wm. Theodore de Bary

Contents

Acknowledgments

I wish to express special appreciation to my three teachers to whom this book is dedicated: Professor James B. Parsons, Jr., whose expertise in the Ming period stimulated my initial interest in early modern Chinese history; Professor Donald M. Lowe, from whom I have learned that thinking need not be positivistic and that intellectual history is indeed possible as a disciplined form of knowledge; and Professor Wm. Theodore de Bary, who, as my mentor at Columbia and the primary driving force for the development of Neo-Confucian studies in this country, has taught me that the Chinese intellectual tradition is worth pursuing not only because it is historically meaningful and relevant as a scholarly concern but because it is philosophically significant as a humanistic undertaking.

During my career as a graduate student at Columbia, I benefited a great deal from the instruction of Professors Yoshito S. Hakeda and Philip B. Yampolsky, who initiated me into the technicalities of Chinese Buddhist texts. Without the training I have received from them, a large portion of this book could not have been written. I thank them profoundly. I am also deeply indebted to Professor Wing-tsit Chan, whom I cannot formally claim as my teacher but from whom I have learned immensely through his voluminous writings on Chinese philosophy and his critical reading of an early draft of this book.

Many friends and colleagues have helped with this book. I should like particularly to thank Dr. Irene T. Bloom and

Professor David T. Roy, who read the first draft with meticulous care and sensitivity. Their constructive criticisms have saved me from a number of embarrassing errors. Professors Guy S. Alitto, Ping-ti Ho, Leo Ou-fan Lee, and Tang Tsou also read the first draft either in part or in its entirety and offered many helpful comments for which I am grateful. My thanks also go to the staff of the Far Eastern Library of the University of Chicago, especially to Mr. James K. M. Cheng and Mr. Wen-pai Tai for their help in obtaining copies of rare books from across the Pacific and to Mr. Tai-loi Ma for his generous bibliographical counsel. Matthew A. and Amy Sanders Levey prepared the index. Their assistance is much appreciated.

Three of my previously published articles have been incorporated into this book, and I am grateful to the editors and publishers concerned for permission to use this material: "Chiao Hung and the Revolt Against Ch'eng-Chu Orthodoxy," in Wm. Theodore de Bary et al., *The Unfolding of Neo-Confucianism* (New York: Columbia University Press, 1975); "The Neo-Confucian Confrontation with Buddhism: A Structural and Historical Analysis," *Journal of Chinese Philosophy* (1982) 9; and "The Conception of Language and the Use of Paradox in Buddhism and Taoism," *Journal of Chinese Philosophy* (1984) 11.

Finally, I wish to thank my wife, Anne, who, as a fellow-traveler in Chinese intellectual history, has often performed the frustrating and thankless job of being my constant critic. She has contributed much more to this book than she would take credit for.

CHAPTER ONE

The Problem

Rectification of Names

THOUGH IT FOCUSES on a single individual, this book is concerned with three broad issues in late Ming: syncretism, especially as it prevailed among the Neo-Confucians; the historical controversy between the Ch'eng-Chu and Lu-Wang schools of Neo-Confucianism; and the emergence of "evidential research" (*k'ao-chü* or *k'ao-cheng*) as a formation. The term "syncretism" has been used frequently by scholars in religious studies. Among those who use it, however, there is no consensus on a precise definition, and in some cases there are even ambiguities in the use of the term within the work of a single scholar. For instance, Helmer Ringgren, in his article "The Problems of Syncretism," defines syncretism as "any mixture of two or more religions ... where elements from several religions are merged and influence each other mutually."[1] This definition does not explicitly distinguish syncretism as a process whereby "elements from several religions are merged" from syncretism as the result of such a process, i.e., as "any mixture of two or more religions." For the most part, Ringgren seems to have intended the term to refer to both. But he did not remain consistent in his use of the term, for in the same article he also talked about "the final product, the result of syncretism,"[2] thus restricting the meaning of syncretism to designate only the process of mixing and not the resultant mixture.

Unlike Ringgren, Ake Hultkrantz draws a distinction between syncretism as a process of mixing and its end product as the mixture. He called the latter "fusion" and reserved the term syncretism solely for "the process of religious fusion, irrespective of the presence of fusion in its advanced sense."[3] In this book, I will generally follow Hultkrantz's definition, but with a few modifications. On the one hand, I will retain Hultkrantz's distinction between the process of mixing and its end product and will use, as Hultkrantz does, the term "syncretism" only for such a process. On the other hand, I will include in the term not only the process of mixing but also a certain consciousness which offers justification for such a process. This type of consciousness, though not to be found in all those who do the mixing, nevertheless prevails among many of them and is included here not as a necessary but as a sufficient condition for syncretism.

Moreover, I will use the term "synthesis" in place of Hultkrantz's "fusion." As used in this book, "synthesis" is comparable to Hultkrantz's "fusion," defined as "complete religious amalgamation."[4] It is not, however, an overall concept for the end product of syncretism. "Fusion" or synthesis is only one kind of possible product resulting from syncretism. Although synthesis can be a product of syncretism, it bears no necessary relationship to syncretism. As will be shown, while there are cases in which both syncretism and synthesis are present, there are also cases in which there is only syncretism without synthesis or synthesis without syncretism.

Syncretism: Late Ming Departure from a Tradition

Syncretism has long had its advocates and practitioners in Chinese history. Buddhism, for instance, was accepted as another aspect of the native Taoism when it was first introduced into

China. As the cases of Prince Ying of Ch'u (d. A.D. 71) and Emperor Huan (r. 146–167) of the Eastern Han dynasty (25–220) indicate, the Buddha then was worshiped together with Confucius in the same temple that also enshrined the Yellow Emperor and Lao Tzu.[5] To some extent, this early mixture in popular religious worship of Buddhism with the native cults of Confucius and Taoist deities may be regarded as a reflection of inadequate understanding on the part of the Chinese during their initial encounter with Buddhism. Nevertheless, it persisted as a salient feature of Chinese religious practice down to modern times.[6]

In the realm of ideas, conscious efforts also began early to reconcile Buddhism as a foreign religion with the native systems of Confucianism and Taoism. Already in the latter half of the second century A.D., there appeared in eastern China the fantastic story of Lao Tzu's disappearance to the west and his conversion of the "barbarians." This story, which was systematized during the Western Chin (265–316) by the Taoist Master Wang Fu as the *Sūtra on Lao Tzu's Converting the Barbarians (Lao Tzu hua-hu ching)*, was cited repeatedly by Taoists in later times to prove the superiority of their religion over Buddhism. Initially, however, the story was intended as a justification for accepting the foreign Buddha on an equal footing with the native deities such as the Yellow Emperor and Lao Tzu.[7] As such, the *Sūtra on Lao Tzu's Converting the Barbarians* suggests in terms of a common progenitor the idea of "Three Teachings—One Source" (*san-chiao i-yüan*) which was to be reiterated throughout later Chinese history as one of the two basic justifications for asserting the oneness of the Three Teachings.

The second justification, "Different Paths—Same Ending" (*shu-t'u t'ung-kuei*), is derived from an expression in the *Book of Changes*, where it occurs as part of a commentary on hexagram 31, *Hsien* or "Influence." However, in its original context, the expression has no syncretic significance. In fact, the term *t'u* or "paths" in this instance does not even refer to schools of thought or sects of religion but to the various processes of deliberate calculation which the *Book of Changes* tries to discredit as contrary to the spontaneous operations of the universe.[8]

Nevertheless, in the post-Han periods of prolonged disunity, the expression became a syncretic formula and was widely cited as a justification for the harmonization of the Three Teachings. Hui-yüan (334–417), for instance, while defending the Buddhist doctrine of *karma* against Confucian rationalism, conceded to Confucianism a certain validity and asked his followers "not to be puzzled by the variety of paths or be afraid of their differences" because, he said, "the principle in which they meet is necessarily the same."[9] Hui-lin, though often characterized as a Buddhist renegade because of his essay "On Black and White" *(Pai-hei lun)* which was critical of Buddhism, actually acknowledged in this essay the significance of Buddhism as a teaching. He regarded the Buddhist doctrines of "compassion" *(tz'u)* and "commiseration" *(pei)* as paths which were different from but tending toward the same goal as the Confucian virtues of "truthfulness" *(hsin)* and "obedience" *(shun)*. He also considered the Buddhist Six Pāramitās *(liu-tu)*[10] to run parallel to the Confucian Five Norms *(wu-chiao)*.[11] For these reasons, he gave his essay "On Black and White" the subtitle "On [the Two Teachings as] Equally Good" *(Chün-shan lun)*.[12]

The same idea of "Different Paths—Same Ending" was also invoked by Yen Yen-chih (384–456), a Buddho-Confucian of the Sung state (420–479) in southern China. Yen distinguished three kinds of learning: "the doctrine of the Way" *(yen-tao che)*, "the theory of the mind" *(lun-hsin che)*, and "that which does the investigation of principles" *(chiao-li che)*. "The doctrine of the Way," which Yen explicitly identified with Taoism, had its basis in "Nature" *(t'ien)* and valued the "exercise of the body" *(lien-hsing)*. "The theory of the mind," which Yen equated with Buddhism, focused on men and stressed the "cultivation of the mind" as especially important. The third kind of learning, "that which does the investigation of principles," which Yen did not identify with any particular teaching but by which he presumably referred to Confucianism, centered around "matters" *(wu)* and "affairs" *(shih)*. The Three Teachings thus seemed to Yen to be different in emphasis and concern. And yet, they were identical in terms of their "essentials" *(yao)* since their differences were like those of the divergent paths which would all converge in the same terminus. "When viewed from the standpoint of perfect understanding," Yen said, "[the Three Teachings] are equally good."[13]

As the above examples indicate, there existed in China a long tradition of syncretism, the two basic ideas of which were already well developed early in the Six Dynasties (265–589). This tradition of syncretism constituted a symbolic resource from which syncretists of later periods including the Ming (1368–1644) drew for inspiration and articulation. However, although the relevance of the syncretic tradition before the Ming as a symbolic resource is not to be denied, late Ming syncretism cannot be viewed simply as its continuation. Syncretism in late Ming is unique in both strength and significance, especially in terms of its implications for the constitution of Confucianism as a philosophy. It has therefore been claimed that there was "penetration of Taoism into the Ming Neo-Confucian elite"[14] and that "only with a better understanding of these [Taoist] elements can we arrive at a real understanding of both Wang Yang-ming and the various branches of his philosophical school in Chekiang, T'ai-chou, and Kiangsi."[15] The same claim may be made for a number of late Ming Neo-Confucians with regard to Buddhism. Many members of the T'ai-chou school, such as Kuan Chih-tao (1536–1608), Li Chih (1527–1602), Yang Ch'i-yüan (1547–1599), Chou Ju-teng (1547–1629) and Chiao Hung (1540–1620), drew freely from Buddhist as well as Taoist sources to interpret the Confucian Classics.[16] They became known as "wild Ch'anists" (*k'uang-ch'an*). Yang Ch'i-yüan, in particular, has often been singled out as the first person in the Ming to have used Buddhist and Taoist ideas for writing civil service examination essays. The tendency to inject Buddhism and Taoism into Confucianism was perhaps most pronounced in the T'ai-chou school. It was not, however, confined to this school. The late Ming world of classical scholarship was full of works of commentary which were written in the syncretic vein.[17]

In this regard, late Ming syncretism is notably different from its antecedent tradition, which operated mainly in the framework of Buddho-Taoist concerns with little actual effect upon Confucianism as a philosophy. During the late Han and

early Six Dynasties periods, for instance, "matching concepts"
(*ko-i*) was a popular explanatory device through which much of
the exchange of ideas between Buddhism and Taoism took place.
It did not bring about in Confucianism any kind of philosophical
synthesis on the level of the *prajñā* ontology. Identification of
elements in Buddhism and Confucianism was sometimes done by
Buddhist monks like Hui-lin as a matter of open-mindedness
which entailed no reinterpretation of the concepts of one teaching
in terms of those of the other. Or, as in the case of Hui-yüan, it
was practiced as a conscious mechanism for proselytizing. Hui-
yüan was explicitly authorized by his master Tao-an (312–385)
to use the *Chuang Tzu* as a medium to explain Buddhism; and his
essays on *karma*, rebirth, the rights of the *saṅgha*, etc. included
quotations from the *Lao Tzu*, the *Chuang Tzu*, the *Book of
Changes* and other works of classical literature. But, in his
extensive correspondence with Kumārajīva (344–413), Hui-yüan
did not refer even once to the Chinese scriptural writings or
philosophical concepts of any kind except for a reference to *yin-
yang* which occurred only once.[18] Therefore, for monks like Hui-
yüan, allusions to the Confucian Classics were merely a means of
appealing to the cultured Chinese public. They were tactical
concessions made to the Confucians for reasons of expediency
and were not intended to impinge upon the doctrinal integrity of
Confucianism for the formulation of synthesis.

　　Awareness of the value of the Confucian Classics as a
tactical means of propaganda was most obvious in Mou Tzu, the
alleged author of the "Disposition of Error" (*Li-huo lun*). When
asked why he had drawn upon the *Book of Odes* and the *Book of
History* instead of the Buddhist sūtra to support his arguments,
Mou Tzu said,

> I have quoted these things, sir, which I knew you would under-
> stand. Had I preached the words of the Buddhist scriptures or
> discussed the essence of non-action, it would have been like
> speaking to a blind man of the five colors or playing the five sounds
> to a deaf man.[19]

Mou Tzu's purely Machiavellian use of the Classics and his blunt confession of it may be viewed as personal eccentricities not commonly shared by the Buddho-Confucians of this time, whom he was supposed to represent but whose acceptance of the Confucian canon was probably firmer than his. Nevertheless, his apologetic tone in the "Disposition of Error" was rather characteristic of the syncretic literature of that time. The Buddho-Confucians of that period continued to pair the Buddhist and Confucian elements as parallels even after *ko-i* fell into disuse as an explanatory device.[20] They also invoked in various forms the two standard ideas of syncretism to justify their pursuit of Buddhism, which they embraced alongside Confucianism but did not try to integrate with Confucianism. As an example, we may cite Yen Chih-t'ui (531–591). Yen deplored the "delusion" (*mi*) of those who "took refuge in the Duke of Chou and Confucius while turning against Buddhism." He said that the teachings of Buddhism and Confucianism were "originally of one substance" and that the Buddhist Five Precepts (*wu-chung chih-chin*)[21] were each in "perfect agreement" (*fu-t'ung*) with the Confucian Five Norms (*wu-ch'ang*).[22] In thus correlating concepts to demonstrate the fundamental oneness of Buddhism and Confucianism, Yen was following a syncretic practice which, by Yen's time, had become almost a convention among the Buddhist-inclined Confucian literati.[23] But, characteristically, Yen's syncretism occurred in an apologetic context where he tried to answer certain criticisms of Buddhism in order to affirm for his descendants its validity as a teaching. There was no fusion in doctrinal terms between these two teachings, which were in fact accepted by Yen as both valid but each in its own sphere. Yen looked to the classical tradition of Confucianism for ideal patterns of social behavior but reserved for Buddhism all systematic speculations on ultimate values and the nature of the universe.[24]

Thus, for Yen and the majority of the Buddho-Confucians of this period, the tension between Buddhism and Confucianism was resolved through a syncretic logic which was predicated upon the principle of compartmentalization. This logic presumed the idea of difference in identity and, as the harmonizing agent, managed to draw the teachings together only by keeping them apart. Essentially the same situation seems to have prevailed during most of the later periods of Chinese history. Like their predecessors in the Six Dynasties, the open-minded monks and the Buddhist-inclined Confucians of the Sui (589–618), T'ang (618–907), Sung (960–1279), and Yüan (1279–1368) dynasties asserted the oneness of the Three Teachings by balancing concepts and equating terms without attempting to involve Confucianism in a philosophical synthesis. With the monks of these later periods, syncretism was sometimes expressed in what may be regarded as an extension of the *p'an-chiao* ("judging the teachings") practice which was done in earlier times to systematize and reconcile the internal contradictions of the Buddhist doctrine,[25] but which was now used also to accommodate such non-Buddhist teachings as Confucianism and Taoism. Therefore, Chih-i (538–597) constructed not only a comprehensive system of classification to harmonize the diverse and frequently conflicting scriptures of Buddhism[26] but also an elaborate theory of "contemplating the mind" (*kuan-hsin*), into which he tried to assimilate Confucianism. Confucianism, according to Chih-i, with its Five Norms, Five Phases (*wu-hsing*), Five Classics, etc., was a "worldly dharma-medicine" (*shih-chien fa-yao*) comparable to Buddhism in having the Triple Refuge (*san-kuei*), Five Precepts, Ten Good Deeds (*shih shan-tao*), and Four Dhyānas (*ssu-ch'an*), etc.[27] It provided a "view of the temporary" (*chia-kuan*) and, when thoroughly understood, would eventually lead the practitioner to the "dharmas universally destroyed" (*p'o-fa p'ien*), which was the fourth of Chih-i's Ten Dharma-Gates (*fa-men*) of contemplating the mind.[28] In his view, Confucianism was necessary for those who were unable to achieve "profound transformation" because of their "thin and weak" capacities; and it performed in China the historical function of setting the stage for the introduction of Hīnayāna and Mahāyāna Buddhism.[29]

Tsung-mi (780–841) too, while rendering judgments on the various sects of Ch'an Buddhism in his *Chart of the Master-Disciple Succession of the Ch'an School (Ch'an-men shih-tzu ch'eng-hsi t'u)*,[30] broadened his scope in the *Treatise on the Original Nature of Men (Yüan-jen lun)* to include Confucianism and Taoism, which he discussed before he took up the "doctrine concerning man and god" *(jen-t'ien chiao)* for evaluation.[31] In his preface to this treatise, Tsung-mi stated:

> Confucius, Lao Tzu, and Shākyamuni were all perfect sages who established teachings as different paths according to the demands of the age and the needs of the various beings.

Buddhist and non-Buddhist teachings were thus different but mutually complementary. Taken as a whole, they would

> benefit people, encourage them to perfect all good deeds, clarify the beginning and end of causal relationship, penetrate all phenomena *(dharmas)*, and throw light on the relationship between root and branch by which all things come into being.

Moreover, by encouraging good deeds through the punishment of the wicked and the rewarding of the virtuous, the Three Teachings would all lead to the creation of an orderly society and should all be observed with respect. "However," Tsung-mi said, "scholars of the present day cling each to his own school so that they, and students of Buddhism as well, are perplexed as to what is the truth." To redress the "obstruction" *(chih)* and "partiality" *(p'ien)* which he felt was prevalent among his contemporaries, Tsung-mi tried in his *Treastise* "to examine all phenomena according to both Buddhist and non-Buddhist doctrines," which he scrutinized one by one by proceeding "from the superficial to the profound."[32]

Compared with the monks of the Six Dynasties, Chih-i and Tsung-mi had a syncretic consciousness which was less facile and haphazard. It was manifested as a systematic attempt to incorporate the Three Teachings into a common scheme of classification which was unitary and hierarchical. It did not, however, alter the principle of compartmentalization which characterized the logic of the earlier Buddho-Confucians. The arrangement by Chih-i and Tsung-mi of the Buddhist and non-Buddhist teachings into a unitary scheme of hierarchical order was a mechanical act of pigeonholing. It prescribed for each teaching a definite place without authorizing the transposition of ideas from one teaching to the other. Moveover, the liberal catholicity which seemed to lie at the base of the expanded *p'an-chiao* practice of Chih-i and Tsung-mi was constrained by an ultimate exclusiveness with which they guarded Buddhism as their own teaching. Therefore, Chih-i's Confucianism was a mere "worldly dharma-medicine" which provided no "ultimate cure" (*pi-ching chih*). It needed to be transcended if salvation was to be attained.[33] For Tsung-mi, the difference between the Buddhist and non-Buddhist teachings was no less vital than their complementarity; and he said in his preface to the *Treatise*,

> Although the Three Teachings equally reflect the intentions of the sages, differences exist in that there are real and provisional doctrines. . . . In going to the root of things, only Buddhism—since it examines all phenomena and, using every means, investigates their principles in an attempt to reveal their nature—is definitive and final.

Confucianism and Taoism were thus discussed by Tsung-mi in the *Treatise* only to be refuted as "delusions."[34] For both Chih-i and Tsung-mi, the purpose of syncretism was still to uphold Buddhism. They tolerated Confucianism as a non-Buddhist teaching and were no more interested than the earlier monks in engaging the Confucians in a philosophical dialogue to establish a Buddho-Confucian discourse as synthesis.

This mixture of initial tolerance with ultimate exclusiveness was a common phenomenon among the eminent monks after the Sui, who were not always such ambitious systematizers as Chih-i and Tsung-mi but who were nonetheless ostensibly all-embracing. Chih-yüan (976–1022), just to cite another example, considered the Three Teachings as the "same" (*t'ung*) in "[making people] move toward the good and depart from evil and [in helping them] overcome cruelty and weed out murder." But, he said, "[Confucianism and Taoism], though extensive and complete, only briefly point to the general aim of reaching to the spirit and investigating ultimate principles. That which fully expounds their wonders [i.e., of the spirit and of the ultimate principles] consists in the teachings of Shākyamuni."[35]

A notable exception exists, however; and in the midst of the monkish exclusiveness, Ch'i-sung (1007–1072) is conspicuous for his wholehearted acceptance of the non-Buddhist teachings of Confucianism and Taoism. Like Chih-i and many others before him, Ch'i-sung compared the Buddhist Five Precepts and Ten Good Deeds to the Confucian Five Norms.[36] But, unlike Chih-i and many others, Ch'i-sung did not insist on the sectarian necessity of Buddhism as the "ultimate" teaching. He said,

> The teachings of the sages are no more than goodness. The Way of the sages is no more than uprightness (*cheng*). When the man is upright, he is treated as a man. When the event is good, it is taken as an event. He or it does not have to be in accord with Buddhism. Nor does he or it have to be in accord with Confucianism.[37]

Thus, Ch'i-sung accepted Buddhism and Confucianism, and the doctrines of the Hundred Schools as well, as equals and considered them to be equaly indispensable for maintaining the world order because they were all "paths to goodness." "When one of these teachings is lacking," he said, "one path to goodness is lost in the world. When one path to goodness is lost, the evil in the world cannot but increase."[38]

In addition to his nonhierarchical attitude toward the non-Buddhist teachings, Ch'i-sung is also remarkable for having written a number of essays on "filiality" (*hsiao*), "rites" (*li*), "music" (*yüeh*), "public morals" (*feng-su*), and "good government" (*ta-cheng*),[39] which were characteristically Confucian concerns. The contents of these essays, however, are not nearly so memorable as the fact that they were written by a Buddhist monk. Ch'i-sung discussed these problems almost entirely in orthodox Confucian terms. As a matter of fact, with one exception, none of these essays contained even a single reference to the Buddhist scriptures or concepts. They cannot therefore be regarded as an effort to synthesize Confucianism with Buddhism. The one exception is the essay on "filiality," which is probably the most systematic and comprehensive statement on the subject by a Buddhist monk in premodern Chinese history. In this essay, Ch'i-sung tried to affirm filiality as a Confucian as well as a Buddhist virtue. "Filiality," he said, "is the beginning (*tuan*) of the [Buddhist] precepts (*śīla* or *chieh*)" and, as such, is "contained" (*yün*) in all the Five Precepts. For this reason, "in order to be sincere in [the practice of] filiality, nothing is better than cultivating the Precepts." Specifically, the precept of "nonkilling," which is the first of the five, "can [help] develop the filial son's mind for 'reverence toward death and remembrance of the remote ancestors' (*shen-chung chui-yüan*)"[40] because "nonkilling" is not just a matter of being compassionate toward all sentient beings; it embodies the "concern" (*lü*) for parents.[41] Ch'i-sung said,

> The sages thought that the spirit, in the process of change and transformation, might alternately become a man and a beast. [As a result, they asked themselves,] "With the passage of time from the ancient to the present, would there not be confusion [as to what had become of this spirit]?" The ordinary man, however, is not of himself aware of [this transformation of the spirit]. Lest the buffalo or the sheep, which they see in the present, be what has become of the spirits of their parents in the past, the sages prohibited killing. Not allowing the violation of one minute being is to be sincere in thought about one's parents.[42]

This interpretation of filiality is unmistakably synthetic; it uses the Buddhist theory of transmigration to provide a karmic sanction for the Confucian idea of filiality, which in turn gives the Buddhist precept of "nonkilling" a distinctly familial orientation. As a synthesis, however, it did not actualize from Ch'i-sung's syncretism, the logic of which is still one of compartmentalization. He characterized Buddhism as the sages' teaching concerning the transcendence of the world and Confucianism as a teaching concerning the government of the world.[43] In this regard, he was no different from the Buddho-Confucians of the Six Dynasties. Not surprisingly, therefore, his synthetic interpretation of filiality was achieved in an apologetic context where he tried to demonstrate to the critics of Buddhism that "filiality, which all teachings venerate, is particularly adored in Buddhism even though its doctrines in this regard are not very well known to the world."[44] It happened accidentally as a by-product of his need to defend his faith in Confucian terms in the face of Confucian hostility, which had been growing since the T'ang owing to the Neo-Confucian ascendancy. It is thus significant as an indication of the sinicization within Chinese Buddhism and is not an expression of an attempt to reconstitute Confucianism for synthesis.

As Zürcher has noted, the apologetic literature of the Buddho-Confucians early in the Six Dynasties was written in a "stereotyped" fashion with "the same answers to the same questions repeated *ad nauseam*."[45] By comparison, the syncretic efforts of the later Buddho-Confucians were stated in more imaginative and variegated terms. Aside from the kind of apologetic literature which the earlier Buddho-Confucians had written and which the Buddho-Confucians after the Six Dynasties, such as Liu Mi and Shen Shih-jung, continued to write,[46] the latter now also used metaphors to suggest the oneness of the Three Teachings. Li Shih-ch'ien (523–588), for instance, was a pious Buddho-Confucian who would not eat meat or drink liquor even during the semiannual clan reunion. When questioned about the comparative values of the Three Teachings, he said, "Buddhism is the sun, Taoism is the moon, and Confucianism is the five stars."[47] There also appeared diagrams of which T'ao Tsung-i's (c. 1320–1402) "Diagram of the Three Teachings—One Source" (*San-chiao i-yüan t'u*) was probably the most elaborate.[48] But, in spite of the growing complexity in expression, the later Buddho-Confucians were not noticeably more interested than their predecessors in synthesizing Confucianism with Buddhism; and we find a perfect latter-day Yen Chih-t'ui in the life and thought of Yeh-lü Ch'u-ts'ai (1189–1234). When criticized by a friend for being excessively involved in Buddhism and thereby neglecting Confucianism, Yeh-lü Ch'u-ts'ai replied,

To grasp fully the universal principle and get to the bottom of one's Nature, nothing is better than the Buddhadharma. To help society and pacify the people, nothing is better than the teachings of Confucius. In office, I follow the constant Way of Hsüan-ni [Confucius]; in private, I enjoy the Absolute Truth of Buddhism. Surely this is not wrong.[49]

Therefore, for the Buddho-Confucians after the Six Dynasties, the logic in operation remained one of compartmentalization, the dominance of which as a syncretic formula is attested to by the popularity of the "tripod" as a metaphor. Liu Mi attributed this metaphor to the monk Chih-yüan;[50] it served as a perfect symbol for the kind of syncretism which had prevailed during most periods of Chinese history and which, in being pluralistic but compartmentalizing, argued only for accepting Buddhism and/or Taoism alongside Confucianism, but not for synthesis.

A notable change, however, occurred in the syncretic situation of late Ming, during which a number of Buddhist- and Taoist-inclined Neo-Confucians attempted to formulate a synthesis involving Confucianism as well. As I indicated earlier, this attempt manifested itself as the "wild Ch'an" of the T'ai-chou school. But it also found an expression in the altered structure of the syncretic logic. For a syncretist like Chiao Hung, the principle of pluralism still prevailed, but it ceased to be compartmentalizing. As will be shown later, Chiao Hung was highly critical of some of his fellow syncretists in late Ming for maintaining the logic of compartmentalization, for he regarded the Three Teachings as one not because they stood apart like the legs of a tripod but because they possessed the integrity of a single entity and were mutually explanatory and illuminating.[51] Lin Chao-en (1517–1598) who, as will be seen later, founded a popular cult of syncretism, also departed from the logic of compartmentalization and insisted that the Three Teachings not be viewed in separate terms as three compartments.[52] It is true that in Lin's temple his followers were accommodated in three different chambers, depending on whether they were originally Buddhists, Confucians, or Taoists. This segregation, however, is not inconsistent with Lin's holistic vision; it was meant as a reminder that since the Three Teachings were one, there was no need to renounce one's original teaching in order to embrace the other two. It is also true that Lin characterized Confucianism as the teaching which "establishes the basis" (*li-pen*), Taoism as the teaching which "enters the gate" (*ju-men*), and Buddhism as the teaching which "makes principles ultimate" (*chi-tse*). But he regarded these characterizations as having pedagogical value only. They were made in order to provide for an orderly process of cultivation which, according to Lin, should proceed from Confucianism as the "beginning" (*shih*), through Taoism as the "middle" (*chung*), and to Buddhism as the "end" (*chung*). In the final analysis, the Way or Tao as the ultimate truth is embodied in all three teachings as the common concern for the sagely mind. For this reason, Lin also said, "The teachings of Confucius, Lao Tzu, and Shākyamuni all have the beginning, middle, and end."[53]

In thus enunciating an altered logic of syncretism, Chiao Hung and Lin Chao-en may or may not have been typical of their fellow syncretists in the late Ming. Their typicality in this regard, however, need not be an overriding concern, for, quite apart from the question of the extent to which their noncompartmentalization actually displaced compartmentalization as an explicitly stated principle, there remains the fact that they advocated noncompartmentalization, which had so far been inconceivable and, in the case of Chiao Hung, did so to controvert compartmentalization, which so far had been taken for granted. That fact, in and of itself, is an expression of late Ming syncretism as a new mode of operation in which Buddhism and Taoism were held not only to coexist but also to intermix with Confucianism. This newness of the syncretic situation in the late Ming has been noted by a number of orthodox traditional Chinese thinkers, who saw in late Ming syncretism an unprecedented threat to the purity of Confucianism. Kao P'an-lung (1562–1626), for instance, said,

When the Way of the sages is not made clear and practiced, the Buddhists and Taoists will have an opportunity to exploit in order to delude the people. However, those who deluded the people in the past stood outside our Way and used what seemed to be true to confuse the Truth, whereas those who delude the people today are based right in the midst of our Way and use what is truly false to eliminate the Truth. Those who pursued Buddhism in the past borrowed from Confucianism nonetheless in order to exalt Buddhism, whereas those who follow Confucianism today extol Buddhism in order to slight Confucianism. When the doctrine of the Three Teachings was first formulated, it was considered fortunate if [Buddhism and Taoism] could be listed together with our Way to constitute three [teachings]. But then there appeared the one-school doctrine, which considers it fortunate if [Buddhism and Taoism] could be merged with our Way to become a single [teaching]. . . . Alas! The use of the barbarian [Way] to change the Chinese [Way] has now reached its extreme. The words [which advocate this change] did not come from the barbarians, but from the Chinese; they did not come from the disciples of the Buddha, but from the followers of the sages. If this [situation] could be tolerated, what else could not be tolerated?[54]

A similar observation was also made by Ku Yen-wu (1613–1682) who condemned the "pure discussions" (ch'ing-t'an) in both the Six Dynasties and the late Ming as being responsible for the repeated triumphs of "barbarians" in Chinese history, but found the late Ming situation to be particularly reprehensible because it involved not only Lao Tzu and Chuang Tzu but also Confucius and Mencius.[55] It is possible to question these statements by Kao and Ku as exaggerations, especially in view of the fact that the purity of the whole Neo-Confucian undertaking as a Confucian development has sometimes also been held in doubt. The influence of Buddhism and Taoism on the development of Neo-Confucianism can certainly not be denied. Chou Tun-i's (1017–1073) "Diagram of the Great Ultimate" (T'ai-chi t'u) is most likely Taoist in origin, though not in intent, and, as de Bary has pointed out, Buddhism contributed to the deepening of Neo-Confucian spirituality which so much characterized the Chin-ssu lu.[56] However, with a few notable exceptions, the Neo-Confucians before late Ming were not syncretists. Their avowed aim was to defend the Confucian tradition, and they regarded Buddhism and Taoism more as a challenge to be met than as a positive source of doctrinal interest to be integrated with Confucianism. The hostility of the Ch'eng brothers and Chu Hsi (1130–1200) toward Buddhism and Taoism is well known; and Lu Hsiang-shan

(1139–1192), though an archrival of Chu Hsi, was no less firm than Chu Hsi in rejecting Buddhism and Taoism as heterodox. Even Ch'en Hsien-chang (1428–1500) whose "philosophy of the natural"[57] has been alternately criticized for being Buddhist and for being Taoist affirmed the existence and significance of "principle" (*li*) as a Confucian idea. He held Chuang Tzu in high esteem,[58] but spoke of the Taoistic "natural" in terms of the idea of "principle" with which he also distinguished Confucianism from Buddhism. He said,

> Men cannot be apart from affiars;
> Affairs cannot be apart from the Principle.
> [Affairs and the Principle] are what the Buddhists call the
> "two obstacles."
> How can we Confucians concur in this?[59]

Ch'en Hsien-chang has often been regarded as the predecessor of Wang Yang-ming (1472–1529) who had more than a passing interest in the Taoist cult of longevity and couched some of his ideas in both Ch'an and Taoist terms.[60] But, as Tu Wei-ming has pointed out, Wang in his later years regretted his earlier involvement with the cult of immortality, which he came to reject as "wasteful and deceitful"; and he used Ch'an and Taoist symbols to "revitalize" the Confucian tradition and not to synthesize Confucianism with Buddhism and Taoism.[61] Moreover, although Wang, as will be shown later, was decidedly more tolerant of Buddhism and Taoism as heterodoxies than the Ch'eng brothers, Chu Hsi, and Lu Hsiang-shan, he was nonetheless insistent that Confucianism be distinguished from Buddhism and Taoism and that he be identified as a Confucian.[62] In these regards, Wang contrasts as strongly as the Ch'eng brothers, Chu Hsi, and Lu Hsiang-shan do with the left-wing Neo-Confucians of the late Ming, who were both syncretists and synthesizers and who tried, rather self-consciously, to unite the Three Teachings into one doctrine.

As mentioned a little earlier, there were exceptions to the pattern exemplified by the Ch'engs, Chu, Lu, Ch'en, and Wang. As examples, we may cite Yang Shih (1053–1135), Chang

Chiu-ch'eng (1092–1159), Ch'en Kuan (1057–1122 or 1060–1124), and Yang Chien (1141–1226). Yang Shih was a disciple of the Ch'eng brothers[63] and was once praised by Ch'eng I (1033–1107) as one of the two disciples who had not given up Confucianism for Buddhism when Ch'eng I was away from K'aifeng during an exile in Szechwan.[64] Nevertheless, in his later years, Yang became interested in Buddhism and resorted to the Yogācāra theory of consciousness to reconcile the occurrence of both good and evil in the empirical world with Mencius' doctrine of man's Nature as originally good. He maintained that the *amalavijñāna* which is "pure and spotless" is what Mencius means by the "goodness of Nature," whereas *ālayavijñāna* which contains the "seeds of both good and evil" accounts for the "sprouting" (*meng*) of good and evil.[65] He also took what Layman P'ang (i.e., P'ang Yün, fl. late eighth century) had talked about as the "spiritual power and marvelous use" of "drawing water and carrying firewood" to be the same as the "Way of Yao and Shun," which, he said, "lies in between going and stopping or being fast and slow."[66] He further compared the "Four Ailments" (*ssu-ping*) of the *Sūtra of Perfect Enlightment* (*Yüan-chüeh ching*) to what Mencius had proscribed as the mistaken ways of nurturing Nature, saying, "'work' (*tso*) is the so-called 'helping the corn to grow long' (*chu-chang*), 'stop' (*chih*) is the so-called 'not weeding the corn' (*pu yün-miao*), and 'letting it be' (*jen*) and 'annihilation' (*mieh*) are the so-called 'not practicing constantly' (*wu-shih*)."[67] He condemned opposing man with Heaven and considered Mencius' view of "physical form" as "heavenly in nature" to be the same as the Buddhist idea that "*rūpa* is *śūnyatā*."[68] He thus proclaimed that "Confucianism and Buddhism actually do not advocate two different principles" because they both consider the "true mind" to be the "place of enlightenment."[69]

   Chang Chiu-ch'eng was a disciple of Yang Shih, but he also studied with the Ch'an monk Ta-hui Tsung-kao (1089–1163) and became a Buddhist layman, styling himself the "Spotless Layman" (*wu-kou chü-shih*).[70] Ta-hui advised him to "change the appearance of Ch'an and talk about it in Confucian terms"; and he put the advice into practice. In his *Record of Mind Transmission* (*Hsin-ch'uan lu*), Chang followed Ta-hui in characterizing the relationship between the three concepts of "Nature" (*hsing*), "Destiny" (*ming*), and "instruction" (*chiao*) in the opening passage of the *Doctrine of the Mean* in terms of the Buddhist theory of *trikāya*. In doing so, however, Chang did not exactly replicate Hui-yüan and Mou Tzu who, as noted before, also quoted from the Confucian Classics to facilitate propaganda. Chang's purpose was not wholly propagandistic, but rather syncretic so that "the different paths can be made to converge in the same terminus" and that "there will be no regrets in either this world or the other world." The result of Chang's syncretism was a definite Buddho-Confucian synthesis in which the distinction between Buddhism and Confucianism became blurred. He was thus condemned by Chu Hsi, who regarded the "harmfulness" of his *Record of Mind Transmission* as "even greater than [the destruction caused by] beasts, barbarians, and the Great Flood," for in the words of a traditional Chinese scholar, "whenever Shang-ts'ai [Hsieh Liang-tso (1050–1103)] talked about Ch'an, he was obviously talking about Ch'an because he did so rather straightforwardly. However, since the elderly Ta-hui instructed Heng-p'u [Chang Chiu-ch'eng] to change the appearance of Ch'an and talk about it in Confucian terms, [those who were involved with Ch'an] no longer recognize themselves to be Ch'an. This is substituting falsehood for truth, and as a result, few do not become confused."[71]

Ch'en Kuan was apparently close to Yu Tso (1053–1123), who was a disciple of the Ch'eng brothers. The two were "friends in intellectual discussion" (*chiang-yu*).[72] Moreover, many of Ch'en's disciples eventually ended up studying with Yang Shih, who, as noted earlier, was also a disciple of the Ch'eng brothers. Ch'en himself never formally studied with the Ch'eng brothers even though he had a special admiration for Ch'eng Hao (1032–1085). It was said that "whenever he obtained Ch'eng Hao's writings, he would dress formally with his cap and gown and read them immediately." He was also an expert on Shao Yung (1011–1077), whose contribution, he said, "does not lie in numerology but in the study of mind."[73] In addition to these interests and accomplishments as a Neo-Confucian, Ch'en also embraced Buddhism as a serious undertaking, saying that Buddhism and

Confucianism represented two individual "entrance gates" but
were "actually identical."[74] He admitted that he had "studied
Buddhism all his life." "As a result," he said, "I have absolutely no
fear of death." He was particularly fond of the *Diamond Sūtra*,
which, he said, "relegates all those with names, forms, feelings,
and senses to [the category of] illusion" and "establishes" in their
stead "enlightenment" (*chüeh*). He understood "enlightenment" in
synthetic terms to be the same as "sincerity" (*ch'eng*) in the
Doctrine of the Mean. For him, therefore, "enlightenment" was
not, as it was in the *Diamond Sūtra*, just a cognitive and spiritual
term for the attainment of the Buddha-knowledge of *anātman* as
nonattainment.[75] It was also an ontogenetic concept for the
principle of reality which generates and constitutes all things in the
universe, for, as the *Doctrine of the Mean* states, "Sincerity is the
end and beginning of things; without sincerity there would be
nothing."[76] Ch'en pointed out that what was called *chüeh* in
Chinese, known in Sanskrit as *anuttara-samyak-sambodhi*, was
also transliterated into Chinese with nine characters. However, he
said, "although the characters are nine, the thing they designate is
one." The "one" in this regard, he emphasized, is not the "numeral
one" but the "one" of "one thread"; and the "thing" that the
"one" describes is not a thing among the "ten thousand things"
but the "thing that cannot be without sincerity."[77]

In contrast with Yang Shih, Chang Chiu-ch'eng, and
Ch'en Kuan, who all had a direct or indirect relationship to the
Ch'eng brothers, Yang Chien was a disciple of Lu Hsiang-shan.[78]
But, like Chang Chiu-ch'eng, he has been accused of carrying on
the Buddhist discourse in Confucian disguise.[79] He has also been
compared to Wang Chi (1489–1583), who was a follower of
Wang Yang-ming. Both Yang Chien and Wang Chi, it was said,
accentuated the Ch'an tendencies of their masters with the result
that their masters' thought, which "was close to but was not
Ch'an," lost the Confucian character and became indistinguishable from Ch'an.[80] As a thinker, Yang Chien was preoccupied
with the problem of "egotism" (*wo*). He wrote an essay on "Being
Free from Four Things" (*Chüeh-ssu chi*)[81] which is obviously
inspired by, and may in fact be regarded as a sustained

philosophical commentary on, the statement in the *Analects* that Confucius was free from "arbitrariness of opinion" (*i*), "dogmatism" (*pi*), "obstinacy" (*ku*), and "egotism" (*wo*).[82] His understanding of "egotism," however, has an unmistakable Buddhist dimension: it is the *ātman* in *anātman*. He held "egotism" responsible for man's inability to "see the Way." It is, he said, a universal "affliction" (*huan*) from which even the "famous gentlemen" (*ming-shih*) who have transcended worldly concerns cannot always escape. As a result, they often mistake "hearing and seeing as the Way." Using a metaphor derived from the *Śūraṅgama Sūtra* and the *Sūtra of Perfect Enlightenment*, he likened this mistaking of "hearing and seeing as the Way" to "accepting a thief as one's son." Just as a person who has accepted a thief into his household as his son will never succeed in accumulating wealth, a person who holds *ātman* as true reality will never gain enlightenment and see things as they really are. *Anātman* or *wu-wo*, according to Yang Chien, characterizes the "mind of Yao and Shun"; its attainment enables a person to "advance naturally every day without cultivation and effort."[83]

As the above examples show, the syncretically inclined Neo-Confucians of late Ming were not unprecedented in being both syncretists and synthesizers. Moreover, among these Sung predecessors, a sense of likemindedness or even affinity apparently prevailed. Not surprisingly, therefore, as noted earlier, Chang Chiu-ch'eng and a number of Ch'en Kuan's students ended up following Yang Shih. However, notwithstanding their affinity, the Sung predecessors remained loosely associated individuals; they did not possess the organizational coherence and group identity that characterize their counterparts in late Ming. The latter were viewed by orthodox opponents as a group and were collectively condemned as "wild Ch'anists." Significantly also, there emerged in late Ming the cult of the "Three-in-One Doctrine" (*san-i chiao*) as an organized religion. This cult revolved around Lin Chao-en who, as noted earlier, ceased to compartmentalize the logic of syncretism. Lin believed that the Three Teachings were originally one, as they were all embodiments of the Way, and that they become differentiated as three

only when the later followers of Confucius, Lao Tzu, and
Shākyamuni lost sight of their original unity. To recapture the
original vision of unity, Lin established a religious organization
which was dedicated to the task of "combining the Three
Teachings into one" (*san-chiao ho-i*) and which incorporated
followers of all three teachings. Basing themselves in Lin's home
town in P'u-t'ien, Fukien, Lin and his disciples traveled extensively
in southeast China, proselytizing along the road and erecting
"Shrines of the Three Teachings" (*san-chiao tz'u*) for the worship
of Lin as the "Master of the Three Teachings" (*san-chiao hsien-
sheng*). They also published collections of Lin's writings to help in
the dissemination of his ideas.[84] Lin's cult of syncretism as an
organized religion was unprecedented in Chinese history. It
exemplifies the organizational impulse and group consciousness
that distinguished late Ming syncretism as a unique phenomenon.

      Lin and his disciples might have been exceptional in
their singleminded dedication to spreading the gospel of syncretism, but they were hardly alone among the late Ming syncretists
in being organization minded and group conscious. Organization
and group consciousness also characterized the highly syncretic
lay Buddhist world of late Ming, during which lay Buddhist
associations proliferated in number and, as will be seen later, came
to have a changed status and ideology that bear the fresh imprint
of late Ming syncretism. These associations were rather unlike
their earlier counterparts, which consisted of an indeterminate
number of people meeting at unspecified times. By contrast, the
lay Buddhist associations of late Ming were formally established
institutions with definite rules for both group conduct and
individual behavior.[85] It is also noteworthy that, toward the end of
the Ming, attempts were made to compile a biographical work
exclusively devoted to the lay Buddhists. The result was the
Record of Lay Buddhists Who Shared the Lamp (*Chü-shih fen-
teng lu*), which was begun by Chu Shih-en around 1610 and
completed by Wang Yüan-jui in 1631. This work, published in
1632 with contributions from the lay Buddhists, was the first of its
kind.[86] It is a firm indication that the lay Buddhists in late Ming,

like their fellow syncretists who gathered around Lin Chao-en, also came of age in their mutual identification as a syncretic group.

The organization-mindedness and group conscious-ness that thus prevailed among the syncretists in late Ming suggest that syncretism during this period was not simply a haphazard tendency toward what Nakamura has characterized as the "easy compromise" between the Three Teachings,[87] but a purposive movement to synthesize the teachings. It was a movement of tremendous strength and significance. It provoked from the orthodox circles of both the late Ming and the early Ch'ing a vigorous reaction which testifies to its strength; and its implications for late Ming society and culture as a whole can readily be seen in a number of developments which were distinctly late Ming. For instance, there appeared during this period a new kind of "morality book" (*shan-shu*) which shifted the emphasis of their earlier Sung prototype from religious salvation in the other world to conduct in this world. These new "morality books" were also invariably synthetic. They retained the popular Buddho-Taoist notion of retribution, but transformed it from a religious belief in the divine dispensation of reward and punishment into a self-enforcing ethical bookkeeping with strong Confucian over-tones.[88]

A similar shift to this-worldly orientation also oc-curred among Buddhists. In spite of Hui-neng's (638–713) statement in the *Platform Sūtra* that "if you wish to practice, it is all right to do so as laymen; you don't have to be in a temple,"[89] the *sangha* vis-à-vis the "household" had always been viewed as the necessary or preferred route to salvation. This privileged position, however, began to be widely questioned in late Ming not only by laymen like Chiao Hung but also by the leading monk Chu-hung (1535–1615), who provided much of the impetus for the development of lay Buddhism in the late Ming. Chiao Hung, as will be seen later, regarded the *sangha* as different from the lay world only in vocational terms. For him, it was neither distinct from nor more efficacious than the lay world as a path toward enlightenment.[90] Chu-hung, on the other hand, treated his lay disciples as the equals of monks under his supervision and assured the former in unequivocal terms that "as long as one can realize the nature of his own mind and obtain salvation, it is unnecessary to ask if he has shaved his head or not."[91] As the attitude toward the lay world thus became affirmative, lay Buddhist associations grew numerically and organizationally, involving both the common people and also the educated literati-gentry elite, who, though steeped in the Confucian tradition, embraced with all seriousness certain Buddhist principles and practices in their daily lives. In fact, many of the lay Buddhist associations in the late Ming were organized by the literati-gentry themselves for the purpose of "releasing life" (fang-sheng), i.e., setting captured animals free, as a way of observing the Buddhist precept of "nonkilling."[92] It is also noteworthy that, of the twenty laymen listed by P'eng Shao-sheng (1740–1796) as Chu-hung's disciples, nine achieved the chin-shih degree in the official civil service examinations and, of these nine, two attained such prominence in public life that they were included in the biographical section of the standard Ming dynastic history.[93]

To be sure, literati-gentry sponsorship of lay or monastic Buddhism and their participation in such Buddhist activities as vegetarianism and "release of life" were not unprecedented.[94] Nevertheless, the rationale for such participation changed somewhat in the late Ming, reflecting the changed orientation of syncretism as a movement to form a synthesis. Chu-hung, for instance, justified the precept of "nonkilling" and the practices of vegetarianism and "releasing life" not only in traditional Buddhist terms of "compassion" (tz'u-pei) and "filial obedience" (hsiao-shun) as prescribed in the Sūtra of Brahma's Net (Fan-wang ching) but also in terms of the "Mind of Heaven" (t'ien-hsin), which he specified as the intent to "love life" (hao-sheng). Characteristically, Chu-hung prohibited the slaughter of animals for the wedding ceremony because, he said, "marriage is the beginning of the bringing forth of new life."[95] Conceptually, the specification of the "Mind of Heaven" as the intent to "love life" is a Neo-Confucian and not Buddhist practice. The Neo-

Confucians regarded the universe as intrinsically creative. Basing themselves on the *Book of Changes*, they identified the "great virtue of Heaven and Earth" as the life force of "generation and regeneration" (*sheng-sheng*). They also equated this life force of the universe with the cardinal Confucian virtue of "humanity" (*jen*) which, for the Neo-Confucians, constituted the "Mind of Heaven and Earth to produce things" and was inherent in man as the feeling for life.[96] It is difficult to determine whether Chu-hung was actually aware that the concept of the "Mind of Heaven" was a Neo-Confucian formulation and thus consciously made use of it to fuse the Buddhist idea of "nonkilling" with the Neo-Confucian vitalistic view of the universe as creativity. There is, however, no doubt that his rationale for "nonkilling" was shared by many lay Buddhists in the late Ming and was understood by them as a Buddhist as well as a Confucian articulation.[97]

The impact of syncretism on the classical scholarship of the late Ming has been noted before. It should, however, be pointed out further that the Confucian stronghold of the civil service examination system was also affected by syncretism in the late Ming, during which the use of Buddhist and Taoist ideas for the writing of supposedly Confucian examination essays was a rather popular practice. As Sakai has observed, "Although the examinations were officially based on the Ch'eng-Chu commentaries on the Classics, the minds of both administering officials and competing candidates were strongly influenced by currents of heterodox thought."[98] The resulting erosion of the Confucian orientation of the examination system caused alarm among defenders of the official orthodoxy. It led the Ministry of Rites to submit in 1588 a protest memorial which asked the emperor to order the local officials to "burn" all the "bizarre interpretations and twisted discussions" (*hsin-shuo ch'ü-i*) of the Confucian canon and to punish the students who should dare even to "quote one sentence from Buddhist books."[99] It also become a symbol in the factional politics of late Ming. As will be seen later, Chiao Hung was demoted and sent into exile because of the allegation that he passed examination papers which contained unorthodox statements.[100]

The Neo-Confucian Impulse

The strength and uniqueness of late Ming syncretism have often been attributed to the policy and practice of some of the Ming emperors. As is well known, many of the Ming emperors were interested in Buddhism and Taoism and employed Buddhist monks and Taoist priests for high governmental positions.[101] The founding father of the dynasty, Emperor T'ai-tsu (r. 1368–1398), in particular, maintained a syncretic stand on the Three Teachings, the oneness of which he proclaimed in a number of public pronouncements. He dismissed as "shallow in views and superficial in perception" those who considered the Three Teachings to be incompatible, saying, "There are not two Ways under Heaven; and the sages are not of two minds." Moreover, in order to consolidate the ideological foundation of his newly established regime and to recruit talent before he could secure the support of the scholar-gentry officials, he appointed to offices many Buddhist monks and Taoist priests who were also versed in Confucianism. In the words of a Japanese scholar, Emperor T'ai-tsu's syncretic pronouncements and recruitment practice epitomized a "Ming dynastic policy" which was a "major condition" that "precipitated" the growth of syncretism in the Ming.[102]

     As a historian of ideas, I will not address the question of whether there was in fact a "policy" of syncretism in the Ming, which is an issue for the institutional historians to settle. I will simply acknowledge that Emperor T'ai-tsu's pronouncements on the oneness of the Three Teachings had an evident appeal to the late Ming syncretists, many of whom referred to, quoted from, or even commented upon these pronouncements. Granting the reality of this appeal, however, I still wish to question its significance as a "condition" for the flourishing of syncretism. Ming emperors, it may be noted, were not the first or only rulers in Chinese history to have displayed a favorable attitude toward Buddhism and Taoism; and Emperor T'ai-tsu's syncretic pronouncements were not without precedents of which the essay by Emperor Hsiao-tsung (r. 1162–1189) of the Sung on the "Origin of the Way" (*Yüan-tao lun*) may be cited as an example. There is therefore the question of how the Ming emperors were able, as their earlier counterparts were not, to "precipitate" the kind of syncretism that was uniquely Ming. Moreover, the "policy" statements of Emperor T'ai-tsu and the personal religious preferences of some of his successors neither ensured the acceptance of syncretism as an indisputable creed nor so legitimized the Ming syncretists as to secure them from the charge of "heterodoxy" as a basis for condemnation or persecution. I have already noted syncretism as a symbol in the factional politics of late Ming and the strong reaction that it provoked from the orthodox circles; and the fact that Li Chih cited emperor T'ai-tsu's syncretic pronouncments as a justification for his own syncretic outlook[103] but died in jail as a "heretic" should stand as a poignant reminder that if there was indeed "balance" between "orthodoxy" and "heterodoxy" in the Ming, as is sometimes claimed,[104] the "balance" was by no means necessarily maintained in favor of the syncretists. A further question thus arises: in what sense did the Ming syncretists enjoy, as their predecessors did not, a socially and politically privileged position which made it possible for them to pursue syncretism the way they did? Finally, many of the syncretists in late Ming were highly independent minded. The T'ai-chou advocates of syncretism, for instance, though citing Emperor T'ai-tsu's syncretic pronouncements, were also openly critical of Ch'eng-Chu Neo-Confucianism as state orthodoxy. A third question thus arises: why did these independent-minded syncretists feel compelled to follow and champion the state's policy in one regard while challenging it in another?

Obviously, these questions cannot be dealt with satisfactorily without a careful analysis of the constitution of the authority of the Ming state. With the exception of the third one, however, I will not attempt to deal with these problems, which have been raised here not so much to elicit consideration as to indicate my reservations about a particular interpretation. The third question deserves some attention, as it holds a clue to our understanding of late Ming syncretism as a distinctly Ming occurrence. The fact that many of the syncretists in the late Ming were critical of the Ch'eng-Chu school of Neo-Confucianism suggests that syncretism in the late Ming, or at least as it prevailed among the Neo-Confucians, needs to be understood as part of what I have elsewhere referred to as the "revolt against Ch'eng-Chu orthodoxy,"[105] which in turn derived much of its impetus from Wang Yang-ming's doctrine of "original-good-knowing" (*liang-chih*). Wang rejected the Ch'eng-Chu school's emphasis on the primacy of Principle (*li*) over Mind (*hsin*) and advocated *liang-chih* as the basis for moral judgment and action. In so doing, Wang undermined what in Araki Kengo's terms was the "high embankment" maintained during the Sung between Buddhism and Confucianism and redefined the whole issue of orthodoxy and heterodoxy in terms of the "self-awareness of the inner mind." For Wang, the determination of heterodoxy was no longer a matter of systemic identity; it became a consideration of "whether or not one had awakened to this innate knowledge [i.e., *liang-chih*]."[106] As Wang once said, "If learned correctly, even the Taoist teaching, which is of no benefit to the world, would not be harmful to the world; if learned incorrectly, even our Confucianism cannot be without evil."[107] Wang's doctrine of *liang-chih* and liberal view of heterodoxy did much to loosen the grip of Ch'eng-Chu orthodoxy on the Ming intellectual scene. As a result, there emerged an intellectually fluid situation in which many of the Neo-Confucians set out on personal quests and became involved with Buddhism and Taoism. Not surprisingly, therefore, the growing prominence of Wang Yang-ming and his schools coincided with the thriving of syncretism in the late Ming.[108]

Wang, of course, was not the first person in the Ming to have become dissatisfied with the Ch'eng-Chu tradition; and the syncretically oriented Ming intellectuals who were dissatisfied with the Ch'eng-Chu tradition were not all under Wang's influence. If Wang's accomplishments as a philosopher must be viewed as unique and original in the Ming, what he tried to deal with through these accomplishments cannot be considered so. The agony that he experienced after a seven-day investigation in the bamboo grove[109] was preceded by Ch'en Hsien-chang's "pathetic outcry of 'return to the natural'";[110] and Wang's contemporary Chu Yun-ming (1461–1527), who was both syncretically oriented and critical of the Ch'eng-Chu tradition, was obviously independent of Wang's influence.[111] In a very real sense, therefore,

Wang himself was an expression of the Ming intellectuals' growing dissatisfaction with the Ch'eng-Chu tradition. Nevertheless, as an expression, Wang not only exemplified but helped organize this sense of dissatisfaction. It was largely through Wang that there was in the Ming a revived interest in Lu Hsiang-shan, whose school went into decline by the end of the Sung. As Wing-tsit Chan has observed, the "Neo-Confucianism of the Yüan period is mainly the Neo-Confucianism of Chu Hsi"; and not long after Lu's death, even his home district in Kiangsi "came under the influence of Chu Hsi's followers."[112] Moreover, as the case of Chiao Hung indicates, Wang and the revived Lu became symbols for many of the dissatisfied Ming intellectuals and provided them with much of the language and vocabulary for articulating their revolt against Ch'eng-Chu orthodoxy. This being the case, syncretism in late Ming as it prevailed among the Neo-Confucians needs to be considered both as part of the general revolt against the orthodox Ch'eng-Chu tradition and, specifically, in conjunction with the ongoing Ch'eng-Chu versus Lu-Wang controversy in the Ming.

The syncretic-mindedness of some of the late Ming Neo-Confucians has often led to their being characterized either as un-Confucian or as suspiciously un-Confucian. Later on in this book, there will be occasions when I will discuss this characterization in detail on the basis of Chiao Hung's thought as a syncretist. Suffice it to note here that the interest of a thinker like Chiao Hung in Buddhism and Taoism did not result in his rejection of Confucianism, and that his revolt against Ch'eng-Chu orthodoxy was accompanied by an affirmation of Confucius and the Confucian tradition as mediated by Lu Hsiang-shan and Wang Yang-ming. Unlike the Sung Neo-Confucian Ch'eng Hao, who drifted from Buddhism to Confucianism as an alternative to Buddhism, Chiao Hung came to Buddhism and Taoism via Confucianism, not as an alternative to but as a further elaboration of Confucianism. He appropriated certain Buddhist and Taoist elements, which, however, were redeployed in a typically Neo-Confucian framework to articulate concerns arising from the controversy between the Ch'eng-Chu and Lu-Wang schools of Neo-Confucianism. Chiao Hung's interest in Buddhism and

Taoism must thus be understood symbolically. It was Neo-Confucian in intent and was informed in its meaning by what may be termed a restructured Neo-Confucianism which developed as a concomitant of the revolt against Ch'eng-Chu orthodoxy.

Briefly stated, this restructured Neo-Confucianism challenged the Ch'eng-Chu school's dichotomous view of *li* and *ch'i*, or Nature and Mind, as a duality and its exaltation of *li* over *ch'i*, or Nature over Mind. The result of this challenge was what some scholars have referred to as the "monism of *chi'i*," which desacralized and desubstantialized the concept of *li*. *Li* was no longer the *li* in *chi'i*, but became the *li* of *ch'i*.[113] This restructured Neo-Confucianism has significant implications for a number of developments that continued to pertain to the early Ch'ing. Most notably, it constituted the context in which the Ch'ing "evidential research" operated. The latter has often been viewed either as a reaction to or as a departure from the Ming Neo-Confucianism of the Lu-Wang persuasion, especially as it was professed by the left-wing "wild Ch'an" followers of Wang Yang-ming. This view of the Ch'ing "evidential research" is not totally without basis in fact. It is certainly undeniable that the early Ch'ing advocates of "evidential research" were extremely critical of both Wang Yang-ming and his syncretically oriented left-wing followers. However, as I will try to argue later, these criticisms were made according to the logic of the above-mentioned restructured Neo-Confuciaism which originated in Ming. Like the two rivals in a chess game, the "wild Ch'anists" of the late Ming and the early Ch'ing advocates of "evidential research," though playing against one another, were nevertheless playing the same game. Mutually contradictory as they may seem, the Han Learning of early Ch'ing and the syncretism that characterized the left-wing followers of Wang Yang-ming in the late Ming need to be considered together with the Ch'eng-Chu versus Lu-Wang controversy in their inter-connectedness as expressions which define the historical parameters of the restructured Neo-Confucianism as a discursive formation.

CHAPTER TWO

The Man

Family Background and Early Education

WE ARE NOT absolutely certain about the year in which Chiao Hung was born. According to his official biography in the *Ming Shih*, Chiao Hung "died in the forty-eighth year of Wan-li [i.e., 1620] at the age of eighty"[1], (or seventy-nine in Western terms), suggesting that he was born in the twentieth year of Chia-ching, i.e., 1541. His biography in Huang Tsung-hsi's (1610–1695) *Ming-ju hsüeh-an* also takes 1620 as the year of his death but says that he died at the age of eighty-one,[2] thus bringing the year of his birth one year back to the nineteenth year of Chia-ching, i.e., 1540. The *Ming chuang-yüan t'u-k'ao* offers still a third possibility. It states that Chiao Hung passed the Palace Examination as *chuang-yüan* at the age of fifty-one in the seventeenth year of Wan-li,[3] i.e., 1589. Thus we figure that he was born in the eighteenth year of Chia-ching, i.e., 1539. Of the above mentioned three dates, it is not really possible to determine precisely which one is correct. I have, however, tentatively decided upon 1540 as the year of Chiao Hung's birth, not so much because it represents a compromise as because it has the confirmation of a letter that Chiao Hung received from his teacher, Keng Ting-hsiang (1524–1596). In this letter, which is a primary contemporary source, Keng noted the coincidence that Chiao Hung achieved the smashing success as *chuang-yüan* in 1589 at exactly the age of "knowing Heaven's will,"[4] i.e., fifty. If Chiao Hung was fifty in 1589, he would have been born in 1540.

In any case, Chiao Hung lived from the middle of the Chia-ching period (1522–1567) through the entire reign of Emperor Wan-li (1572–1620), corresponding to a crucial phase in Chinese social and intellectual history when Chinese society witnessed the activation of "new forces on several levels" and when Chinese thought experienced "a near revolution."[5] It was also a period in which Chinese classical and historical scholarship went through a reorientation toward what was to become the "evidential research" of early Ch'ing.[6] Chiao Hung was an active participant in this "near revolution" in Chinese thought; he was also a pioneer in critical studies of the Classics and history and made important contributions to the new emerging scholarship of "evidential research."

The *Ming Shih* describes Chiao Hung as a man of Chiang-ning (modern Nanking).[7] His ancestral home, however, was in Jih-chao, Shantung, from whence his ancestor, Chiao Wu-lüeh, had migrated early in the Ming dynasty as a military officer of low rank (i.e., as *ch'ien-fu chang*).[8] We have no information of the Chiao family in its early years in Nanking, probably because it produced no members who were socially or politically prominent. Nevertheless, we may assume that it fared reasonably well. It apparently grew in size until the periods of Cheng-te (1506–1522) and Chia-ching, when the family was almost completely wiped out by a series of famines and epidemics save for Chiao Hung's father, Wen-chieh (1503–1584).[9] Wen-chieh was orphaned at the age of three, but he lived to maturity and inherited, at the age of sixteen, the position as battalion commander (*ch'ien-hu*) in Nanking's Banner Bearers Guard (*ch'i-shou wei*).[10] He thus became involved in military administration for more than forty years.[11] As a battalion commander, Wen-chieh was apparently well liked by his men, with whom he seems to have achieved a feeling of rapport. Therefore, when the soldiers of the Chen-wu Ying mutinied during Chia-ching's reign, Wen-chieh was able to maintain control over his men, who remained loyal and orderly.[12]

He retired from the Ming military establishment with the honor-ary title of Ch'i-tu-wei.[13]

As a person, Wen-chieh was "lofty and forthright" (*k'ang-chih*), and his "thoughts were straightforward like a cord that could be drawn out with a mere pull." He was also frugal, unassuming, and very much at ease with himself. Throughout his life, he "never sought anything from the world or contracted a hatred for anybody." While still young, he "circulated among those of wealth and high station without becoming affected by their grandeur." In his middle age, he "taught his children to read books, but not to do so for personal gain." At sixty, he decided not to trouble himself any longer with the worldly activities of social intercourse and so became secluded in a small chamber, abstaining from both meat and liquor and devoting himself entirely to worshiping the Buddha, reading the sūtras, and sitting in meditation.[14] He died of a "minor illness" at the age of eighty-two.[15] Chiao Hung remembered him as "the only person whom [I] Hung have ever known who has never gone against his conscience in [so much as] a word or deed."[16]

In addition to Chiao Hung, Wen-chieh had another son named Jui, who was Chiao Hung's elder brother. Jui was said to be "pure, honest, sincere, and upright." (*ch'ing-fang yüan-ch'ih*). As the eldest son, Jui did some private tutoring to supplement the family's income. But whenever a student came to pay his due, Jui always asked him to demonstrate his learning before accepting his money; and there were times when a student would go for a whole year without paying because Jui felt that the student had not sufficiently benefited from the tutoring. As a young man, Jui attended the Ying-t'ien Prefectural School (*Ying-t'ien fu-hsüeh*) and tried but failed repeatedly in the civil service examination. He was finally chosen to be a "specially selected tribute student" (*hsüan-kung*) and thereby obtained an appointment as the magistrate of Ling-shan, Kwangtung. He was obviously a concerned and conscientious county administrator. He suppressed the banditry which had been rampant in the area and strengthened security by revitalizing the local defence forces. He personally supervised the studies of the local students, whom he examined regularly once a month. He also stringently enforced the Single Whip Law and abolished the miscellaneous tribute levies of jade, pearl, and bear's gall, etc. which had been imposed on Ling-shan. As a result, he was well liked by the local populace but so alienated his superiors that he had to resign. As a final gesture of protest from an upright official, he refused to ride in the official sedan and went on foot to his superior's office to tender his resignation. He died on his way back to Nanking.[17]

Chiao Hung had a great deal of respect for his brother, with whom he seems to have identified as a child and whom he later recalled to be one of the three most admired men in his youthful world.[18] He received his childhood education essentially from his brother, who tutored him in the Confucian Classics and commentaries.[19] This private tutoring lasted until 1555, when Chiao Hung, at the age of sixteen, was selected to attend the Metropolitan Prefectural School (*Ching-chao hsüeh)* as a *sheng-yüan.*[20] In 1558, he had his first try, without success, at the provincial examination.[21] Three years later, in 1561, he married the third daughter of the "old venerable Confucian scholar" Chu Ting. The marriage lasted fourteen years until 1574 when his wife died of illness. In 1575, Chiao Hung remarried, this time the second daughter of a Mr. Chao who was a military *chü-jen.*[22] In many regards, the two wives were contrasting personalities, reflecting perhaps their difference in family background. The Chu daughter, being from a Confucian scholarly family, was said to be "going after success," "immersed in Confucian arts," and "demanding with regard to the children's education but lenient in managing others." The Chao daughter, on the other hand, came from a military family and was said to be a person who "had no worries and understood the art of nourishing life" and who was "genial and warm with her children but rather harsh in dealing with the servants."[23] They both were equally devoted to Chiao Hung, who was apparently not easy to get along with. Judging from the tone of his writings, Chiao Hung was contentious and opinionated; and according to Huang Tsung-hsi, he was considered by Keng Ting-hsiang's brother, Keng Ting-li (b. 1541), to be one of the "three people in the world who cannot be persuaded and who are difficult to live with."[24] Nevertheless, he seems to have been close to his wives, of whom he had fond memories. In his tombstone inscription for the combined tomb of his wives, he compared the two wives' personalities, reminisced about his first wife helping him with her dowry to obtain dainties for his parents and his second wife's patient care of his aged father, and said:

> Alas! There have been men of extraordinary character and independent action who, being at odds with the world, drifted from place to place and yet were able to maintain their integrity. They all, however, had to have understanding and virtuous wives who, by yielding to and standing by them, enabled them to forget their worries. I dare not claim to be a man of extraordinary character. But my health has been failing lately, and my death may come shortly. The two *an-jen*[25] could not wait and have abandoned me. How can I not but be grieved![26]

Chiao Hung's first marriage produced two sons and two daughters and his second, one son and two daughters.[27] Of the three sons, the one by the second marriage, Jun-sheng, seemed most successful in pursuing a career which, however, ended tragically. Jun-sheng held the *chü-jen* degree and served as prefect (*chih-fu*) at Ch'ü-ching, Yunnan, during the difficult years of Southern Ming. In April 1647, he was captured by the rebel forces under the leadership of Sun K'o-wang (d. 1660) and was urged to surrender. But he refused and died a martyr's death. For his loyalty to the Ming, the Ch'ing court granted him the posthumous name Chieh-min.[28]

Association with the T'ai-chou School

As mentioned above, Chiao Hung failed in his first try at the provincial examination, which he did not pass until 1564.[29] Thereafter, he took the metropolitan examination quite regularly once every three years except in 1580 and 1586.[30] But he failed repeatedly and did not obtain his *chin-shih* degree and therefore his first official appointment until 1589, as a Hanlin compiler (*Han-lin yüan pien-hsiu*)[31]. In terms of his intellectual growth, the years before he was twenty-three (i.e., before 1562) were relatively dull and uninspired. He attended the Metropolitan Prefectural School, studied at some of the temples in Nanking, and read such Taoist works as the *Lao Tzu* and the *P'an-shan yü-lu*.[32] But such intellectual pursuits were desultory and superficial. His reading of the *Lao Tzu*, for instance, did not involve real "tasting" or understanding of the text and, by his own admission, was "no different from eating with the ears."[33] The turning point came in 1562, when he met Keng Ting-hsiang and began to "set his mind on learning."[34]

Keng was a prominent member of the T'ai-chou school. He came to Nanking in 1562 to take charge of educational administration in the Southern Metropolitan Area and remained there for six years until 1567, when he was promoted to be an assistant minister of the Grand Court of Revision (*Ta-li ssu ch'eng*).[35] These six years in Nanking, though hardly the peak of Keng's official career, were nevertheless a high point in his life, during which he made a deep personal imprint on the intellectual world of Nanking. In a commemorative essay for the completion of Keng's shrine in Nanking, Chiao Hung wrote, "The beauty of literary accomplishments in Nanking has been especially celebrated in our time, but its opening to learning of the Way actully began with the Master [Keng]."[36] This account by Chiao Hung was confirmed by the local gazetteer, *Shang-yüan Chiang-ning hsiang-t'u ho-chih*, which also stated that the doctrine of "original-good-knowing" (*liang-chih*), though first enunciated by Wang Yang-ming in the middle of the Ming dynasty, was not widely propagated in Nanking until Keng Ting-hsiang arrived there and established the Ch'ung-cheng Academy at Mount Pure Coolness (*Ch'ing-liang shan*).[37] As a result, Chiao Hung was able to say that "even to this day, whoever speaks of the place to which the Master [Keng] was most attached necessarily speaks of Nanking, and those who speak of Nanking's learning necessarily speak of the Master."[38]

When Keng first arrived in Nanking, the students were, in Chiao Hung's words, "mostly without head and brain." Keng advised them to "make their effort on the basis of humanity (*jen*)." As a result, "many gained understanding"; and, as Chiao Hung later said to his own students, "If we today have any sense of direction, it is all my teacher's accomplishment."[39] In order to help the students in the cultivation of humanity, Keng organized informal meetings which became institutionalized in 1566 as the Ch'ung-cheng Academy.[40] Chiao Hung later recalled his experience at these meetings:

> The teacher came to us from time to time, and we brought up our doubts and difficulties to question him. He opened [us as if] with the key to the springs [of the mind]. There were none of us whose minds were not awakened and whose vision was not made clear. We leapt for joy. Sometimes it was without a word of explanation and with only a look that he made us understand. It happened often that we came [to the meetings as if] empty but went away filled.[41]

Chiao Hung was soon accepted by Keng as a disciple and, through Keng, gained the acquaintance of Keng's two younger brothers, Ting-lii (1534–1577) and Ting-li (b. 1541).[42] Of all the disciples, Keng seems to have placed particular confidence in Chiao Hung, who not only participated in the organization of the Ch'ung-cheng Academy but was chosen by Keng to take charge of it when the academy was formally founded in 1566.[43] Over the years, Keng also continued to refer students to Chiao Hung for instruction. Thus, for instance, when Tsou Shou-i's (1491–1562) grandson, Te-han (1538–1681), was experiencing agony and neglected eating and sleeping during an intense struggle to break an intellectual and spiritual impasse, Keng advised him to spend some time with Chiao Hung.[44] At another time when an uneducated peasant, Hsia T'ing-mei, came to Hupeh to ask Keng about learning, Keng sent him to study with Chiao Hung.[45] Still another time when P'an Shih-tsao (1537–1600) was about to leave Peking after having studied some time with Keng, Keng suggested that he further broaden his learning by visiting Wang Tsung-mu (1523–1591) at Huai-an, Wang Pi (1511–1587) at An-feng, and Chiao Hung at Nanking.[46]

Both the *Ming Shih* and the *Ming-ju hsüeh-an* state that Chiao Hung also studied with Lo Ju-fang (1515–1588),[47] another prominent member of the T'ai-chou school. Lo came to

Nanking several times and was active in Nanking's circles of intellectual discussion.[48] But, as Jung Chao-tsu has pointed out, there is in Chiao Hung's writings only one brief reference to his meeting with Lo, which took place in 1586.[49] As far as I am aware, Chiao Hung never referred to Lo as "my teacher." Therefore, if there existed a teacher-student relationship between Lo and Chiao Hung, it was apparently never personalized into the kind that prevailed between Keng Ting-hsiang and Chiao Hung. Nevertheless, Chiao Hung was well acquainted with Lo's ideas, which he quoted from time to time in his own works. He certainly had a great deal of respect for Lo, who, he said, left "nothing further to unravel" in developing the teachings of Wang Yang-ming and Wang Ken (1483–1541).[50]

Chiao Hung also had high esteem for Wang Ken, the founding father of the T'ai-chou school. He considered Wang Ken to be as influential as Wang Yang-ming and said that the disciples of the two Wangs "divided the state of Lu in the middle."[51] His relationship with Wang Ken's son, Wang Pi, was close. He wrote the tombstone inscription for Wang Pi, and his collected works contain six poems that were dedicated to Wang Pi.[52] He was a fellow disciple of P'an Shih-tsao, who, as noted earlier, also studied under Keng Ting-hsiang. Shih-tsao's brother, Ssu (1523–1578), was a heroic type of personality. Or, as Chiao Hung put it, he was "indomitable and possessed of an extraordinary spirit" (*t'i-t'ang fu ch'i-ch'i*). As such, Ssu was not only decisive and spontaneous in action but accomplished in the martial arts and military strategy. In 1566, for instance, he assumed command of the government forces as a private citizen and routed the bandits at his native town of Hsin-an (in modern Anhwei) when the government forces were on the verge of total disintegration after their commander was killed by the bandits. Chiao Hung had firm connections with both P'an brothers, but he particularly admired the heroic exploits of Ssu and praised him as "an extraordinary man" (*ch'i nan-tzu*).[53] He was also on friendly terms with Kuan Chih-tao, who not only studied along with Chiao Hung under Keng Ting-hsiang but was an independent-minded syncretist and, as such, was regarded by Chiao Hung as a kindred spirit. In his tombstone inscription for Kuan, Chiao Hung characterized Kuan in terms that could well have applied to himself. He said that Kuan "attempted to encompass the Three Teachings and fuse the Nine Schools of thought in order to formulate a doctrine of his own."[54] But, above all, Chiao Hung was a special friend of Li Chih, who became his "soul mate" and "sworn brother."[55]

Li Chih first heard of Chiao Hung in 1563 when Li, emerging from his mourning for his father, went to Peking to be reinstated in the National University (*Kuo-tzu chien*) as an erudite (*po-shih*). But he did not get to know Chiao Hung until three years later, and their friendship did not really begin to develop until 1572, when Li Chih was reassigned to Nanking as vice director (*Yüan-wai-lang*) in the Ministry of Justice.[56] Li spent the next six years in Nanking, during which, through long frequent meetings, he established a special rapport with Chiao Hung. Li Chih later recalled of these meetings:

Jo-hou [Chiao Hung] and I sat close to each other, knee to knee from morning till night, each of us delving exhaustively into the real being of the other. Either we were not to delve at all, or we were to delve deeply in this manner. Consequently, our minds intimately coincide like the halves of a tally.[57]

By then, Chiao Hung had already acquired a reputation for broad learning and filiality and was being sought after by various kinds of people. As Li Chih said of him:

There are a great many in the world who would like to associate with Jo-hou. Those who are engaged in literature and desire to become established in words take Jo-hou as their teacher. Others who pursue the civil service examinations in order to advance and to gain glory with meritorious and ever-lasting accomplishments also take Jo-hou as their teacher. As for those who are truly great, they say, "He, though poor and thus only able to provide porridge to eat and water to drink, is nevertheless good at attending on his parents. He is indeed established in virtue." Therefore, I, Hung-fu, am not the only one in the world who associates with Jo-hou in order to gain immortality [by becoming as accomplished as he is in words, meritorious service, and virtue.].[58]

"However," Li Chih said, "it is only I, Hung-fu, who knows Jo-hou profoundly well; and, as a result, Jo-hou also regards Hung-fu as a friend who truly knows him."[59]

This close relationship between Li Chih and Chiao Hung endured the vicissitudes of time. Many of Li Chih's early friends left him when tension developed between him and Keng Ting-hsiang, whom he eventually came to despise as a "hypocrite."[60] But his friendship with Chiao Hung remained firm even though Chiao Hung was a favorite disciple of Keng Ting-hsiang. It was a chief source of consolation for Li Chih during his many years of trial and persecution. Therefore, in 1579, when Li Chih was despairing over Ho Hsin-yin's (1517–1579) death in a Hupeh prison, it was to Chiao Hung that he confided his agony.[61] Later in 1602 when he was preparing for his own death and wrote his last will, it was again Chiao Hung whom he asked to write his name to be inscribed on his tombstone.[62]

Li Chih's strong feelings for Chiao Hung were fully reciprocated. After Li's split with Keng Ting-hsiang, Chiao Hung was one of the few friends who remained loyal and provided refuge for Li.[63] Chiao Hung also wrote a preface to Li's *A Book To Be Hidden Away (Ts'ang Shu)*, thus endorsing Li's indictment of Confucian moralism in Chinese history.[64] During Li's final days in a Peking prison, the thought that his trusted friend, Chiao Hung, continued to stand by him must have been very comforting, especially because his contempt for Keng Ting-hsiang was partly a result of his belief that Keng, being concerned for wealth and position, had not tried hard enough to save Ho Hsin-yin, who was Keng's "friend in intellectual discussion."[65] Later in 1602 after Li's suicide, Chiao Hung composed a "petition" (*shu*) to Heaven for use in a Buddhist prayer service (*chui-chien*) in honor of Li Chih. In this "petition," Chiao Hung compared Li's suicide to the Buddha's allowing himself to be mutilated by Kaliṅgarāja, which Chiao Hung understood in the tradition of the *Diamond Sūtra* as both an illustration of the Buddha's perfection in patience (*jen-ju*) and as Buddha's way of demonstrating the idea of "emptiness" or "no self."[66]

Shen Te-fu (1578–1642) stated in his *Yeh-huo pien* that Li Chih's "intelligence overwhelmed his generation" and that

Chiao Hung "extolled him as a sage."[67] What Shen said of Chiao Hung in this regard was probably an exaggeration. It was flatly contradicted by Huang Tsung-hsi, who stated explicitly that Chiao Hung "did not necessarily regard Li Chih as a sage but rather as a person who could bear on his shoulders the word *k'uang* or 'wild' and who might sit next to a sage."[68] P'eng Shao-sheng (1740–1796), however, was quite right in saying that Chiao Hung "sincerely believed in Li Chih."[69] As his preface to Li Chih's *A Book To Be Hidden Away* testifies unequivocally, Chiao Hung not only believed in the "loftiness" of Li Chih's character and the truth of Li Chih's ideas but was confident that Li Chih's works would "definitely go down in history" and be regarded by later scholars as "scales and mirror," i.e., as the yardstick to distinguish between right and wrong.[70] Because of his unswerving faith in Li Chih and also because of his association with other members of the T'ai-chou school, Chiao Hung was ridiculed by some of his contemporaries as a "Ch'anist."[71]

As a "Wild Ch'anist"

The term "Ch'an" or "Ch'anist" has often been used by traditional Chinese scholars in describing the movement of the T'ai-chou school. It is not an entirely improper term. As we have already seen, quite a few members of this school maintained an interest in, and came under the influence of, Ch'an or Buddhism in general. Of these syncretic-minded T'ai-chou Neo-Confucians, Chiao Hung was apparently exposed to Buddhism at an early stage of his life. In fact, Buddhism was an integral part of his upbringing as a child, since his father was a devout Buddhist who, as I mentioned earlier, retired from official life to worship the Buddha. But, in spite of this early exposure, Chiao Hung's interest in Buddhism as a serious intellectual undertaking seems to have begun relatively late. There are in his writings a few fragmentary references to his studying at the various temples in Nanking shortly after he came of age.[72] However, we do not know whether he studied there to pursue his interest in Buddhism or to prepare for the civil service examinations. Moreover, these were the years before he "set his mind on learning." Therefore, whatever he might have read in Buddhism during this period was not likely to have produced a deep imprint on his mind; and he probably did not begin to study Buddhism seriously until he was in his late twenties or early thirties. After he had obtained his *chin-shih* as *chuang-yüan*, Chiao Hung wrote a letter to a monk named Lu-an in which he stated that he had "cultivated *karma (hsiu-yeh)* for twenty years," more than half of which time he had spent at Lu-an's temple under Lu-an's care.[73] The term *hsiu-yeh* as used in this letter can mean either "cultivation of *karma*" or "study for the civil service examination." I have chosen to render it as "cultivation of *karma*" because the twenty-year period indicated in the letter could not possibly have corresponded with the length of time which Chiao Hung spent preparing for the civil service examinations. He began his study for the examinations at least as early as 1555[74] and would have been engaged in such study for at least thirty-six years by the date of this letter, which was written when he passed the metropolitan examination in 1589. If by 1586 Chiao Hung had only "cultivated karma for twenty years," he could not possibly have begun his pursuit of Buddhism as an active interest much before he was thirty. By then, he had already become a disciple of Keng Ting-hsiang and had earnestly studied Confucianism for six or seven years. Apparently, the problems arising from his study of Confucianism compelled him to look into Buddhism, which, he said, could best clarify "the cardinal meaning of the teachings of the sages and worthies."[75] In this regard, Chiao Hung was a precise contrast to his Neo-Confucian predecessor Ch'eng Hao (1032–1085). Whereas Ch'eng Hao drifted from Buddhism to Confucianism as an alternative to Buddhism, Chiao Hung came to Buddhism via Confucianism, not, however, as an alternative but as a further elaboration.

Unfortunately, the letter to Lu-an does not specify how Chiao Hung did his "cultivation of *karma*." Presumably, this cultivation involved a great deal of reading; and there is no doubt that Chiao Hung was well acquainted with a wide range of Buddhist literature. His writings are full of quotations from or references to the standard Buddhist scriptures like the *Lotus, Diamond, Heart, Laṅkāvatāra, Śūraṅgama,* and *Avataṁsaka Sūtras,* the *Awakening of Faith,* and the *Āgamas,* etc., as well as to other works by eminent Chinese monks such as Seng-chao (374–414), Hsüan-tsang (596–664), Hui-neng (638–713), Tsung-mi (780–841), Tsung-kao (1089–1163), and Lin-chi (d. c. 867), etc. Of these Buddhist texts, the *Śūraṅgama Sūtra,* the Āgamas, and the *Avataṁsaka Sūtra* may be singled out as particularly important, since they played a decisive role in three stages of Chiao Hung's transformation as a syncretist. During the first stage, Chiao Hung read the *Śūraṅgama,*[76] which, like many other Buddhist scriptures, is concerned with the two interrelated problems of ignorance and enlightenment, but with a particular focus on the workings of the "storehouse consciousness" (*ālayavijñāna*) as the source of ignorance.[77] It was probably the most popular Buddhist text among Ming Neo-Confucians, who found the sūtra's analysis of the innermost consciousness relevant to the Confucian tradition of self-examination, especially as that tradition was conceived in the post–Wang Yang-ming era.[78] Wang's rejection of the priority of Principle over Mind led not only to the attempt to find Principle from within one's own mind but to a heightened awareness of the importance of purifying the mind of its falsehood[79] so that egotistical ideas could not masquerade as the truth of *liang-chih.* The *Śūraṅgama* so impressed Chiao Hung that he came to feel that "Confucianism was inferior to Buddhism."[80] This sense of inferiority about Confucianism was then replaced during the second stage by a sense of equality about the two teachings when he read the *Āgamas,*[81] which contain the most fundamental tenets of Buddhism such as the Fourfold Noble Truth, the Eightfold Noble Path, the doctrine of "dependent origination," etc. During the third and final stage of Chiao Hung's transformation as a syncretist, he read the *Avataṁsaka,*[82] which is a basic scripture for the Hua-yen school of Buddhism and which is reputed to be a record of what the Buddha preached immediately after his enlightenment. This text enabled Chiao Hung to transcend his earlier sense of equality about Buddhism and Confucianism and to realize that no distinction could be made between these two because they both taught the same thing, which he took to be the "realization of Nature and the fulfillment of Destiny" (*chin-hsing chih-ming*).[83]

Chiao Hung's realization that Buddhism and Confucianism were not different as teachings caused some uneasiness in his teacher Keng Ting-hsiang. Citing Ch'eng Hao's charges against Buddhism, Keng expressed to Chiao Hung a deep sense of concern for "people who are fooled by heterodox learning." In response, Chiao Hung made a well-reasoned, point-by-point rebuttal of Ch'eng Hao who, he said, "was lofty in character but still had biases in what he had obtained."[84] Keng, who was criticized by Huang Tsung-hsi for having an ambiguous attitude of "half belief and half disbelief" toward Buddhism,[85] retreated before Chiao Hung's reply and said that Ch'eng Hao's charges against Buddhism were probably attributed to him by mistake or were distorted when they were recorded by his disciples.[86] Subsequently, Chiao Hung was able to keep up with his interest in Buddhism until the end of his life without Keng's further interference. As many of his poems testify, Chiao Hung made frequent visits to Buddhist temples and monasteries[87] and was on good terms with quite a few monks. In addition to his aforementioned relationship to Lu-an, he was also close to Tsu-hsin, Lang-mu (d. 1605), Yü-an, and Te-ch'ing (1546–1623). His collected works contained poems dedicated to Tsu-hsin and Lang-mu, a commemorative essay in honor of Yü-an's sermon on monastic discipline, and a letter to Ch'en Ch'ien-shih in which he expressed his concern over Te-ch'ing's exile to Lei-yang (in modern Kwangtung) and asked Ch'en to send Te-ch'ing his personal regards.[88] Chiao Hung was also a member of a Lotus Association (*lien-she*) and was active in the Buddhist community as a layman. He composed laudatory verses in honor of statues and paintings of the various bodhisattvas and arhats, compiled commentaries on Buddhist sūtras, wrote prefaces to a number of secondary works on Buddhism, and helped in the building and repairing of temples and monasteries either by making and soliciting contributions or by writing commemorative essays. In his old age, he was a regular guest at the Ch'i-hsia Ssu outside Nanking and practiced the "samādhi of invoking the Buddha" (*nien-fo san-mei*).[89]

As the case of Chiao Hung indicates, there is ample justification for labeling some members of the T'ai-chou school as "Ch'an" or "Ch'anist." The term suggests a certain syncretism which was admittedly a chief characteristic of this school, even though some of us today might wish to dispute the term's implication that the school was necessarily un-Confucian. However, the term has also been coupled with the word *k'uang* to form the expression *k'uang-ch'an*. The word *k'uang* was used during the Ming by both adherents and opponents of the T'ai-chou school to characterize its peculiarities. It was, for instance, used by Chiao Hung, who, as noted earlier, described Li Chih as *k'uang*. In doing so, Chiao Hung placed Li in one of the two personality categories whom Confucius, in the absence of men who could act according to the Mean, preferred to have as transmitters of his teaching.[90] Therefore, when Chiao Hung spoke of Li Chih as a person who, being *k'uang*, "might sit next to a sage," his point was not to deprecate Li for falling short of the ideal of sagehood but to distinguish Li's passionate and untrammeled personality from the banality of the conventional Confucians and to affirm Li's worth as a transmitter of the Confucian Way.

On the other hand, however, when the word *k'uang* was used by the opponents of the T'ai-chou school, as in the expression *k'uang-ch'an*, it became a special term of opprobrium with which traditional Chinese scholars condemned the school as morally corrupt and philosophically anti-intellectual.[91] The sense of moral outrage that this use of *k'uang* connoted in traditional times no longer prevails in modern scholarship, but the view of the T'ai-chou school as anti-intellectual has persisted, with the result that the flourishing of "evidential research" in the early Ch'ing is still seen as an "intellectualist" reaction against the alleged anti-intellectualism of this school.[92] De Bary has discussed this view of the T'ai-chou school and has proposed some rivisions according to his own and other scholars' researches in Ming Neo-Confucianism.[93] Later in this book, I will further examine this persistent notion of the T'ai-chou school in terms of Chiao Hung's accomplishments as a philosopher and scholar. Here I will merely point out that Chiao Hung, while maintaining firm connections with Li Chih, was also a close associate of Ch'en Ti (1541–1617). He discussed problems of phonetics and philology with Ch'en Ti, composed biographies for Ch'en Ti's parents, and wrote prefaces and postfaces to many of Ch'en Ti's works, including the *Mao-shih ku-yin k'ao*, the *Fu-hsi t'u-tsan*, and the *Shang-shu shu-yen*.[94] Ch'en Ti, as Ch'ien Mu has observed, was a great late Ming master of "evidential research" and anticipated Ku Yen-wu (1613–1682) in making some of the most important discoveries in Chinese classical scholarship.[95] A painstaking scholar, Ch'en Ti would seem diametrically opposed to Li Chih, who was probably the wildest of the "wild Ch'anists." If the standard interpretation of the T'ai-chou school were accepted as valid, Chiao Hung's simultaneous friendship with Li Chih and Ch'en Ti would have to be regarded as an inconsistency in his intellectual temper. But, as we shall see, Chiao Hung was not being ambivalent. What appears contradictory in his personal relationships is perfectly understandable in terms of his position as a late Ming Neo-Confucian syncretist. His varied intellectual associations symbolize his remarkable ability to integrate and hold in balance the divergent systems of Buddhism, Taoism, and Confucianism, from which his own philosophy evolved as a synthesis.

Political Involvement and Critical Scholarship

As mentioned earlier, Chiao Hung's official life did not start until 1589, when at the relatively advanced age of fifty, he finally obtained his *chin-shih* degree by passing the palace examination as *chuang-yüan* and was made a Hanlin compiler. His smashing success as *chuang-yüan* was said to have been the fulfillment of a dream. While in Peking for the examination, Chiao Hung stayed at a Taoist temple. A priest of this temple had a dream in which a spirit appeared to announce that there was a future *chuang-yüan* in the temple. As it was later interpreted, the future *chuang-yüan* was Chiao Hung.[96] There is no need to take this dream as evidence of prophecy, but it should be noted that Chiao Hung's achievement was greeted by some of his contemporaries as more than a personal triumph. For his teacher Keng Ting-hsiang, it could not have been a coincidence that Chiao Hung obtained his *chin-shih* as *chuang-yüan* at precisely the age of fifty. Keng saw in this event the guiding hand of providence. As he said in a letter to Chiao Hung, he was exhilarated on hearing of Chiao Hung's success. But he soon became fearful and could not sleep for several nights as he came to realize that Chiao Hung's success coincided with the age of "knowing Heaven's will." He explained:

> Heaven did not bestow fame and glory on you in vain. I should think that Heaven has so decreed with a most profound intent. Do not tell yourself that you have just taken off the clothes of the lowly and can afford to be relaxed and leisurely. You still have great and heavy burdens to bear.[97]

It might seem possible to interpret Keng's words as conventional utterances of Confucian ceremony, but Keng himself cautioned that they should be taken otherwise. He asked Chiao Hung "not to regard these words of mine as ordinary words of encouragement" but to "think deeply about them in the quiet of the night."[98]

As for Chiao Hung himself, we may assume that he was overjoyed. He must have felt a tremendous sense of relief and confirmation after almost twenty-five years of repeated failure. He did not, however, see this success as an occasion for personal celebration. He declined the offer of a monument of celebrity from his clansmen at Jih-chao, Shantung, and suggested that the money be invested in land to help in the upkeep of his ancestral temple and the care of his poor relatives at Jih-chao.[99] He also turned down a similar offer from the authorities in Nanking who wanted to build an arch of triumph at the gate of his residence to publicize his accomplishment, saying that the money should be used for famine relief.[100]

Chiao Hung's success as *chuang-yüan* probably did not add substantially to his fame, as he already enjoyed quite a reputation as a private scholar. But he had never held a government position before 1589, and his first official appointment as Hanlin compiler filled him with a grave sense of responsibility. He proceeded to study the laws and institutions of the dynasty[101] and became deeply involved in the instruction of the eunuchs.

At the outset of the Ming dynasty, eunuchs had been prohibited by Emperor T'ai-tsu (r. 1368–1398) from obtaining an education.[102] But T'ai-tsu's policy of keeping the eunuchs illiterate was not observed by his successors. Emperor Ch'eng-tsu (r. 1402–1424), for instance, assigned a teacher to instruct Fan Hung, Wang Chin (d. 1451), Juan An (d. 1453), etc. in the Classics and history. They acquired a fairly good knowledge of reading and writing and later served Emperor Ying-tsung (r. 1435–1449 and 1457–1464) as trusted eunuchs.[103] Emperor Hsüan-tsung (r. 1426–1435) further disregarded T'ai-tsu's prohibition by institutionalizing the education of eunuchs. He estalished the Palace School (*nei-shu t'ang*) for the eunuchs and transferred Liu Ch'ung as a secretary from the Ministry of Justice (*hsing-pu chu-shih*) to the Hanlin Academy as a compiler with the special responsibility of teaching the eunuchs. Later, the Grand Secretary Ch'en Shan (1365–1434) was also assigned to this job; and by Chiao Hung's time, it had become standard practice to select four officials from the Hanlin Academy to teach the eunuchs at the Palace School.[104] As a rule, these Hanlin officials did the teaching merely as a matter of "formality." Chiao Hung, however, took the job seriously and often lectured his eunuch-students on the "good and evil deeds of past eunuchs."[105] He said,

> The emperor has loftily folded his arms in the deep recess of the palace. There are only eunuchs running around to attend to his affairs. If we can enlighten the eunuchs just a little so that they know what to aspire to, then even a thought that is as insignificant as a trickle of water or speck of dust can be used to make us effective.[106]

Chiao Hung was thus well aware of the reality of eunuch power during his time. But, unlike some of his fellow officials who either fought against or cooperated with the eunuchs, he used his position in the Hanlin Academy to try to subvert the eunuchs' consciousness by giving them moral indoctrination in the Confucian scheme of values. For this purpose, he also began to compile a work on the conduct of eunuchs in Chinese history for use at the Palace School. The work was never finished as he was soon relieved of his duties in teaching the eunuchs and was given a new function of keeping the Diaries of Activity and Repose (*ch'i-chü chu*).[107]

In 1592, Chiao Hung was appointed co-examiner (*t'ung-k'ao-kuan*) for the metropolitan examination,[108] after which he was sent out by the emperor to confirm the succession of the district princes at Ku-yüan (in modern Kansu), Shang-jao (in modern Kiangsi), Shen-ch'iu and Ta-liang (both in modern Honan), etc.[109] While on his way to Ta-liang, he obtained a set of Su Ch'e's (1039–1112) commentaries on the *Book of Odes* and the *Spring and Autumn Annals*. These commentaries were later put together with Su Shih's (1036–1101) commentary on the *Book of Changes* in a single volume as the *Liang-Su ching-chien*, to which Chiao Hung wrote a preface. In this preface, Chiao Hung emphasized the significance of the Su brothers as classical scholars in contrast to their conventional reputation as mere men of literature. "Literature," Chiao Hung said, "reached its ultimate in the Classics" because "the Classics are the literature that the previous Confucians used to convey the Way (*Tao*)" and because "no one in the world can abandon the Way and still be able to do literature." Literature and the Classics are thus inextricably related; the latter, being the embodiment of the Way, authenticates the former as its very source. Therefore, "to say that there can be literature when classical learning is abandoned is [like saying that] there can be water when the spring is abandoned." According to Chiao Hung, what distinguished the literature of the Su brothers as "immortal" and not subject to the changing "likes and dislikes" of various ages was precisely the fact that their literature was a spontaneous outgrowth of their singular understanding of the Classics, which was in turn a result of their "self-

attainment" (*tzu-te*). However, their commentaries on the Classics
were often neglected because, Chiao Hung said,

> The world, confined as it is to the words of one school, looks down
> upon them as the works of literary men. . . . Now the Way is not
> something that can be exhausted by a single sage. Those who came
> earlier opened it while those who came later extended it. Where
> sketchy it was expanded, and where obscure it was clarified. Then
> and only then is its principle made clear. That is why the Classics
> have accumulated to become six in number. But there are those
> who, in their discussion of the Classics, desire to follow the words
> of only one teacher and feel that the Classics consists entirely in
> these words. How can they not be mistaken![110]

In thus reevaluating the Su brothers as classical
scholars, Chiao Hung seemed to be echoing the idea of literature
as a vehicle for the Way which had been a standard theme in Neo-
Confucianism since Han Yü (768–824) and his *ku-wen* movement.[111] Nevertheless, for Chiao Hung the Way could no longer
be "exhausted by a single sage" and was not confined to what
Han Yü had regarded as the orthodox transmission from Yao to
Confucius and Mencius. Rather, it was the result of "self-
attainment." As we shall see later, such a view of the Way
provided Chiao Hung with a basis for challenging the supremacy
of Ch'eng-Chu orthodoxy and enabled him to embark on a career
as a syncretist and synthesizer.
     The second half of the Wan-li period witnessed the
long struggle between Emperor Shen-tsung (r. 1572–1620) and
his bureaucracy over the choice of an heir apparent. The
bureaucracy pressed for the early appointment of the emperor's
eldest son, Chu Ch'ang-lo (1582–1620), as heir apparent, while
the emperor tried to procrastinate so that he could find a way to
appoint as heir apparent Chu Ch'ang-hsün (1586–1641), the son
of his favorite "precious concubine" née Cheng (c. 1568–1630).
The problem went unresolved for fifteen years until 1601, when
the emperor finally yielded to the pressure from the bureaucracy
and named the nineteen-year-old Ch'ang-lo as heir apparent.[112]
As a central government official during this period of struggle

over the imperial succession, Chiao Hung was outspoken in support of Ch'ang-lo as the legitimate heir to the throne. He also submitted a memorial requesting the emperor to allow Ch'ang-lo out of the inner palace to receive formal education. In doing so, Chiao Hung was apparently trying to help establish Ch'ang-lo's status as de facto heir apparent. For, as Chiao Hung indicated in his memorial, there were two aspects to this problem of imperial succession, the appointment and the education of the heir. The emperor, Chiao Hung said, might prefer not to act on the first aspect of the problem immediately, but he could not afford to delay action on the second, because education had to be pursued early, when "the original mind/heart of the heir apparent is still pure and firm." Lest the emperor refuse his request on the pretext that Ch'ang-lo was not yet officially designated as heir apparent and therefore could not be allowed to emerge from the inner palace, Chiao Hung cited Emperor Ch'eng-tsu's (r. 1402–1424) practice as precedent. Emperor Ch'eng-tsu, Chiao Hung pointed out, also declined repeated requests for the early appointment of an heir apparent, but he did not delay in securing a proper education for his eldest son.[113] Therefore, in Chiao Hung's memorial, Emperor Shen-tsung was made to appear entirely legitimate in putting off Ch'ang-lo's appointment; he was merely following in the steps of Emperor Ch'eng-tsu. But this analogy could easily backfire, since Emperor Ch'eng-tsu did eventually appoint his eldest son as heir apparent.[114]

It is difficult to evaluate the effect of Chiao Hung's memorial on Emperor Shen-tsung who, secluded as he was at the time in the interior of the palace, might not even have read it. But in 1594, when Ch'ang-lo was finally allowed to emerge from the inner palace to receive formal education, Chiao Hung was appointed his lecturer (*chiang-kuan*). Others who were appointed lecturers at the same time included Tsou Te-p'u (*chin-shih* 1583), Kuo Cheng-yü (1554–1612), and others who were all Chiao Hung's fellow officials in the Hanlin Academy.[115] As a lecturer, Chiao Hung was dissatisfied with lecturing as the standard way of teaching. Consequently, he proposed to supplement lecture with discussion, which had prevailed among the Neo-Confucians as a favorite method of education. Ch'ang-lo was said to have liked the idea of discussion, except that he did not seem able to raise questions. Thereupon, Chiao Hung took the initiative in posing questions to Ch'ang-lo. The latter soon acquired proficiency in both "questioning and replying," which was duly regarded as a manifestation of his bright nascent intelligence but which was also attributed to Chiao Hung's ability to stimulate thinking.[116] For Ch'ang-lo's moral edification, Chiao Hung compiled the *Yang-cheng t'u-chieh*, which was an illustrated thesaurus of golden sayings and noble deeds of past heirs apparent drawn from history.[117] The book was presented to the throne in 1597[118] but was never actually used by Ch'ang-lo because of the jealousy and opposition of Chiao Hung's fellow lecturers, who felt that he compiled the book as a gimmick to "buy reputation."[119]

In 1594, through the recommendation of the then Minister of Rites Ch'en Yü-pi (1545–1597), Chiao Hung was appointed compiler-official (*tsuan-hsiu-kuan*) and placed in charge of the Ming state history. This project was originally proposed by Ch'en Yü-pi in a memorial of September 1593, but it was not approved by the emperor until May 1594. Ch'en, in proposing the project, cited as precedent similar undertakings during the Sung dynasty.[120] Actually, however, the T'ang dynasty preceded the Sung in launching projects of this kind and the tradition of the reigning dynasty compiling its own history can ultimately be traced to the *Han Record of the Eastern Library* (*Tung-kuan Han-chi*) of the Eastern Han dynasty.[121] These histories are different from the *shih-lu* in that they were usually written in the composite style.[122] They are commonly known as "state" or "national histories" (*kuo-shih*), although Ch'en Yü-pi in his memorial to the emperor referred to his projected work as "standard history" (*cheng-shih*).

As compiler-official for the Ming state history, Chiao Hung made a four-point proposal. The first point concerned the "annals" (*pen-chi*) part of the projected work. It was an attempt by Chiao Hung to restore Emperors Hui-ti (r. 1398–1402) and Ching-ti (r. 1449–1457) to their rightful positions as legitimate rulers. Hui-ti, Chiao Hung pointed out, reigned for four years and

Ching-ti for seven or eight years. Neither one of them, however, even had an independent set of *shih-lu*.[123] Chiao Hung noted:

> This is not considered correct. People have always kept [separate] records for each of the rulers of a victorious state because the fact that they have all ruled at one time or another cannot be blotted out. This is what it means to say that a state can be destroyed but its history cannot be destroyed.[124]

Consequently, he suggested that these two rulers be treated individually in two independent sections of the annals.[125]

The second point of his proposal concerned the biographical section of the state history. It suggested that the old principle of including in this section only officials above the rank of third grade be abandoned, and that there be no regard for position as a necessary criterion for inclusion or exclusion. "History," Chiao Hung said, "has as its purpose the praise and blame of the various kinds of people." As such, it should not discriminate between "the illustrious and the lowly" so that "the public Way (*kung-tao*) can be clarified and made manifest to future generations." It should also include both "the good and the evil." He noted that many biographical works of his time dealt only with the famous and not with the infamous officials, with the result that "the chief evildoers and the night prowlers" escaped the judgment of history. "Praise and blame," however, should not be a result of the historian's personal "likes and dislikes" as was the case of parts of the *Ming shih-lu* which Chiao Hung criticized for misrepresenting Fang Hsiao-ju (1353–1402) as "begging for forgiveness" rather than opposing Emperor Ch'eng-tsu as a usurper. Mistakes of this kind, he suggested, should be rectified in accordance with the "impartial views of social consensus" (*kung-lun*).[126]

The third point of his proposal had to do with the problem of personnel. It suggested that the people to be enlisted for the project should be not only of the right kind but also limited in number. He said that except for finding specialists to handle the three subjects of the calendar, music, and water control, it was not

necessary to search for new recruits outside the court to work on
the project, since the court already had a bigger historiographical
staff than was actually needed.[127] The fourth and final point of his
proposal was an appeal for a concerted effort to collect material
of all kinds, including rare books in ancient editions.[128]

Taken together, these four points reflect Chiao Hung's
belief in the responsibility of the historian as the custodian of
moral truth and in the "authority" (*ch'üan*) of history as an
objective, impartial embodiment of the "public Way." This
"authority of history," he said in an essay "On History" (*Lun-
shih*), "is coequal with the authorities of Heaven and the emperor"
and could best be maintained if the writing of history were
entrusted to a single historian. "In ancient times," he said, "the
state histories were all produced by one man. That is why they can
be deposited in the Famous Mountain and be handed down
through a hundred generations." In later times, however, the
practice of collective compilation developed. As a result, the
historian lost the "exclusive charge" that had formerly been his,
and with a "supervisor" to whom he "had to report for every
word or event that he intended to record," he became "like a
general who is hampered by interference from the center [i.e., the
court]." "How,"Chiao Hung asked, "is he able to succeed?"[129]

There is not much that is extraordinary in Chiao
Hung's ideas of history. Traditional Chinese historians had
always believed in the moral intent and didactic function which
constituted the "authority of history."[130] Truthfulness and impartiality also had long been cherished values of traditional historiography. Even the idea of history as one man's work, which was
undoubtedly the rationale for the third point of Chiao Hung's
proposal to limit the size of the staff, had been voiced before by
Liu Chih-chi (661–721) and for essentially the same reasons.[131]
Nevertheless, it is noteworthy that "impartiality" for Chiao Hung
was no longer simply a matter of personal virtue, consisting of
fairness or lack of bias on the part of the historian. It involved the
"impartial views of social consensus" which, according to Chiao
Hung, the historian should bring to bear upon his material in
rendering "praise and blame." This concern for the "impartial
views of social consensus" was most strongly stated in Chiao's

essay "On History," where he deplored the prevailing practice of descendants' uncritically eulogizing their ancestors in the tombstone inscriptions and suggested that the tombstone inscriptions and memorials be checked against "community appraisals" (*hsiang-p'ing*) and "contemporary discussions" (*shih-lun*).[132] Chiao Hung's emphasis on "community appraisals" and "contemporary discussions" was partly a manifestation of the growing rigidity in the concept of objectivity, which occurred as a reaction against the post-Sung tendencies "to offer more eulogy than discussion."[133] Partly it was an expression of the heightened social consciousness among the educated elite during the late Ming, an era when Chinese society experienced a tremendous blurring of class lines and status distinctions.[134] It may, however, also be regarded as a corollary of Chiao Hung's idea of truth as public. This idea, as will be shown later, is constitutive of a whole conceptual universe which is distinctly Confucian; and Chiao Hung, for all his reputation as a "wild Ch'anist," remained in this regard a true Confucian.

The impetus for the project of the Ming state history was provided primarily by Ch'en Yü-pi, who, as I noted earlier, proposed the project to the emperor and recommended Chiao Hung as compiler-official. But Ch'en died in 1597. His death and a palace fire in the same year which caused damage to the materials collected for this project brought it to an end before it was ever completed.[135] By then, however, Chiao Hung had already finished the bibliographical section in six *chüan* which was later independently published as the *Bibliographical Treatise of the [Ming] State History* (*Kuo-shih ching-chi chih*).[136] The *Imperial Catalogue* (*Ch'ing-ting ssu-k'u ch'üan-shu tsung-mu*) was extremely critical of this work and said that it was the "most unreliable" work of its kind in the entire history of Chinese bibliography because it failed to distinguish the books which were extant from those which were lost at the time of its compilation.[137] This criticism by the editors of the *Imperial Catalogue* still prevails in contemporary scholarship. Hsu Sze-in (Hsü Shih-ying), for instance, writing in 1954, continued to dismiss the work as one that "indiscriminately incorporated [the book titles of] previous times."[138] But, as Naitō Torajirō has pointed out in his

Shina shigaku shi, the same criticism can actually be made of many bibliographical works before Chiao Hung's, the bibliographical treatises in the *T'ang Shu* and *Sung Shih* being examples. Moreover, Chiao Hung revived in his work the practice of writing a preface to each classification, a practice which had persisted through the *Sui Shu* but had been interrupted since the *Chiu T'ang-shu.*[139] In these prefaces, and also in the one supplementary *chüan* of corrections, Chiao Hung discussed the history of each classification, evaluated the various theories concerning the authenticity of such classical texts as the *Shang Shu* and the *Chou Li,* and proposed revisions for what he considered to be the misclassifications in practically all the major bibliographical works of earlier times. Naitō considered this work to typify the best bibliographical tradition in China as exemplified by Cheng Ch'iao's (1108–1166) *Chiao-ch'ou lüeh.*[140]

Probably also for the abortive project on the Ming state history, Chiao Hung compiled 120 *chüan* of biographies known as *A Record of the Worthies of the Reigning [Ming] Dynasty (Kuo-ch'ao hsien-cheng lu).*[141] In this work, Chiao Hung was true to his principle of nondiscrimination. He included all men of distinction regardless of their status from the beginning of the Ming dynasty to the end of the Chia-ching period (i.e., from 1368 to 1567), with those possessing official status grouped according to their titles or positions and others treated under such headings as "men of filiality and brotherly love" (*hsiao-yu*), "men of righteousness" (*i-jen*), "artists and writers" (*i-yüan*), etc.

As a collection of biographies, *A Record of the Worthies* was based largely on tombstone inscriptions of one kind or another which were, however, supplemented by materials drawn from government records, local gazetteers, and other works written or compiled by private individuals.[142] It was therefore a mixture of sources of the official kind with those which are usually referred to as "private records and unofficial histories" (*chia-ch'eng yeh-shih*)[143] and which, based as they often were on gossip and hearsay, were not accepted by traditional Chinese historians as legitimate sources for writing serious history.[144] In making use of these sources, Chiao Hung was implementing his view that "contemporary discussions" were a form of the "impartial views of social consensus." But he was criticized for this by the *Imperial Catalogue*, which, though recognizing Chiao Hung's thoroughness in gathering material, rejected *A Record of the Worthies* as "not entirely trustworthy."[145] Actually, however, Chiao Hung's use of the "private records and unofficial histories" did not result in an uncritical dependence upon them, since they were only one of the many varieties of sources that he had consulted. We do not know precisely how he made use of materials of this particular kind, especially because he did not specify in all instances the sources of his information. Nevertheless, judging from what he said in "On History," there should be no doubt that he used them to check and balance the accounts in sources of the official kind. The result of this simultaneous use of official and unofficial sources was wholly beneficial. By drawing on unofficial works, Chiao Hung preserved a wide range of information which modern scholars have been able to use to supplement or even correct the official sources. For instance, Wada Sei, on the basis of the information obtained from this work, was able to refute the *Ming shih-lu*'s claim that the capture of the Mongol chieftain Esen Tügel (d. 1431) was a result of his voluntary submission, and to demonstrate as popular nonsense the *Ming Shih*'s statement that the Prince of Yen, who later became Emperor Ch'eng-tsu, was assisted by barbarian troops from Uriyangqad (Wu-liang-ha) in revolting against Emperor Hui-ti.[146] Conversely, by putting private, unofficial works against such legitimate sources as the *Shih-lu* and tombstone inscriptions, *A Record of the Worthies* subjected the unofficial accounts to scrutiny and verification. The work is therefore also significant as an attempt to historicize the "private records and unofficial histories." As such, it marked the beginning of a change in private historiography, which was to become increasingly based upon "evidential research."

This change in Chinese private historiography is perhaps nowhere more evident than in the so-called *chang-ku* learning.[147] Naitō noted the large number of *chang-ku* books listed as the "historical sources of the great Ming dynasty" in Chu

Ch'üan-tsai's *Wen T'ung* and considered the flourishing of *chang-ku* learning to be a distinct feature of Ming historiography. The vogue of writing books of this kind did not, of course, begin with the Ming. As Naitō has pointed out, about half of the works contained in Tso Kuei's (d. c. 1274) *Pai-ch'uan hsüeh-hai* were *chang-ku* books written during the Sung. The practice, however, developed to a much greater extent during the Ming and, when compared with the *chang-ku* books of the Sung period, those of the Ming were larger in number and wider in scope. While the Sung *chang-ku* books usually recorded the events and ceremonial matters of the Imperial Court as they were observed or experienced by the authors as public officials, those of the Ming tended to go beyond the mere recording of court events and incorporated whatever court gossip seemed interesting or extraordinary. As a result, the Ming *chang-ku* books became a mixture of true facts with unverified and even unverifiable hearsay. As such, they are strongly characterized by the fictitious flavor of "unofficial history" (*yeh-shih*) and, according to Naitō, are hardly distinguishable from the latter. They are not always accurate, even though they may have been written in the composite or chronicle style of legitimate history. The growth during the Ming of the *chang-ku* learning may thus be judged as unfortunate: its expansion in scope and quantity was achieved at the expense of its value as reliable history. But, as Naitō was quick to point out, this was only the case with Ming *chang-ku* books produced before the middle of the Chia-ching period (c. 1550). Further development during the late Chia-ching and Wan-li periods tended to transform the Ming *chang-ku* learning from the pursuit of hearsay-based gossip literature into a serious undertaking of writing truthful history. Wang Shih-chen (1526–1590) and Chiao Hung are, according to Naitō, the two pioneers primarily responsible for this change, which continued into the Ch'ing. Wang, in writing his *Yen-chou shih-liao*, not only used the *Shih-lu* as a basic source of information but went through a meticulous process of collating the *Shih-lu* with a variety of other materials available at his time. The same process was also followed by Chiao Hung when he wrote *A Record of the Worthies*, which later became the model for the *Pei-chuan chi* of the Ch'ing dynasty[148] and was used by Wan

Ssu-t'ung (1638–1702) as a major source for the *Ming Shih*.[149] Wan, I might also point out, though generally critical of the historical scholarship of the Ming, recognized Chiao Hung as a master historian for his accomplishment in *A Record of the Worthies*.[150]

In 1597, Chiao Hung was appointed deputy examiner (*fu-chu-k'ao*) for the provincial examination in the metropolitan area of Shun-t'ien.[151] As such, he was censured by two supervising secretaries (*chi-shih-chung*), Hsiang Ying-hsiang (*chin-shih* 1580) and Ts'ao Ta-hsien (1555–1613), for the unorthodox statements which were said to have appeared in the examination papers of nine successful examinees.[152] The fact that Chiao Hung himself was rather unorthodox as a thinker might seem to lend credence to this censure. Actually, however, he was quite innocent, and the censure was largely motivated by narrow political considerations. As he tried to explain in his memorial to the emperor, he could not really be held responsible for eight of these nine examinees because he had nothing to do with their examination papers, which had been graded by the chief examiner (*chu-k'ao*). As for the one examinee whose paper he had read and whom he had passed, he stated his willingness to submit the paper to the rest of the court for further examination, even though the grading of examination papers had traditionally been the "exclusive responsibility" of the Hanlin officials. He thus pleaded not guilty and appealed to the emperor to dismiss the whole matter as a political conspiracy among some of his fellow officials who were trying to oust him from court.[153] The reason for this conspiracy, which he did not specify in this memorial but which he revealed in the privacy of his personal correspondence, was his outspoken support of Ch'ang-lo as the legitimate heir to the throne. This support which, he claimed, aroused the anger of the "many scoundrels"[154] would certainly also have displeased the emperor. Therefore, it is not surprising that his appeal to the emperor did not result in his exoneration. Instead, he was demoted and exiled to Fukien, where he served for about a year as vice magistrate (*t'ung-chih*) of Fu-ning subprefecture. In 1599, he tendered his resignation and went into retirement, thus terminating his career as a government official.[155]

Retirement

Chiao Hung retired back to Nanking where he spent the last twenty years of his life. In retirement, he engaged in a wide variety of activities which kept him far from being idle or secluded. He was continually beset by requests for funerary inscriptions, commemorative essays, and prefaces and postfaces to the various works of friends and acquaintances.[156] Nevertheless, he was able to find time for gardening[157] and, as mentioned previously, made frequent visits to the Ch'i-hsia Ssu. He also did a great deal of reading,[158] for which he amassed a superb personal library. He was reputed to have a collection which filled five rooms with every volume carefully annotated in his own hand.[159]

His scholarly pursuits, however, were not limited to reading and annotating; for we know that at least eleven of the works that he either wrote or edited were published during his years of retirement.[160] Moreover, in 1604, he had a meeting with Ch'en Ti, with whom he discussed the problem of "rhyming pronunciation" (hsieh-yin)[161] Chiao Hung had long been dissatisfied with the term "rhyming pronunciation" as a description of the end-rhymes in ancient songs and poems. As a result, he set out on a philological quest and, after analyzing some samples taken from ancient sources, came up with the theory that the end rhymes in ancient odes, which no longer fitted into modern schemes of rhyming, were all natural rhymes whose pronunciations had changed in the course of time.[162] This theory stimulated Ch'en Ti, who came to Nanking to meet with Chiao Hung. Emerging from this meeting and armed with a number of books loaned to him by Chiao Hung, Ch'en Ti was able to systematize and further elaborate Chiao Hung's theory in *An Inquiry into the Ancient Pronunciations of the Book of Odes (Mao-shih ku-yin k'ao)* and *On the Ancient Pronunciations of the Rhymed Songs by Ch'ü Yüan and Sung Yü (Ch'ü-Sung ku-yin i)*,[163] for which Ch'en Ti has been acclaimed as a late Ming master of "evidential research." The discovery of the theory on ancient natural rhymes has often been accredited to Ch'en Ti.[164] Actually, however, and by Ch'en Ti's own admission, his analysis of the problem was much indebted to Chiao Hung.[165]

In addition to his purely scholarly endeavours, Chiao Hung also continued to teach. In 1603, he traveled to Hsin-an to conduct a series of discussions at the Huan-ku Academy, where Chan Jo-shui (1466–1560) and Tsou Shou-i had taught in their time. Since the late 1580s and through the mid-1620s, however, the academy became closely affiliated with the T'ai-chou school and could claim among its teachers, aside from Chiao Hung, such renowned T'ai-chou thinkers as Lo Ju-fang, Yang Ch'i-yüan, and Chu Shih-lu (1539–1610).[166] Chiao Hung's arrival in 1603 drew an audience of more than 2,000 from all classes and age groups ranging from well-established members of the gentry to youthful herdboys.[167] In 1606, Chiao Hung led another series of discussions at Lo Ju-fang's shrine in Nanking.[168] Notes kept by students who attended the two series of discussions have been compiled and incorporated into Chiao Hung's collected works.[169] These notes suggest that both were truly discussion meetings, with no rigid structure or formal lectures by Chiao Hung. From time to time, Chiao Hung would pose a question or make a statement to elicit response, but more typically it was the students who asked the questions. Some students requested clarification of certain sayings in the classical works of Confucianism and Neo-Confucianism. Others asked about abstruse concepts like Nature (*hsing*), Destiny (*ming*), *liang-chih*, etc. Still others raised questions that had emerged out of their personal experience of self-cultivation, such as how to overcome "wild thoughts" (*wang-nien*). Chiao Hung's answers ranged from the purely theoretical to the concrete, earthy, and anecdotal. An atmosphere of intimacy and liveliness characterized the exchanges between Chiao Hung and the students, who were often overjoyed, chastened, and inspired.

As a teacher, Chiao Hung may not be comparable to Wang Yang-ming in the magnitude of his influence. As de Bary has observed, aside from Confucius, few people in Chinese history matched Wang in the number of students he had taught and the schools he and his students established.[170] However, Chiao Hung was no less resourceful with his students than Wang; and like Wang, he was forceful, dynamic, and provocative and resorted to exhortation, scolding, cajoling, and the use of paradox or reversal of conventional reasoning for effect. Nevertheless, there are

notable differences between Chiao Hung and Wang in pedagogical style. Wang believed that "study must be for one's own
sake."[171] As a result, he maintained a view of learning which
stressed individual experiential apprehension and practiced a
teaching method which was intensely personal. Indeed, the first
and third chapters of the *Instructions for Practical Living
(Ch'uan-hsi lu)*, which recorded Wang's activities as a teacher,
may be read as a series of his personal encounters with students,
during which he talked about his own agonized struggles to
become a sage and often inquired about what the students had
achieved for themselves in their efforts.[172] Interestingly, however,
although Wang in his discussions with students was always ready
to go beyond the immediate circle of his group for concepts and
doctrines, he seldom referred to experiences and practices other
than his own and those of his students. By contrast, Chiao Hung,
though equally personal in his interactions with students and
equally strong in his belief in learning as autodidactic, was fond of
citing the experiences and practices of others, especially as they
engaged in personal encounters.

Chiao Hung's incorporation into his teaching of the
experiences of those who were not involved in his "intellectual
discussion" must be distinguished from, say, the inclusion by Chu
Hsi and Lü Tsu-ch'ien (1137–1181) of an account of the sages
and worthies as a chapter in the *Reflections on Things at Hand
(Chin-ssu lu)*. While the conduct and dispositions of the sages and
worthies were presented in the latter work as models for
"contemplation" (*kuan*) and emulation, the experiences and
practices to which Chiao Hung alluded in his teaching were not
always intended for homiletic purposes. Rather, they were
frequently given either as elaborations of Chiao Hung's points or
as answers to specific questions from students. Whether as
elaborations or as answers, they often have a *kōan*-like sense of
enigma. For example:

1. [A student] asked, "The meaning of forming one body with
   things is known to me; but whenever I see someone at fault, I
   cannot help becoming angry. Where does the meaning of
   forming one body with things lie?"

The teacher [Chiao Hung] replied, "This requires the application of effort. In the past, Mr. Lo [presumably Lo Ju-fang] said to a friend, 'Your appearance is so strict and cold. How do you expect to deal with people?' The friend answered, 'My appearance is something that I was born with. How can I change it?' Mr. Lo said, 'Didn't Confucius say that in regard to countenance, [the gentlemen] was careful to be kindly?' On hearing this, that man's anger dissolved without his being aware of it."[173]

2. A friend asked, "Confucius spoke of 'one thread.' What Master Yang-ming talked about as the 'original-good-knowing' refers only to the 'thread' but not to the 'one.' [Am I right?]"
The teacher said, "In response to a friend who made a point similar to yours, Hsia Yün-feng asked, 'What is the one?' That man said, 'It is what is without sound or smell.' Smiling, Yün-feng said, 'Do you mean to say that the original-good-knowing has sound or smell?'"[174]

3. The teacher said, "In the study of the Way, there is nothing extraordinary. One need only stop seeking greedily and find a clear-sighted person to point it [the Way] out directly. [If one does this,] one will be back in one's original homeland [i.e., one's own Nature] immediately. What other affairs are there? My teacher Mr. Keng [once] said to me, 'My learning really began as a result of the stimulation by my oldest younger brother Tzu-yung. When I returned home from my mission as a messenger (hsing-jen), my oldest younger brother had also just come back from a study trip afar. He was full of vitality as if he had acquired something. At that time, P'eng Tung-o and I were studying laboriously. My oldest younger brother, however, did not approve [of what we were doing]. He said, 'The Classics and canonical works of the sages and worthies are voluminous. But they contain only a few essential sayings; [the rest] are ramblings and banterings which are insufficient to exhaust the mind.' Suprised, I asked him, 'What are the essential sayings?' He said, 'The saying that pleasure, anger, sorrow, and joy in their unaroused state are called centrality is the most essential.' I did not believe him. However, I had already studied for a long time and was agonizing for having no place to enter [the Way]. [Therefore,] I could not help being suspicious. One morning after I got up, I asked him, 'What is centrality?' My brother raised his hand and pointed. Suddenly, I gained understanding.

Later when I told others [about this incident], many experienced enlightenment."[175]

As the above examples indicate, the exchanges which
had taken place between two parties who were not present at
Chiao Hung's "intellectual discussions" were cited by him both as
answers to questions (1 and 2) and as further statements of his
own points (3). As such, however, their relevance to the question
or point at issue is not immediately obvious; and their apparent
irrelevance was clearly accepted by Chiao Hung and his students
as legitimate. The way Chiao Hung responded to the question in
example 1, for instance, was regarded by the note-taker as a
demonstration of his "skillfulness in teaching" (*shan hui-jen*),
whereas his reply in example 2 was said to have effected an
"enlightenment" (*hsing*) in "all those present." The note-taker
provided no comment for example 3 which, whatever its impact
on the audience, Chiao Hung made no attempt to clarify further.
In this regard, Chiao Hung again differed from Wang Yang-ming.
Wang, as is well known, often responded to his students in
ambiguous and paradoxical terms. But ambiguity and paradox
are not irrelevance. Besides, some of Wang's ambiguities and
paradoxes may only seem incompatible with one another as
individual statements, but are not truly ambiguous and paradoxical. They are simply different responses to different students
and, as such, are understandably inconsistent in terms of Wang's
idea of the teacher as a physician who cannot rely on a set
formula but must vary his prescriptions to suit the needs of
students as individual patients.[176] Moreover, Wang rarely left his
ambiguities and paradoxes unexplained or without further probing. On one occasion, he even tried to explain a Buddhist story
which, if it had not actually been used as a *kōan*, can certainly
pass as one:

A friend related a Buddhist story saying, "A Buddhist
pointed his finger and asked,'Have you seen this?' 'Yes,' replied the
monks. He then put his finger in his sleeve and asked, 'Do you still
see it?' The monks said, 'No.' According to the Buddhist interpretation, this means that they had not seen the Buddha-nature. I do
not understand this."

The teacher [Wang] said, "Fingers may or may not be seen. Your seeing of your Nature always rests with the human mind which, however, [often] runs only after what can be seen or heard and does not make the real effort on what is not seen or heard. Now, the substance of the original-good-knowing consists in what is not seen or heard and the effort to extend the original-good-knowing consists in the mind's being cautious [over what is not seen] and apprehensive [over what is not heard]. The student must at all times and at every moment see what he does not see and hear what he does not hear. Then his effort will be rooted in reality. When after a long time he has mastered the task, he does not need to exert energy, and without any caution or control the true Nature will operate without cease. How can seeing or hearing external things be any trouble?"[177]

To some extent, Chiao Hung's pedagogic differences from Wang can be seen as a result of Ch'an Buddhist influence, which is obvious and not surprising in view of Chiao Hung's orientation as a syncretist. Nevertheless, this influence needs be understood in context and, as will be shown later, is informed by a type of linguistic skepticism which considers language to be both continuous and asymmetrical with the *Tao* and which advocates, not the reduction of speech to silence as in Ch'an, but the transcendence of speech in the realization of the *Tao* as experience.

After a full and energetic retirement, Chiao Hung died in 1620, apparently of old age. Emperor Hsi-tsung (r. 1620–1627) honored him posthumously with the position of Mentor (*Yü-te*) in recognition of his service as lecturer to Chu Ch'ang-lo, who was Emperor Hsi-tsung's father. Further tribute was paid to him by the Prince of Fu who, on ascending the throne in Nanking after Peking had fallen to the Manchus, granted him the posthumous name Wen-tuan.[178] The Prince of Fu, ironically, was the son of Chu Ch'ang-hsün, Ch'ang-lo's competitor for the position of heir apparent.

CHAPTER THREE

A Syncretist's Critique of Ch'eng-Chu Orthodoxy

"Extreme Rigidity" and "Narrowness"

AS A SYNCRETIST who advocated unequivocally the "oneness of the Three Teachings" and as a member of the T'ai-chou school, known for its radical spirit of iconoclastic independence, Chiao Hung was almost an exact antithesis of Chu Hsi, who established the orthodox line of Confucian transmission and was determined to uphold it in opposition to Buddhism and Taoism. Not surprisingly, therefore, Chiao Hung was critical of Chu Hsi for indulging in anti-Buddhist parochialism, which he in turn held responsible for what in his view was Chu's misrepresentation of Confucianism. Chu Hsi, according to Chiao Hung, took pains to avoid Ch'an Buddhism as "heretical" (*i-tuan*). He was unwilling to use ideas which would have served well to elucidate the truth of Confucianism but which might have been suspect because of their Ch'an derivation. Therefore, whenever he encountered "subtle and abstruse words" in the Classics, he "became invariably afraid that they resembled Ch'an and explained them in terms other than those of Ch'an." As a result, his commentaries on the Classics missed the "cardinal meaning" (*ta-chih*) of the sages' teachings which, Chiao Hung believed, could best be clarified by the mystical doctrines of Ch'an Buddhism.[1]

In thus avoiding Ch'an as "heretical," Chu Hsi exhibited an "extreme rigidity" (*t'ai-yen*) which Chiao Hung considered to be a fundamental weakness of the "Sung" Neo-Confucians. "Rigidity," according to Chiao Hung, leads inevitably to "narrowness" (*lou*), for "just as a country becomes poor if its goods do not circulate in all directions, so a person's views become narrow when his learning does not reach out in all directions." Chu Hsi's "extreme rigidity" not only made him "afraid" of Ch'an and precluded him from an adequate understanding of the Confucian Classics but produced an impoverished vision of "orthodoxy" (*cheng-hsüeh*). It prevented him from being able to accept diversity of thought and to appropriate from a variety of doctrines which happened to be different from his own but which he should in principle have appreciated as the individual soundings of what Chiao Hung, borrowing a phrase from the *Chuang Tzu*, called the universal chorus of the "piping of Heaven" (*t'ien-lai*).[2] Therefore, Chu Hsi was "unsparing in his effort when he appraised the ancients, evaluated the Hundred Schools, hammered at the famous scholars, and picked at a multitude of doctrines." But he never indicated that he had "selected this or that strong point from this or that person." Nor did he ever proclaim, "Each sings according to his skill, but all are the same in being the one blowing and are to be regarded as the 'piping of Heaven.'" Instead, he was "afraid of falling into heresy" and "refrained from speaking" whenever he came across that which was "easy, simple, and free-flowing" (*i-chien shu-ch'ang*). In particular, he dismissed "all the discussions on spiritual awakening, luminous enlightenment, discerning understanding, and wonderful penetration as Ch'an" from which he feared "contamination" (*wo*). "Can it be said," Chiao Hung chided, "that a Confucian must be obstructed and befuddled (*chih-chih hun-yü*) before he can become orthodox?"[3]

"Tzu-ssu," Chiao Hung pointed out, "maintained [in the *Doctrine of the Mean*] that 'of all under Heaven, it is only he who, being of quick apprehension, luminous discernment, far-reaching intelligence, and all-embracing knowledge, is fit to rule.'"[4] Moreover, Chiao Hung continued, "it is said in the *Hsi Chuan* [section of the *Book of Changes*] that 'those in ancient times who were of quick apprehension, luminous discernment, far-reaching intelligence, and all-embracing knowledge could overcome [things] without killing.'"[5] These statements by Tzu-ssu and in the *Hsi Chuan* convinced Chiao Hung that Confucianism was not comprised of "dust or turbid matter" and that the "abstruse words and wonderful meanings" were not the "sole possession of the Ch'an school." Therefore, what was claimed to be Chu Hsi's "synthesis [lit., "unification," *t'ung-i*] of the various philosophers" was judged by Chiao Hung to be decidedly un-Confucian. It "could not match Confucius' half of the tally"; and Chu's criticisms of these philosophers, though "skillful" and "thorough," "could only appease the mouth but could not appease the heart." Chiao Hung said that he had very much wanted to write a book to exonerate all the philosophers who had been attacked by Chu Hsi and thereby to demonstrate that they "each had a purpose (*tsung*) in their learning." After some consideration, however, he gave up on the idea, knowing that such a book "would involve a great deal" and that he "might not be able to get it done soon."[6] Nevertheless, we may regard as a minor fulfilment of this wish the prefaces that he wrote to the "Philosophers" (*tzu*) section of his *Bibliographical Treatise*, where he discussed the reasons for all the seventeen schools of his classification and may therefore be said to have demonstrated that they "each had a purpose."[7]

In being thus "extremely rigid" and "narrow," Chu Hsi was viewed by Chiao Hung as a precise contrast to Grand Historian Ssu-ma T'an (d. 110 B.C.) who "discussed the essentials of the Six Schools" and selected strong points from each school. In doing so, Ssu-ma T'an exemplified for Chiao Hung an ideal attitude which Chuang Tzu had advocated in the essay "Ch'i wu lun." Chuang Tzu, according to Chiao Hung, came after Confucius, when the "abstruse teaching" was in eclipse and when the world was full of scholars who "were fond of food and drink but lacking in the sense of shame and integrity." Like the "Confucians" in the *Chuang Tzu*, who robbed graves on the supposed authority of the *Odes* and *Rites*,[8] these scholars abused the Classics for ego indulgence. They "each took what they considered right to be right and what they considered wrong to be wrong." As a result, Chuang Tzu "desired to equalize the theories about things" and wrote the essay "Ch'i wu lun."[9]

To Chiao Hung's regret, Chuang Tzu's "elegant intent" in this essay had never been truly understood, since the title of the essay had always been read as "Ch'i-wu lun" (i.e., as "A Discussion on the Equality of Things"). This way of reading the essay's title had come about by dismissing the third word *lun* as inconsequential and by taking the second word *wu* to be the same in usage as the *wu* in the statement by Mencius that "it is the nature of things (*wu*) to be of unequal quality."[10] The first two words, *ch'i* and *wu*, thus formed a phrase by which Chuang Tzu was alleged to have expressed the wish to equalize things. On this account, Chuang Tzu had often been criticized. The critics considered Chuang Tzu to be wrong in trying to equalize things intrinsically unequal. For Chiao Hung, however, it was the critics who were mistaken as their criticism was based on a misunderstanding of the text resulting from an erroneous reading of the three characters in the title. The third word, according to Chiao Hung, was far from being inconsequential, but was of crucial importance. With the character *wu*, it formed the term *wu-lun* or "theories about things," which Chuang Tzu had used to designate the contending views of the different schools of thought. What Chuang Tzu really wanted to do in this essay was therefore to "equalize," or *ch'i*, the "theories about things" and not intrinsically unequal things. In doing so, Chuang Tzu's hope was to demonstrate the senselessness and futility of being self-righteous and to stop the petty squabbles among the philosophers so that they would "together forget themselves in the art of the Way."[11]

In thus challenging what he regarded as the standard way of interpreting the "Ch'i wu lun," Chiao Hung cannot be considered original. The idea was apparently well known during the Sung dynasty. As Ch'ien Ta-hsin (1723–1804) has noted, it was first proposed by Wang An-shih (1021–1086) and Lü Hui-ch'ing (1031–1111) and was later expounded by Wang Ying-lin

(1223–1286).[12] Two of Wang An-shih's essays on the *Chuang Tzu* were copied *in toto* into Chiao Hung's *Chuang-tzu i*, which also incorporated some of Lü Hui-ch'ing's commentaries on the *Chuang Tzu*.[13] It would therefore seem that Chiao Hung was acquainted with these two men's ideas on this problem, even though he made no acknowledgment to that effect. Originality aside, we may also question the validity of the reinterpretation. As Chang Ping-lin (1869–1939) has pointed out, the new reading of the essay's title as "Ch'i wu-lun" does not fully correspond to the essay's content, which stands for a lot more than the title would then suggest.[14] The "equality of things" is demonstrably a concern of the essay and cannot be explained away by merely changing the reading of the title, however imaginatively.

It is noteworthy that Chiao Hung himself did not include the reinterpretation in his *Chuang-tzu i*, where he merely quoted from the commentaries of Kuo Hsiang (d. 312) and T'ang Shun-chih to emphasize Chuang Tzu's attempt to expose the subjectivity of value judgments without pressing further for the new reading of the title.[15] His proposal that the title be read as "Ch'i wu-lun" was actually made in connection with his critique of Chu Hsi and ought to be appreciated in its context. As a criticism of Chu Hsi, it is significant not so much in being a statement for a revised reading of the title as in being a plea by Chiao Hung for the necessity of redressing what he perceived to be the failings of Chu Hsi's intellectual outlook. In rejecting Ch'an and all other teachings except his own as "heterodox," Chu Hsi became for Chiao Hung as senseless as what in Chuang Tzu's terms were the "howlings of the myriad hollows" (*chung-ch'iao chih-hao*)[16] which, though caused by the same wind, contended among themselves for the exclusive claim to being indentical with the wind. Moreover, in being thus senseless, Chu Hsi fell prey to the twin weaknesses of "extreme rigidity" and "narrowness" which, according to Chiao Hung, could best be rectified by Chuang Tzu's "Ch'i wu-lun" theory as practiced by Grand Historian Ssu-ma T'an. What Chuang Tzu had thus advocated and what Ssu-ma T'an had thus practiced constituted for Chiao Hung an ideal which would be maintained by "all those who valued syncretising the multitude of doctrines" (*so kuei-yü che ch'ün-yen chih-chung che*).[17]

Syncretism, then, was the thesis that Chiao Hung tried to establish through his criticism of Chu Hsi when he proposed that "Ch'i-wu lun" be read as "Ch'i wu-lun." It is a thesis which he invoked over and over again, especially when he was confronted with the charge of "heresy" or *i-tuan*. I have rendered *i-tuan* as "heresy," but it is not an exact equivalent. In its use as a concept in Christianity, heresy has been understood not only as the antithesis of orthodoxy but in contradistinction to infidelity (i.e., of pagans), schism, and apostasy. To the extent that both heresy and infidelity reject what is normatively defined as the Christian dogma, they may both be regarded as species of unbelief.[18] Nevertheless, they are distinguishable in that while infidelity is simply a denial of faith never professed, heresy can occur only to a person who has once accepted but has since repudiated or doubted the rule of faith. For this reason, I will follow Bauer in designating infidelity as "unbelief" and heresy as "false belief." As "unbelief," infidelity can certainly be transformed into heresy, but not without first being converted into orthodoxy as the pure and genuine belief which must precede heresy as "false belief."[19]

The specific content of heresy varied over time as the criteria for orthodoxy changed. Nicolaitism, for instance, was increasingly condemned as immoral by the church. But it did not become heretical until the eleventh century, when it was anathematized as such.[20] However, whatever its doctrinal constitution is at a given moment, heresy is never a matter of personal knowledge or conviction; it must be a decision by the church, which alone has the authority to fix a body of dogmas as orthodox. By withholding assent to what the church regards as the doctrinal norm and thereby denying the church's authority as the sole arbiter of faith, heresy entails separation from the communion of the church and is necessarily schismatic. Indeed, the original meaning of heresy in Greek (*hairesis*) is schism. Historically, however, schism need not always be heretical although it became so in Catholicism with the definition of papal infallibility. Schismatics may simply be rebellious and unconcerned with matters of doctrine. They may separate themselves from the church without relinquishing what the church proposes as the faith, while heretics in their opposition to the church are invariably motivated by doctrinal considerations. What the heretics commit is thus always a double offense; they defy the authority of the church and suffer what from the church's point of view is a loss of faith.[21]

Heresy also admits of varying degrees. At one extreme, there is heresy in the first degree. It is heresy pure and simple and implies the holding of a doctrine which directly contradicts what the church has explicitly pronounced as an article of faith. At the other extreme, there is what in the church's terms is merely "an opinion suspected or savouring of heresy" (*sententia de hoeresi suspecta, hoeresim sapiens*). It consists of a doctrinal violation which is not strictly demonstrable and is only probable. These two types of heresy define the outer boundaries of heresy, which does not include and must therefore be distinguished from apostasy. As the abandonment of both the church and the faith, apostasy may logically be viewed as the culmination of heresy, but it is not deemed as such because the apostate ceases to believe in Christ and is no longer a Christian whereas the heretic still retains faith in Christ and professes himself to be a Christian.[22]

The above differences between heresy on the one hand and infidelity, schism, and apostasy on the other suggest that heresy as a Christian concept is necessarily intrasystemic in reference, distinctly doctrinal in orientation, and must be an exclusively ecclesiastical determination which only the church has the authority to establish.

By comparison, the Neo-Confucian *i-tuan* is not so restricted in application. It is both intrasystemic and intersystemic in reference. Therefore, in "sifting the heterodoxical doctrines," the *Chin-ssu lu* condemned not only such Confucians as Tzu-chang and Tzu-hsia for deviating from the "Sage's Way of the Mean" but also a number of non-Confucians ranging from Yang Chu and Mo Ti to Lao Tzu and the Buddha. Likewise, Hu Chü-jen (1434–1484) in early Ming, while criticizing the views of fellow Confucians like Ch'en Hsien-chang and Lou Liang (1422–1491) as heretical, also rejected Buddhism and Taoism as *i-tuan* or *i-chiao*.[24] Moreover, in Neo-Confucianism, there did not exist an institutional apparatus comparable to the Christian church as the privileged authority on faith. Accordingly, *i-tuan* in Neo-Confucianism need not wholly be an institutional decision. It can be a matter of private concern which an individual may entertain as a personal conviction. To be sure, after the thirteenth century when Neo-Confucianism gained recognition as the official ideology, the state became the guardian of Neo-Confucian orthodoxy and had the power to censure certain ideas as heretical. But the state's power in this regard, though substantial or even devastating at times, was not absolute. It did not in principle preclude private individuals from exercising the same power, with the result that the private individual often adhered to doctrines which deviated from the official norm and even rendered judgments which were an explicit challenge to the state's verdict on orthodoxy and heresy. I have already noted Chiao Hung's abiding faith in the truth of Li Chih's ideas in spite of their condemnation by the state. Though a syncretically minded "Ch'anist," Chiao Hung was by no means atypical of the Ming–Ch'ing intellectuals in expressing dissent from the established dogma. The state's sanction of the Ch'eng-Chu school as orthodoxy during both the Ming and the Ch'ing did not prevent rival schools from proliferating in late Ming or save Ch'eng-Chu orthodoxy from scathing attacks by critical thinkers in early Ch'ing. Yen Yüan (1635–1704), for instance, denounced the orthodox Ch'en-Chu school in no uncertain terms as a "collection of all the evils of textual scholarship, pure discussion, Ch'an Buddhism, and pharisaism," which, he said, "obscured the sagely Way" of Confucius and Mencius and was "more harmful than [the doctrines of] Yang [Chu] and Mo [Ti]."[25] Significantly, in staking claims against the official orthodoxy, the dissidents in Ming-Ch'ing times made no attempt either to organize or to appeal to an alternative institutional structure for authentication. For, in Neo-Confucianism, the authority for truth is institutionally inconclusive; the state as the guardian of Neo-Confucian orthodoxy is, curiously, not the indisputable spokesman for the

Neo-Confucian truth, which, as will be seen a little later, is directly accessible to every person and does not require institutional dispensation.

The fact that the Neo-Confucian concept of *i-tuan* was both intrasystemic and intersystemic in reference has been noted by Paul Cohen, who distinguished the Neo-Confucian *i-tuan* from its Christian counterpart as "broader" in scope. Cohen, however, interpreted this difference between the two conceptions of heresy as a result of two contrasting situations between the growing intellectual coherence in Sung and post-Sung China and the increasingly "pluralistic" outlook of the postmedieval West. He said,

> as postmedieval Western society became more and more pluralistic in nature, an increasing number of heterodoxies developed, each referring back to a different orthodoxy. In Sung and post-Sung Chinese society, on the other hand, as Confucianism to an ever-increasing extent became the only orthodoxy worthy of the name, *all* [sic] departures from the Confucian norm became heterodox.[26]

This interpretation of the "broadness of application" of the Neo-Confucian *i-tuan* implies an obviously anachronistic view of the concept of heresy in Christian history. The restricted use of heresy in Christianity as an intrasystemic category was not a post-medieval development. It was already an established practice during the Patristic era. As Bauer has pointed out, Origen was stating a widely held notion when he said unequivocally, "All heretics at first were believers; then later they swerve from the rule of the faith."[28] Origen's straightforward statement on heresy has a metaphorical parallel in Tertullian's formula which compared heresy to the wild olive or fig tree springing from a cultivated seed which is orthodoxy.[29]

Aside from being anachronistic, Cohen's interpretation also underestimates the intellectual diversity in Sung and post-Sung China. Philosophically, Buddhism may be said to have passed its peak by Sung. It could no longer compete with Neo-Confucianism as the dominant system in creative vigor. Nevertheless, it did not cease to be a viable alternative to the revived

Confucianism. The many syncretic-minded Neo-Confucians whom I have discussed in the first chapter are an unmistakable demonstration of the continued appeal of both Buddhism and Taoism to the Chinese elite. Moreover, different and contending schools did emerge within Neo-Confucianism in Sung and post-Sung China. Their existence was duly recognized and recorded by Huang Tsung-hsi in the *Sung-Yüan hsüeh-an* and the *Ming-ju hsüeh-an*. It led to the development in late Ming of what I shall call a preoccupation with intellectual genealogies[30] of which the two above-mentioned works by Huang may be cited as examples. But it did not effect any change in the scope of the Neo-Confucian conception of *i-tuan*. The persistence in late Ming of the Neo-Confucian *i-tuan* as a "broader" category in the midst of acknowledged diversity suggests further the need to reexamine the meaning of the Neo-Confucian *i-tuan* as an issue.

As mentioned above, the Neo-Confucian *i-tuan* differs from Christian heresy not only in being "broader" in scope but also in lacking an institutional center as the privileged authority. These two distinguishing traits of the Neo-Confucian *i-tuan* need to be considered together in their adjacency; and when so considered, what appears to be the "broadness" of the Neo-Confucian *i-tuan* suggests, not an overall intellectual coherence, but a certain referential diffuseness which may be regarded as a correlate of what has been noted earlier as institutional inconclusiveness. Moreover, as correlates, they are both informed by a theory of man, which is characteristically Neo-Confucian. In Neo-Confucianism, man's Nature (*hsing*), whether conceived dualistically by the Ch'eng-Chu school as distinct from the Mind (*hsin*) or monistically by the Lu-Wang school as one with the Mind, is identical with the divine Principle of Heaven (*t'ien-li*). Man thus has access to the divine truth by virtue of being a man and not on account of his conversion to or membership in a particular faith. There is no need of an institution to provide for mediation in the Neo-Confucian relationship between the human and the divine, which, though not unproblematic, is definitely continuous. Besides, an institution with the claim to being vouchsafed the truth as a special revelation is not conceivable in Neo-Confucian terms whether it be in the form of an ecclesiastic hierarchy as in Roman Catholicism or in the form of a corporate community as in Protestantism. Similarly, since truth is existentially embodied in every man, orthodoxy as the correct perception of truth is also necessarily the true belief of every man. The individual man may deviate from his heavenly Nature and fall into heresy, which he will need to rectify. But, being born with the true belief, he does not have unbelief as a problem to contend with. Understandably, orthodoxy in Neo-Confucianism as the true belief is only opposed to heresy as false belief, and not distinguished from infidelity or apostasy as unbelief. As the systemic locus of the Neo-Confucian orthodoxy is not restricted by other belief systems as unbelief, the Neo-Confucian *i-tuan* as the antithesis cannot logically be exclusive in its application as a mere intrasystemic reference to false belief.

Notwithstanding their differences in meaning, both Neo-Confucian *i-tuan* and Christian heresy presume a systemically defined norm and stigmatize beliefs and practices which deviate from the presumed norm. Chiao Hung, however, while challenging Chu Hsi's claim to orthodoxy, also advocated a modified conception of *i-tuan*. For him, the term means first and foremost a teaching or practice which is different from one's own. He said, "I have a strand of learning. Others differ from me. That is a 'different strand' (*i-tuan*)." Mere difference as such, however, is not a sufficient reason for condemning a teaching or practice as heretical. To condemn a teaching or practice as heretical simply because it is different is, according to Chiao Hung, "like living in the wilds while laughing at the houses of others as being ugly."[31] Obviously, this rather literal interpretation of *i-tuan* as "different strand" did not oblige Chiao Hung to accept just any teaching. As a committed syncretist, Chiao Hung was necessarily pluralistic, but not nihilistically skeptical. He did not refrain from disputing the truth claims of Chu Hsi's teaching and was unequivocal in his affirmation of a norm which he enunciated in terms of the "daily uses of the people" (*pai-hsing jih-yung*):

Whatever corresponds to the daily uses of the people is common virtue. Whatever is different from the daily uses of the people is heresy. Scholars should try to think about what the daily uses of the people are. They need not be too anxious about attacking heresy.[32]

To the extent that the "daily uses of the people" prescribes for Chiao Hung a norm from which all deviations are regarded as heretical, his conception of *i-tuan* is still unmistakably judgmental. Nevertheless, his norm can no longer be identified with a particular system. As will be seen later, the "daily uses of the people" constitute for Chiao Hung the ultimate reality which transcends systemic distinctions and, in the final analysis, is systemically undefinable. As his norm thus loses its systemic identity, his *i-tuan* also ceases to be systemically determinate. Accordingly, in his conception of *i-tuan*, Chiao Hung was able to avoid the systemic exclusiveness of the orthodox Neo-Confucians and to maintain a pluralistic outlook without abdicating from his responsibility as a critical thinker to judge the truth value of a variety of teachings.

It may be noted that Chiao Hung, in making the above-quoted statement on heresy, traced himself back to Wang Ken,[33] who, as the founding father of the T'ai-chou school, had already attempted to establish the distinction between orthodoxy and heresy on the basis of the "daily uses of the people." Wang Ken said, for instance, "The Way of the sage is not different from the daily uses of the people. Whatever is different [from the daily uses of the people] is heresy."[34] Textually, however, the *locus classicus* for the expression *pai-hsing jih-yung* is to be found in the *Hsi Tz'u* section of the *I Ching*, where it is stated, "The kind man discovers it [the Way or Tao] and calls it kind. The wise man discovers it and calls it wise. The people use it day by day (*pai-hsing jih-yung*) and are not aware of it, for the way of the superior man is rare."[35] The main thrust of this passage is, as Wilhelm has suggested, that the Way is universal, even though it is perceived differently by different kinds of people or, as in the case of the common people, not perceived at all but simply "used."[36] Wang

Ken went beyond the *Hsi Tz'u* when he cited the "daily uses of the people" as the basis upon which to redefine the concept of heresy. In addition to affirming the universality of the Way, he tried to make "the Way answer to the everyday uses of the people."[37] In doing so, he articulated a vision of the Way which fully expresses the "popular nature" (*jen-min hsing*) of his thought and his intensely physical sense of the self.[38] Chiao Hung subscribed to Wang Ken's vision of the Way and its implications for self and society, but with a purpose of his own. Wang Ken was close to the Taoists in his idea of human nature as natural spontaneity (*tzu-jan*).[39] He also originated a school in which syncretism prevailed. But he was not an advocate of the "oneness of the Three Teachings." Rather, as he announced ostentatiously in his door poster, he intended his teaching to be identified with the central line of the Confucian transmission, from Fu Hsi through Yao and Shun to the Duke of Chou and Confucius.[40] His purpose in redefining heresy was "to liberate the potentialities of the individual" and to satisfy man's immediate needs.[41] Chiao Hung, on the other hand, while following Wang Ken's redefinition of heresy, did so with the manifest intention of opening up Confucianism for a dialogue with the non-Confucian teachings, especially Buddhism and Taoism. His above quoted statement on heresy appeared twice in his works, once in a long essay called "Chih T'an" which, though written in the form of fragmentary notes, is a sustained attempt to demonstrate and justify the thesis that the Three Teachings are one.[42]

"Fragmentation," "Compulsion," and "Pharisaism"

As noted earlier, Chiao Hung criticized Chu Hsi for missing the "cardinal meaning" of the sages' teachings, which, he said, could best be understood in terms of the mystical doctrines of Ch'an Buddhism. Specifically, Chu Hsi misinterpreted the two concepts of "investigation of things" (*ko-wu*) and "extension of knowledge" (*chih-chih*), with the result that his alleged "synthesis" failed to match "Confucius' half of the tally" and misled generations of later scholars. Chiao Hung said,

> The learning of Confucius and Mencius became obscured when it came down to the Sung Confucians. This all began with I-ch'uan [Ch'eng I] and Yüan-hui [Chu Hsi] who misinterpreted the "investigation of things" and the "extension of knowledge," with the result that scholars exhausted their energies in seeking principles in external things with no regard for the cultivation of their bodies and minds.[43]

According to Chiao Hung, it was not until the Ming dynasty that the truth of Confucianism was made clear again when Hsüeh Hsüan (1389–1464) reemphasized the importance of "restoring Nature" (*fu-hsing*). Hsüeh Hsüan, however, came long after Confucianism had been "obscured." Hence, "his doctrine was still not lucid." But he was followed in time by Ch'en Hsien-chang and Wang Yang-ming, whose "forceful exposition and direct pointing" (*heng-fa chih-chih*) finally made "the purpose of Confucius and Mencius" shine like "the sun and the moon in the sky." Wang Yang-ming, in particular, was said by Chiao Hung to have made "a great contribution" with his doctrine of *liang-chih* which, by establishing *liang-chih* as the existential identity of man as man, "demonstrated to scholars that they should return to themselves and seek [principles] within themselves."[44]

As a latter-day follower of Wang Yang-ming, Chiao Hung continued to affirm *liang-chih* as the existential identity of man as man. He said,

> *Liang-chih* is what everyone possesses. If you call for it and offer it to the practitioner of the Way, he would not accept it because he has this *liang-chih*. If you trample on it and offer it to a begger, he would only spurn it because he also has this *liang-chih*.[45]

As the existential identity of man as man, *liang-chih* is further equated by Chiao Hung with "humanity" (*jen*) which, he said, is also "what a man naturally possesses." On the other hand, however, though inherent in man's being as man, like *liang-chih*, "humanity" cannot be realized without "learning" (*hsüeh*), which, according to Chiao Hung, has "doing humanity" (*wei-jen*) as its very purpose. That is why, he said, "the compilers of the *Analects* spoke of learning first and of filiality and brotherly respect as the root of humanity immediately afterwards." Moreover, as "the root of humanity," "filiality" and "brotherly respect" are analytically distinguishable from "humanity," which, for Chiao Hung as it was for Confucius, is the general virtue denoting the supreme excellence of man. It pervades every aspect and activity of man. As Chiao Hung put it, "Daily uses, food and drink are humanity. Coming, going, activity, and repose are humanity. Speech, silence, and a smiling face are also humanity." By contrast, "filiality" and "brotherly respect" are particular virtues and, according to Chiao Hung, are singled out in the *Analects* as "the root of humanity" because, of all the activities and aspects of man, they are "the most basic and easy to understand." But, different as they are from "humanity" as concepts, "filiality" and "brotherly respect" are existentially identical with "humanity." All three are but "names" (*ming*) for "one and the same thing" (*i-wu*) which is the "human mind" (*jen-hsin*). This being the case, "doing humanity" as the purpose of learning requires not only the cultivation of "filiality" and "brotherly respect" as particular virtues but the apprehension in these particular virtues of "humanity" as the general virtue or, in Chiao Hung's terms, the "knowing of filiality and brotherly respect as humanity" (*chih hsiao-t'i chih wei jen*).[46]

Ultimately, "filiality," "brotherly respect" and *liang-chih* are identified by Chiao Hung not only with "humanity" which defines man's existence as man but also with the very "substance" (*t'i*) which constitutes the "norm of Heaven" (*t'ien-tse*). He said, "Humanity is sometimes called filiality and brotherly respect and at other times *liang-chih*. But it is also called propriety (*li*); and propriety is the substance or norm of Heaven." Since "filiality," "brotherly respect," *liang-chih*, and "humanity" are all thus identified with the "substance" or "norm of Heaven," "doing humanity" cannot be different as a process from the "attainment of the Way" (*chih-tao*). Therefore, while affirming "doing humanity" as the purpose of learning, Chiao Hung was able to declare further that "the superior man's learning is for nothing but the attainment of the Way" which, for Chiao Hung, is also necessarily and simultaneously an achievement of what in the *I Ching*'s terms are the "realization of Nature" (*chin-hsing*) and the "fulfillment of Destiny" (*chih-ming*).[47] Thus he said, "With the attainment of the Way, all the mystery and profundity of Nature and Destiny . . . will become illuminated in the mind."[48]

Chiao Hung's identification of the particular virtues of "filiality" and "brotherly respect" with the general, existential virtues of "humanity" and *liang-chih* and with the "substance" or "norm of Heaven" as one and the same exemplifies his mode of thought as a discursive formation which enabled him to accord every ethical or empirical specificity epistemologically legitimate status as a datum of perception and to approach it in ontologically ultimate terms as a metonymic instance of the holistic Way. For Chiao Hung, therefore, "filiality" and "brotherly respect" are to be known both as "humanity" and as the "substance of the Way" (*tao-t'i*). "The sages," he said, "demonstrate the substance of the Way in the daily course of things directly and decisively to the people." And this, according to Chiao Hung, is precisely what Confucius tried to accomplish during his meeting with the music master Mien.[49] Confucius, Chiao Hung maintained, did what he did and said what he said while receiving the music master in order to make a "direct demonstration" of the Way to his disciple Tzu-chang. The reason why Confucius and other sages were able to do so is that they "obtained the One" (*te-ch'i-i*) in their "learning" and apprehended the world holistically. Consequently, they were able to "pick up a thing at random with everthing else falling in line" (*hsin-shou nien-lai t'ou-t'ou shih-tao*). In this regard, the sages are markedly different from "later Confucians who fragment (*chih-li*) and trivialize and who patch and repair, gaining here and missing there."[50]

That "later Confucians fragment and trivialize" is, according to Chiao Hung, a result of their failure to have a "true understanding of the word 'learning'." Chaio Hung compared learning to "shooting" (*she*) and said, "Just as there is a target in shooting, so there must be a purpose in learning. With the target lying ahead of us, we may go after it with the bow and arrow and can hit it without fail." If, however, we "do not recognize the target," we may try as hard as we can, but in the end the effort will be in vain. It is even likely that "the more diligently we apply our effort, the farther we shall be from hitting the target."[51] We may, of course, hit the target by chance. But, Chiao Hung said, "hitting the target by mere chance is what Confucius means by 'conjecture' (*i*)."[52] It happens only "once in every thousand" tries and is highly unreliable. Assuming, however, that the rare chance does occur, there is still no "benefit" (*i*) to be derived from its occurrence because, "in method, [conjecture] is no different from 'guessing at the identity of an item beneath an overturned cup' (*she fu-yü*)."[53] This in turn is nothing but "wild imagination" (*wang-hsiang*). It does not have anything real to go by, since the identity of the item is "known only to the person who put the item there"; and there is always the chance that "nothing was ever placed beneath the overturned cup." In the latter case, the person who does the guessing "labors in vain" (*t'u-lao*).[54]

The target of which Chiao Hung spoke as the purpose of learning he specifies as "my original mind" (*wu chih ch'u-hsin*) which, though "mine," is not exclusively mine and is in fact what "everyone possesses." As such, "my original mind" is just another designation for the existential quality of man, which he also termed "humanity" and *liang-chih* and which, as noted earlier, he identified with the Way or Nature. Like the Way which is "self-sufficient" (*tzu-tsu*) and like Nature which is "not lacking in anything" (*wu pu-pei*), "my original mind" is never mistaken and always functions properly as a matter of course. Thus, "when the infant is first born, he does not seek milk with eyes, nor does he turn to light with ears, nor does he try to walk with hands or to feel around for things with feet." But self-functioning as it is, "my original mind" does not preclude the necessity of "learning," for, Chiao Hung said analogically, "There is fire in the wood, but the wood does not burn without being drilled. There is also water in the earth, but the water is not to be reached without digging."[55]

On the other hand, since the "original mind" which is the purpose of learning is "mine" and is what "everyone possesses," learning for Chiao Hung cannot and must not be undertaken as a "search from without;" this, as noted earlier, was where he believed Ch'eng I and Chu Hsi had erred in their "investigation of things."[56] The injunction against the "search from without" is, of course, the hallmark of the Lu-Wang school, which has often been characterized as "subjective-idealist" or "anti-intellectualist."[57] I will discuss this characterization of the Lu-Wang school in detail later. For the moment, we need to become aware that the Neo-Confucian categories of "within" (*nei*) and "without" (*wai*) or "mind" and "things" (*wu*) are coded expressions which must be decoded for their meaning through an analysis of the Neo-Confucian language as an encoding proce- dure. They cannot readily be described in terms of such European philosophical categories as "subjectivism," "idealism," or "anti- intellectualism." Surely, Chiao Hung's rejection of the "search from without" does not require the mind to withdraw into itself as the "world of truth."[58] Rather, he said, "According to Mencius, '[Shun] clearly understood the multitude of things and closely observed human relationships.'[59] Now the complexity of human life is not separate from these two words—'relationships' and 'things.' Amidst this complexity, [relationships and things] must be observed with particular care."[60] This statement indicates unequivocally that, for Chiao Hung, the mind as the knowing faculty must not be disengaged from the world of phenomena in order to achieve truth and that his "learning" necessarily involves "things" and "relationships." It is only that "things" and "rela- tionsips" are to be observed not as ends in and of themselves but for the sake of "seeing into Mind" (*chien-hsin*) or "knowing Nature" (*chih-hsing*), which, according to Chiao Hung, is also what Confucius took to be the "target" of his teaching.[61]

Of the Sung Neo-Confucians, Chiao Hung confessed "deep admiration" for Chou Tun-i, Ch'eng Hao, Shao Yung (1011–1077), and Lu Hsiang-shan, who, he said, "all had attainment with regard to the Way." As for Ch'eng I and Chu Hsi, their "learning did not enter from the realization of Nature as the purpose." As a result, they became just like the "conventional Confucians" who "examine and check every affair" but who only grow "daily farther from the Way." Moreover, the fallacy which Ch'eng I and Chu Hsi thus committed in their "learning" is not simply epistemological in nature, as it also has unfortunate implications in terms of psychology and morality. As noted earlier, "Mind" or "Nature" is equated by Chiao Hung with the ontologically ultimate "substance of the Way." Specifically, he spoke of Mind or Nature as the "foundation" (*pen*) of "things" and "relationships." For him, "seeing into Mind" or "knowing Nature" implies the concomitant establishment of the "foundation" upon which "propriety" as the "norm of Heaven" naturally and necessarily prevails among "things" and "relationships."[62] This being the case, learning for Chiao Hung cannot simply be an intellectual process of cognition; it must also be a matter of moral and psychological fulfillment.

In terms of personal cultivation, establishing the "foundation" is comparable to "first having a master within." Here, the "master" is defined as "the Substance in its original state." It is "not that which I first take possession of and then use as a master." "Taking possession of it first and then using it as a master" is like "straightening the inside with reverence" (*i-ching chih-nei*), which, Chiao Hung insisted, must not be confused with "straightening the inside by being reverent" (*ching-i chih-nei*). The difference between "straightening the inside with reverence" and "straightening the inside by being reverent" is subtle and crucial. One is artificial and contrived, while the other is natural and spontaneous. It is the kind of difference in which, he said, "the least divergence in the beginning will lead many miles astray in the end."[63]

The "master" of which Chiao Hung spoke as "the Substance in its original state" is the a priori condition for self-cultivation. Without this a priori condition or, as Chiao Hung put it, "not first having a master within, " one is likely to resort to the "Four Interdictions" (*ssu-wu*)[64] and become "compulsive" (*ch'iang-chih*). Morally, "compulsion" manifests itself as "pharisaism" (*hsiang-yüan*), which is an attempt "to take over the old traces of the ancients and to imitate their forms and appearance."

The "pharisee," he said, is a "fox" which can disguise its true identity and "deceive" people by "putting on the appearance of being a man." As such, the "pharisee" is very difficult to identify unless one has the eye of a Confucius or Mencius, who was able to recognize the "pharisee" as the "thief of virtue."[65] Nevertheless, the "pharisee" must be seen for what he really is and be "opposed vigorously," for just as the fox in disguise is not actually a man, so the "pharisee" as a personality can never be "genuine" (*chen*).[66]

"Not knowing the purpose of learning," Ch'eng I and Chu Hsi were said by Chiao Hung to have "taken the imitation of forms and appearance as accomplishment." They thus fell into the category of the "pharisee" and could no longer take Confucius as their "refuge" (*i-kuei*). Confucius, as noted earlier, was said by Chiao Hung to have also taken "seeing into Mind" or "knowing Nature" as the "target" of his teaching. This "target" is what Confucius obtained as the "One" which, Chiao Hung lamented, not even all of Confucius' disciples were able to achieve, still less the later Confucians who were "misled and submerged by the commentaries and subcommentaries."[67] "The T'ang commentaries and Sung subcommentaries," Chiao Hung declared, "are fetters on my intelligence."[68] By contrast, Buddhist literature "points directly to man's mind" and does not suffer from the "fragmentation" and "convolution" (*ch'an-jao*) of conventional Confucianism. That is why, Chiao Hung said, Wang Yang-ming realized the truth of *liang-chih* only after he had studied Buddhism, even though the doctrine of *liang-chih* had always been the "essence of the sages' teachings."[69]

Mencius and the Aberration

Chu Hsi was, of course, not alone among the Confucians in rejecting Ch'an or Buddhism in general as heretical. Nor, for that matter, was he unprecedented. Indeed, "much of the ground work" for anti-Buddhist and antiheretical thought in later Confucianism was "hammered out in the thick of ideological combat" long before "a genuine Confucian orthodoxy became firmly established in China."[70] For instance, the argument that Buddhism was a foreign religion and therefore not acceptable to the Chinese was an integral part of Han Yü's (768–824) polemics against it. But the core of Han's argument was already formed at the time of Mou Tzu and achieved a high level of elaborateness in Ku Huan's (390–453) "Treatise on the Barbarians and the Chinese" (*I-hsia lun*), in which Ku condemned the Indian religion as "evil" on grounds of its being foreign.[71] Xenophobic arguments of this kind may have become "increasingly ineffective as Buddhism was domesticated."[72] In Chiao Hung's time, however, they were apparently still strong enough and popular enough for him to address them as a challenge. He noted that Buddhism was sometimes rejected because the Buddha was not Chinese. But, he quipped, the Chinese do not always reject something on account of its being foreign in origin. In fact, they had accepted and cherished for generations such foreign weapons and precious stones as Su-shen's arrows and Ch'üan-fu's jade. It was only with regard to the Buddha's "subtle words and wonderful discussions" that the Chinese chauvinists "covered their ears and would not listen." They are, Chiao Hung said disdainfully, "surely to be considered bizarre."[73]

In spite of the Buddha's having been an Indian prince, Chiao Hung does not regard Buddhism as a foreign doctrine. Rather, he believed that Buddhism, if properly understood, could be appreciated as part of China's ancient philosophical heritage, since it dealt with the problems of Nature and Destiny which, he said, had also been concerns of Confucius and Lao Tzu. Chiao Hung was aware that Confucius did not pursue problems of this sort at great length. He admitted that "Confucius rarely spoke about them." But, he explained, Confucius was waiting for a qualified person to emerge, with whom it would be appropriate to discuss these problems. "That is why," Chiao Hung said, "[Confucius] stated that 'to those who are less than mediocre, the highest subjects may not be revealed.'"[74] Obviously, Confucius had waited in vain. Nevertheless, as Chiao Hung was quick to point out, the *Analects* does contain a few more than casual remarks on Nature and Destiny, which Buddhism had made its special field of inquiry. In doing so, Buddhism clarified what Confucius wanted to but did not have the chance to clarify, thereby providing "a commentary on the teachings of Confucius and Mencius." Consequently, Chiao Hung said, "Once the Buddhist scriptures are penetrated, the sayings of Confucius and Mencius will be understood immediately. There are not two separate principles [in Buddhism and Confucianism]." As "a commentary on the teachings of Confucius and Mencius," the Buddhist scriptures also compared favorably with the writings of Han and Sung Confucians, for "what the Buddhists have commented on is the essence of Confucius and Mencius, whereas what the Han and Sung Confucians have commented on are their chaff and dregs." To "worship" the "chaff and dregs" while "rejecting" the "essence" is, according to Chiao Hung, "not penetrating the principle."[75]

Chiao Hung's argument that Buddhism pursued the kind of problems which had also concerned Confucius and Lao Tzu and that its scriptures were "a commentary on the teachings of Confucius and Mencius" sounds suspiciously like an appeal to Chinese nativist sentiments. He may thus seem to be an example of what has been described as the gentry-dominated tradition of "Sinomania" which had first looked down upon Buddhism as a mere corruption of native Taoism and which later accused Christianity of plagiarizing the then relatively domesticated Buddhism.[76] In reality, however, any imputation to Chiao Hung of such "Sinomania" would be unwarranted. He did not consider foreignness to be a good reason for repudiating a doctrine and was in any case advocating the acceptance and not the rejection of Buddhism. Although in a sense he viewed Buddhism as part of China's own heritage, he did not claim it as uniquely Chinese. For him, it was simply a doctrine which could help clarify the truths of Nature and Destiny. He said:

> Nature and Destiny are the treasures of our own household. We [Chinese] have an inexhaustible deposit of these treasures which have long been buried while we remained poor and with nothing to live on. There then comes a barbarian merchant [i.e., the Buddha] who points them out to us. Can we reject his words because he is

not Chinese? Although that man is a barbarian merchant, the treasures are our own possession. There may be differences among men between aliens and Chinese, but the treasures recognize no such differences. Moreover, Chinese and alien are not fixed terms. They are what people use to refer to one another. I may refer to him as an alien. But how do I know that he does not refer to me as an alien? Those who understand may simply laugh![77]

Chiao Hung thus appropriated Buddhism as "a commentary" on Confucianism not so much to deny its Indian source of origin as to affirm its universal validity as a teaching.

The rejection of Buddhism by Chu Hsi and other "conventional Confucians" (shih-ju) as heretical was, according to Chiao Hung, a deviation from the classical norm of high antiquity. He was of the conviction that the sages in ancient times were open-minded. Instead of wrangling among themselves for the exclusive claim to orthodoxy, they tried to learn from one another in spite of their differences in systemic identity. He compared the history of doing scholarship "from the ancient past to the present" to that of "governing the state" and said, "Just as there were times when meetings were held [for lords who came from different regions] with jade and silk [as tribute], so there was a period during the Three Dynasties and before when [the state] circulated the goods of all under Heaven to provide for the needs of all under Heaven. There was then no exclusiveness due to differences in locality."[78] To contrast this open-mindedness of the ancient sages with the exclusiveness of later generations, Chiao Hung cited Yü and Lao Tzu. Yü, Chiao Hung pointed out, happily doffed his clothes when he ventured into a country of nudists, and Lao Tzu imitated what was obviously a barbarian language while residing in the land of the Western Barbarians (hsi-jung).[79] Later Confucians often waged their campaigns against Buddhism and Taoism on the supposed authority of Confucius. But, Chiao Hung retorted, Buddhism had not yet been introduced to China in Confucius' time. Therefore he could not possibly have attacked it as heretical. Nor would he have been likely to do so, since he never attacked Lao Tzu as unorthodox. "Why," Chiao Hung asked, "do people today attack what Confucius himself did not attack?"[80]

For Chiao Hung, therefore, a genuine spirit of open-mindedness had prevailed in ancient China until the late Chou period, when Mencius launched an overly zealous crusade against Mo Ti and Yang Chu. "For the most part," Chaio Hung said, "the teachings of these two philosophers had their origins [in the ancient sages]." Mohism was based on Yü's teachings, and the philosophy of Yang Chu was derived from the traditions of the Yellow Emperor and Lao Tzu. Mencius, Chiao Hung believed, had certainly inquired deeply into the teachings of the early sage-kings and could not be accused of being ignorant of the sources of the ideas of Mo Ti and Yang Chu. Nevertheless, he denounced them as beasts and must therefore be said to "have held his views with extreme rigidity."[81]

The scholarly world had since become increasingly partisan. Taking their cue from Mencius, Confucians of later generations often attacked Buddhism and Taoism as unorthodox without really knowing what these two teachings were about. This, according to Chiao Hung, was the case with Han Yü and Ou-Yang Hsiu (1007–1070). Han Yü, Chiao Hung noted, was much impressed by his acquaintance with the monk Ta-tien, whom he described in his letter to Meng Chien (d. 823) as "having no impediments in his breast" and as "being able to transcend the bounds of the body, thereby conquering the self by means of reason and not permitting himself to be invaded or thrown into confusion by things and events."[82] What thus impressed Han Yü about the monk Ta-tien was, according to Chiao Hung, the greatest possible benefit to be derived from the "field of blessngs" (*fu-t'ien*).[83] Yet, in this same letter to Meng Chien, Han Yü denied any personal interest in Buddhism, saying, "It is not that I worship or believe in his [Ta-tien's] *dharma* or seek benefits [from the field of blessings]." Han Yü, Chiao Hung taunted, must have become involved in Ta-tien's teachings "without himself being aware."

Ou-yang Hsiu, on the other hand, was said by Chiao Hung to be "particularly stubborn." Toward the end of his life, he heard about Fu Pi's (1004–1083) obtaining the *dharma* from the monk Ching Tz'u and was obviously impressed, as he always had trusted and admired Fu Pi as a man who "did not carelessly stoop before people." As a result, he himself started making inquiries into the teachings of Hua-yen Buddhism. But he never got very far in these inquiries because he died shortly afterward. By Chiao Hung's standard, Han Yü and Ou-yang Hsiu "never really had much grasp of the Confucian principles" and were not the kind of people who "touched the ground with their heels." They need not be taken seriously in their opposition to Buddhism and Taoism, which they opposed out of the mere desire to imitate Mencius in his crusade against Mo Ti and Yang Chu.[84]

If, however, Han Yü and Ou-yang Hsiu in their opposition to Buddhism and Taoism seemed to Chiao Hung to be partisan without yet being quite certain of themselves, the rejection of these two teachings by the Ch'eng brothers and Chu Hsi was both firm and calculated. It was almost like a deliberate cultivation of ignorance and prejudice. I have already discussed Chiao Hung's criticism of Chu Hsi's anti-Buddhist parochialism, which he held responsible for Chu Hsi's failure to perceive the "cardinal meaning" of the sages' teachings. As for Ch'eng Hao, Chiao Hung respected him as a "lofty" personality but found him to be "still biased in what he had attained."[85] His charges against Buddhism were, according to Chiao Hung, quite without foundation. They were based on his own "surmises" and not on any genuine understanding of Buddhism, which he or his brother Ch'eng I advised their followers not to investigate thoroughly but to judge only by its practical consequences.[86] Thus, like a judge handling a lawsuit, Ch'eng Hao or Ch'eng I had rendered an arbitrary decision without giving the defendant a chance to speak out. "Being the judges ourselves," Chiao Hung asked, "shall we say that there ought to be no following of the conventional world and that the sentence ought to be reversed to make it a happy thing for both the past and the present?"[87] Actually, Chiao Hung said, Ch'eng Hao was not entirely unaware of the "silent correspondence" between Buddhism and Confucianism. He once expressed great admiration for the manners of a group of monks whom he chanced to see in a Ch'an monastery, and said, "Herein lies all the majesty and decorum of the Three Dynasties."[88]

Nevertheless, he insisted on the incompatibility of Buddhism with Confucianism and "confined himself to the practice of partiality, narrow-mindedness, and obstinacy." In this regard, he was like all other "conventional Confucians" who "were entangled with names without investigating facts."[89]

Three Teachings: Truth and Untruth

To uphold his charge that Ch'eng Hao and other "conventional Confucians" were "entangled with names without investigating facts," Chiao Hung struck out at a number of anti-Buddhist and anti-Taoist arguments which the Confucians had advanced over the years and which Chiao Hung now tried to expose as spurious and contrary to the "facts" of the Three Teachings. In so doing, he came up with a series of counterarguments which were probably the most sustained and thoroughgoing refutations of the orthodox Confucian criticisms of Buddhism and Taoism.

Of all the Confucian charges against Buddhism and Taoism, the one concerning Buddhist and Taoist metaphysics emerged relatively late in time. The Confucians did not seriously engage the Buddhists and Taoists on the metaphysical level until the Neo-Confucian revival in the Sung. But, emerging late as it did, the metaphysical charge must be viewed as the most basic in terms of the philosophical consciousness of the orthodox Neo-Confucians. It is ironic that while the importance of metaphysics in Neo-Confucianism is usually recognized, the metaphysical significance of the Neo-Confucian confrontation with Buddhism and Taoism is not always fully appreciated. It has been said, for instance, that the Ch'eng brothers' criticisms of Buddhism were largely based on "morality and common sense" and that their "fundamental objection" to Buddhism consisted in their judgment that "the ultimate motive of the Buddhist is selfish."[90] Actually, Ch'eng I had insisted that the "foundation" or *pen-ling* of Buddhism was wrong. In response to a student's enumeration of the similarities between Buddhism and Confucianism, Ch'eng I said, "Although there are many similarities like these, simply because their [the Buddhists'] foundation is wrong, everything of theirs is wrong."[91] Together with his brother Ch'eng Hao, Ch'eng I had also rejected any suggestion that the "mind" or *hsin* of Buddhism might be right whereas its "practice" or *chi* was wrong. Repeatedly, the two Ch'engs singled out Wang T'ung's (583–616) distinction between "mind" and "practice" for criticism,[92] suggesting that they regarded their differences from the Buddhists as more than a mere matter of moral practice and that their apparently ethical and commonsensical arguments against Buddhism were grounded in fundamental considerations of metaphysics. In point of fact, the orthodox Neo-Confucians had always considered their metaphysics to be different from those of the Buddhists and Taoists. Thus it is said in the *Chin-ssu lu*, "The Buddhists do not understand *yin* and *yang*, day and night, life and death, or past and present. How can it be said that their metaphysics is the same as that of the Sage?"[93] As for Taoist metaphysics, Chu Hsi noted Chang Tsai's (1020–1077) condemnation of the doctrines of being and nothingness as "vulgar" and considered Lao Tzu as "wrong" in maintaining that "things come from being and being comes from nothingness."[94]

In metaphysics, the orthodox Neo-Confucians developed the theory of "Principle" (*li*) with which they opposed the Taoist idea of Nothingness (*wu*) and the Buddhist doctrine of Emptiness (*k'ung* or *śunyatā*). As propounded by the Ch'eng brothers and Chu Hsi, Neo-Confucian Principle "is not just an idea or something abstract,"[95] not only because it is embodied in concrete things but also because it exists metaphysically as the essence of things and is that which gives reality and universality to things. As the essence of things, Principle is inherent in all things and is never in actuality separate from things or material force (*ch'i*), for, as Chu Hsi said, "it is only when there is material force that Principle finds a place to settle."[96] In this sense, Principle is necessarily immanent. On the other hand, Principle is also transcendent, as it exists "above physical form" (*hsing-erh-shang*) and is itself without "form."[97] Therefore, although Principle is inherent in things and is actually inseparable from things, it does not depend on them for existence. It has a metaphysical existence of its own which does not transform with the transformation of things. In other words, Principle is immaterial but nonetheless real in the sense that it is "eternal and unchanging" and that it forms the "essence of things" and is "indestructible."[98]

As such, Neo-Confucian Principle was often contrasted with Taoist Nothingness and Buddhist Emptiness, both of which the orthodox Neo-Confucians understood in a negative sense as a denial of the reality of their Principle. I have already noted Chu Hsi's rejection of Lao Tzu for maintaining that "things come from being and being comes from Nothingness." He opposed Lao Tzu in this regard because Lao Tzu's Nothingness seemed to him to negate the "existence" of Principle, which he, like the Ch'eng brothers before him, tried to affirm as the foundation of Neo-Confucianism and which he held to be both "uncreated and imperishable" (*pu-sheng pu-mieh*).[99] He said,

> Nothingness means nonexistence of a thing but the existence of its Principle. Since there is the Principle, there is being. But Lao Tzu said that things come from being and being comes from Nothingness. Even Principle is considered nonexistent. This is wrong.[100]

However, in thus rejecting as "wrong" Lao Tzu's Nothingness as the source of being and things, Chu Hsi did not make an unconditional condemnation of Taoist metaphysics as a whole. In comparison with Buddhist Emptiness, Taoist Nothingness was apparently considered by Chu Hsi the lesser of the two evils. He seems to have felt that the Taoist concept of Nothingness, though negative, is sufficiently ambiguous as to allow for some residual Principle still to be contained in it. Thus he said,

> For the Taoists, there is still being after all. For example, the saying, "Let there always be Nothingness so we may see their subtlety and let there always be being so we may see their outcome," is an evidence of this.[101]

Buddhist metaphysics, on the other hand, did not seem to Chu Hsi to be characterized by such redeeming ambiguity, and he made no qualifications whatsoever in his denunciation of the Buddhist idea of Emptiness, which, he said, "means complete nothingness."[102] He accused the Buddhists of regarding Heaven and Earth as "illusory and erroneous" and the Four Elements as "temporary [i.e., unreal] aggregates"[103] and said,

The Buddhists talk about Emptiness whereas the Confucians talk about reality, and whereas the Buddhists talk about Nothingness, the Confucians talk about being.[104]

He also criticized the Buddhists for mistaking mind for Nature and for being "most afraid of the very mention of the word Principle," saying,

With us Confucians, although the mind is vacuous, Principle is real. The Buddhists, on the other hand, go straight to their destination of Emptiness and void.[106]

He thus rejected the view that the distinction between righteousness and selfishness was the "only difference between Buddhism and Confucianism and insisted that the "starting points" (yüan-t'ou) of these two teachings were different because, he said, "we Confucians say all principles are real while the Buddhists say all principles are empty."[107]

Chu Hsi's metaphysical criticisms of the Buddhist idea of Emptiness are standard among the orthodox Neo-Confucians and can be traced back to anti-Buddhist arguments of Chu's early Sung predecessors such as Chang Tsai (1020–1077) and the Ch'eng brothers. Chang Tsai accused the Buddhists of "not knowing to investigate Principle to the utmost." As a result, "the Buddhists do not know Heaven's decree and consider mind-dharma as the reason for the rise and extinction of Heaven and Earth." He said,

The Buddhists have false ideas about our Heaven-endowed Nature and do not know how to shape and bring into completion the functioning of Heaven. On the contrary, they regard such small things as the Six Sense Organs to be the causes of the universe. They cannot thoroughly understand these things, and consequently falsely assert that heaven, earth, the sun, and the moon are illusory and false.... Can they be said to have investigated

Principle to the utmost? Can they be said to have fully developed
their Nature? . . . [108]

Ch'eng Hao, who was the prime target of Chiao
Hung's refutations of the Confucian anti-Buddhist arguments,
also condemned the Buddhists for trying to "do away with the
Four Elements" and to "annihilate the normal Nature completely" in order to "achieve the Way." In doing so, he said, the
Buddhists would only "deviate very far from the Way" and end
up with "having no reality." The Buddhists, according to Ch'eng
Hao, also "want to eliminate Principle." But, he said, all things
have and come from "this Principle," which is "the reason why it
is said that all things form one body." For Ch'eng Hao, "to
eliminate this Principle" is utterly impossible and becomes
possible "only in death."[109]

Compared with Chang Tsai and Ch'eng Hao, Ch'eng
I is not particularly known for his metaphysical criticisms of
Buddhism. As Wing-tsit Chan has pointed out, Ch'eng I criticized
Buddhism mostly on moral and social grounds.[110] But even
Ch'eng I denounced the Buddhists as those who "do not
understand Principle" and contrasted them with the Sage as a
follower and practitioner of Principle. He said,

Heaven has this Principle. The Sage follows and practices it
[Principle]. This is what is called the Way. The Sage bases himself
on Heaven whereas the Buddhists base themselves on mind."[111]

In coping with this metaphysical challenge from the
orthodox Neo-Confucians, Chiao Hung as a syncretist denied
that Nothingness and Emptiness were negative concepts. He
claimed that "Lao Tzu did not talk about the Nothingness of
Nothing but only clarified the Nothingness of being." "The
Nothingness of Nothing" is, according to Chiao Hung, achieved
through the "destruction of being." He called the pursuit of
Nothingness of this kind "lopping away at the corners" (wan-
tuan), a phrase which was originally used in the Chuang Tzu to
characterize Shen Tao's attempt to "discard knowledge" and to
"do away with self" in order to follow the Way. However,

according to the *Chuang Tzu*, Shen Tao in doing so "did not really understand the Way"; he only "heard something of what it was like."[112] Chiao Hung used this allusion from the *Chuang Tzu* to distinguish the "Nothingness of Nothing" from the "Nothingness of being " which, he said, "is realized in the midst of being" and is so "realized" by cultivating what in Lao Tzu's terms is the learning of the "return to the root" (*kuei-ken*).[113] The "Nothingness of being" is not a rejection or negation of "being"; it is the "ultimate of attaining vacuity and observing tranquillity."[114] It is only because "things all return to their roots" that they, "though rising in teeming multitudes," cannot be said to have "being."[115]

Thus understood as the "Nothingness of being," Taoist Nothingness is regarded by Chiao Hung not as a contradiction of but as a concept "subsumed" (*yü*) in the Confucian idea of "being." He said that Confucius and Mencius talked about "being" because they wanted to "guide" (*yin*) the world by "using what was already understood by the world." This, he said, is "the so-called learning the lower subjects in order to penetrate the higher subjects." However, many Confucians became thus "confined" (*chü*) to the realm of "being," and few could "penetrate" the higher subjects. Consequently, Lao Tzu and Chuang Tzu propounded the idea of Nothingness. In doing so, their "elegant intent" was not to "advocate becoming high-flown" but to affirm that in order to make use of Confucian "being," it would be "necessary first to penetrate Nothingness."[116]

Similarly, it is because the world "sees only form/ matter [*se* or *rūpa*] but not Emptiness" that the Buddha preached that "form/matter is Emptiness."[117] Buddhist Emptiness is thus no more a rejection or negation of "form/matter" than Taoist Nothingness is a rejection or negation of "being." Chiao Hung flatly denied as untrue Ch'eng Hao's charge that the Buddhists wanted to "annihilate the normal nature completely" in order to "achieve the Way." He said,

> How can there be these words [by Ch'eng Hao]? Such [views as Ch'eng Hao has attacked] are the nihilistic views of the two vehicles [of Śrāvakahood and Pratyekabuddhahood] and are precisely what the Buddha himself has condemned.[118]

He also said,

> According to the perfect teaching of Hua-yen Buddhism, nature
> has no self-nature, and yet there is no nature that is not *dharma*.
> This *dharma* is not a different *dharma*, for there is no *dharma*
> which is not nature.[119]

The fact that "nature" is here both denied for its "self-nature" and
affirmed as *dharma* is, according to Chiao Hung, evidence that
Hua-yen Buddhism does not advocate "rejecting the world and
leaving the mind with no support." Rather, the purpose of this
"perfect teaching" is "to demonstrate the uncreated in the realm
of the created and to indicate that the uncreated *dharma* is not
destructive of the created *dharma*."[120]

Related to the orthodox Neo-Confucian rejection of
Buddhist and Taoist metaphysics was the charge that Buddhism
and Taoism were amoral, escapist, and selfish. As Mou Tsung-san
has noted, Neo-Confucian metaphysics is "moral metaphysics"
(*tao-te ti hsing-shang-hsüeh*).[121] Thus, as the metaphysical
essence of things, Neo-Confucian Principle is creative of a
universe which is both real and moral. Principle is simultaneously
the reason for creation and the source of goodness. Not
surprisingly, therefore, Buddhist Emptiness and Taoist Nothingness were viewed by the orthodox Neo-Confucians as metaphysically nihilistic and morally hollow. Thus Ch'eng Hao, while
accusing the Buddhists of attempting to "do away with the Four
Elements," also criticized them for having only "seriousness to
straighten the internal life" but "no righteousness to square the
external life." As a result, he said, "those who are rigid become like
dry wood and those who are relaxed end up in recklessness."[122]
Ch'eng Hao's dual rejection of Buddhism as metaphysically
nihilistic and morally hollow was also voiced by Ch'eng I and Chu
Hsi, both of whom attacked what appeared to them to be the
amorality of Buddhism on the basis of their belief in the moral
character of Principle. Ch'eng I denounced the Buddhists for
"desiring to forget about right and wrong" and said, "How can
right and wrong be forgotten? The Principle of the Way naturally
exists in abundance. Why bother to forget [about right and

wrong]?"[123] Chu Hsi, on the other hand, took pains to draw a distinction between the Confucian and Buddhist conceptions of Nature. The Confucians, he said, maintain that Nature is "intrinsically possessed of Principle of the Way in abundance" and that it embodies a definite sense of "right and wrong" whereas the Buddhists regard Nature as an "indeterminate" (*hun-lun*) state of "things and affairs" without any sense of "right and wrong." Consequently, the Buddhists take "seeing" of any kind as Nature regardless of whether or not the "seeing" involved is in accord with Principle. "That is why," he said, the Buddhists "are topsy-turvy and are never right anywhere."[124]

As is well known, a large part of the orthodox Neo-Confucian attack on Buddhism as amoral was focused on the Buddhist institution of monasticism or "leaving the home" (*ch'u-chia*), which was an obvious affront to the Neo-Confucian valuation of family as the basis of the Neo-Confucian ethical system of the Five Human Relationships (*wu-lun*). For the Ch'eng brothers, "leaving the home" was an attempt on the part of the Buddhists to "cut off" or "destroy all human relationships" by deserting family as a social institution. "The home," said one of the Ch'eng brothers, "is no more than the relationships between the ruler and minister, father and son, husband and wife, and elder and younger brothers," which in turn are what the Way is comprised of. As such, the home constitutes a set of natural, existential relationships which are impossible to "leave." The Buddhists, according to Ch'eng I, did not actually succeed in "leaving the home." What they called "leaving the home" was merely an attempted escape from home by not treating their parents as parents. It symbolized the kind of escapism that was prevalent among the Buddhists who, the Ch'eng brothers charged, wanted to "live alone in the mountains and forests" and to seek "goodness only for themselves."[125]

In being thus escapist, the Buddhists were said to be motivated by the selfish concern for "gain" or "advantage" (*li*), which in turn was viewed as the reason why the Buddhists held to the doctrine of "birth and death" or *saṁsāra*. The Buddhists, Ch'eng I said, "are basically afraid of death and fond of life" and their teachings "can finally be reduced to a pattern of selfishness and self-interest."[126] He or his brother Ch'eng Hao also accused the Buddhists of "frightening people with the doctrine of birth and death," saying,

> The sages and worthies regarded birth and death as our lot, which there is no reason to fear, and so they did not discuss birth and death. The Buddhists, however, because they are afraid of birth and death, never stop talking about them. The lowest class of man of course has many fears, and is easily moved by self-interest. As for the Ch'an school, although they claim to be different, in essentials their viewpoint is the same—it all comes to self-interest.[127]

The charge that the Buddhists were escapist, selfish, and concerned for "gain" or "advantage" was made by a large number of Neo-Confucians who, whatever their disagreements on other issues, all agreed that the Buddhists were terrified of "birth and death" and were bent on a selfish quest for transcendence. Even Lu Hsiang-shan, whose doctrine Chu Hsi criticized as Ch'an in disguise,[128] condemned the Buddhists for their escapist and selfish view of life:

> I have used the two words "righteousness" and "personal gain" to distinguish between Confucianism and Buddhism. I have also used the terms "public-spiritedness" and "selfishness," but actually they mean righteousness and personal gain.... Buddhists consider man, living in the world, as consisting of a chain of birth and death, a wheel of transmigration and afflictions resulting from passions, and regard them as most painful, and seek to escape from them.... Therefore they say, "Birth and death are a great matter." What you [i.e., Wang Hou-chih (1131–1204)] called resolution to become a Bodhisattva is merely for the sake of this great matter. This is the basis on which the Buddhist teachings are founded. Therefore, we call them self-seeking and selfish. Being righteous and public-spirited, Confucians are engaged in the management of the world; being self-centered and self-interested, the Buddhists withdraw from the world.[129]

From the Confucian and Neo-Confucian point of view, which demands that man achieve self-fulfillment within the temporal limitations of birth and death and the ethical framework of the Five Human Relationships, the Buddhist search for enlightenment appears selfish. It is selfish because it requires a person to "leave the home" and thus to assert his independence egotistically by renouncing his responsibilities as a man among men. It is also self-interested because the quest thus made is for the "advantage" of being able to transcend the sufferings of birth and death.

Chu Hsi, as noted earlier, did not reject Taoist Nothingness out of hand as hopelessly nihilistic and accepted it in preference to Buddhist Emptiness. A similar preference also characterized his moral criticisms of Taoism. It was, however, a preference which was highly tentative and extenuated. Therefore, although he maintained at one point that the teachings of Lao Tzu and Chuang Tzu were less harmful than Ch'an Buddhism because Lao Tzu and Chuang Tzu "did not completely destroy moral principles" whereas Ch'an Buddhism "wiped out all moral principles from the very start," he soon corrected himself by stating that they were all harmful "just the same" because "in the matter of doing harm, there has never been a case which does not proceed from the smaller to the greater degree." In most instances, therefore, Chu Hsi did not distinguish Taoism from Buddhism as morally more acceptable. Instead, he lumped them together as "destructive of the Three Bonds and the Five Norms" and charged Taoism with the same kind of indictments that he and the Ch'eng brothers directed against Buddhism. For instance, he denounced the Taoists for being exclusively concerned for "gain" or "self-interest" and for being engrossed in "preserving the body and avoiding harm" with no regard for the "oughtness of the moral principle." He also criticized the Taoists for being "selfish" and considered them different from the Buddhists only in that their "selfishness" manifested itself as "trickery" (*ch'iao*) whereas the "selfishness" of the Buddhists assumed the form of "disliking human affairs and taking them lightly." Accordingly, he said, the Buddhists wished "to turn everything into a void" while the Taoists tried "to take advantage of the critical situations and opportunities" and provided ideas for developments in "military strategy, the art of calculation, and the technique of debate." But, despite this difference in form, the Taoists did not become any less "selfish" than the Buddhists in the eyes of Chu Hsi, who rejected both kinds of "selfishness" as "transgressions" (*shih*).[130] Finally, the Taoists were said by Chu Hsi to be as much obsessed with the problem of "birth and death" as the Buddhists. "The Taoists," he said, "are greedy for life and the Buddhists are terrified of death." But they are equally "perverse" (*pei*) in this regard because, he said,

> There is birth when *ch'i* coagulates and there is death when *ch'i* disperses. One simply follows it [the operation of *ch'i*], and that is all.[131]

Compared with Chu Hsi, the Ch'eng brothers were not nearly so extensive in their moral criticisms of Taoism, partly because they felt that Taoism had been on the decline and was thus less influential and harmful than Buddhism in their time. As one of the Ch'engs said

> As to the harm of heterodox teachings today, Taoism has nothing further to be refuted. It is only Buddhism which spreads, confuses, and inundates most profoundly. Today it is Buddhism which is flourishing while Taoism has fallen into decay.[132]

Nevertheless, there is no doubt that the Ch'eng brothers found Taoism morally objectionable. Ch'eng Hao, for instance, spoke of "the harm of Yang Chu and Mo Ti" as "greater than that of Shen Tzu and Han Tzu" and of "the harm of the Buddha and Lao Tzu" as still "greater than that of Yang and Mo."[133] Ch'eng I, on the other hand, condemned Taoism for what in his terms was "an element of treachery" (*ch'üan-cha*) and underscored the charge that the Taoists were self-interested when he rejected the theory of "immortals" (*hsien*) and denounced those who engaged in the cult of longevity as "thieves in the world" because, he said, they tried to "steal the secret of creation and transformation."[134] He also implicitly criticized the Taoists for being amoral when he accused Lao Tzu of separating the Way from "virtue" (*te*), "humanity" (*jen*), "righteousness" (*i*), and "rites" (*li*) which were all integral parts of the Neo-Confucian idea of the Way as Principle. He said,

Lao Tzu said, "When the Way is lost, there then arises virtue; when virtue is lost, there then arises humanity; when humanity is lost, there then arises righteousness; when righteousness is lost, there then arise the rites." He thus divided the Way, virtue, humanity, righteousness, and the rites into five separate entities.[135]

Needless to say, Chiao Hung as a syncretist rejected as invalid the orthodox Neo-Confucian accusations that Buddhism and Taoism were amoral, escapist, and selfish. He dismissed the notion that the *Lao Tzu* as a book had anything to do with military affairs and maintained that "the words about fine weapons and skilful warfare" in the *Lao Tzu* were nothing but metaphors which were used to "open up" (*ch'i*) for the reader the significance of "softness" (*jou*). "Of all under Heaven," Chiao Hung said, "no one values strength more than the soldier." Therefore, if the soldier, despite his strength, can be shown to "yield" (*ch'ü*) to "softness" as he was in the *Lao Tzu*, there will be the recognition that "there is softness wherever one goes." "Softness," Chiao Hung said further, "is the antithesis of hardness (*kang*)." But it "can never be apart from hardness." The two coexist in the Way as a pair of interrelated opposites of which, however, "softness" is the more important. In Chiao Hung's terms, "softness" is the "host" (*chu*) and "hardness" is the "guest" (*pin*) because "softness, though not being the Way as such, is close to nonactivity (*wu-wei*) whereas hardness, though not lying outside of the Way as such, is far from nonactivity." "That is why," he said, "one can hope to reach nonactivity if one seeks it through softness." For Chiao Hung, therefore, the purpose of the *Lao Tzu* as a book is to "clarify the Way" (*ming-tao*) while the military metaphors in the book merely form figures of speech for the discourse on "softness" which, being "close to nonactivity," best symbolizes the true functioning of the Way.[136]

Moreover, according to Chiao Hung, "nonactivity" as the true functioning of the Way is "rooted in constant Nothingness" (*ch'ang wu-yu*)[137] which he takes both as the source of being and as the basis of morality. He denied that the Taoist idea of Nothingness was morally hollow and said that Nothingness as propounded by Lao Tzu and Chuang Tzu "did not abandon social and moral teachings" but was "that by which social and moral teachings were established."[138] As the source of being, Nothingness is comparable to what in Chiao Hung's terms is the "substance in its original state," which, as noted before, is considered by him as the *a priori* basis of moral self-cultivation and without which one is apt to resort to "compulsion" and thereby become a "pharisee." Also, since "social and moral teachings" do not exist independently and are "established" on the basis of Nothingness, the cultivation of morality entails going beyond "humanity and righteousness," etc. as particular virtues so that Nothingness can be realized as the reason for these particular virtues as virtues. Failure to push on to Nothingness as the moral and metaphysical ultimate will lead to the fragmentation of one's moral being or to what Chiao Hung characterizes as the "endless" pursuit of the particular virtues as ends in and of themselves with the result that "one matter is performed while a hundred others are abandoned."[139] It was, Chiao Hung said, only because "the world held to terms and concepts and clung to vessels and numbers" that Lao Tzu declared, "When the Way is lost, there then arises virtue; when virtue is lost, there then arises humanity; when humanity is lost, there then arises the rites." In making this statement, however, Lao Tzu's purpose was not to separate the "rites" from the Way or to present the Way as amoral. Rather, Chiao Hung claimed, Lao Tzu had hoped that the world would "advance" beyond the "rites" and seek the Way as the basis of the "rites." Seeking the Way and obtaining it, "true harmony" (*chen-ho*) would prevail between the Way and the "rites" with the result that all "terms, concepts, vessels and numbers" could be "instituted" without "obstructing" the operation of the Way.[140]

The same, according to Chiao Hung, may also be said about Chuang Tzu's alleged rejection of "humanity," "righteousness," "rites," and "music." The "conventional Confucians," Chiao Hung maintained, considered Chuang Tzu's ideas to be incompatible with those of the Confucians because they seized upon Chuang Tzu's seemingly negative statements about humanity, righteousness, rites and music. Actually, however, Chuang Tzu did not make a simple rejection of humanity, righteousness, rites, and music; and the "conventional Confucians" in their condemnation of Chuang Tzu as amoral had only a partial and one-sided understanding of Chuang Tzu. They focused on some of Chuang Tzu's arguments which seemed to be directed against humanity, righteousness, rites, and music but ignored others which advocated their acceptance. As an example, Chiao Hung cited a passage from chapter eleven in which Chuang Tzu stated, "What seems to apply only to distant relationships and yet must be observed is righteousness; what seem to be confining and yet must be repeatedly practiced are the rites."[141] Positive statements such as this about righteousness and rites convinced Chiao Hung that Chuang Tzu's rejection of these virtues was only apparent and not real and that Chuang Tzu ultimately affirmed these virtues as inherent in the Way as Nothingness.

Furthermore, Chiao Hung said, Chuang Tzu held the Way to be all-embracing and even regarded "tiles, pebbles, chaff, and husks" as "wonders of the Way." He could not therefore have possibly had the "intention" of discarding humanity, righteousness, rites, and music as extraneous to the Way. Indeed, Chiao Hung claimed, Chuang Tzu never really wanted to do away with these virtues per se. He only rejected them as they were held by the "conventional Confucians." What the "conventional Confucians" held as humanity, righteousness, rites, and music were, according to Chiao Hung, only the outward appearances or "traces" (chi) of the Way and should not be cultivated apart from the Way. But the "conventional Confucians" did not recognize the "traces" as "traces." Instead they confused the "traces" with the Way, clinging tenaciously to humanity, righteousness, rites, and music without knowing the Way as the underlying basis. As a result, Chuang Tzu felt compelled to reject humanity, righteousness, rites, and music in order to urge the "conventional Confucians" to seek the Way beyond these virtues.[142]

For Chiao Hung, therefore, Lao Tzu and Chuang Tzu did not propound an amoral concept of the Way as Nothingness. To him, the kind of social and moral nihilism which prevailed among the Taoistically inclined "pure conversationalists" of the Six Dynasties came about only because the "pure conversationalists" were "blind" (mei) to the true meaning of the Way as

Nothingness. He condemned them for their amorality as being contrary to the intrinsically moral Way of Lao Tzu and Chuang Tzu as Nothingness. He quoted Chuang Tzu as saying, "It is the nature of water that if it is not mixed with other things, it will be clear, and if nothing stirs it, it will be level. But if it is dammed and hemmed in and not allowed to flow, then it will cease to be clear."[143] The "pure conversationalists" in their socially and morally nihilistic attempt to realize the Way as Nothingness were, according to Chiao Hung, like "having water dammed and hemmed in and still expecting it to remain clear."[144]

As for the Buddhist concept of Emptiness, Chiao Hung also denied that it implied any kind of amorality or escapism. He took issue with Ch'eng Hao on the characterization of Buddhism as having only "seriousness to straighten the internal life but not righteousness to square the external life." He said that "enlightenment" (*chüeh*) as the realization of the truth of Emptiness did not make the distinction between the internal and the external as a dichotomy. What, therefore, existed as inner "seriousness" would necessarily manifest itself as outer "righteousness." Since the Buddhists were said to have "seriousness to straighten the internal life," they could not be said to be without "righteousness to square the external life." Chiao Hung denounced those who indulged in what he called the "mind of excessive desire" and who tried to excuse their conduct by claiming the doctrine of "nonego" (*wu-wo* or *anātman*). The doctrine of "nonego," he said, was formulated to help "perceive the uncreated as the original substance in the midst of the created." It was never meant to be a license for amorality. As a teaching, Buddhism never taught that "good and evil were mixed without differentiation" or that "evil could be practiced and good could be relinquished." Rather it always distinguished between the good and the bad *karma*.[145]

For Chiao Hung, therefore, Buddhism could not be faulted for being morally hollow; it did not lack a sense of righteousness. Nor was it ever intent upon the "destruction of human relationships." According to Chiao Hung, only the Śrā-vakas and Pratyekabuddhas were bent on the "destruction of human relationships." The Buddha, however, was not to be blamed for the views of these "two vehicles" because he had condemned them himself for being "nihilistic" and had not himself repudiated Suddhodana as his father or Rāhula as his son. He desired to save all the sentient beings in the world and did not spurn his family as the Śrāvakas and Pratyekabuddhas did.[146] Admittedly, the Buddha asked the monks "to bid farewell to their relatives and to leave their homes" to join the *saṅgha*. But, Chiao Hung tried to argue, the Buddha did so not because he rejected the family as a social institution or the human relationships embodied therein. He did so for the same reason that Confucius tried to discourage Fan Ch'ih from studying "farming and gardening."[147] "The way of man," Chiao Hung said, "cannot flourish without farming and gardening." And yet, there must be in the world those who "do not study farming and gardening" so that they can provide peace for others who engage in farming and gardening. Therefore, when Confucius berated Fan Ch'ih for requesting to study these pursuits, his purpose was not to deny their vital importance but to urge Fan Ch'ih to become one who would secure peace for those who practiced them. Similarly, when the Buddha asked the monks to "leave the home," he was not rejecting the family or human relationships as such. He only wanted monks to become detached from their "wives and children" so that they could save all those who remained attached to wives and children.[148]

Chiao Hung did not specify how the monks could accomplish this mission by becoming detached. Nevertheless, it is clear that, for him, this mission constituted the *raison d'être* of the *saṅgha*, which was instituted not so much to satisfy the personal spiritual needs of the monks as to perform the function of effecting universal salvation. The *saṅgha*, in other words, was not apart from the lay world as a place where one pursued a particular religious way of life. Rather, it was a place where the monks congregated for the task of saving all under Heaven. It differed from the lay world only in vocational terms and was not distinct as a separate path for the quest of enlightenment, which, according to Chiao Hung, could be cultivated in the lay world as well as in the *saṅgha*. "The Way," he said, "is all pervasive" and cannot be "divided in terms of black [robes of the *saṅgha*] and white [garments of the lay world]." Therefore, although the "dusty realm" has to be transformed into the "realm of truth," it must also be realized that "the monk's home is the home of the layman."[149]

With the distinction between the *sangha* and the lay world thus eliminated except in vocational terms, membership in the *sangha* ceased to be necessary as a prerequisite for enlightenment. While enlightenment as a goal is appropriate for all men, "leaving the home" as a practice need not be undertaken by all men. For Chiao Hung, home life is not incompatible with the journey toward enlightenment. One may remain in the household and be a good family man but still follow the teachings of the Buddha as a seeker of enlightenment. To justify his stance that the lay man could achieve enlightenment without having to "leave the home," Chiao Hung cited the fact that the Buddha, while preaching the *dharma*, addressed all manner of beings from gods to common laymen and that only a fraction of the audience was composed of monks. He also pointed out that although the Buddha became a monk and observed monastic discipline, the "Golden Grain Tathāgata" (*chin-su ju-lai*) manifested himself as Vimalakīrti, who was able to achieve enlightenment as a householder. To Chiao Hung, these instances from the lives of the Buddha and Vimalakīrti were further proof that Buddhism did not reject family or human relationships and that "the Six Relationships were not obstacles to the Way."[150]

In regard to the charge that the Buddhists and Taoists were pursuing their own self-interest in seeking to transcend birth and death, Chiao Hung contended that the doctrine of transcending birth and death was not meant to be taken literally and that the pure and original forms of Buddhism and Taoism never claimed that a person could achieve the state of "no extinction" (*pu-mieh*) or "everlasting life" (*ch'ang-sheng*). He pointed out that the ideas of "no extinction" and "everlasting life" were contrary to Emptiness and Vacuity as central concepts of Buddhism and Taoism. He said, "Since everything is empty, where can that which is not extinguished come to rest? Since everything is vacuous, what thing is there that can have everlasting life?"[151]

What the Buddha and Lao Tzu urged the people to transcend, therefore, were not the physical occurrences of birth and death but the "mind of birth and death" and the human emotions regarding the physical occurrences of birth and death. The "mind of birth and death" is, according to Chiao Hung, what *The Awakening of Faith* speaks of as the "aspect of Mind in terms of phenomena."[152] As such, it is characterized by an endless flow of "thoughts" (*nien*), and the transcendence of the mind of birth and death is simply the stopping of the succession of these thoughts so that the mind can "abide in its place" and "realize *Bhūtatathatā* in the midst of *saṃsara*."[153]

As for the human emotions regarding the physical occurrences of birth and death, they manifest themselves as "love of life" and "fear of death" which, Chiao Hung said, were "basic emotions of man" and from which the Confucians suffered as much as anyone else, even though they might "regard [the thought of] transcending birth and death as self-interested." Seeing that these emotions were common to man, the Buddha and Lao Tzu talked about transcendence of birth and death with the hope that the people in the world could be "induced to enter the Way." Once the Way is entered, there will be the realization that originally there is neither birth nor death. Thus the Buddha and Lao Tzu could not be accused of "frightening people with the doctrine of birth and death" because the purpose of this doctrine was precisely to relieve the people of the emotional afflictions of love of life and fear of death by bringing about the realization that these emotions were unfounded and had no basis in the Way. Nor, for that matter, could the Buddha and Lao Tzu be considered to be "self-interested" in the sense that they were after the "gain" of "no extinction" or "everlasting life"; they did not intend to resist birth and death as natural occurrences of the life process but only to overcome the mind of birth and death and the emotional fear of death.[154] Chiao Hung condemned the various cults of physical longevity or immortality as later corruptions of original Taoism. These corruptions, he claimed, came about because the "conventional Confucians" rejected Lao Tzu as heterodox. As Lao Tzu was thus abandoned by the conventional Confucians, he fell into the hands of the "recipe dispensers" (*fang-shih*) who made him a patron of the "doctrines of alchemy and sexual hygiene" (*huang-pai nan-nü chih shuo*). Chiao Hung deplored this misuse of Lao

Tzu in later Taoism and said that it was "not only a misfortune for the scholars but also an insult to the Way." He proclaimed that a person, by "nurturing Nature," would be able to achieve "identification" with the eternal "Way of Heaven" and to become in this sense "inextinguishable." But, he said, the "recipe dispensers" did not understand that "nurturing Nature" was what was meant by "prolonging life." As a result, what they "talked about as prolonging life" was nothing but an attempt to "bore through and chisel away at" things which were "external to Nature and Destiny." Chiao Hung wanted the recipe dispensers repudiated and Taoism restored to its original purity so that there would be the recognition that what the sages had regarded as the "realization of Nature and fulfilment of Destiny" was the "essential secret of nourishing life."[155]

In addition to refuting the orthodox Confucian criticisms of Buddhism and Taoism as untrue, Chiao Hung also tried to argue that certain concepts which had been rejected by the orthodox Confucians as Buddhist and/or Taoist were actually also Confucian. In particular, he singled out the two concepts of birth and death (i.e., *saṁsāra*) and Emptiness which, he claimed, could be found in the *Analects* of Confucius. He referred to *Analects* 4:8, which Legge has translated as follows: "The Master said, 'If a man in the morning hear the right way, he may die in the evening without regret'."[156]

As Legge has pointed out, this passage has also been read by some traditional Chinese commentators as "a lament of Confucius that he was likely to die without hearing of right principles prevailing in the world." Thus understood as "a lament," this passage may be translated: "Could I hear the prevalence of right principles, I could die the same evening!"[157] But, whether as "a lament" or not, Legge took this passage to be a statement which Confucius made in order to emphasize the "importance of knowing the right principles." Legge was somewhat "perplexed" by the term "Way" or *tao*, but did not seriously entertain the possibility that it implied an "apprehension of some higher truth."[158] However, what was thus dismissed by Legge as a possibility is precisely what was proposed by Chaio Hung as the correct interpretation. According to Chaio Hung, the person who hears the Way and is thus identified with it becomes oblivious to birth and death just as the Way itself is. He can therefore die without regret because he has come to realize that death has no reality in the Way which has neither birth nor death and which transcends them both.[159]

Legge's interpretation represents a convention which, though never wholly abandoned by traditional Chinese scholars in later periods, prevailed essentially before the Sung; both Ho Yen (190–249) and Huang K'an (488–545) subscribed to it.[160] Chiao Hung's interpretation, on the other hand, exemplifies a position which did not become prominent until the Sung, during which a number of commentators began to read this passage from the *Analects* in the light of the *Book of Changes*' idea of birth and death as the "beginning"and "end" of things in the rhythmic operation of the Way[161] and/or Chang Tsai's concluding statement in the *Western Inscription* (*Hsi-ming*) that "in life I follow and serve [Heaven and Earth]; in death I will be at peace."[162] Ch'en Hsiang-tao (1053–1093), for instance, while commenting on this passage, stressed the necessity of "investigating the beginning" of things and "following" them "to the end" in order to understand birth and death, saying that a person, on "obtaining the Way," will become at ease wherever he goes because he "knows that past and present are one time and birth and death are one thread."[163] Chu Hsi, too, in his commentary on this passage, advocated following life and accepting death in accordance with the Way, which he understood not only as the "principle of oughtness in events and things"[164] but, as noted earlier, as "uncreated and imperishable." He also claimed in his commentary on the *Western Inscription* that what Chang Tsai tried to express in the concluding statement was what Confucius meant by "hearing [the Way] in the morning and dying [without regret] in the evening."[165] However, none of the Sung commentators whose commentaries on the *Analects* have been incorporated into Yen Ling-feng's *Wu-ch'iu-pei chai Lun-yü chi-ch'eng* ever went so far as to take this saying by Confucius as an example of the Confucian counterpart of the Buddhist doctrine of birth and death. A few like Chen Te-hsiu (1178–1235) and Chang Shih (1133–1180) in fact disclaimed explicitly that the Confucian doctrine of birth and death was comparable to the Buddhist kind because it was informed by the Confucian concept of the Way as the "real Principle" and because, as Chang Shih said in an obvious reference to the Buddhist idea of transmigration, it did not involve "theories of frightening ghosts and elusive [apparitions]."[166] By contrast, Chiao Hung used this statement of "morning Way" and "evening death" as a basis of his argument that the doctrine of "birth and death" was a shared concern of Buddhism, Taoism, and classical Confucianism as well.[167] He would also most definitely have rejected the disclaimer by Chen Te-hsiu and Chang Shih as both unnecessary and unjustified because, as we have seen before, he believed that the Buddhist and Taoist concept of the Way was no less "real" for being "empty" and "vacuous" and that the Buddhist and Taoist theories of birth and death were not meant to be taken literally as referring to the physical occurrences of birth and death but should be understood as a discourse on the mind of birth and death and the emotional fear of death.

As for the concept of Emptiness, Chiao Hung said that it was a designation for the "original substance of Heaven's decree." As such, it refers to that which a person obtains on "becoming a sage through learning" and is not alien to Confucius, who, according to Chiao Hung, actually described himself as "empty-like" (*k'ung-k'ung ju-yeh*). Since, Chaio Hung said, Confucius was a sage and "self-attained his original mind," he could not but regard himself as "empty-like."[168] The textual basis for this interpretation of Confucius is *Analects* 9:8, which Legge has translated as follows: "The Master said, 'Am I indeed possessed of knowledge? I am not knowing. But if a mean person, who appears quite empty-like, ask anything of me, I set it forth from one end to the other, and exhaust it.'"[169]

Obviously, Legge's translation of this passage is based upon a reading which differs from Chiao Hung's. While Legge viewed the expression "empty-like" as a description of the "mean person," Chiao Hung took it to be a reference which Confucius made to himself. Legge's reading has been followed by other translators, such as Arthur Waley and James Ware.[170] It also conforms to a well-established Chinese tradition which began at least as early as the Han dynasty and which was still dominant in the Ming. Of the more than thirty pre-Ch'ing commentators in the *Wu-ch'iu-pei chai Lun-yü chi-ch'eng*, eleven glossed or commented on the term *k'ung-k'ung*. Of these eleven, some understood it to mean "empty" just as Legge did, while others followed Cheng Hsüan (127–200) and took it to be synonymous with the homonymic compound *k'ung-k'ung*, which means "sincere" or "humble."[171] However, with the exception of the monk Chih-hsü (1599–1655),[172] they all agreed that the term described the "mean person." It is also noteworthy that Chiang Ch'ien, who wrote a supplementary commentary appended to Chih-hsü's commentary, reverted to the traditional reading of *k'ung-k'ung* as a description of the "mean person" and said that it designated the Buddha Nature that the Buddha and the "mean person" held in common.[173] Chiao Hung departed from this tradition. His departure may or may not be justified textually. But it embodies a kind of concept-matching which is reminiscent of and yet significantly different from the kind that prevailed before the Ming. As will be seen below, Chiao Hung's practice of concept-matching is produced on the condition of a type of syncretic consciousness which is no longer constituted by the logic of compartmentalization.

CHAPTER FOUR

Mysticism and Pluralism

Language and Reality in Chiao Hung

IN HIS *Ways of Thinking of Eastern Peoples*, Nakamura Hajime noted syncretism as a characteristic of traditional Chinese thought and religion and considered it to be a reason for what he believed to be the "very great extent" of "freedom of belief" in traditional China. He pointed out that the Chinese in traditional times, though not allowed to have a "personal choice in marriage," had nevertheless "enjoyed absolute freedom in the choice of religion." He said,

> From ancient times, the Chinese governing class acknowledged Confucianism as the correct religion and tried to suppress the other religions in an attempt to maintain the authority of their class and social position. They tried to make the teaching of Confucianism the chief font of literary studies. Nevertheless, they failed to suppress the compromising and syncretic traditional Chinese way of thinking.[1]

Thus impressed by the strength of traditional Chinese syncretism, however, Nakamura was also disappointed by its character, which he found to be "arbitrary" and "without deep logical

reflection." "What stands out in this sort of [syncretic] reasoning," he said, "is a certain sort of utilitarianism and easy compromise, with cold logical consideration completely abandoned."[2]

One can readily sympathize with Nakamura's sense of
ambivalence. Few of the syncretists whom I examined in the first
chapter ventured much beyond equating concepts and using
"pictorial or intuitive similes."[3] Most of them proclaimed the
"oneness" of the Three Teachings in terms of a single "source" or
"ending." But no attempt was made to establish the identity of this
source as a unity or to analyze its relationship to the Three
Teachings in their doctrinal specificity as "streams" or "paths."
There was no demonstration of how the supposedly same
"source" or "ending" would validate the claims of the Three
Teachings as paths and comprehend them as one. Without
exploring questions of this kind and yet maintaining that the
Three Teachings are one, these syncretists may indeed be faulted
for what Nakamura has termed "the non-logical and political
compromise tendency."[4]

Nevertheless, if Nakamura is justified in his disap-
pointment over the tendency of traditional syncretism toward
"easy compromise," the large number of syncretists who constituted what I have called a "tradition of syncretism" are also
understandable for not pursuing certain "cold logical" considerations. Considerations, logical or otherwise, are never so cold as to
have a necessary or self-possessing existence. They come into and
remain in existence through the occupation of a discursive domain
to which they are related reciprocally.[5] A discursive domain
vocalizes certain considerations and allows them to emerge and
exist as objects of its discourse while maintaining silence about
others as nonobjects. In doing so, it also achieves articulation as a
discursive formation which is constituted by both the presence of
certain considerations as objects of its discourse and by the
absence of others. A discourse is thus comprised of two parts, the
said and the unsaid, with the unsaid just as significant as the said
to our understanding of a given discourse. When viewed discur-
sively as the unsaid, the silence of certain syncretists before the
Ming on the identity of the source or its relationship to the Three
Teachings as streams need not be deplored as a failure. Rather, it

can be seen as an absence which both informs and is informed by their syncretism as a discourse.

As noted before, a large number of syncretists before the Ming subscribed to the logic of compartmentalization as the principle of their syncretism. They did so either as apologists, such as Yen Yen-chih and Yen Chih-t'ui, or as supremacists, such as Chih-i and Tsung-mi. The apologists embraced the Three Teachings in all their differences with no necessary sense of hierarchy, whereas the supremacists ranked the teachings in a scheme of classification which invariably culminated in their own teaching, either logically according to an ascending order of universality (as in Tsung-mi) or sometimes also sequentially according to a stage theory of development (as in Chih-i). But they were all preoccupied with the differentiation of the Three Teachings as an undertaking which they were compelled to sustain as syncretists. For, according to the logic of compartmentalization, their success in affirming the oneness of the teachings depends on their ability to distinguish the Three Teachings as three. Not surprisingly, therefore, the focus of their syncretism was placed on the interrelationship of the Three Teachings as differences which they tried to specify through comparison. The source or ending functioned as an unproblematic, unanalyzed given and existed silently as a nonobject of their syncretism as a discourse. It did not and was not permitted to enter the flow of discourse as the said, for, as the said, it would intrude upon and jeopardize the very differences that the logic of compartmentalization strives to establish and maintain. The metaphors of "source" and "ending" were not employed in vain. They refer to that which initiates or concludes the logic of compartmentalization as a discursive activity to differentiate the Three Teachings as doctrinal specificities. In doing so, however, the source or ending does not itself become specified, because it remains at the edge of the logic of compartmentalization as the silent unsaid, is aloof from the Three Teachings as discursive objects, and has an existence which comes either before or after the logic of compartmentalization as a discursive activity. Far from being a logical failure, the silence of the source or ending as the unsaid is entailed by the logic of compartmentalization which in turn requires this silence as a condition of possibility for its own formation as a discursive activity.

Moreover, as a silent nonobject occasioned by the logic of compartmentalization, it can and did transform to emerge as the said when the constitution of syncretism changed in late Ming and became noncompartmentalizing. I have already mentioned Lin Chao-en, who viewed the Three Teachings holistically and considered them all to be concerned with the Tao as the sagely mind. Lin's *Tao* is comparable to the "source" or "ending" of the apologists and supremacists in being a concept which comprehends the Three Teachings as one. However, as his syncretism is no longer compartmentalizing, his Tao also ceases to be a silent and unproblematic nonobject. As noted before, Lin regarded his division of the Three Teachings into "beginning," "middle," and "end" as a mere pedagogical device and not as a statement of their respective distinctness. For him, the Three Teachings inextricably involve and imply one another because the Tao as an undifferentiated whole has not only the beginning but also the middle and the end as a unity and is embodied as such in each of the Three Teachings. As that which is embodied in the Three Teachings, Lin's Tao is not removed from the Three Teachings as discursive objects. Instead, it is implicated in the Three Teachings as a constant presence and is itself an object. As such, it needs to be established in its identity in terms which can ensure its own coherence as a unity and also provide for the oneness of the Three Teachings as doctrinal specificities. Understandably, Lin's Tao is specifiable as the sagely mind, which he tried to affirm as the common concern of the Three Teachings by refuting "errors" among the followers of each teaching and by defining a "true" line of transmission as the "correct understanding" for each teaching. In doing so, Lin produced a highly "selective reinterpretation" of China's religious and philosophical heritage. The selectiveness of this reinterpretation can no doubt be attributed to the particularity of his "syncretic vision."[6] But it is also entailed by his logic of noncompartmentalization, which requires him to explain away the incompatibilities of the teachings as "errors" and to demonstrate that the three in their "true" transmission do indeed cohere in the Way as a unity.

The same logic of noncompartmentalization also prevailed in Chiao Hung's activities as a syncretist. Unlike Lin, Chiao Hung did not formally propose a "true" line of transmission for each of the teachings. But he was unequivocal in articulating what he considered to be their "correct understanding" and was no less involved than Lin in the refutation of "errors." As we have seen before, he confronted the Confucian critics head on by exposing their criticisms of Buddhism and Taoism as contrary to "facts" and by challenging their conceptions of Confucianism. In the process of this confrontation, he tried to establish the oneness of the Three Teachings not only in terms of their interrelationship as doctrinal specificities but also in terms of their status as linguistic embodiments of the Tao as the ultimate reality. Like the Tao in Lin Chao-en's syncretism, Chiao Hung's Tao is also a discursive object. It is present in the Three Teachings and is specifiable in terms of their composition as theories of "Nature" and "Destiny" which, as noted before, he took to be the common concerns of Confucius, Lao Tzu, and the Buddha.

In their shared concern with the Tao as "Nature" and "Destiny," the Three Teachings were conceived by Chiao Hung to be noncompartmentalizable. For him, they were "one" not in the sense that they were united as differentiated parts of a composite assemblage but in the sense that they had the fused integrity of a single entity and were mutually identified and indistinguishable. To be sure, he still used some of the old arguments of the earlier syncretists who compartmentalized the Three Teachings. He continued to match the Buddhist *vinaya* (*lü*) with the Confucian rites (*li*),[7] and reiterated the formula of "different paths—same ending." He said,

> It is said in the *Book of Rites*, "The fulfillment of Nature is called the Way, and the cultivation of the Way is called teaching."[8] The teachings of the sages are different, but they are one in regard to the cultivation of the Way for the purpose of restoring Nature.... The sages in ancient times had different paths [which, however, all tended toward] the same ending. Of the Six Classics, the *Analects*, and the *Mencius*, there is none that is not Ch'an. Yao, Shun, the Duke of Chou, and Confucius are the Buddha.[9]

However, if in the above statement Chiao Hung seems to have reverted to the compartmentalizing rhetoric of his syncretic predecessors, the reversion is only apparent. He retained the "path" image as a description of the complementarity of the Three Teachings. But it did not mean to Chiao Hung what it used to mean to the earlier syncretists because he had a different sense of complementarity, which was no longer compartmentalizing. For him, the Three Teachings were complementary not because they each explicated a part of the Way as the other two did not but because they could be understood in terms of one another and were mutually explanatory and illuminating in approximating the Way as truth. As a result, he did not expound the view that each of the teachings was equally valid but only in its own sphere, as Yen Yen-chih and others had done before. Instead, he spoke of Buddhism and Taoism as "commentaries" on Confucianism not in the sense that they were subordinate or inferior to it but in the sense that they could help clarify what was obscure and underdeveloped in Confucianism.

Moreover, though retaining the "path" image, Chiao Hung denied that the Three Teachings could stand divided like the legs of a tripod or be viewed as different "streams" from the same "source." For him, the Way as the source is one and indivisible and its differentiation in representation as three separate teachings was a later development which the sages had never intended. The sages, Chiao Hung said, were among the first people to have penetrated the Way as reality. What they have thus penetrated has been transmitted in their teachings as Buddhism, Taoism, and Confucianism. As carriers of the sages' insight into the Way as reality, the Three Teachings cannot but be viewed as "one" not only because they all have the Way as their common concern but also because the Way as their common concern is itself one and its oneness is necessarily invested in them as the transmission of the sages' perception of the Way as one.[10] In the minds of some people, however, the Three Teachings were not one. These people followed one or the other of the teachings or else divided the teachings into distinct schools of thought as though "carving up a melon." They did so because they saw the teachings but not the Way. They did not have the anchorage in reality to enable them to apprehend the Three Teachings as one.[11] The divisive view of the Three Teachings as three is thus attributable as a direct consequence to the loss of sight of the Way. As such, it can best be rectified by going beyond the teachings to reach the Way as reality. It cannot be overcome by a movement for the "union of the Three Teachings" (*san-chiao ho-i*), which Chiao Hung rejects as the "piling of one absurdity upon another." He said,

> Recently, people like Wang Ch'un-fu [Wang Tao, 1487–1547], Mu Po-ch'ien [Mu K'ung-hui, 1479–1539], and Hsüeh Chün-ts'ai [Hsüeh Hui, 1489–1541], etc., boldly came out into the open and desired to unite the Three Teachings as one. They felt themselves to be rather great. But they do not realize that the Way does not exist as three. It does not become three [in spite of our attempt] to make it three. [On the other hand,] the Way is also not one [in the sense of being a unified assemblage of distinguishable parts]. It does not become one [in this sense in spite of our attempt] to make it one. [These syncretists] are like those who loathe the absurdity of someone dividing the void with his hand and then try to unify it with their own hands. They ratify what cannot be ratified. Interpreting a dream while in a dream, they pile one absurdity upon another.[12]

For Chiao Hung, the Three Teachings are not self-possessing. They embody the sages' perception of the Way as reality and depend for their meaning on the Way whose oneness validates their claim to being one. As the Way itself is always one, the Three Teachings must also be always one. To suppose that they could have been otherwise is an absurdity which the movement for the "union of the Three Teachings as one" further promotes into a double absurdity because it presupposes the absurdity that the Three Teachings were once divided and compounds it by trying to have them reunited.

Implied in Chiao Hung's argument is his belief in the continuity between the Tao as reality and language as a medium of representation. Unlike the Western scholastics,[13] Chiao Hung did not distinguish the divine Word from the human word. For him, language was never a primal existence coeval with the Way as reality. Rather, it began as a human activity as a result of human necessity. He pointed out that the *Book of Changes* was originally a text without words and consisted only of "trigrams, hexagrams, and the component lines" (*hsiang-kua*)[14] which constituted the "wordless teaching" of Fu Hsi. It was in later times when the meaning of the *Changes* was no longer understood and the Way was no longer practiced that the Duke of Chou and Confucius "felt compelled" to use words. As an occasioned human activity, language contrasts with the Way, which is mute and indifferent to naming. "What the sages had spoken of as the Way," Chiao Hung said, "is like what people have called heaven. While the Chinese people call it *t'ien*, the Hsiung-nu people call it *ch'eng-li*. How could there be two heavens? Heaven itself certainly does not know what it is being called. It is only the people who have forcibly given it a name."[15] Moreover, while the Way is unity, language is multiplicity. Words, according to Chiao Hung, vary from time to time and place to place in both pronunciation and form. His awareness that *ch'eng-li* as the Hsiung-nu word for heaven is *t'ien* in Chinese indicates his sensitivity to language as a system of changing sounds. It is this sensitivity that prompted him to embark on an inquiry into the end rhymes of ancient odes. The results of this inquiry enabled him to account for the discrepancy between the ancient and the modern schemes of rhyming and to advocate that "modern poems be written according to modern rhymes and ancient poems be read according to ancient rhymes."[16]

The same kind of sensitivity also characterized his analysis of the changing forms of written characters in Chinese history. He was accomplished in traditional Chinese etymology and discussed with facility a large body of etymological theories including those of Hsü Shen (30–101) and Cheng Hsüan (126–200) of the Han, Wu Yü (d. 1154) and Cheng Ch'iao (1104–1162) of the Sung, and Yang Shen (1488–1559) of the Ming.[17] He believed that the ancients, while creating the written characters, often "invested the dots and strokes with meaning."[18] As a result, he was opposed to interpreting characters according to "philosophical principles" (*i-li*) and was particularly critical of such scholars of the Han period as Liu Hsiang (77–6 B.C.), Cheng Hsüan, and Pan Ku (A.D. 32–92), etc. who, he said, "often missed the ancients' intent in creating the characters." As examples, he cited a group of kinship words like *mu* or "mother" and *tzu* or "child" which these Han scholars took to be the same in meaning as the homonymic *mu* or "to tend as a shepherd" and *tzu* or "diligent." They did so because they thought that the mother in raising her child was like a shepherd tending his flock and that a child would always be diligent in his filial attendance on his father. In reality, however, the two characters for "mother" and "child" are pictographs. The word for "mother" is composed of two parts: the part which stands for "woman" or *nü* and the part with two dots which depict a woman's breasts. When combined, these two parts represent a woman with breasts as an accentuated feature, which is what a mother uses in nursing her child. The character for "child," on the other hand, is analyzed by Chiao Hung into three parts: (1) the top part which represents a person's head, (2) the horizontal stroke in the middle which stands for a pair of outstretched arms, and (3) the hooked verticle stroke at the bottom which portrays the two legs wrapped up in a bundle. They together form a pictorial symbol for a child in swaddling clothes. The meanings of characters of this type are, according to Chiao Hung, to be sought in the arrangements of the "dots and strokes." The mistakes that Liu Hsiang, Cheng Hsüan, Pan Ku, and others had committed are a result of "projective thinking" (*fu-hui*) and can easily be avoided if one makes a careful study of the seal form of writing."[20]

In his concern for language as multiplicity, Chiao Hung was interested not only in the variability in pronunciation and written form of characters but also in the difference in the rules of lexical and "stylistic" (*ko-chih*) formation. He contrasted the Chinese characters with the "barbarian words" and pointed out that the "barbarian words" were all phonetically constructed whereas the Chinese characters were governed in their formation by the six principles of "pictorialization of objects" (*hsiang-hsing*), "denotation of events" (*chih-shih*), "implication of ideas" (*hui-i*), "phonetic correspondence" (*hsieh-sheng*), "figurative extension of meaning" (*chuan-chu*), and "borrowing of one character to stand for another" (*chia-chieh*). Quoting Kuei Yu-kuang (1507–1571), he also noted that "writing styles" change over time and that later people, no matter how much they try, can never even hope to come close to reproducing the styles of the ancient sages. "Stylistic" differences can thus be used as a sure guide to the determination of whether or not a given work is a forgery.[22]

The multiplicity of language presents a difficulty in communication and understanding. Therefore, a modern man cannot possibly appreciate an ancient poem adequately without knowing and using the ancient scheme of rhyming.[23] This difficulty, however, is not insurmountable. It can be overcome through the acquisition of a particular linguistic skill and is therefore technically problematical but not metaphysically disturbing. It was not regarded by Chiao Hung, as it was by the medieval scholastics, as a reflection of the confusion of the human word or the imperfection of the human mind.[24] For Chiao Hung, the mind of man is ontologically identical with the Tao, and what the multiplicity of language means is not a falling away from the Tao but the variety of possible ways of articulating the same Tao and its embodiments as things and situations. Just as the same heaven is called *t'ien* by the Chinese and *ch'eng-li* by the Hsiung-nu, so the Tao is also known by a number of different names.[25] Moreover, Chiao Hung noted, different characters were used in ancient China not only in different times and places but often in the same period of time as designations for the same thing or situation. There can certainly be different words which, however, are not to be taken as necessarily different in reference or "meaning."[26]

That language in spite of its multiplicity can represent one and the same Tao as the unified order of things and situations is an inherent power that language possesses as a humanly originated activity. As a humanly originated activity, it consists of a series of signs (*semeion*). These signs are artificially constructed, but they do not constitute and, as will be shown in the following, must not be allowed to become an arbitrary system of signification with an ideality of its own meaning. For, according to Chiao Hung, linguistic signs are created by man for the sole purpose of representing the Tao as reality, without which language would become babble. Or, as Chiao Hung put it, it would stumble like a "blind man." He said that the Tao as the Ancestor or *tsung* "is the source of speech. [A person who] establishes a doctrine without the Ancestor is like a blind man on a journey. He will run into obstacles wherever he turns."[27] This conception of language as a human activity to represent the *Tao* as reality means not only that *mimesis* has a share in the construction of language as a human creation but that language as a human creation to render a mimetic representation of the Tao as reality is not self-possessing. In Chiao Hung's terms, language is "emptiness" (*k'ung*) and is devoid of selfhood. "Ink and paper," he said, "are originally empty and words and literature are not real." As "emptiness," language does not distinguish the subject "within" from the object "without" or admit of the "space in between."[28] It has no content or meaning in itself and is for this reason able to function as the signifier to point to whatever object is to be signified. However, in its pointing function as the signifier, language not only makes visible what it signifies; it also incorporates into itself the truth of the object signified and thereby acquires a content or meaning as *eikon*. Language, in other words, is both *semeion* and *eikon*. It can assume the existence as *eikon* because of its origin as *semeion*. Therefore, though artificially constructed and infinitely variable, language is continuous with the Tao. It can embody the "oneness" of the *Tao* as reality in the interrelatedness of the Three Teachings as one, and it can serve as a notation of the Tao as the truth of "liberation" (*chieh-t'o or mokṣa*). For Chiao Hung, as it was for the Goddess in the *Vimalakīrti Nirdeśa Sūtra*, whom he quotes, "speech, words and literature are all marks of liberation" and "liberation can not be preached apart from words and literature."[29]

On the other hand, although language is created to represent and can actually represent the Tao, its efficacy in doing so is not unproblematical, not merely because it can be abused to misrepresent the Tao but because it is intrinsically limited in its power as a medium of representation. The Tao as reality is conceived by Chiao Hung as a mystical existence which is not only pre-scriptive but also ineffable. It is a dynamic, holistic process which can best be comprehended through a lifelong cultivation of experience and realization but which cannot be stated adequately in words. All-embracing and all-permeating, it is temporally and spacially nondeterminate and is not a thing with distinguishable attributes which can be "grasped" (chih) or "pointed to" (chih).[30] For this reason, it cannot be designated by names,[31] which cannot function without making distinctions and are necessarily exclusive while being inclusive. Therefore, Chiao Hung said, "When highness is spoken of, lowness is left out. The Way of the sages is without highness. When purity is spoken of, impurity is left out. The Way of the sages is without purity."[32] All names for the Tao, including the name Tao, are "forcibly" given to the Tao. They are viewed by Chiao Hung as "traces" (chi) and "images" (hsiang) which are suggestive of what the Tao is but which cannot be held onto as the Tao itself. In an apparent allusion to the Book of Changes, he said, "That which is the Tao stands prior to the images and transcends the surface of the 'Appended Remarks.'"[33] Isomorphic correspondence does not prevail in the relationship between language and the Tao, which, though continuous, is also asymmetrical.

Being asymmetrical with language, the Tao cannot be sought entirely in language,[34] which one must transcend in order to become "silent" (mo) so that the mind will cease its "intellection" (ssu-lu) and be without preoccupation with the "slightest dharma" and can "follow" and "respond" to things and situations as embodiments of the Tao.[35] By contrast, a person who "abides in the realm of language and thought" will not be able to reach "what language does not reach."[36] Therefore, according to Chiao Hung, when the commentaries by the Duke of Chou and Confucius began to "circulate in isolation" from the "wordless teaching" of Fu Hsi, the Tao of the Changes became "obscured."[37] Similarly, the divisive view of the Three Teachings as three resulted from loss of sight of the Tao and could not be rectified without going beyond the teachings to reach the Tao as reality.

Nevertheless, to the extent that language is also continuous with the Tao, it can be used as an instrument for apprehending the Tao. Thus viewed instrumentally, language is likened by Chiao Hung to what in Chuang Tzu's terms is the "fish trap" (ch'üan) or "rabbit snare" (t'i),[38] which is useful for fish-catching or rabbit-snaring but which ought to be forgotten as soon as the fish or rabbit is caught. As an artificial system of signs, language must not be allowed to assume an independent existence detached from its association with the Tao. It is useful as a representation of the Tao and can remain so only if its own existence is effaced in the presence of the Tao. Chiao Hung described the proper attitude toward language or its specific constructions as teachings through the analogy of a horse and the shadow of a whip. The horse symbolizes a man with the proper attitude toward language, whereas the whip's shadow stands for the role of language as an instrument which the man may use in his quest for the Tao as truth. A good horse, on seeing the mere shadow of a whip, gallops forward instantaneously.[39] That is to say, the pursuit of the Tao's inexplicable truth should be an ongoing process of racing forward, spurred on by the shadow of the symbolic whip but always going beyond it. There can be no stopping or standing still, no attachment to language and still less engagement in ideological controversies for the exclusive claim to "orthodoxy." To do otherwise, as did the Ch'eng brothers and Chu Hsi, is to commit the error of confusing language with the Tao and to become trapped in the ideality of teachings which, as the mere "images" of the Tao, have only a shadowy and dependent existence and are without meaning or content in themselves. Chiao Hung compared the Confucians' attack on Buddhism as "heterodox" to a "person's counting other people's treasures without himself possessing half a penny":

> At a different time [in the future] when one arrives at the other shore, on will know automatically what they [the teachings] point to—and indeed that is not a subject which can be fully explained by tongue or brush. But, before then, one can only make the effort to care for one's self unceasingly.[40]

Deviation from the Classical Confucian Norm

Embodied in Chiao Hung's idea of the Tao as ineffable truth and his uncertainty about the teachings as mere "images" of the ultimately imageless Tao is a type of mystical thinking which intersects with Buddhist and Taoist mysticism and which is un-Confucian in the sense that it deviates from the classical Confucian norm. To be sure, mysticism is not an exclusively Buddhist or Taoist affair in Chinese thought. Awareness of the ultimate reality as pre-scriptive silence and of language as a problematical human undertaking also prevailed among the early Confucians. Confucius, for instance, once claimed the abiltiy to "remember silently" what he had learned (*mo-erh chih-chih*) as one of his accomplishments. He said, "To remember silently [what I have learned], to learn untiringly, and to teach others without being wearied—that is just natural with me."[41] He also expressed the wish "not to speak" (*wu-yen*); and when his disciple Tzu-kung wondered how the disciples could ever learn anything to "pass on to others" if he did not speak, Confucius replied, "Does Heaven say anything? The four seasons run their course and all things are produced. Does Heaven say anything?"[42] Mencius too characterized Heaven as "not speaking" (*pu-yen*). In response to a question from Wan Chang, Mencius affirmed the transfer of power between rulers as a divinely directed process, saying that Yao as the emperor could not give the empire to Shun as his successor and that it was Heaven which gave the empire to Shun. In doing so, however, Heaven did not issue verbal commands. For, Mencius explained, "Heaven does not speak. It simply showed its will by [Shun's] personal character and his conduct of affairs."[43]

      The above statements by Confucius and Mencius exemplify a Confucian type of mysticism, according to which Heaven is forever silent; it exists as doing and never as speaking. These statements had a tremendous appeal in late Ming. They so captivated the philosophical imagination of late Ming that Ku Yen-wu was led to complain that scholars at his time became obsessed with problems of "one thread" (*i-kuan*) and "not speaking" (*wu-yen*) and were no longer concerned about the "essential teachings of Confucius on learning and government."[44] Ku's complaint, of course, cannot be taken at face value. It is part of a patterned indictment that the loyalist scholars lodged against the Ming in the wake of the Ming's overthrow by the Ch'ing. As recent scholarship has demonstrated, in what has often been described as the corrupt and degenerate atmosphere of late Ming, there was no lack of serious scholars involved in social reordering and intellectual rebuilding, which were in fact closely related to what Ku has denounced as "empty" speculations on mind and nature.[45] Nevertheless, there is no doubt about what Ku has sensed as the importance of the mystical elements in classical Confucianism for the late Ming during which the syncretic-minded latter-day Confucians seized upon these elements as a symbolic resource in their quest of a synthetic universe. Chiao Hung, for instance, capitalized on the statement of *mo-erh chih-chih* and interpreted it not as "silent remembrance" but as "silent comprehension" which, he said, means "illumination without words" (*wu-yen ch'i-chih*). According to Chiao Hung, what Confucius called "silence" in this statement is not the "silence of the mouth" but the "silence of the mind" which occurs when mind ceases its intellection and is poised for the onrush of "sudden illumination" (*huo-jan yu-ch'i*).[46] It is a form of what a modern philosopher has called the "deep silence" of the "to be said" which, being "beyond all saying," is "not intrinsically correlated with any specifiable utterance," but which "tests all that is said" and which "the encountered world presents to man for his originary response."[47] Chiao Hung identified it with "enlightenment" or *bodhi*, which, though devoid of all things and thoughts, is capable of "responding" (*ying*) to all things and thoughts as they are.[48] Because, Chiao Hung said, Confucius learned and taught with "silence" and did not insist on anything in particular to learn or to teach, he was "never tired of learning" nor became "weary of teaching." For this reason, Confucius was able to proclaim, "What is being to me?"[49]

The Chinese original for "what is being to me" is *ho-yu yü-wo tsai*, which is the concluding sentence of the "silent remembrance" passage and which I have followed Wing-tsit Chan in rendering as "that is just natural with me." What this sentence really means is somewhat uncertain, however, and there is no consensus among the commentators and translators with regard to its precise interpretation. Chu Hsi took it to mean "which one [of these three accomplishments] am I capable of?" (*ho-che neng-yu yü-wo*) and considered the whole passage to be an expression of Confucius' "humility."[50] Chu Hsi's interpretation is followed by Legge, who translated the sentence as "which one of these things belongs to me?"[51] Waley translated this sentence as "these at least are the merits which I can confidently claim." He glossed the phrase *ho-yu* as "there is no further trouble about" and considered it to be the same in usage as the *ho-yu* in the *Analects* 4:13, where the phrase is rendered by Waley as "there is no more to be said."[52] Waley's interpretation is consistent with that of Chan who, as noted above, rendered the sentence as "that is just natural with me." Chiao Hung, however, gave the sentence a characteristically metaphysical interpretation. He equated the word *yu* in the phrase *ho-yu* with the *yu* in *yu-wu* and took it to mean "being" as the correlate of "nonbeing" or "nothingness" (*wu*).

I will not try to justify Chiao Hung's interpretation, which is provocative but not incontrovertible. I need, however, to emphasize that he was consistent in his interpretation of this sentence, which also occurs in the *Analects* 9:15, where, according to Chiao Hung, Confucius is supposed to have said:

> Abroad, to serve the high ministers and nobles; at home, to serve one's father and elder brothers; in all the duties to the dead, not to dare not to exert one's self; and not to be overcome with wine—what is being to me?[53]

This passage, Chiao Hung suggested, is to be understood in the same vein as the "silent remembrance" passage. Just as Confucius was "never tired of learning" nor became "weary of teaching" because he approached learning and teaching as a "silent" nonbeing, so he was able to perform all these activities with perfect ease as the occasion arose because his mind was not a "being" and "had not even the slightest *dharma* to obtain."[54]

It is also noteworthy that Chiao Hung's consistent interpretation of this particular sentence is in line with his interpretations of "silent remembrance" as "silent comprehension" and of "empty-like" as a description of what Confucius had "self-attained" as the "original substance of Heaven's decree."[55] All three interpretations attempt to understand the *Analects* in the light of Buddhism and Taoism and are exemplary of a coherent synthetic formation in which the "silent comprehension" interpretation is the linguistic counterpart of the other two interpretations as metaphysical and ontological statements on the reality of the universe and the being of man. The coherence of this synthetic formation and the significance of the "empty-like" and "what is being to me" interpretations will be explored in the next chapter. Here, I will only deal with the "silent comprehension" interpretation as a linguistic statement which claims to be rooted in, but is actually quite different from, Confucius' idea of "silence," and which could not have been made without Buddhist and Taoist mediation. There is no necessary continuity between the *mo-erh chih-chih* and "not speaking" of Confucius and the "silent comprehension" of Chiao Hung either in terms of commentarial history or in terms of the meaning of silence as an idea. In terms of commentarial history, a number of commentators, including Chu Hsi, stood between Confucius and Chiao Hung. Chu Hsi took the second and unnominalized *chih* in *chih-chih* to be a reference to the metaphysical "Principle" or *li* and explicitly rejected "silent comprehension" as a possible interpretation of *mo-erh chih-chih*, which, he said, means "keeping [the *li*] in the mind without talking about [it]" (*pu-yen erh ts'un-chu hsin*) and not "mental comprehension [of the *li*] without talking about [it]" (*pu-yen erh hsin-chieh*). Similarly, Chu Hsi did not take Confucius' "not speaking" as an expression of Confucius' wish to go beyond language and become silent. Rather, he understood it as a statement on the transparency of the Heavenly Principle. He said, "The circulation of the four seasons and the production of the hundred things are all [a matter of] the reality of the Heavenly Principle which can be seen without being talked about. [Likewise] the sage in his every activity and repose has nothing that is not the springing forth of the Wonderful Way .... Does [Sagehood] become manifest only after it has been talked about?"[56]

Conceptually, both Confucius and Mencius considered Heaven to be "not speaking." They did not proceed to claim, as did Chiao Hung, that Heaven was beyond all saying and indescribable. They spoke of Heaven's "not speaking" as a matter of doing and not in contrast with speech as a notation of Heaven as the ultimate reality. Consequently, their conception of Heaven, though mystical, did not entail Chiao Hung's kind of linguistic skepticism which viewed language as an intrinsically limited medium of representation. It is true that both Confucius and Mencius were deeply suspicious of speech as a human activity. Therefore, Confucius pointedly expressed his wish "not to speak" to Tzu-kung, who ranked with Tsai-wo as the two disciples most accomplished in speech.[57] Mencius, on the other hand, had to defend his frequent engagement in debates, saying, "Indeed, I am not fond of disputing, but I am compelled to do it."[58] He also said that "men's being ready with their tongues arises simply from their not having been reproached."[59] Nevertheless, the suspicion that Confucius and Mencius entertained about speech is, strictly speaking, not linguistic. It did not arise from a consideration of the power of language as representation, but from the moral concern for the possible discrepancy between words and deeds. Just as Heaven acts but does not speak, so men ought to cultivate deeds rather than words which can often be deceptive and are not always reliable.

For Confucius, therefore, "the superior man acts before he speaks and then speaks according to his action."[60] The "superior man" also "wishes to be hesitant in speech and earnest in action"[61] and is "ashamed to let his words exceed his deeds."[62] "Hesitancy in speech" (*no*) is, according to Confucius, "close to humanity" or *jen* as the perfect virtue.[63] By contrast, "clever speech" (*ch'iao-yen*) is "shameful"[64] and is "rarely" associated with "humanity."[65] For, according to Confucius, "a man of humanity" realizes the "difficulty of doing" and is therefore necessarily "chary" (*jen*) of speech.[66] Similarly, Mencius valued deeds over words and considered morality to be a matter of doing which, he claimed, had nothing to do with the "tone of a voice" or a "smiling countenance." He said, "He who is respectful does not insult others. He who is frugal does not plunder others. A ruler who insults and plunders others will be solely preoccupied with the fear that the people will not be compliant. How can he be respectful and frugal? Can respectfulness and frugality be practiced with the tone of a voice or a smiling countenance?"[67]

Thus concerned with the possible discrepancy between words and deeds, however, Confucius and Mencius did not insist that words be necessarily carried out as deeds. In fact, they both regarded the strict observance of words in deeds as a characteristic of the "small man" (*hsiao-jen*). Confucius said, "He who always stands by his word and necessarily sees his action through to the end is a stubborn small man."[68] Mencius, on the other hand, said, "The great man (*ta-jen*) does not always stand by his word or necessarily see his action through to the end."[69] For both Confucius and Mencius, the morality involved in the consistency between words and deeds is not so much a matter of doing what one says as a matter of judiciously exercising tact in speech. Tact entails a form of silence and, as Gadamer has observed, is characterized by "inexplicitness and inexpressibility."[70] Nevertheless, to speak with tact is not "to avert the gaze from something."[71] Rather, it is to speak with due regard for circumstances. A person speaks according to the propriety of a given situation; he says certain things in certain ways, but maintains silence about other things, including those which cannot be done in such a situation.

Confucius had a deep concern for tact in speech. As a result, he urged modesty in speech, saying, "He who speaks without modesty will find it difficult to make his words good."[72] Specifically, "lofty speech and action" are appropriate only "when the Way prevails in the land." "When the Way does not prevail in the land," one should still remain "lofty" in action but become "reserved" in speech.[73] Moreover, according to Confucius, one must relate to one's audience while one speaks. He said, "Not to talk to a person who could be talked to is to be amiss with regard to the person. To talk to a person who cannot be talked to is to be amiss with regard to one's own words. The wise are never amiss either with regard to the person [they talk to] or with regard to their own words."[74] He also said, "There are three mistakes that a person is likely to make while waiting on a superior man. To speak before it is time for him to speak; this is called rashness. Not to speak when it is time for him to speak; this is called secretiveness. To speak without first noting the expression on [the superior man's] face; this is called blindness."[75]

Confucius exemplified his tact in his own pattern of speech, which showed a remarkable sensitivity to situations. Therefore, while at home in his native village, "he looked simple and unassuming as if he were not able to speak." However, "when he was in the ancestral temple or the court [of the Duke of Lu], he spoke readily, though carefully."[76] Also, "When conversing with the Under Ministers at court, he spoke freely and friendlily. When conversing with the Upper Ministers, he spoke formally and honestly. When the ruler was present, he was respectful and attentive, but not constrained."[77]

A similar concern for tact also characterized Mencius' approach to speech. Just as Confucius maintained that "the wise are never amiss either with regard to the person [they talk to] or with regard to their own words," so Mencius said, "To speak to a knight who cannot be spoken to is to use words as a bait. Not to speak to a knight who could be spoken to is to use silence as a bait. To speak or not to speak like this is the same as boring through or climbing over other people's walls [to commit robbery]."[78] Mencius also singled out "those who do violence to themselves" (tzu-pao che) and "those who are not humane" (pu-jen che) as two types of people with whom it would be impossible to speak, saying, "If it were possible to talk to a man who is not humane, there would not have been annihilated states or ruined families."[79] He also said that he would not answer questions from those "who rely on the advantage they posses of position, capability, age, merit, or status as an old acquaintance."[80] Tact demands that there be both speech and silence which, according to Mencius, shall be undertaken in accordance with the sense of i or "righteousness." "Righteousness," as Chung-ying Cheng has noted, is "a universal principle of specific application" and, as such, has a strong situational orientation.[81] It is this sense of "righteousness" that Mencius cited as the reason why "the great man does not always stand by his word or necessarily see his action through to the end." For the "great man," Mencius said, this is "solely" a matter of "where righteousness is."[82] The same sense of righteousness also guides Mencius' own pattern of speech. On the one hand, he felt "compelled" to engage in frequent debates because he wished to "guard the Way of the former kings," to "rectify the minds of the people," and to "put an end to the perverse doctrines" of Yang Chu and Mo Ti.[83] He also criticized Po-i as "narrow-minded" (*ai*) for being unwilling to "speak with an evil man."[84] On the other hand, in spite of his previous success in doing so, he himself would not grant the wish of the people of Ch'i to ask the ruler to open the state granary at T'ang for famine relief. "To do so," he said, "would be to act like a Feng Fu," who did not know when and where to stop. He then proceeded to tell about Feng Fu: "There was a man in Chin by the name of Feng Fu. He was at one time an expert at seizing tigers bare-handed, but later became a good knight. Once, traveling in the countryside, he found a crowd pursuing a tiger. The tiger turned at bay and no one dared go near it. Seeing Feng Fu, the crowd hastened to greet him. Feng Fu rolled up his sleeves and got off his carriage. The crowd was delighted, but the knights laughed at him."[85]

　　For both Confucius and Mencius, therefore, silence is no mere absence of speech; it is transcendence of speech in action and, as such, authenticates speech both as moral fulfillment and as sensible practice.[86] In this sense, silence is a form of activity and, as T'ang Chün-i has observed, is comparable in its relationship with speech to "retreat" (*t'ui*) as a correlate of "advance" (*chin*).[87] Just as a Confucian gentleman in his involvement with the world advances or retreats according to circumstances, so he speaks or remains silent as the situation demands. "The Way of the superior man," says the *Book of Changes*, "consists in going forth (*ch'u*) at certain times and staying put (*ch'u*) at other times and in speaking at certain times and remaining silent at other times."[88] Nevertheless, as a form of activity comparable to retreat, silence is also subtly different from retreat. While the decision to advance or to retreat is purely a matter of circumstances and implies no necessary valuation of advance over retreat or retreat over advance, silence is preferred by both Confucius and Mencius as superior to speech. They did not regard silence with the kind of deep suspicion that they entertained about speech. Their preference for silence follows logically from their conception of Heaven as "not speaking." This conception of Heaven, as noted earlier, implies no recognition of language as an intrinsically limited medium of representation. It does, however, entail the view that language as the signifier not only is extraneous to but must also be kept in accord with the signified as reality or truth. Therefore, Confucius advocated the "rectification of names" (*cheng-ming*), saying,

> If names are not rectified, then language will not be in accord with truth. If language is not in accord with truth, then things cannot be accomplished. If things cannot be accomplished, then rites and music will not flourish. If rites and music do not flourish, then punishment will not be just. If punishments are not just, then the people will not know how to move hand or foot. Therefore, the superior man will use only names that can be applied in speech and say only what can be carried out in practice. The superior man is never careless with regard to his speech.[89]

A similar concern for anchoring language in reality also characterizes the linguistic outlook of Mencius, whose sense of reality has a distinct psychological dimension and is often couched in terms of the feelings of the mind. For him, language functions, at least partly, to express the feelings of the mind and must not be pursued apart from the feelings of the mind. Consequently, he rejected Kao Tzu's position that "what is not attained in words is not to be sought in the mind."[90] He also warned against literal reading of the *Odes* with no regard for the "intended meaning" (*chih*), saying,

> in explaining an ode, one should not allow the words to obscure the sentence or the sentence to obscure the intended meaning. The right way is to meet the intention of the poet with sympathetic understanding. If a sentence were all there is, then there is the ode *Yün Han* which says, "Of the remaining black-haired people of Chou, not a single one survived [the drought]." If we were to believe in this statement as literally true, then the Chou had no subjects left.[91]

In his rejection of Kao Tzu's position that "what is not attained in words is not to be sought in the mind" and in his warning against literal reading of the *Odes*, Mencius sounded suspiciously like the Neo-Taoists of the Wei and Chin periods, who viewed reality as linguistically transcendental and who disputed the possibility of language being able to express the "intended meaning" (*i*) fully.[92] Actually, however, Mencius was not like the Neo-Taoists. His rejection of Kao Tzu's position on "words" and his warning against literal reading of the *Odes* are mere expressions of an awareness which he shared with Confucius that the relationship between language and reality could be problematical. This awareness, however, did not affect in the slightest the confidence that Confucius and Mencius maintained in the power of language to represent reality. For both Confucius and Mencius, the adequacy of language as a representation of reality is in principle indisputable and will remain so if language is not allowed to be used apart from reality and does not become self-referential. Moreover, the use of language apart from reality constitutes an abuse which is rectifiable through the "rectification of names" and readily recognizable if one cultivates the art of "knowing words" (*chih-yen*). Not surprisingly, therefore, both Confucius and Mencius valued the art of "knowing words." Confucius, for instance, put the "knowing of words" on the same footing with the "knowing of Heaven's will" and the "knowing of rites." He said, "Without knowing Heaven's will, it is impossible to be a superior man. Without knowing the rites, it is impossible to conduct oneself. Without knowing words, it is impossible to know men."[93] Mencius, on the other hand, took tremendous pride in his ability to "know words." He claimed that he was "good at nurturing the vast overflowing *ch'i*" (*hao-jan chih-ch'i*) and accomplished in "knowing words." When asked what he meant by "knowing words," he replied, "From biased words, I can see wherein the speaker is blind; from extravagant words, wherein he is depraved; from heretical words, wherein he has strayed from the right path; from evasive words, wherein he is at his wits' end."[94]

The confidence that Confucius and Mencius held in language is shared by Hsün Tzu, who made what I should regard as the most elaborate and systematic statement on language in classical Confucianism. Like Confucius and Mencius, Hsün Tzu also preferred doing to speaking and viewed speech as a form of activity to be performed according to the propriety of a situation and the imperatives of moral fulfillment. He maintained that the "wise ruler" had no need of "discourse" (*pien*) and "explanations" (*shuo*), saying,

> The wise ruler controls them [the people] with power, guides them with the Way, instructs them with commands, enlightens them with the maxims [of the former sages] and prohibits them [from evil] with punishments. Hence his people are converted to the Way as though by supernatural power. What need has he of discourses and explanations?

Moreover, Hsün Tzu said,

> Names are used when reality is not understood. Descriptions are used when names are not understood. Explanations are used when descriptions are not understood. Discourses are used when explanations are not understood.

For Hsün Tzu, "explanations" and "discourses" are a last resort and become necessary only with the "demise of the sage-kings" when "the world is in confusion" with the proliferation of "evil doctrines" and when the "superior man" no longer has the "power" or "punishments" with which to "control" or to "prohibit" the people from evil.[95]

As a last resort, however, explanations and discourses have a vital function to perform. Together with "names" and "descriptions," they constitute "the major forms to be used in conducting practical affairs" and are regarded by Hsün Tzu as the "beginning" (*shih*) of the "kingly enterprise" (*wang-yen*).[96]

Understandably, therefore, Hsün Tzu was critical of those who "took former kings as models, followed rites and righteousness and consorted with scholars" but who "were not fond of speaking," saying that they were "definitely not men of true breeding" (*pi-fei ch'eng-shih yeh*).[97] He also condemned Tzu-hsia's disciples as "contemptible Confucians" (*chien-ju*) because they "wore hats and clothes straight and were dignified in countenance, but would not utter a word the whole day as if they were gagged."[98] The "superior man," according to Hsün Tzu, is different. He is not only "fond of speaking" but also "committed to debate" (*pi-pien*) because he speaks and debates for the sake of "humanity" (*jen*). "All men," said Hsün Tzu, "are fond of talking about what they cherish, and this is especially so with the superior man." What the "superior man" cherishes is "humanity"; and as he "does not ever become tired of practicing humanity," he is "never tired of speaking."[99]

On the other hand, however, the "superior man" is considered by Hsün Tzu to be a man of "few words" (*shao-yen*),[100] because he speaks only of what is "in accord with humanity." If, therefore, what is spoken of is not in accord with humanity, he would rather remain silent than speak and rather be "hesitant" (*na*, read as *no*) than eager in debate.[101] Moreover, the "superior man" does not create his own doctrines; he merely follows what the sages have established as the "norm" (*fa*). In this regard, the "superior man" differs from the sage, who exemplifies for Hsün Tzu the ideal of highest achievement in speech. The sage is a man of "many words" (*to-yen*). His words, however, are orderly and systematic, as they are structured by "categories" (*lei*) which are consistent with reality.[102] What the sage says is also entirely spontaneous and situationally appropriate. Therefore, while engaged in a debate, he "does not deliberate beforehand or plan early," but is always "appropriate in what he utters" and is able to "respond endlessly" to whatever he encounters from the opponent. The superior man in his speech falls short of the sagely ideal. He has to "deliberate beforehand or plan early" for a debate.[103] Nevertheless, he is far superior to the "small man" who is "talkative without any sense of norm" (*to-shao wu-fa*—reading *shao* as *yen*) and is "submerged" (*mien*) by his own talk "without knowing when and where to stop" (*liu*). The "small man" has no understanding of silence, which, according to Hsün Tzu, is to be cultivated as well as speech. "Proper speech," said Hsün Tzu, "is wisdom. Proper silence is also wisdom. Therefore, knowing silence is comparable to knowing speech."[104]

In his valuation of debate, Hsün Tzu resembles Mencius but is rather unlike Confucius, who, as T'ang Chün-i has noted,[105] is not much given to argumentation. When Tsai-wo complained that the three years' mourning for parents was too long and that one year should suffice, because if the "superior man" had to disengage from "rites" and "music" for three years on account of mourning, then rites and music would "certainly decay" or "be ruined," Confucius made no attempt to refute Tsai-wo even though he had a perfectly good reason to do so. Children, according to Confucius, are supposed to observe the three years' mourning for their parents because they do not "leave their parents' arms" until they are three years old. But, characteristically, Confucius did not argue with Tsai-wo, to whom he simply said, "Would you then [after a year] feel at ease in eating good rice and wearing silk brocades?" When Tsai-wo said that he would indeed be "quite at ease," Confucius replied, "If you would really feel at ease, then do so. But when a superior man is in mourning, he does not find good food to his liking, is not pleased on hearing music, and is uncomfortable in his normal resting place. That is why he abstains from these things. But if you would really feel at ease, there is no need for you to abstain."[106]

However, in being argumentative like Mencius, Hsün Tzu is also different from Mencius in the mode of argumentation. As T'ang Chün-i has observed, [107] Mencius tends to argue from a psychological perspective in terms of subjective feelings, which, Mencius believed, can be subjectively experienced by every man and are therefore constitutive of man's being as man. Mencius said,

> Now things of the same kind are all alike. Why should we have doubts when it comes to man? The sage and I are of the same kind. Thus Lung-tzu said, "When someone makes a shoe for a foot he has not seen, I am sure he will not produce a basket." All shoes are alike because all feet are alike. All palates show the same preferences in taste. I-ya was simply the first to discover what would be pleasing to our palates. If taste were to vary from man to man in the same way as horses and dogs differ from me in kind, then how is it that all palates in the world show the preferences of I-ya? The fact that in taste the whole world looks to I-ya shows that all palates are alike. It is the same also with the ear. The whole world looks to Shih-k'uang for truly musical sounds, and this shows that all ears are alike. It is the same also with the eye. The

whole world appreciates the good looks of Tzu-tu; whoever does not is blind. Hence it is said: all palates have the same preference in taste; all ears in sound; all eyes in beauty. Can it be that in our minds alone we are not alike? What is it that we have in common in our minds? It is the sense of principle and righteousness. The sage is simply the man first to discover what is common in our minds. Therefore, principle and righteousness please our minds just as beef, mutton, pork, and dog meat please our palates.[108]

This belief in the universality of the feelings of the mind informs Mencius' frequent citation of sages like Yao and Shun. Mencius, as the quotation indicates, considered Yao and Shun to be of the same kind as every other man. He did not invoke them as authorities to be appealed to but as exemplifications of totally fulfilled personalities who, being the "first" to "discover what is common in our minds," charted the path to and provided the assurance for the perfection of sagehood as an ideal that every man could achieve through self-cultivation. Therefore, when Duke Wen of T'eng was still crown prince and stopped by to see Mencius while on his way to Ch'u, Mencius talked a great deal of Yao and Shun while expounding the theory of human nature as intrinsically good. The crown prince, however, was not convinced and paid Mencius another visit on his way back from Ch'u. Obviously incensed, Mencius burst out in a recitation of the names of those who had confidence in themselves and aspired to become sages, saying,

Crown prince, do you doubt my words? There is one Way and one only. Ch'eng Chien said to Duke Ching of Ch'i, "They [the sages and worthies] are men. I am also a man. Why should I be in awe of them?" Yen Yüan said, "What sort of man was Shun? What sort of man am I? Anyone who would make something of himself will be like that." Kung-ming I said, "The Duke of Chou was indeed not fooling me when he said that he modeled himself on King Wen." Now, T'eng, averaging its length and its width, amounts to about fifty *li*. [It is small but] can still become a good state. The *Book of History* says, "If the medicine does not make the head swim, the illness will not be cured."[109]

The same belief in the universality of the feelings of the mind formed the basis of Mencius' objection to those who "talked about human nature" merely in logical terms of "therefores" (*ku*) with no regard for the natural tendencies of man. As a result, their use of "therefores," though "clever," was nothing but "forced reasoning" (*tso*, literally, "chiseling away at something") which Mencius contrasted with Yü's way of handling the flood waters; Yü followed the natural tendencies of water and drained the flood waters effortlessly as if he "had not done anything."[110] In his own arguments for the intrinsic goodness of man's nature, Mencius avoided this type of forced reasoning. He appealed to our feelings, which he regarded as natural and spontaneous promptings of the mind. He said, "All men have the mind which cannot bear to see the suffering of others . . . . Now, if a man sees a child about to fall into a well, he will experience a feeling of alarm and distress, not because he wishes to gain friendship with the child's parents and to seek the praise of his neighbours and friends or because he dislikes the cry of the child. From such a case, we see that a man without the feeling of commiseration is not a man; a man without the feeling of shame is not a man; a man without the feeling of deference is not a man; and a man without the feeling of right and wrong is not a man."[111] These four feelings are the "beginnings" (*tuan*) of the four cardinal virtues of humanity, righteousness, ritual propriety, and wisdom,[112] which, being rooted in the natural and spontaneous feelings of the mind, "are not drilled into us from outside" but are "what we have originally." Therefore, when confronted by Kung-tu Tzu with the possibility that "man's nature may be made good or evil" because "when King Wen and King Wu were in power people loved virtue," but "when King Yu and King Li were in power people loved violence," Mencius replied, "As far as their feelings are concerned, they are able to do good. This is what is meant by saying that human nature is good. If man does evil, it is not the fault of his natural endowment."[113]

Similarly, when Mencius argued for humane government, rites, and music, he did so in terms of feelings. The humane government, according to Mencius, is nothing but an extension into the public realm of "the mind which cannot bear to see the suffering of others." He said, "The former kings had the mind which cannot bear to see the suffering of the people. Therefore, they had a government that could not bear to see the suffering of the people. When a govenment that cannot bear to see the suffering of the people is conducted from a mind that cannot bear to see the suffering of the people, the empire will be as easy to rule as if it could be rolled around in the palm . . . . Man has the Four Beginnings just as he has four limbs . . . . If a man knows how to extend and develop the Four Beginnings that he possesses, the result will be like a fire beginning to burn or a spring beginning to shoot forth. When fully developed, the Four Beginnings will be sufficient to protect all within the four seas [i.e., the whole world]."[114]

Likewise, rites are an outgrowth of feelings. Therefore, in his rejection of I Chih's Mohist principle of economy for funerals, Mencius said, "In great antiquity, there were those who did not bury their parents. When their parents died, they simply picked up and threw the bodies into a ditch. Then one day while passing by the dead bodies of their parents, they saw foxes and wild cats gnawing at the bodies and flies and gnats biting at the flesh. With perspiration breaking out on their foreheads, they looked away to avoid the sight. The perspiration was not put on for others to see. It was an expression on the face of feelings felt deep in the heart. Thereupon, they returned home and came back with baskets and spades to cover the dead bodies of their parents. If it was right for these people to cover the dead bodies of their parents, then filial sons and men of humanity must also be acting in accordance with the Way when they bury their parents [the way they do]."[115] Also, when his disciple Ch'ung Yü made the observation that he seemed to have used wood of "excessively fine" quality for his mother's coffin, Mencius justified himself in terms of feelings. He said,

In high antiquity, there were no regulations governing the inner and outer coffins. In middle antiquity, it was prescribed that the inner coffin was to be seven inches thick with the outer coffin to match. This applied to all men, ranging from the Son of Heaven to the commoner. The prescription was not instituted for the sake of mere appearance. Rather, the feelings of the mind cannot be fulfilled without it. If a person is not allowed to use this type of coffin, he will not be satisfied. Or, if a person does not have the money to afford this type of coffin, he will not be satisfied. The ancients, when they both were allowed and had the money to do so, had always used this type of coffin. Why should I alone not do so? Moreover, does the mind not feel pleased for being able to prevent the earth from getting close to the dead body which is about to decompose? I have heard it said that the superior man would not for all the world be niggardly to his parents.[116]

As for music, Mencius considers it to have originated in the sense of joy that one feels in the performance of humanity and righteousness. He said,

The reality of humanity consists in serving one's parents. The reality of righteousness consists in obeying one's elder brother. The reality of wisdom consists in knowing these two things and not departing from them. The reality of ritual propriety consists in regulating and providing these two things with cultured forms. The reality of music consists in rejoicing in these two things. [As these two things are rejoiced in,] a sense of joy is produced. Once the sense of joy is produced, how can it be stopped? Since it cannot be stopped, the feet will dance and the hands will move spontaneously.[117]

Feelings also concern Hsün Tzu, not however as the ontological "beginnings" of man's innately good nature, but as the ineradicable source of man's inherently evil nature as being antisocial. Hsün Tzu is suspicious of feelings which he more or less equated with "desires" (*yü*). "Desires," according to Hsün Tzu, "are the responses of feelings" (*ch'ing chih ying*) and, as such, "cannot but" seek gratification.[118] If left uncontrolled, they will inevitably lead to social contention and disorder. He said, "Man is born with desires. When these desires are not gratified, he cannot remain without seeking their gratification. When this seeking for gratification is without measure or limit, there can only be contention. When there is contention, there will be disorder. When there is disorder, there will be impoverishment [of material goods]."[119] Therefore, in contrast to Mencius who viewed feelings, mind, and man's nature in structurally unitary terms and regarded the goodness of man's nature as the direct outgrowth of the intrinsically moral feelings, Hsün Tzu birfurcated feelings from the mind and considered man's nature to be evil because it is constituted by feelings. Consequently, although Hsün Tzu advocated morality, rites, and music as much as Mencius did as the basis of "kingly" government,[120] he did so by appealing to the mind and not feelings for justification.

The mind, according to Hsün Tzu, is "vacuous" (*hsü*), "unified" (*i*), and "tranquil" (*ching*). He said,

> Man is born with an intellect, and where there is intellect there is memory. Memory is what is stored up in the mind. Yet the mind is said to be vacuous because what has already been stored up in it does not hinder the reception of new impressions. Therefore, it is said to be vacuous. The mind is born with an intellect, and where there is intellect there is an awareness of differences. An awareness of differences means that one can have an understanding of a variety of facts at the same time, and where there is such understanding, there is diversity. And yet the mind is said to be unified because it does not allow the understanding of one fact to impinge on that of another. Therefore it is said to be unified. When the mind is asleep, it produces dreams; when it is unoccupied, it wanders off in idle fancy; and when it is used, it engages in deliberation. Hence the mind is constantly moving. And yet it is said to be tranquil, because it does not allow dreams and anxieties to disturb its understanding. Therefore it is said to be tranquil.[121]

Being thus "vacuous," "unified," and "tranquil," the mind can "know the Way"[122] and is spoken of by Hsün Tzu as the "supervisor of the Way" (*tao-chih kung-tsai*) which he in turn regards as the "constant principle of good government" (*chih-chih ching-li*).[123] As the "supervisor of the Way," the mind can "choose" from among a variety of feelings and generate moral conduct through "conscious activity" (*wei*),[124] which is the source of "goodness" (*shan*). "Man's nature," said Hsün Tzu, "is evil; goodness is the result of conscious activity."[125] Therefore, although desires or feelings are inherently antisocial and cannot be eradicated because they are inborn, they are not really relevant to the question of "order" (*chih*) or "disorder" (*luan*) which, according to Hsün Tzu, hinges on the dictates of the mind. He said,

> All those who maintain that desires must be gotten rid of before there can be order do not know how to guide (*tao*) desires and are therefore perplexed by the sheer existence of desires. All those who maintain that desires must be lessened before there can be order do not know how to control (*chieh*) desires and are therefore perplexed by the numerousness of desires. Beings that possess desires and that do not belong to two different categories—the categories of the living and the dead. But the possession or nonpossession of desires has nothing to do with order or disorder.... Desires arise without waiting to make certain that satisfaction is possible. The search for satisfaction, however, follows what is possible. That desires arise without waiting to make certain that satisfaction is possible comes from man's natural endowment at birth. That the search for satisfaction follows what is possible comes from the direction of the mind.... Therefore, although a man's desires are excessive, his actions need not be so, because the mind will stop them short. If what the mind considers to be possible is in accord with just principles, then, although desires are many, how can they do any harm to order?... [Conversely,] if what the mind considers to be possible is not in accord with just principles, then, although desires are few, how can disorder be stopped? Therefore, order or disorder depends on what the mind assents to, not on what feelings desire.[126]

The "guidance" and "control" of desires is accomplished through the observation of rites, music, and such ethical values as filiality and deference (*tz'u-jang*), etc., which Hsün Tzu characteristically did not consider, as did Mencius, to be the spontaneous outward expressions of the natural feelings within. Rather, he viewed them as human artifices created by the "conscious activity" of the minds of the ancient kings and sages to provide for guided and controlled satisfaction of man's natural feelings so that there would be no disorder.[127] The observance of the humanly constructed rites, music, and morality is what makes a sage like Yü a sage who is not different in nature from the man in the street, or even such archetypical evil personalities as the tyrant Chieh and the robber Chih.[128] "What," said Hsün Tzu, "made Yü a Yü is simply that he practiced humanity and righteousness and abided by the proper rules and standards."[129] He also said,

> Heaven was not partial to Tseng Tzu, Min Tzu-ch'ien, and Hsiao I to the exclusion of the common multitude. And yet Tseng Tzu, Min Tzu-ch'ien, and Hsiao I were particularly accomplished in the realization of filiality and won perfect fame for filiality. Why? Because they fully observed rites and righteousness. Heaven was not partial to the people of Ch'i and Lu to the exclusion of the people of Ch'in. And yet, with regard to the normative relationship between father and son and the distinction between husband and wife, the people of Ch'in cannot compare to the people of Ch'i and Lu, who are filial and reverential [reading *hsiao-chü* as *hsiao-kung* according to Wang Nien-sun] toward their fathers and respectful and courteous [reading *ching-fu* as *ching-wen* according to Wang Nein-sun] toward their husbands. Why? Because the people of Ch'in give free rein to their feelings and nature, are content to indulge their passions and neglect rites and righteousness. There is certainly no difference in nature between these two groups of people.[130]

Hsün Tzu's bifurcation of the mind from feelings or nature runs parallel to and may in fact be regarded as an instance of a general distinction which he maintained between the human and the natural and which has implications not only for his theories of human nature and culture but also for his conceptions of Heaven and language. Again, in contrast to Mencius, who advocated the identity of man and Heaven in structurally unitary terms and stated that "he who realizes his mind knows his nature and he who knows his nature knows Heaven,"[131] Hsün Tzu insisted that man be viewed as categorically different from Heaven, saying, "He who knows the distinction between Heaven and man may be called a perfect man (*chih-jen*)."[132] This insistence on the categorical difference between man and Heaven involves a naturalistic conception of Heaven, which, according to

Hsün Tzu, consists of a series of processes in the physical universe and is nonpurposive. He said, "Heaven operates with constant regularity. It does not exist because of a sage like Yao or cease to exist because of a tyrant like Chieh."[133] He also said, "Heaven does not suspend the winter because men dislike cold. Earth does not stop being vast because men dislike distance."[134] Because of his belief in a naturalistic Heaven, Hsün Tzu has been characterized as "positivistic" and "Taoistic."[135] It is noteworthy, however, that Hsün Tzu's naturalistic conception of Heaven entails no attempt to reduce man to Heaven. In this regard, he is different from both the positivists and the Taoists. Although he argued against the teleological notion of Heaven and said that order and disorder had nothing to do with the revolution of the heavenly bodies or the succession of the seasons, he did so in order to affirm the value of human endeavor.[136] For this reason, he dismissed the unusual natural occurrences like the "appearance of strange stars" and the "eclipses of the sun and moon" as not worth worrying about, but counseled caution for what he called the "human portents" such as the "mutual suspicion of fathers and sons," the "wanton mingling of men and women," and the "estrangement between the superior and the inferior," etc., which he regarded as truly "fearsome."[137] Similarly, while extolling the "perfect man" as the ideal person who "does not compete with Heaven's work," he also condemned those who "set aside what belongs to man and long for what belongs to Heaven."[138] He said, "The superior man is serious about what lies in himself and does not desire what pertains to Heaven. The inferior man sets aside what lies in himself and desires what pertains to Heaven."[139] Far from trivializing man and his culture, Hsün Tzu's naturalistic conception of Heaven expresses a humanistic outlook on the universe, which, according to Hsün Tzu, has a distinctly human dimension not reducible to nature. For Hsün Tzu, precisely because the human realm is distinct from the natural realm, man can form a triad with Heaven and earth. He said, "Heaven has its seasons, earth has its riches, and man has his government. This is how they are able to form a triad."[140] He also said, "Heaven and earth are the beginning of life, rites and righteousness are the beginning of order, and the superior man is the beginning of rites and righteousness . . . . Therefore, Heaven and earth produce the superior man and the superior man brings order to Heaven and earth. The superior man forms a triad with Heaven and earth."[141]

When translated into his theory of language, the distinction between the human and the natural means that, for Hsün Tzu, names relate to reality only indirectly. In this regard, he differed from both Confucius and Mencius, who structured their notion of language in dyadic terms and were of the view that a direct relationship prevailed between names and reality, which either corresponded to one another or did not. By contrast, Hsün Tzu approached the phenomenon of language in triadic terms and did not believe the relationship between names and reality to be possible without the mediation of social conventions. For this reason, he denied that names could have intrinsic reality, saying, "Names have no intrinsic appropriateness. People agree on calling something by a certain name. When the agreement is established and becomes a matter of custom, then the name is said to be appropriate. If, however, the name is contrary to the agreement, it is said to be inappropriate. Names have no intrinsic reality. People agree on calling a certain reality by a certain name. When the agreement is established and becomes a matter of custom, then the name is said to be a real name."[142] This statement by Hsün Tzu indicates a strong awareness of language as a socially regulated activity and is consistent with his belief that language fulfills a definite social purpose. He said,

> When different forms are referred to by the same name at cross purposes by minds which are not coordinated and when different things are referred to by names whose relationship to realities is obscure and entangled,[143] the distinction between the noble and the base will not become clear and the differentiation between things that are the same and those that are different will not be properly maintained. Under these circumstances, there will certainly be the danger of intentions being misunderstood and the mishap of affairs not being carried out. For this reason, men of wisdom established distinctions and instituted names to refer to realities so that the noble will be clearly distinguished from the base and things that are the same will be properly differentiated from things that are different. When the noble are clearly distinguished from the base

and when things that are the same are properly differentiated from things that are different, there will certainly be no danger of intentions being misunderstood and no mishap of affairs not being carried out. This is the reason for having names.[144]

On the other hand, though strongly social in orientation, Hsün Tzu's theory of language does not entail the view that names as signifiers are arbitrary constructions discontinuous with realities as the signified. For, according to Hsün Tzu, the differences and similarities that names are intended to establish and maintain are rooted in the differences and similarities inherent in the realities, which form the "essential standard (*shu-yao*) to be used in instituting names." He said,

> There are things which share the same form but occupy different places and things which have different forms but occupy the same place. These two types of things can be distinguished. Things which share the same form but occupy different places are said to be two different realities even though they may be grouped under the same name. Things which change form and appear to have become different but which remain the same in reality are said to have been transformed. When things undergo transformation without becoming actually different, they are said to be the same reality. This is how realities are examined and their number determined. It is the essential standard to be used in instituting names.[145]

Moreover, names bear a relationship of necessary correspondence to realities because they are established as expressions of the perceptions of man's "natural faculties" (*t'ien-kuan*), which can distinguish between things that are the same and those that are different. Hsün Tzu said,

> On what account are things that are the same to be distinguished from those that are different? On account of the natural faculties. Things which are of the same kind and form are apprehended by the natural faculties as the same.[146] Therefore, through comparison, things that seem alike are identified as being of the same

kind and are thereby given a common name which people have agreed upon and which they expect each other to use. Differences in shape, color, or marking are distinguished by the eye. Differences of tone, timbre, pitch, or modulation are distinguished by the mouth. Aromatic and putrid smells, the fragrance of fresh flowers and grass, the smell of rotten plants, rankness, rancidness, the sour smell of a hot humid summer day, and other unusual smells are distinguished by the nose. Pain, itchiness, cold, heat, smoothness, roughness, lightness, and heaviness are distinguished by the body. Enjoyment of doing something because one likes to, distress about doing something because one is forced to, pleasure, anger, grief, joy, love, hate, and desire are distinguished by the mind. The mind also possesses an overall understanding. Because of this overall understanding, sound can be known through the ear and form can be known through the eye. On the other hand, however, this overall understanding must always wait until the five sense organs [reading *t'ien-kuan* as *wu-kuan* according to Yü Yüeh] have registered the sense data according to proper categories .... This is how things that are the same come to be distinguished from those that are different. Following the distinctions thus established, names are given to things. Things that are the same are given the same name and those that are different are given different names.[147]

For Hsün Tzu, therefore, names as social conventions can represent reality which they signify. In spite of his structural differences from Confucius and Mencius in the theorizing of language, he had as much confidence as they did in the power of language as a medium of representation. Therefore, while denying that names had intrinsic appropriateness or reality, he nevertheless affirmed that "there are names which are intrinsically good (*ku-shan*)," saying, "Names which are straightforward, simple and not at odds (*pu-fu*) with [the reason for having names, the ways according to which things that are the same are distinguished from those that are different, and the essential standard used in the instituting of names] are said to be good names."[148] For the same reason, he said, "Reality can be understood when names are mentioned. Therein lies the function of naming."[149]

Intersection with Buddhist and Taoist Articulations

In contrast to Confucius, Mencius, and Hsün Tzu, who, though viewing language as a distinctly human and problematical undertaking, never doubted its adequacy as a medium of representation, the Buddhists and Taoists advocated a form of linguistic skepticism, according to which the ultimate reality is mute in the sense of being pre-scriptive and unsayable. Both Lao Tzu and Chuang Tzu are known for their pronouncements on the Tao as nameless and unnameable. Lao Tzu said that the Tao is "infinite, boundless and unnameable" (*sheng-sheng pu-k'o ming*).[150] He also said, "The Tao is forever nameless. Though the uncarved block is small, no one in the world dare claim its allegiance . . . . Only when it is cut are there names. As soon as there are names, know that it is time to stop."[151] Likewise, Chuang Tzu said that "the Great Way is not named" (*ta-tao pu-ch'eng*)[152] and that although "the ten thousand things differ in principle," the Tao shows "no partiality" (*pu-ssu*) among them and is therefore itself undifferentiated and "nameless" (*wu-ming*).[153] Among the Buddhists, Vimalakīrti's "silence" is proverbial and paradigmatic. As the anticlimactic climax of a series of attempts by thirty-three Bodhisattvas including Mañjuśrī to define the Dharma-Gate of Nonduality (*pu-erh fa-men*),[154] it examplifies a conventional Buddhist wisdom that the Tathāgata as the ultimate truth is, as Vimalakīrti put it, "beyond the paths of word and speech" and "cannot be revealed by word, speech, discerning and pointing."[155]

To be sure, neither the Buddhists nor the Taoists did away with language entirely. To say that the ultimate reality is unsayable is already a form of saying. In fact Lao Tzu, Chuang Tzu, and Vimalakīrti all said a good deal more than that. In spite of their injunction against saying, they all engaged in speech and affirmed a mode of language use as an activity. In doing so, however, they were not necessarily contradicting themselves, for, as will be shown, the mode of language use that they each affirmed not only is consistent with but actually articulates their linguistically skeptical belief that the ultimate reality is ineffable.

Lao Tzu, for instance, made a number of statements on the Tao. These statements, according to T'ang Chün-i, can be categorized into six distinct but not mutually exclusive types:[156]

1. Statements concerning the Tao as the principle of regularity in the universe. Here, the word *Tao* stands for what the myriad things in the universe share in common. It does not refer to the ultimate reality, but to what in T'ang Chün-i's terms is a "vacuous principle" (*hsü-li*) and is likened by him to an air route in the sky. An air route has no reality in and of itself and becomes manifest only because of a flying airplane. Similarly, the Tao as the principle of regularity in the universe does not exist in its own right and has no independent existence to speak of. It depends on the myriad things for existence and can be talked about only as an observed commonality of the myriad things. Examples of this type of statement may include: (1) chapter 40 of the *Lao Tzu*, where it is said: "Reversal is the movement of the Tao"; and (2) chapter 77, where the Tao is compared to the "bending of a bow": "Heaven's Way is indeed like the bending of a bow. When (the string) is high, bring it down. When it is low, raise it up. When it is excessive, reduce it. When it is insufficient, supplement it. The Way of Heaven reduces whatever is excessive and supplements whatever is insufficient."[157]

2. Statements concerning the Tao as a metaphysical existence, or, in T'ang Chün-i's terms, the metaphysical "substance of the Tao (*tao-t'i*)." Here, the word *Tao* is a designation for the ultimate reality which has an independent and eternal existence not only in and of itself but prior to the existence of the myriad things and is the source of the myriad things. An example of this type of statements appears in chapter 25, where it is said: "There is something undifferentiated and yet complete, which is born before heaven and earth. Soundless and formless, it stands alone and does not change. It goes round and does not weary. It is capable of being the mother of the universe. I do not know its name; I call it the Tao."[158]

3. Statements concerning the attributes of the metaphysical "substance of the Tao." The metaphysical substance of

the Tao is in and of itself "undifferentiated" and has no attributes to speak of. However, since it is the "mother" of the myriad things which have attributes, it bears a relationship to the myriad things and, as a result, takes on a set of attributes which are contingent upon this relationship and which can and must be talked about in terms of what the attributes of the myriad things both are and are not. The Tao in its metaphysical "substance" must be talked about in terms of what the attributes of the myriad things both are and are not because its relationship to the myriad things consists of both identity and contrast and is a necessary contradiction which is entailed by the Tao's movement as "reversal" and which can only be stated in paradoxical terms. For this reason, Lao Tzu stated in chapter 78 that "straightforward words sound paradoxical" (*cheng-yen jo-fan*). In contrast to the myriad things which have "shape" (*chuang*) and "thingness" (*wu*) and which are nameable and susceptible to sensory perception through seeing and hearing, the Tao in its metaphysical "substance" is said to be a "shape without shape" and a "thing without thingness" and to be "unnameable," "invisible," "inaudible," and beyond "touch." Thus it is said in chapter 14, "We look at it and do not see it; it is called invisible. We listen to it and do not hear it; it is called inaudible. We touch it and do not find it; it is called minute and subtle .... Infinite, boundless, and unnameable, it reverts to nothingness and is what is known as the shape without shape and the thing [*hsiang*, literally "image" or "concrete phenomenon"] without thingness."[159] Conversely, the Tao in its metaphysical "substance" can also be talked about as having attributes in terms of its identity with the myriad things which it generates. Therefore, since things have "being" (*yu*) and are spoken of as "things" with "names," the Tao in its metaphysical substance can also be said to have "being" and to be a "thing" whose "name ever remains" (*ch'i-ming pu-ch'ü*). Thus, when Lao Tzu spoke of the "undifferentiated and yet complete" Tao in chapter 25, he referred to it as a "something" which "is" (*yu*). Similarly, he said in chapter 21, "As a thing, the Tao is elusive and vague. Vague and elusive, there are images (*hsiang*) in it. Elusive and vague, there are things in it .... From the time of old until now, its name ever remains so that we may see the beginning of all things. How do I know that the beginnings of all things are so? By means of this."[160]

4. Statements in which the Tao is spoken of in terms of *te* or "virtue." In the *Lao Tzu*, Tao as a concept is usually distinguishable from *te*. Tao is the "mother" of the myriad things and is what they all hold in common whereas *te* pertains to the individuality of the myriad things and is what they each obtain from the Tao and must observe in order to become what they are as particulars. In this regard, Lao Tzu is rather different from Chuang Tzu, who does not distinguish Tao from *te* as much as Lao Tzu does and who is unequivocal in advocating both "letting the *te* be in [one's] actions" (*fang-te erh-hsing*) and "following the Tao in [one's] journey" (*hsün-tao erh-ch'ü*).[161] Not surprisingly, therefore, the statements in which the Tao is spoken of in terms of *te* are relatively few in the *Lao Tzu*. Nevertheless, since *te* is what the myriad things each obtain from the Tao and has the Tao as its source, it bears to Tao the same kind of relationship that prevails between the myriad things and the Tao as metaphysical "substance." Therefore, just as the Tao as metaphysical "substance" can be talked about in paradoxical terms of what the attributes of the myriad things are and are not, so the Tao in its relationship to *te* can also be spoken of in terms which both identify and contrast the Tao with *te*. In terms of its identification with *te* which is embodied in things, the Tao is said to be a possession of things. As such, the Tao is viewed by Lao Tzu as a "treasure" which can even be "offered" as a present. Thus, it is said in chapter 62, "Tao is the storehouse of all things. It is the good man's treasure and the bad man's refuge.... Therefore on the occasion of crowning an emperor or installing the three ministers, rather than present large pieces of jade preceded by teams of four horses, it is better to kneel and offer this Tao."[162] As a contrasts to *te*, the Tao is distinguished from the *te* of things and is spoken of by Lao Tzu as the "superior virtue" (*shang-te*) or "profound and mysterious virtue" (*hsüan-te*). It is said in chapter 38, "The man of superior virtue does not keep to virtue, and that is why he has virtue. The man of inferior virtue never strays from virtue, and that is why he is without virtue. The man of superior virtue never acts, but leaves

nothing undone. The man of inferior virtue acts, but there are things left undone."[163] It is also said in chapter 65, "In ancient times those who practiced Tao well did not seek to enlighten the people, but to make them ignorant. People are difficult to govern because they have too much knowledge. Therefore he who rules the state through knowledge is a robber of the state; he who rules a state not through knowledge is a blessing to the state. One who knows these two things also knows the norm. Always knowing the norm is called profound and mysterious virtue. The profound and mysterious virtue is deep and far-reaching. And with it all things return to their original natural state with the result that complete harmony is established."[164] Statements in this category are closely related to but analytically distinguishable from those in category 3 because *te*, though embodied in things as the principle of individuation, is nonetheless different as a concept from things understood in terms of attributes.

5. Statements in which the Tao is understood in a practical sense, a technique of realizing or conforming to the Tao, such as the correct method of cultivation, the right way of living, and the art of good government, etc. Statements of this type are numerically most significant in the *Lao Tzu*. But they are not concerned with the Tao per se as the ultimate reality, even though they have implications which are relevant to any metaphysical consideration of the Tao as the ultimate reality. Examples may include: (1) chapter 15, where it is stated, "He who embraces this Tao does not want to fill himself to overflowing. It is precisely because there is no overflowing that he is beyond wearing out and renewal";[165] (2) chapter 30 where it is said, "He who assists the ruler with Tao does not dominate the world with force. The use of force usually brings requital. Wherever armies are stationed, briers and thorns grow. Great wars are always followed by famines. A good [general] achieves his purpose and stops, but does not seek to dominate the world . . . . [For] after things reach their prime, they begin to grow old, which means being contrary to Tao. Whatever is contrary to Tao will soon perish";[166] and (3) chapter 37 where it is said, "Tao invariably takes no action, and yet there is nothing left undone. If kings and barons can keep it, all things will transform spontaneously. If, after transformation, they

should desire to be active, I would restrain them with simplicity, which has no name. Simplicity, which has no name, is free of desires. Being free of desires, it is tranquil. And the world will be at peace of its own accord."[167]

6. Statements in which the discourse on the Tao is a description of a state of existence which has realized the metaphysical "substance" of the Tao, spoken of in the *Lao Tzu* in terms of whatever can be said of the *Tao* as the ultimate reality. Just as the Tao in its metaphysical "substance" is said to be beyond "inquiry" because it is "invisible," "inaudible," and "minute and subtle" (chapter 14), so the "best rulers of old," who were "genuine like a piece of uncarved wood" and "undifferentiated like muddy water," are also said to be "subtly mysterious, profoundly penetrating, and too deep to comprehend" (chapter 15). Other examples may include: (1) chapter 8 where it is said, "The best [man] is like water. Water is good; it benefits all things and does not compete with them. It dwells in [lowly] places that all disdain. This is why it is so near to the Tao"; and (2) chapter 16 where it is said, "To know the eternal is called enlightenment. Not to know the eternal is to act blindly so that disaster results. He who knows the eternal is all-embracing. Being all-embracing, he is impartial. Being impartial, he is kingly. Being kingly, he is one with Nature. Being one with Nature, he is in accord with Tao. Being in accord with Tao, he is longlasting and free from danger till the end of his life."[168] Statements in this category are closely related to those in 3 and 4 above. They differ, however, in focus or point of reference and represent two different procedures of talking about the Tao as the ultimate reality. While category 6 proceeds from that which is differentiated to the Tao as the undifferentiated in terms of what has become of the differentiated, 3 and 4 begin with the undifferentiated Tao as the "mother" of all differentiated things and speak of the undifferentiated Tao in terms of what the differentiated things are and are not.

In terms of our concern with Lao Tzu's theory and use of language, T'ang Chün-i's six types may be regrouped as two: (1) 2, 3, 4, and 6, which all refer to the Tao as the ultimate reality; and (2) 1 and 5, which do not refer to the Tao as the ultimate reality. 1 and 5 are obviously compatible with the mystical/

skeptical belief in the ineffability of the Tao as the ultimate reality which is simply not their concern. As for 2, 3, 4, and 6, it is noteworthy that what they say of the Tao as the ultimate reality, including the saying that the Tao as the ultimate reality is unsayable, is said in terms of what can and cannot be said of the sayable things and says nothing of the Tao in itself. Thus the saying affirmed in 2, 3, 4, and 6 does not contravene Lao Tzu's mystical/skeptical vision. Rather, it is informed by, and may in fact be viewed as an articulation of, his mystical/skeptical belief that the Tao as the ultimate realtity is ineffable.

Chuang Tzu, as noted a little earlier, differed from Lao Tzu in maintaining an unequivocally unitary view of the Tao and the *te*. As a logical correlate of this difference, Chuang Tzu advocated a form of mysticism/skepticism which is even more radical than Lao Tzu's. He extended his sense of ineffability to things as concrete embodiments of the individualizing *te* and considered both the Tao and things to be ultimately beyond speech and silence. He said, "The perfection of the Way and things—neither words nor silence are worthy of expressing it. Not to talk, not to be silent—this is the highest form of debate."[169] Nevertheless, Chuang Tzu also spoke. He even debated, sometimes with a sense of relish. He obviously enjoyed Hui Shih as a debating partner and felt a sense of loss after Hui Shih's death, saying, "There's no one I can talk to any more."[170] Chuang Tzu's feelings for Hui Shih as a debating partner are indeed unsettling, not only because these feelings seem to contradict his belief in the ineffability of the *Tao* and things but also because he explicitly condemned debate as a result of deficiency in "seeing" (*chien*). He said, "debates arise because there is that which [the debaters] do not see. The Great Tao is not named. Great debates are not spoken .... If the Tao is made clear, it is not the Tao. If debates are put into words, they do not suffice."[171] He also criticized the Confucians and the Mohists for arguing over what they each regarded as the right and the wrong and considered them both to have "closed" minds which, for Chuang Tzu, are what makes an argument possible. Alluding to one of Hui Shih's paradoxes, he said, "Not being closed in mind and yet having a sense of right and wrong is [as impossible as] going to Yüeh today but arriving there yesterday."[172] He also said, "Because right and wrong appeared, the Way was injured...."[173]

However, if Chuang Tzu in his engagement in speech and debate seemed to be contradicting himself, he was perfectly aware of his own contradiction. He said of himself, "Now I am going to make a statement here. I don't know whether it fits into the category of other people's statements or not. But whether it fits into their category or whether it does not, it fits into some category which is still a category in comparison with theirs. So in this respect it is no different from their statements."[174] This statement embodies a sense of irony which is typical of Chuang Tzu. It exemplifies his impulse to double back upon himself to de-center himself as a speaker. Therefore, as a critic, Chuang Tzu is forever self-critical. He claims no privileged position for his statements, which are in fact intended to be self-erasing because, as statements, they are all constituted by the principle of alterity and necessarily imply their opposites as a condition of existence. For Chuang Tzu, statements and counterstatements exist for one another and are interpenetrating and mutually producing. For this reason, he views them as intrinsically self-disrupting; there is always "this" in "that" or "right" in "wrong" and vice versa. He said,

Everything has its "that," everything has its "this." From the point of view of "that " you cannot see it, but through understanding you know it. So I say, "that" comes out of "this" and "this" depends on "that"—which is to say that "this" and "that" give birth to each other. But where there is birth there must be death; where there is death there must be birth. Where there is acceptability there must be unacceptability; where there is unacceptability there must be acceptability. Where there is recognition of right there must be recognition of wrong; where there is recognition of wrong there must be recognition of right. Therefore the sage does not proceed in such a way, but illuminates all in the light of Heaven. He too recognizes a "this," but a "this" which is also "that," a "that" which is also "this." His "that" has both a right and a wrong in it; his "this" too has both a right and a wrong in it. So, in fact, does he still have a "this" and "that"? Or does he in fact no longer have a "this" and "that"? A state in which "this" and "that" no longer

find their opposites is called the hinge of the Way. When the hinge
is fitted into a socket, it can respond endlessly. Its right then is a
single endlessness and its wrong too is a single endlessness.[175]

   Moreover, as that which contains within itself the
principle of its own negation, a statement is viewed by Chuang
Tzu as infinitely substitutable by any other statement. For this
reason, Chuang Tzu advocated "walking on two roads" (*liang-hsing*), according to which "the sage harmonizes with both right
and wrong and rests in Heaven the Equalizer."[176] Significantly,
Chuang Tzu's "hinge of the Way," though it must be fitted into a
"socket," is directionally not hinged anywhere in particular. Being
without a directional center and capable of "responding end-lessly" in all directions, the "hinge of the Way" symbolizes
Chuang Tzu's ideal of language use as a philosophically nomadic
performance which, as the title of his first chapter suggests,
"wanders freely and easily" and which does not yearn for the
certainty of a center. There is in the *Chuang Tzu* an almost
Derridean celebration of the Nietzschean "joyous affirmation" of
"the noncenter otherwise than as loss of the center."[177] On the
other hand, however, this celebration does not for Chuang Tzu, as
it does for Derrida, take place simply on what in Edward Said's
terms is "a field, or space, of language."[178] For, according to
Chuang Tzu, alterity is not just a grammatological principle; it is
also an ontological principle. Therefore, unlike Derrida, for whom
the intersubstitutability of statements is merely a "play" of signs
with one sign leading to another alternately as signifier and
signified,[179] Chuang Tzu envisioned his "play" as a cosmic drama
which acts out not only in the linguistic theater of human signs but
also on the ontological stage of the Tao as the ultimate reality. For
Chuang Tzu, the Tao does not remain self-same, and things
transform from and into one another. Therefore, reality is the
setting up of unitary opposites and is itself self-erasing; it shuttles
perennially and dialectically between "being" (*yu*) and "nothing-ness" (*wu*), between "beginning" (*yu-shih*) and "not yet beginning
to be a beginning" (*wei-shih yu-shih*), and between "not yet begin-ning to be a beginning" and "not yet beginning to be a not yet

beginning to be a beginning" (*yu wei-shih fu wei-shih yu-shih*) as accomplices of one another. Chuang Tzu said,

> There is a beginning. There is a not yet beginning to be a beginning. There is a not yet beginning to be a not yet beginning to be a beginning. There is being. There is nothingness. There is a not yet beginning to be nothingness. Suddenly there is nothingness. But I do not know, when it comes to nothingness, which is really being and which is nothingness. Now I have just said something. But I don't know whether what I have said has really said something or whether it hasn't said something.[180]

As the above quotation indicates, Chuang Tzu's affirmed mode of language use as a self-erasing practice is anchored in his ontological vision; it is an imitation of the Tao as dialectical transformation. As such, it has a doubleness, in its discursive specificity as both statements and counterstatements and in its very being as both speech and silence. Just as things transform from and into one another and just as statements and counterstatements implicate and produce one another, speech and silence are mutually involved and substitutable. There is speech in silence and silence in speech. Because there is speech in silence, silence is capable of erasing itself to become speech. Conversely, because there is silence in speech, speech is also capable of erasing itself to become silence. In this sense, Chuang Tzu spoke of his words as "no words" (*wu-yen*) and said, "With words that are no words, you may speak all your life long and you will never have said anything. Or you may go through your whole life without speaking them, in which case you will never have stopped speaking."[181]

Being an imitation of the Tao, however, Chuang Tzu's language is not assured of adequacy of representation and is in fact forever incomplete and uncertain vis-à-vis the Tao. Precisely because the Tao does not remain stable and has no definable enduring identity, language in its ideal use as an imitative representation of the Tao can never be complete or certain of its meaning. "The Way," Chuang Tzu said, "has never known boundaries; speech has no constancy."[182] If, therefore, language is to be composed for use, it must be decomposed as it is being composed. Chuang Tzu compared this type of language use to the "fish trap" or "rabbit snare" which, as noted before, are useful for fish-catching or rabbit-snaring but which ought to be forgotten as soon as the fish or rabbit is caught. The metaphors of the "fish trap" and "rabbit snare" affirm the use of language for its instrumental value. However, it is an affirmation which entails its own negation. Though somewhat different from Lao Tzu's speaking which does not speak of the Tao as the ultimate reality in and of itself, Chuang Tzu's speaking is also an articulation of a mystical/skeptical vision in which the Tao as dialectical trans-formation ensures its ineffability and permits the use of language only as a self-erasing activity.

In Vimalakīrti's use of language, the principle of alterity also prevails. It is, however, an alterity which differs from Chuang Tzu's in structure and which expresses and articulates a Buddhist form of mysticism/skepticism. While Chuang Tzu's alterity entails a doubleness in which Chuang Tzu's self and the selves of others are interdependent in their coexistence and mutually producing and exchangeable as speaking subjects, the doubleness in Vimalakīrti's alterity postulates Vimalakīrti as a speaking subject who is produced by and for the sake of, but does not reciprocally produce, the selves of others as speaking subjects. Not surprisingly, therefore, the statements by Vimalakīrti are more often than not occasioned by requests, sayings, or thoughts of others as speaking subjects. In this regard, Vimalakīrti as an enlightened layman is very much like the Buddha who does not usually preach unless asked.

This difference between Chuang Tzu on the one hand and Vimalakīrti and the Buddha on the other does not mean that Vimalakīrti or the Buddha never took the initiative to speak. In fact both did; the Buddha's instruction to Maitreya in the last chapter of the *Vimalakīrti-nirdeśa Sūtra* and Vimalakīrti's invitation to the thirty-three Bodhisattvas to speak out on the Dharma-Gate of Nonduality are examples of their initiative as active speakers. However, in taking the initiative as active speakers, the Buddha and Vimalakīrti do not exist as speaking subjects in their own right, but on the condition of an audience of deluded beings as the speaking other. As enlightened beings, neither the Buddha nor Vimalakīrti has a self to speak or to speak of; they come to be possessed of a self in response to the selves of others as deluded speaking subjects who, being deluded, still have selves to speak and to speak of. For this reason, what the Buddha and Vimalakīrti say does not have a determinate subjectivity which is contingent upon the subjectivity of what the audience in their delusion may have to say. Their speech is only provisional saying which makes no ontic reference either to themselves as embodiments of the ultimate reality or to the ultimate reality which they embody and which automatically disappears with the disappearance of the saying of the deluded other. Therefore, instead of being self-erasing like Chuang Tzu's saying, the saying of the Buddha and Vimalakīrti is intended to be other-erasing. It is saying for the sake of the deluded other whose saying needs be erased so that he can be saved from the delusion of himself both as a saying subject and as the subjectivity of his saying. As such, their saying is an exercise of "skillful means" (*upāya* or *fang-pien*)[183] and is no different from their use of magic. In fact, their saying is often accompanied by their use of magic and may be regarded as the verbal counterpart of their visual magical demonstration. Just as their magic produces nothing but conjured-up *māyā* and is in this sense non-producing, their saying also does not say anything real and is a fictitious nonsaying comparable to silence. Therefore, both the Buddha and Vimalakīrti can say a great deal without violating the injunction against saying. Theoretically, their saying will have to go on so long as there is still a deluded being to be saved. All deluded beings must be exposed through the saying as nonsaying so that they can all be erased as saying subjects. For this reason, Indian Buddhist literature is often characterized by an enumerative repetitiousness. It is noteworthy that Vimalakīrti's silence was preceded by an itemized listing of the views of the thirty-three Bodhisattvas who attempted one after another to speak of the Dharma-Gate of Nonduality. This enumerative repetitiousness may tax the patience of a modern reader, but it is theoretically meaningful. It exemplifies both the Mahāyānic ideal of universal salvation and the Buddhist mystical/skeptical affirmation of a legitimate mode of saying as nonsaying.

The legitimate mode of saying which is affirmed in Indian Buddhism and which the saying of the Buddha and Vimalakīrti exemplifies prevailed among Chinese Buddhists as a model. However, in its actual use by Chinese Buddhists, the model changed somewhat in both conception and execution. In the hands of a monk like Seng-chao, the model became a simplified performance which is no longer encumbered by enumerative repetitiousness. In his three essays on "The Immutability of Things," "The Emptiness of the Unreal," and "The Noncognition of Prajñā" in the *Book of Chao (Chao Lun)*, Seng-chao proceeded according to the Mādhyamika theory of twofold truth and the logic of negation embodied therein. Therefore, he maintained the distinction between *chen* and *su*, which Liebenthal has rendered as "truth" and "public view"[184] and which are Seng-chao's terms for *paramārtha-satya* and *saṁvṛti-satya*. He also followed the Mādhyamika logic of negation by arguing for the exact opposite of the "public view" from the same premise. Therefore, he said, "From the fact that things past do not reach up to things present, [the common people] infer that things change and do not remain still while I infer the opposite from the same fact."[185] He also said, "[The common people believe that] things change and do not remain still because they do not come [to the present] . . . . [But I believe that] things remain still and do not change because they do not leave [where they were in the past and come to the present]."[186]

Nevertheless, notwithstanding his subscription to the Mādhyamika theory of twofold truth and its logic of negation, Seng-chao's style of argumentation is notably different from that of Nāgārjuna and Āryadeva. Nāgārjuna and Āryadeva did not use the theory of twotold truth in isolation. Rather, they used it in connection with the "four points of argumentation" to form the so-called "eightfold negation" which is a dialectical process of progressive negation. The ideas of "four points of argumentation" and "eightfold negation" are conspicuously absent from Seng-chao's three essays, which followed the Mādhyamika logic of dialectical negation without, however, becoming entangled in the seriality of progressive negation.

The ideas of four points of argumentation and eightfold negation and the practice of progressive negation are all characteristically Mādhyamikan. But the style of argumentation that they constitute is not peculiar to the Mādhyamika school. It is an instance of what I have referred to above as "enumerative repetitiousness" common in Indian Buddhist literature. Indeed, both Nāgārjuna and Āryadeva were engaged in the ongoing task of erasing the sayings of the deluded other. The so-called Three Treatises of the Mādhyamika school[187] are all preoccupied with the refutation of what Nāgārjuna and Āryadeva regarded as erroneous views, whether the views involved be Hīnayānic, Mahā-yānic, or Brahmanical. In this regard, Seng-chao is again different. He did not itemize the "public views" of "change," "reality," or "cognition" in their variety. Instead, he spoke of them together categorically as "public views" and then proceeded to argue for their opposites by turning them around or standing them on their heads to establish the thesis of what in Liebenthal's rendition is the "coincidence" of opposites.[188] This thesis is unexceptional in terms of the Indian Buddhist insight into the identity of *nirvāṇa* and *saṁsāra*. But the style in which Seng-chao argued for its establishment is simple and direct. It does not involve the use of enumerative refutation or progressive negation as a mediating procedure.

In being simple and direct in his style of argumentation, Seng-chao practiced a type of language use which later became characteristic of Ch'an. Ch'an is known for its doctrine of "direct pointing to the mind of man" (*chih-chih jen-hsin*). This doctrine is part of the contention that Ch'an is a silent "trans-mission from mind to mind" (*i-hsin ch'uan-hsin*) and that it "does not institute words and literature" (*pu-li wen-tzu*).[189] As such, "direct pointing" expresses Ch'an's radical rejection of language use, including the kind of language use entailed by sūtra reading, as unnecessary for attaining enlightenment. Nevertheless, Ch'an masters did not stop talking. The Sixth Patriarch, in spite of his iconoclastic image as an illiterate woodcutter who tore up the sūtras, not only preached and quoted from the sūtras in his preaching but, as part of his last instruction to a chosen group of "ten disciples," told them to "hand down the teaching of the one roll of the *Platform Sutra*" so that they would "not lose the basic teaching."[190] Even Lin-chi (d. 867), who is known for the use of beating and shouting as teaching methods and who condemned those who studied the scriptural literature as "blind idiots" who looked for "juice" in the "dry bones" of "some old fellow, long dead,"[191] did not refrain from preaching or quoting from what in his terms were the "old masters" (*ku-jen*).[192]

That the Sixth Patriarch and Lin-chi could have done so with no sense of contradiction is understandable in terms of the Indian Buddhist conception of the nonsaying as legitimate saying, which both the Sixth Patriarch and Lin-chi continued to affirm as a model. As was the case with the Buddha and Vimalakīrti, neither the Sixth Patriarch nor Lin-chi rejected the use of language unconditionally, but only its use apart from other-generated and other-erasing activity. For the Sixth Patriarch, therefore, "all the sūtras and written words, Hīnayāna, Mahāyāna, and the twelve divisions of the cannon have been established because of men." He said, "all the sūtras exist because they are spoken by man. Among men there are the stupid and the wise. The stupid are insignificant, the wise, great men. Should deluded people ask the wise, the wise will expound the Dharma for the stupid and enable them to understand and gain a deep awakening."[193] Similarly, for Lin-chi, "names and phrases are not names and phrases in and of themselves," but are constructions for the "accommodation and guidance" (*chieh-yen*) of "little children" so that they can be cured of their "illness" of delusion.[194] As such, they are devoid of a determinate self and are unreal like "the moon reflected on water." He said,

The Buddha-realm cannot say of itself "I am the Buddha-realm." It is only the unattached man of the Way who comes forth by riding on circumstances. If a person asks me where to look for the Buddha, I will respond by coming forth in a state of purity. If a person asks me about the Bodhisattvas, I will respond by coming forth in a state of compassion. If a person asks me about Bodhi, I will respond by coming forth in a state of pure mystery. If a person asks me about Nirvāṇa, I will respond by coming forth in a state of tranquillity. Circumstances differ in ten thousand ways, but I as a person do not discriminate. Therefore, I appear in forms in response to things as the moon is reflected on water.[195]

He also asked his followers "not to seize hold of" what he said because what he said was "without evidence and proof" (*wu p'ing-chü*)[196] and said, "I, a simple monk of the mountain, have no Dharma to offer anyone. I merely cure diseases and undo bondage."[197]

      While observing the Indian model of saying as nonsaying, neither the Sixth Patriarch nor Lin-chi indulged in the practice of enumerative refutation or progressive negation. To be sure, the above statement by Lin-chi involves the use of enumeration. But it is enumeration of a different kind which is categorical in orientation and which does not attempt to list the various inquiries about the Buddha or Bodhisattvas as itemizable specificities. In comparison with the Indian masters, both the Sixth Patriarch and Lin-chi tend to focus on the here and now and to pursue speech as an other-generated and other-erasing activity in the intimacy of an immediate personal encounter. Therefore, if Ch'an dialogues are not unprecedented in Indian Buddhism for being dialogical, they are nonetheless distinct in being forthright. They embody what in Ch'an terminology is described as "trigger-fast and razor-sharp" (*chi-feng*)[198] Doctrinally, this Ch'an use of language was advocated by the Sixth Patriarch as the "law of thirty-six confrontations" which requires a person to speak in "symmetrical" terms of paired opposites so that his subjectivity will remain indeterminate and therefore unidentifiable with either affirmation or negation.[199] What was thus advocated by the Sixth Patriarch was also prescribed by Lin-chi when he stated,

Followers of the Way, if you wish to attain the view that is in accord with the Dharma, just do not let yourselves be deceived. Whether you face the inside or the outside, kill whatever you encounter. If you encounter the Buddha, kill the Buddha. If you encounter a patriarch, kill the patriarch. If you encounter your parents, kill the parents. If you encounter a relative, kill the relative.

Only then will you attain release.... There are people who study the Way everywhere, but none come forth without depending on things. When I, a simple monk of the mountain, face them, I beat them down at the very source. If they come forth through the hands, I beat them in the hands. If they come forth through the mouth, I beat them in the mouth. If they come forth through the eyes, I beat them in the eyes.[200]

This statment by Lin-chi and the Sixth Patriarch's "law of thirty-six confrontations" are both informed by the logic of dialectical negation, but they promote a style of its use which is simple and direct like Seng-chao's and which typifies a Chinese affirmation of the Indian Buddhist saying of nonsaying as a simplified performance.

In contrast to Seng-chao, the Sixth Patriarch, and Lin-chi, Chih-i (538–579) complicated the model of nonsaying by constructing an elaborate theory which no longer regarded the Buddha's preaching merely as an other-generated exercise of "skillful means" for the sake of the deluded other. Rather, according to Chih-i, what the Buddha said in his preaching embodies his "original intent in appearing in the world" (*ch'u-shih pen-huai*) and is based upon the truth which he experientially realized under the *bodhi* tree as the culmination of an astronomically long process of cultivation. For this reason, the Buddha's preaching is viewed by Chih-i as consisting of both "the words which follow the minds of others (*sui-t'a-i yü*) and "the words of the Buddha's own mind" (*tzu-i yü*).[201] The precise relationship between them is a main concern of Chih-i's *Miao-fa lien-hua ching hsüan-i*, where Chih-i analyzed the problem in terms of a set of paired categories like "origin" (*pen*) and "trace" (*chi*), the "real" (*shih*) and the "provisional" (*ch'üan*), the "subtle" (*miao*) and the "gross" (*ts'u*), etc. These paired categories were then further analyzed by Chih-i in terms of a number of other paired categories such as "self-practice" (*tzu-hsing*) and "conversion of others" (*hua-t'a*), "principle" (*li*) and "occasion" (*chi*), "following wisdom" (*sui-chih*) and "following situation" (*sui-ch'ing*), and "seven kinds of twofold truth" (*ch'i-chung erh-ti*), etc.[202]

Chih-i's elaborate theory of the relationship between "the words which follow the minds of others" and "the words of the Buddha's own mind" informs his *p'an-chiao* system, according to which the Buddha preached "Four Dharmas of Conversion" (*hua-fa ssu-chiao*) in five periods: (1) the Storehouse Teaching (*tsang-chiao*), which the Buddha preached during the second period; (2) the Pervasive Teaching (*t'ung-chiao*), which the Buddha preached during the third period; (3) the Separate Teaching (*pieh-chiao*), which the Buddha preached during the fourth period; and (4) the Round Teaching (*yüan-chiao*), which the Buddha preached during both the first period when he taught the doctrine of the *Avataṁsaka Sūtra* and the fifth period when he taught the doctrine of the *Lotus Sūtra*.[203] With an analogy that can be traced to the "five flavors" parable in the *Mahāparinirvāṇa Sūtra*,[204] Chih-i compared the Storehouse Teaching to "milk" (*ju*), the Pervasive Teaching to "cream" (*lo*), the Separate Teaching to "butter" (*sheng-su*), the Round Teaching of the *Avataṁsaka* to "boiled butter" (*shu-su*), and the Round Teaching of the *Lotus* to "ghee" (*t'i-hu*). Just as "milk," "cream," "butter," "boiled butter," and "ghee" form a series of progressive refinement in "flavor," so the five teachings in the Four Dharmas of Conversion constitute an ascending hierarchy in which "the words which follow the minds of others" gradually decrease as "the words of the Buddha's own mind" increase. The hierarchy culminates in the *Lotus*, which is comprised of only "the words of the Buddha's own mind." As such, the *Lotus* contains no "grossness," is "absolutely subtle" (*chüeh-tai miao*), and is possessed of both the "real" and the "provisional," which are both "subtle"; it "opens up the provisional as it reveals the real" (*k'ai-ch'üan hsien-shih*).[205]

In using such paired categories as origin/trace and real/provisional for a conceptualization of the Buddha's preaching, Chih-i sounds rather like but is actually different from Chi-tsang (549–623), who also made use of these categories for his theory of twofold truth and practice of *p'an-chiao* and regarded the *Lotus* as a text which "opened up the provisional as it reveals the real." As T'ang Chün-i has pointed out, these categories constituted for Chi-tsang a conception of the Buddha's teaching which is notably different from Chih-i's. As the Buddha's teaching which "opens up the provisional as it reveals the real," the *Lotus* was considered by Chi-tsang to be produced by the Buddha through an exercise of the Buddha's twofold wisdom as both "real" and "provisional" for the purpose of converting the deluded other. For Chi-tsang, therefore, although the Buddha's twofold wisdom is ultimately real, what it "opens up" and "reveals" as the teaching of the *Lotus* is no less a teaching for the sake of others, and is for this reason still provisional.[206] Chi-tsang's concepton of the Buddha's preaching is well within the Indian Buddhist mold, even though it is couched in terms of native Chinese categories of origin/trace and real/provisional.

For Chih-i, the matter is different; the Buddha spoke not only for the sake of others but also as an expression of "the Buddha's own mind." Chih-i thus reconceptualized the Indian model and postulated the Buddha as a speaking subject in his own right who was increasingly implicated in what he spoke until what he spoke as the Round Teaching of the *Lotus* consisted of nothing but "the words of the Buddha's own mind." On the other hand, though postulating the Buddha as a speaking subject, Chih-i denied that the Buddha's speaking had a subjectivity which was ultimately speakable. Commenting on a verse in the *Lotus* where the Buddha instructed Śāriputra to "cease" speaking and pro-claimed that his "dharma is subtle and hard to imagine,"[207]Chih-i said that the Buddha's dharma was "beyond words" (*chüeh-yen*) and "beyond thought" (*chüeh-ssu*) and that it was called "subtle" not because it was relative to what was "gross" but because it was "inconceivable."[208] Moreover, as that of which the subjectivity of speaking is ultimately unspeakable, "the Buddha's own mind" does not have a language of its own to speak or to be spoken of. The words of the Buddha's own mind speak in the borrowed language of "the words which follow the minds of others" and can be spoken of only in terms of the categories which relate to those words. Thus, Chih-i said, "In opening up the traces and revealing the origin, the meaning lies in the traces" (*k'ai-chi hsien-pen i-tsai yü-chi*)[210] Just as "the words which follow the minds of others" can be spoken of in terms of origin/trace and real/provisional, so can the words of the Buddha's own mind. There are, according to Chih-i, not only "the real and the provisional for the conversion of others" (*hua-t'a ch'üan-shih*), which pertain to the realm of *upāya*, but also "the real and the provisional of the Buddha's self-practice" (*tzu-hsing ch'üan-shih*), which pertain to the Buddha's wisdom.[211]

The borrowing of "the words which follow the minds of others" by "the words of the Buddha's own mind" entails the use of paradox, which is necessitated by the speaking of the unspeakable. The words of the Buddha's own mind are implicated in but nonetheless distinguishable from the words which follow the minds of others because, as noted before, they are considered by Chih-i to be possessed of both the real and the provisional, which are both "subtle." For this reason, the categories which relate to the words which follow the minds of others are both affirmed and negated by Chih-i for the words of the Buddha's own mind. Therefore, while speaking of the Buddha's wisdom in terms of the "real" and the "provisional" as "the real and the provisional of the Buddha's self-practice," he also maintained that the Buddha's wisdom was "without boundary" (*wu-pien*) and was "neither real nor provisional" (*fei-ch'üan fei-shih*).[212] He said, "The Principle of Dharmatā is neither past nor present, neither origin nor trace, neither real nor provisional. . . . It comes to be possessed of past, present, and future only because of [the use of] the worldly words and literature."[213] For the same reason, the "revelation of origin" required for Chih-i not only the "opening up of traces" but also the "abandoning of traces" (*fei-chi*).[214]

The use of paradox is common among mystics. Their paradoxes, however, are not always the same in use or meaning. In the case of Chih-i, his paradox differs from those of Lao Tzu and Chuang Tzu and is constituted by a mode of mysticism which is distinctly Buddhist. As noted earlier, Lao Tzu's Tao moves in "reversal" whereas Chuang Tzu's Tao is the setting up of unitary opposites involving the mutual transformation of things. For both Lao Tzu and Chuang Tzu, therefore, the use of paradox is entailed by the structure of the Tao as dialectical change and has in this sense a direct ontic reference. By contrast, Chih-i's paradox makes no direct ontic reference and is engendered by the speaking of the unspeakable in a borrowed language. For Chih-i, the ultimate reality is not intrinsically paradoxical and is neither paradoxical nor nonparadoxical. The words of the Buddha's own mind can be affirmed in terms of the borrowed language of the words which follow the minds of others, not because the former is determinable through the latter, but because the Buddha in his infinite wisdom can always "illuminate" (*chao*) and "penetrate" (*tung-ta*) a "situation" (*ching*) and what he says can therefore always "match" (*hsiang-ch'eng*) the "situation."[215] The subjectivity of the words of the Buddha's own mind is forever indeterminable, and its affirmation in terms of the words which follow the minds of others must be followed by negation. Unlike the paradoxes of Lao Tzu and Chuang Tzu, Chih-i's paradox does not attempt to talk about the ultimate reality as a paradox. Rather, it is a paradoxical attempt to talk *around* the ultimate reality as a semantic enclosure which, ironically, is semantically unoccupied and unoccupiable and for this reason can never become semantically enclosed. Though postulated as a speaking subject, Chih-i's Buddha speaks with a subjectivity which is either indeterminate as the words which follow the minds of others or indeterminable as the words of the Buddha's own mind. In this regard, Chih-i is still identifiably Indian Buddhist. Like the Monkey Wu-k'ung who, though capable of "cloud-somersaulting" a hundred and eight thousand miles in one leap, never jumped clear of the Tathāgata's palm, Chih-i, in spite of all the windings and twistings in his theorizing, was never really out of the mystical/skeptical mold of his Indian Buddhist predecessors for whom the ultimate reality is unsayable and the Buddha's saying is the indeterminate saying of nonsaying.

Mysticism/skepticism of both the Buddhist and the Taoist varieties had an appeal to Chiao Hung who, in articulating his view of language as asymmetrical with the Tao, quoted extensively from Buddhist and Taoist sources and used concepts and metaphors such as *ch'üan, t'i, chi,* and the "horse" which are Buddhist or Taoist in origin and connotation. The terms *ch'üan, t'i,* and *chi* are all derived from the Chuang Tzu. *Ch'üan* and *t'i,* as noted before, affirm language for its instrumental value but underscore the necessity of its becoming invisible as it succeeds in making the Tao visible. The term *chi*, which I have rendered as "traces," has been translated by Watson as "paths."[216] Literally, it means "footprints" and was used in an "outer" chapter of the *Chuang Tzu* where, in an imaginary dialogue between Lao Tzu and Confucius, Lao Tzu compared the Six Classics to "footprints" and the Tao to "shoes" (*lü*) and said to Confucius that the "footprints," though produced by and resembling the "shoes," should not be mistaken for the "shoes" themselves.[217]

The analogy of the "horse," on the other hand, is an established Buddhist convention and has a variety of usages which, though not necessarily mutually inconsistent, do not always refer to the use of language as an activity. It has been used, for instance, in a popular Ch'an *kung-an* (*kōan* in Japanese) which concerns an encounter between the Buddha and a non-Buddhist "outsider" and which, with minor variations in wording, appears in a number of Ch'an texts, such as the *Ching-te ch'uan-teng lu*, the *Pi-yen lu*, the *Wu-men kuan*, the *Wu-teng hui-yüan*, and the *Chih-yüeh lu*:[218]

An outsider said to the Buddha, "I do not ask about the spoken or the unspoken." The World Honored One remained silent. The outsider sighed in admiration and said, "The World Honored One's great kindness and great compassion have opened my clouds of illusion and let me gain entry." After the outsider had left, Ānanda asked the Buddha, "What did the outsider realize, that he said he had gained entry?" The Buddha said, "Like a good horse, he goes as soon as he sees the shadow of the whip."

In this *kung-an*, the Buddha praised the "outsider" as a "good horse." The whip, however, or rather the "shadow of the whip," to which the outsider responded as a good horse, refers to the Buddha's silence and not to the Buddha's preaching as a linguistic performance.

A second usage of the "horse" analogy occurs in the *Saṁyuktāgama Sūtra (Tsa a-han ching)* where the Buddha divided mankind into four hierarchical categories and compared them to four different types of horses. Horses, according to the Buddha on this occasion, differ in their response to the prodding of the "whip." While the best horses go into immediate action on seeing the shadow of the whip, others would not make a move without being actually whipped in varying degrees of severity ranging from the touching of the hair to the gouging of the flesh and the bone. Likewise, some men would take the "correct" path as soon as they "hear about" deaths resulting from illness, while others would not do so unless they "see" or "personally experience the suffering of old age, illness, and death."[219] In this case, the whip is not used exclusively as a symbol for linguistic performance; the use of language is entailed only in the "hearing about" but not in the "seeing" or "personally experiencing" suffering.

A similar classification of horses is also used as an analogy for different categories of men in the *Mahāparinirvāṇa Sūtra* (*Ta pan-nieh-p'an ching*), where, however, the "whip" as a symbol has a strictly linguistic reference; it stands for the Buddha's preaching, either in part or in entirety, of the four sufferings of birth, old age, illness, and death.[220] Chiao Hung's use of the "horse" analogy for the ideal attitude toward the teachings is traceable to the *Mahāparinirvāṇa Sūtra*, which is also the *locus classicus* for its use as a popular metaphor among Chinese monks like Chih-i and the Ch'an master Yüan-wu K'e-ch'in (1063–1135). Chih-i compared the Round Teaching of the *Lotus* to the "shadow of a whip" and said that the *Lotus* was as efficacious in enabling all to "gain entry" as the shadow of a whip in prodding a "fast horse" into action.[221] Yüan-wu K'e-ch'in, on the other hand, used the analogy in his introductory "pointer" (*ch'ui-shih*) for the thirty-eighth *kung-an* in the *Pi-yen lu*, saying, "To a quick person, one word; to a quick horse, one blow of the whip."[222]

Though also used by some Chinese Buddhists like Seng-chao and Chih-i,[223] the metaphors of *ch'üan*, *t'i*, and *chi* in their original use by Chuang Tzu do not cohere with the "horse" analogy, which enunciates a Buddhist instrumental affirmation of a mode of language use and is an expression of the Buddhist form of mysticism/skepticism. For Chuang Tzu, *ch'üan*, *t'i*, and *chi* articulate a mysticism/skepticism which maintains a representational view of language and which both negates and affirms the use of language as a representation. Language is to be negated because it does not represent the Tao adequately and is to be affirmed because it can at least make an inadequate representation of the Tao. Resemblance, though not identity, prevails between language and the Tao to the extent that it does between the trace or footprint and the shoe. For Chuang Tzu, therefore, language can legitimately have an ontic reference and is possessed of an instrumental value which consists in its being a representation. The Buddhists have a different sense of instrumentality in their affirmation of language as the saying of nonsaying. For them, language can be used as an instrument like a "whip," not because it bears any resemblance to what they regard as the truth, which is in fact unrepresentable, but because it can function therapeutically as a cure for the illness of delusion. As the instrumental "whip," the Buddhist saying of nonsaying makes no ontic reference to truth as an object of its discourse. Rather, it operates in a field of mere language and addresses only the saying of saying, the erasing of which can lead to the attainment of truth which, being unsayable, must forever remain unsaid.

Chiao Hung mixed the metaphors of the Buddhist and the Taoist varieties. In doing so, he combined two disparate forms of mysticism/skepticism and constructed a theory of language which is not wholly identifiable with either the Buddhist or the Taoist kind but instead intersects them both. As noted earlier, Chiao Hung viewed language in representational terms as both continuous and asymmetrical with the Tao which is ineffable and indifferent to naming. In this regard, he is well within the Taoist framework, especially as it is articulated by Chuang Tzu. Nevertheless, Chiao Hung's linguistic skepticism also has dimensions which are unmistakably Buddhist. Neither Lao Tzu nor Chuang Tzu ever attempted to account for the continuity between language and the Tao in terms of an ontology of language. Lao Tzu, in spite of his sensitivity to the limitations of language as a medium of representation, did not develop an ontology of language. For him, the being of language per se was not a problem. He discoursed on the Tao's ineffability as a matter of metaphysics and approached the use of language as a problematic in terms of the Tao's paradoxical relationship to *te* or things. Chuang Tzu, on the other hand, had an ontology of language, which, though anchored in his vision of reality as dialectical transformation, was concerned with language's being *qua* being as an issue. But he used his ontology of language to underline the asymmetry between language and the Tao and not to establish their continuity. By contrast, Chiao Hung not only had an ontology of language but used it to explain how language could be both continuous and asymmetrical with the Tao. He spoke of the being of language in Buddhist terms as "emptiness" which, as noted before, enabled him to view language as both *semeion* and *eikon*. As *semeion*, language is devoid of selfhood and is in this sense comparable to the speech of the Buddha as an enlightened being. Just as the Buddha can always "match" a situation in his speech because he has no self and does not speak with a determinate subjectivity, so language as *semeion* can signify in continuity with the signified and incorporate the signified to become *eikon* because it is devoid of selfhood and has no ideality of its own meaning. As *eikon*, however, language can never be a full or symmetrical representation of things as the signified because *eikon's* origin as *semeion* requires that the existence of language as *eikon* be forever dependent on the signified things which are also "empty" in and of themselves and have no stable selves to be represented.

Moreover, according to Chiao Hung, language in its original being as "empty" *semeion* can both be used as *eikon* and function to purify our understanding and thereby to redeem the Way as truth. As noted before, he viewed the use of language as an occasioned human activity which is necessitated by the obscuration of the Way and has the clarification and reapprehension of the Way as its function and purpose. In this regard, he is again different from Lao Tzu and Chuang Tzu, who, though affirming the continuity between language and the Tao, did not believe that the obscured Tao could be reclaimed through the use of language. For this reason, Lao Tzu was nostalgic about a time when "knotted cords" were used in place of writing and advocated its revival.[224] He also said, "As soon as there are names, know that it is time to stop."[225] Similarly, Chuang Tzu would accept the use of language only as a self-erasing activity and was of the conviction that the Tao could not but be linguistically obscure, saying, "If the Tao is made clear, it is not the Tao."[226] In being thus different from Lao Tzu and Chuang Tzu in regarding the use of language as purifying in function and redemptive in purpose, Chiao Hung resembles the Buddhists for whom the Buddha's saying of nonsaying is intended for the removal of delusion so that one's inherently enlightened Buddha-nature can reemerge as truth. Not surprisingly, therefore, he viewed Chinese sages like Confucius and Lao Tzu in Buddhist terms as saviors and saw their appearance in the world as a deeply religious event comparable in meaning to the birth of the Buddha Shākyamuni. He said, "The appearance in the world of Confucius, Lao Tzu, and Shākyamuni is for the sake of sentient beings."[227] He also said, "It is not accidental that Confucius and Lao Tzu appeared together during the Chou era. Since the Yellow Emperor and Shun had by then become increasingly remote, great sages emerged one after another to awaken the masses from their ignorance."[228] As these statements indicate, the value of language for Chiao Hung consists in both its continuity with the Tao as truth and its efficacy as a redeeming device. He did not use the "horse" analogy in vain. What originated as a Buddhist analogy remained for him Buddhist in meaning. It infused his conception of language with a sense of instrumentality which is not subsumable under Chuang Tzu's metaphors of *ch'üan*, *t'i*, and *chi*. Incorporating the Taoist view of language as representation and the Buddhist conception of language as therapy, Chiao Hung's linguistic skepticism affirms a mode of language which is both representational and therapeutic and which can function as therapy because it is representational. Therefore, while declaring that "there is only medicine to remove impediments to vision" but "no medicine to bestow vision,"[229] he also claimed that "the sages demonstrate the substance of the Way in the daily course of things directly and decisively to the people."[230] Similarly, when a student asked him why Confucius gave different answers to inquires about *jen* or "humanity," he replied that it was because Confucius taught by "pointing according to the occasion" (*sui-chi chih-tien*). But, he explained further, although "pointing according to the occasion" may be seen as a matter of "prescribing medicine according to illness," it can better be understood in terms of what the pointing points to as the "original meaning" (*pen-chih*), which is *jen*. Since, according to Chiao Hung, *jen* exists everywhere and is ever present, it can be pointed out in a number of different ways, depending on when and where the pointing happens to occur.[231]

Mysticism as Pluralism: Chiao Hung and the Problem of Textuality

While intersecting the Buddhist and the Taoist conceptions, however, Chiao Hung's view of language cannot be understood simply as a Buddho-Taoist synthesis. For in his appropriation of the mystical/skeptical elements from Buddhism and Taoism, he did not just reiterate the Buddho-Taoist thesis on the ineffability of the Tao or Dharma as the ultimate truth. Rather, he redeployed these elements into a formation in which the affirmed mode of language use was no longer conceived to be merely a performance of reducing speech to silence. Therefore, as noted before, when he quoted the Goddess in the *Vimalakīrti* as saying that "liberation cannot be preached apart from words and literature," he did so not to advocate the saying of nonsaying as an other-erasing practice but to affirm the however limited representational power of language as "empty" *semeion*. It is also noteworthy that he differs subtly but significantly from Chuang Tzu in the use of *ch'üan* and *t'i* as metaphors. Chuang Tzu affirmed the instrumental value of language as representation. This affirmation, however, is predicated on the condition that language be undertaken as a self-erasing activity. Consequently, he used the metaphors of *ch'üan* and *t'i* not so much to acknowledge the continuity between language and the Tao as to express his wish that he could talk to a person who would use language in a self-erasing way, as he himself does. He said, "The fish trap exists because of the fish; once you've gotten the fish, you can forget the trap. The rabbit snare exists because of the rabbit; once you've gotten the rabbit, you can forget the snare. Words exist because of meaning; once you've gotten the meaning, you can forget the words. Where can I find a man who has forgotten words so I can have a word with him?"[232] Chiao Hung, on the other hand, used the same metaphors to indicate both the asymmetry and the continuity between language and the Tao and to underline the instrumental necessity of language as representation. He said, "As the fish and the rabbit have yet to be caught, the fish trap and the rabbit snare cannot be done away with."[233]

In spite of his uncertainties about the teachings as imperfect representations of the ultimately unrepresentable Tao, Chiao Hung did not advocate withdrawal from rational discourse as a way of achieving truth. Rational discourse in the form of "intellectual discussions" (*chiang-hsüeh*) was a favorite teaching method of Ming Neo-Confucians. Chiao Hung used this method extensively and, as noted before, went so far as to introduce it into the Imperial Palace during his tenure as Lecturer to the eldest son of the Wan-li Emperor. Also, he accepted "quiet sitting" (*ching-tso*) only as an *upāya* to help develop "quietude" which, he said, was "a gate to seeing into Nature."[234] The emphasis in "quiet sitting" was thus placed on quietude as a state of mind and not on enlightenment as a mystical experience. For Chiao Hung, therefore, transcendence of the teachings was not just a matter of their negation. His mystical sense of the Tao as ineffable truth was invoked to stress the need not only to go beyond the teachings but to consider the equal, though qualified, validity of a variety of teachings. It was the basis of a pluralism which enabled Chiao Hung to cross the systemic boundary as a Confucian and to engage in a syncretic dialogue with other teachings.

It is true that pluralism also prevails in Buddhism and Taoism. As noten above, Chuang Tzu believed in "walking on two roads" and accepted different and diametrically opposed statements, whereas the Buddhists engaged in an expanded form of *p'an-chiao* practice which accorded both Buddhist and non-

Buddhist teachings varying degrees of recognition and advocated their coexistence. But Chuang Tzu's pluralism stresses the incompleteness and not the representativeness of teachings as representations of the Tao. It assumes the form of philosophical nomadism which regards all statements as intersubstitutable because they are all equal in being equally limited in truth value. As for the Buddhists, they consider all saying as delusion except for the saying of nonsaying. The saying of nonsaying is plural, but its plurality is derived from the plurality of the audience it addresses and has meaning, as it does in the *p'an-chiao* practice, only in terms of its efficacy as therapy and not in terms of what it says of reality as truth which is linguistically indeterminable. Though admitting of the plurality of teachings, neither Chuang Tzu nor a Buddhist like Chih-i attempted to thematize teachings in their plurality as different ways of articulating truth as a positive linguistic presence. Even Chuang Tzu's latter-day follower who surveyed the "world" of philosophy in the last chapter of the *Chuang Tzu* did so to highlight the inadequacy of the various thinkers in late Chou China in contrast with the "breadth and stature" (*po-ta*) of the Barrier Keeper Yin and Lao Tzu and the "fullness and substantiality" (*ch'ung-shih*) of Chuang Tzu. He deplored the fragmentation of the "art of the Way" by the "hundred schools" and acknowledged that they each "have strong points and can be of use at times," but he never specified their strong points or use. Instead, he focused on their "lack of comprehensiveness and universality" (*pu-kai pu-p'ien*) and dismissed their followers as "scholars cramped in one corner" (*i-ch'ü chih-shih*).[235]

Chiao Hung's pluralism is different. It admits of the imperfection of teachings as representations, but values them for what they may reveal of the Tao as truth which, as noted before, is conceived to be unitary in structure but pluralistic in articulation. The unitary conception of the Tao requires that teachings in their variety be viewed in holistic terms as mutually explanatory and illuminating. Therefore, instead of being intersubstitutable as they were for Chuang Tzu, the multiple teachings for Chiao Hung were interdeterminable and called for synthesis. Synthesis, however, is not indiscriminate lumping. As a synthesizer, Chiao

Hung was concerned for the textuality of each teaching which he valued in its individuality as a distinct way of articulating the Tao and as an expression of what an author or school has "self-attained" (*tzu-te*) as the Tao. He considered the Classics to be the "ultimate" of literature because they embodied the Tao, and professed a particular admiration for the literature of the Su brothers because their literature was a spontaneous outgrowth of what they had "self-attained" as the singular understanding of the Classics. In contrast with the author of the last chapter of the *Chuang Tzu*, who acknowledged but did not feel obliged to specify the "strong points" or "use" of the "hundred schools," Chiao Hung desired to thematize the intentionality of all the philosophers attacked by Chu Hsi so that he could demonstrate that they "each had a purpose in their learning." This concern for textuality accounts for his interest in philology and phonetics, which could help him overcome the technical multiplicity of language and thereby restore and reapprehend a text in its original materiality as a linguistic presence. Chiao Hung, as noted before, believed in the necessity of writing modern poems according to modern rhymes and reading ancient poems according to ancient rhymes.

The same concern for textuality informs his opposition to the state's practice of instituting a set of officially sanctioned commentaries as authoritative interpretations of the Classics. The main thrust of his opposition was directed against the T'ang state, which commissioned K'ung Ying-ta (574–648) to write commentaries on the Classics and prescribed them as the standard for scholars to follow. This measure was, according to Chiao Hung, "grossly inappropriate," not only because the truth contained in the Classics could not be molded into definite form in terms of a single school of interpretation[236] but also because the Classics differed from the commentaries as texts. He pointed out that the close association of the commentaries with the Classics was not originally the practice in high antiquity. In ancient times, Chiao Hung claimed, when people wished to comment on the sages' teachings, they did so by writing a book of their own without attaching it to particular Classics. Therefore, in order to elucidate the truth in the *Book of Changes*, Confucius composed the "Ten Wings" (*shih-i*), which he kept separate from the *Book of Changes* as a work in its own right. The same practice was observed by Tzu-ssu, Mencius, and Chuang Tzu when Tzu-ssu and Mencius produced the *Doctrine of the Mean* and the *Mencius* to develop further the ideas in the *Analects* and when Chuang Tzu wrote the *Chuang Tzu* to clarify the ambiguities in the *Lao Tzu*. It was not until the Han dynasty when Mao Ch'ang (second century B.C.) and K'ung An-kuo (c. 156–c. 74 B.C.) ceased writing on their own account but merely wrote as commentators on the *Book of Odes* and the *Book of History* that the formal association of the commentaries with the Classics first became established. This association was then made a firm practice during the Three Kingdoms period (220–265) by Wang Pi (226–249) who incorporated the "Ten Wings" into the text of the *Book of Changes* without realizing that the *Book of Changes* was a work of rhymed literature with an integrity of its own and that it should not be confused with writings of other sorts. Wang Pi, Chiao Hung pointed out further, had also apparently forgotten that the three versions of the *Book of Changes* by Fu Hsi, King Wen and the Duke of Chou, and Confucius were different from one another and could not be lumped together and treated as a consistent whole.[237]

Nevertheless, the practice of associating the commentaries with the Classics persisted and, as time passed, grew in intensity until, as in the case of the *Spring and Autumn Annals*, the commentaries overshadowed the Classics in importance and became the main focus of study while the Classics were pushed into the background as something merely subsidiary. Chiao Hung deplored this excessive emphasis on the commentaries and suggested that scholars go straight to the Classics without relying on the commentaries for mediation. He pointed out that the *Spring and Autumn Annals* was composed by Confucius with no anticipation of others coming along to write commentaries on it, and that it ought to be intelligible as a work by itself.[238] Moreover, the commentaries could sometimes be misleading and obscure the true meaning of the Classics which would otherwise have been clear to the reader. This, according to Chiao Hung, was the case with the *Doctrine of the Mean*, the significance of which as a work of Confucian "mystical teaching" (*wei-yen*) was not always adequately appreciated because scholars "have not known to interpret the *Doctrine of the Mean* through the *Doctrine of the Mean*."[239]

Needless to say, in proposing that the Classics be studied apart from the commentaries, Chiao Hung's aim was not to preclude scholars from reading or writing commentaries. He himself was versed in commentarial literature and compiled two works of commentary on the *Lao Tzu* and the *Chuang Tzu* from a large number of commentaries, including his own. He also wrote a commentary on the *Book of Changes* and ventured into an extensive discourse on the *Analects*, the *Mencius*, and the *Doctrine of the Mean*. But he remained true to the ancient tradition as he envisioned it. He kept his comments on the *Analects*, the *Mencius*, and the *Doctrine of the Mean* as separate notes in his own work, the *Chiao-shih pi-ch'eng*. He also used the terms *ch'üan* and *i* in the titles for his commentaries on the *Book of Changes*, the *Lao Tzu*, and the *Chuang Tzu*. We have discussed the term *ch'üan* or "fish trap" before. The term *i* or "wing" forms part of the title of Confucius' work of commentary on the *Book of Changes*, which was, as noted above, believed by Chiao Hung to be originally an independent work. By using these terms and by keeping his comments in his own work, Chiao Hung left no doubt about the nature of his commentaries as he himself would view it: related to but distinct from the works that they commented upon as texts.

The issue thus involved in Chiao Hung's concern for commentaries pertains not so much to their reading or writing as to the kind of claims that they make on textuality. What he finds objectionable in commentaries is not that they are being read or written as guides to the Classics, but that the commentaries so read or written are discursive commentaries which pretend to speak for the sages rather than for oneself and which, in the guise of commentarial literature, actually propound a philosophy. He contrasted the *Erh Ya* with the commentaries which Wang Pi had appended to the *Book of Changes* and said that the *Erh Ya* as a collection of glosses taken from the *Book of Odes* bore to the *Odes* the kind of relationship which exemplified the true and ideal connection between the Classics and the commentaries as it had existed in ancient times.[240] He also said, "The ancients who commented on the Classics only explained their words but not their meaning, which the reader would have to perceive for himself through deep reflection." This, according to Chiao Hung, was still largely the practice among the Han Confucians; and the change in later times from linguistic analysis to philosophical exposition was held by him to be responsible for increasing superficiality in Confucian scholarship. He said, "As the commentators explain more, the student of the Classics thinks less. Negligent and unmindful, he no longer engages in deep reflection. Like passing by a person in the street, he only sees the person's outward appearance, but does not know the person's inner thoughts and behavior."[241] Chiao Hung advocated the revival of the linguistic approach and proposed that "the *Book of Odes* be discussed in terms of its sound and the other Classics be studied by way of their language."[242] He himself was a pioneer in this approach and, as noted before, made the discovery that the end rhymes in ancient poems were all natural rhymes whose pronunciation had changed in the course of time.

I have indicated in an earlier publication that Chiao Hung, in rejecting discursive commentaries as commentaries and in redefining what proper commentaries ought to be in terms of the *Erh Ya* as a historical model, signaled a reorientation in classical scholarship and anticipated the development in early Ch'ing of "evidential research" as a new mode of inquiry which was distinctly philological in tone.[243] It remains to be emphasized, however, that the impulse of "evidential research" consisted in precisely the kind of concern that Chiao Hung had for textuality, which the scholars of "evidential research" attempted to retrieve through philological reconstruction. As T'ang Chün-i has pointed out, "evidential research" during the Ch'ing, though characterizing itself as Han Learning and claiming descent from the philological scholarship of the Han Confucians, was by no means identical with the Han prototype. The philological activity of the Han Confucians was textually exclusive. It was confined to the Confucian Classics, which they believed to be where the Tao was textually embodied and which they tried to reconstruct in order to recover the Confucian Tao. Moreover, the Han Confucians usually worked within the textual "tradition of a particular school" (*chia-fa*) and regarded the "tradition" of their own school as the true representation of the Confucian Tao. By comparison, the textual horizon of the scholars of Ch'ing "evidential research" was broad. It extended both to the Confucian Classics and to the works of such non-Confucian philosophers as Lao Tzu, Chuang Tzu, Mo Tzu, Han Fei Tzu, etc. The avowed purpose of Ch'ing "evidential research" was not only to recover the Confucian *Tao* but to sort out texts in their variety so that "the learning of Eastern Han would be restored to Eastern Han, the learning of Western Han to Western Han..., and [the learning of] Confucius and Mencius to Confucius and Mencius."[244]

It is also worth noting that the concern for textuality, which distinguishes Ch'ing "evidential research" from Han classicism as a philological undertaking, prevailed both in commentarial scholarship and in a whole body of literature, the purpose of which was to establish the identity of a school or thinker. Both the late Ming and the early Ch'ing witnessed the production of a large number of what I have referred to as "intellectual genealogies." Examples may include Sun Ch'i-feng's (1585–1675) *Li-hsüeh tsung-chuan*, T'ang Pin's (1627–1687) *Lo-hsüeh pien*, Huang Tsung-hsi's *Ming-ju hsüeh-an* and *Sung-Yüan hsüeh-an*, Chiang Fan's (1761–1831) *Han-hsüeh shih-ch'eng chi* and *Sung-hsüeh yüan-yüan chi*, and Chang Hsüeh-ch'eng's (1738–1801) essay on "The Art of Learning in Eastern Chekiang" ("Che-tung hsüeh-shu"), etc., which all tried to individualize a school or thinker either historically in terms of transmission and development or logically in terms of relatedness in the formation of concepts, or both.

Being thus concerned about textuality, however, the "intellectual genealogists" and the scholars of "evidential research" are not necessarily syncretists. In writing the *Li-hsüeh tsung-chuan* and the *Lo-hsüeh pien*, Sun Ch'i-feng and T'ang Pin were motivated by a desire to defend what they regarded as the Confucian orthodoxy against Buddhist encroachment. Sun attributed the "daily decline of the art of learning" to the "lack of clarification of the differences between Confucianism and Buddhism,"[245] while T'ang railed against the "doctrine of the oneness of Confucianism and Buddhism" and underscored Sun's determination to "maintain a rigorous distinction between Confucianism and Buddhism."[246] Huang Tsung-hsi and Chang Hsüeh-ch'eng, on the other hand, though they were confirmed Confucians, did not reject Buddhism outright. Huang defended Lo Hung-hsien's (1504–1564) interest in Buddhism and Taoism and said, "For Master Lo, there is not a place which is not a place of learning; and there is not a person who is not a companion in learning."[247] He also accorded Buddhism a certain degree of truth value and said that "it is not that the Buddhists do not have any true perception whatsoever," but that they "do not probe deeply enough" and as a result fall short of the ultimate.[248] Likewise, Chang Hsüeh-ch'eng was critical of Buddhism for postulating a Tao apart from "events and things," but considered its doctrines on "mind, Nature, principle, and the Way" to be otherwise different from the "words of the sages" only in "names and categories" (*ming-mu*) and not in "meaning and reference" (*i-chih*). He also defended the Buddhist theories of "heavens" and "hells" against Confucian critics and said that they were not "wild falsehoods manufactured" by the Buddhists to "deceive the world," but typified a mode of teaching which, in relying on the use of "symbols constructed by man's mind," was also characteristic of the *Book of Changes*.[249]

Among the scholars of "evidential research," Tai Chen (1724–1777) was unequivocal in his rejection of non-Confucian teachings. He, as Yü Ying-shih has pointed out, regarded the Confucian Classics as the "sole depository of the Tao of the sages." In a 1777 letter which he wrote to Tuan Yü-ts'ai (1735–1815), just a few months before his death, he said of himself, "I have set my mind on hearing the Tao since the age of seventeen, saying that the Tao cannot be obtained unless it is sought in the Six Classics, Confucius, and Mencius."[250] By contrast, Chiao Hsün (1763–1820) criticized those who denounced Buddhism and Taoism as "heretical" and said that they did not understand the concept of *i-tuan* in the *Analects*. Like Chiao Hung, Chiao Hsün also interpreted *I-tuan* literally as a "strand" of teaching which "differed from one's own" and did not consider mere difference as such to be a good reason for condemning a teaching as "heretical." He maintained that a strand of teaching was heretical only if it was held onto as the only strand. For a person who holds on to a strand of teaching as the only strand becomes "self-limiting" (*tzu-hsiao*) in terms of what he may achieve as the Tao. Such a person is the direct opposite of Confucius, who was without "willfulness," "dogmatism," "obstinacy," and "egoism"[251] and who had "no course for which I am predetermined, and no course against which I am predetermined."[252] Therefore, Chiao Hsün claimed, when Confucius said that "*kung-hu i-tuan, ssu-hai yeh-i*," he was not advocating an attack on so-called heresy to eliminate its alleged "harm." Rather, he was suggesting that followers of one strand study other strands so that the harm of opposition between different strands would cease. "How," Chiao Hsün asked, "can words have only one strand?" "Each man has his own nature. Others cannot be compelled to agree with one's self. One's self cannot be compelled to agree with others." For this reason, the "superior man" does not have a "one-track mind" (*i-chih*), but "penetrates the minds of all under Heaven." He "extends to the utmost from his feeling and nature to the feelings and nature of the myriad things" so that they each can "fully develop their use." This, Chiao Hsün said, is what Confucius talked about as the Tao of "one thread" of "truthfulness and reciprocity" (*chung-shu*).[253]

The difference in the attitude of the "intellectual genealogists" and the scholars of "evidential research" toward non-Confucian teachings was a source of creative tension in late Ming and early Ch'ing. As Yü Ying-shih has observed, Chang Hsüeh-ch'eng's historicist thesis that "the Six Classics are all history" was not a shot in the dark but a challenge to Tai Chen's position that the Confucian Classics were the "sole depository of the Tao of the sages"; it was part of Chang's lifelong battle as a "philosopher" with Tai as a "philologist."[254] What is involved in this battle, however, is not the concept of textuality as such, but the question regarding the textual *locus* of the Tao as truth. Both Chang and Tai believed in the possibility of the Tao being textually embodied as a linguistic presence. They both also had a sense of plurality about texts and were sensitive to the intentionality of a text as the expression of what a thinker or school has rightly or wrongly "self-attained" as the Tao. Indeed, the emphasis on "self-attainment" as a value and its use as a criterion for the determination of textuality prevailed as much among those who rejected non-Confucian teachings as those who accepted them. Significantly, Sun Ch'i-feng and T'ang Pin, while rejecting Buddhism as incompatible with Confucianism, did so in terms of its difference from Confucianism in "purpose" (*tsung-chih* or *tsung*). They also advocated the mapping of variations within Confucianism in terms of *tsung*, which they compared to the "lineage" (*hsi*) of a family. Just as the "lineage" of a family often exfoliates into "major branches" (*ta-tsung*) and "minor branches" (*hsiao-tsung*), the *tsung* of a school is likely to differentiate into a variety of persuasions which bear a certain family resemblance but which are distinguishable in terms of "partiality and universality" (*p'ien-ch'üan*) and "profundity and shallowness" (*shen-ch'ien*) because they embody differences in individual "self-attainment" or "perception" (*chien* or *shih*).[255]

It is also noteworthy that Tai Chen disputed P'eng Shao-sheng, for whom he professed respect and admiration, not because P'eng as a syncretist found inspiration in both Confucian and non-Confucian literature. Quoting Mencius as saying that the "superior man," having "self-attained" the Tao, "can draw deeply upon it" and "finds its source wherever he turns,"[256] Tai Chen stated that what P'eng did in that regard simply exemplified what a man of "self-attainment" was capable of doing whether the man was a Buddhist, Confucian, Taoist, or Mohist. But, Tai Chen pointed out, P'eng should not have attributed to Confucius and Mencius what was not Confucian and Mencian.[257] Similarly, when Tai Chen voiced his opposition to the "Sung Confucians," he did so both because he judged them to have misinterpreted Confucianism as a result of influence from Buddhism and Taoism and also because he believed them to have blurred the distinction in "purpose" (*chih-kuei*) between Confucianism on the one hand and Buddhism and Taoism on the other. He pointed out that the "Sung Confucians" like Ch'eng Hao and Chu Hsi studied Buddhism and Taoism before Confucianism and that they achieved their "attainment" via Buddhism and Taoism. They eventually came to realize their "mistake" and returned to Confucianism. But they never succeeded in grasping the "purpose" (*chih-kuei*) of Confucianism at its "root" because they had already been "blinded" (*pi*) by Buddhism and Taoism "without themselves being aware" of this. As a result, they "used the language of the sages and worthies" to talk about what they had "attained" in Buddhism and Taoism. Like a "son or grandson" who has never seen the "face" of his "father or grandfather," they mistook the face of someone else to be the face of their father or grandfather. In doing so, Ch'eng Hao and Chu Hsi made it possible for the Buddhists and the Taoists to pretend that their father or grandfather was the father or grandfather of "our lineage" (*wu-tsung*). It is, Tai Chen said, in order to "expose" (*p'o*) the mistaken identity of the Confucian forefathers and to "rectify" the Confucian intellectual "lineage" (*tsung*) that he wrote the *Meng-tzu tzu-i shu-cheng*.[258]

In being thus concerned about textuality as the expression of the "self-attainment" of a school or thinker, Sun Ch'i-feng, T'ang Pin, and Tai Chen were no different from Chiao Hung, Huang Tsung-hsi, and Chang Hsüeh-ch'eng, who were not systemically exclusive like Sun, T'ang, and Tai. I have already noted that for Chiao Hung synthesis was not indiscriminate lumping. As for Huang Tsung-hsi, he believed in the inevitability of diversity in thought and considered it necessary to distinguish the "purpose" (*tsung-chih*) of a school or thinker. He said, "What suffuses Heaven and Earth is all mind. Mind changes and is unpredictable. It cannot but vary in myriad ways. Mind has no substance (*pen-t'i*) in and of itself. Wherever the effort (*kung-fu*) extends is its substance. Therefore, to make an exhaustive investigation of the Principle is to make an exhaustive investigation of the mind in its myriad variations." For this reason, Huang was critical of his fellow disciple, Yün Jih-ch'u (1601– 1678), for suggesting that "[philosophical] discussions be brought into unity." He said, "With regard to the learning of the different paths and many deliberations, Chung-sheng [Yün] still has a certain rigidity which has yet to be transformed."

Huang was also disparaging of Chou Ju-teng (1547– 1629?) for composing the *Sheng-hsüeh tsung-chuan*, which traced the development of "sagely learning" from the earliest sage-kings through Wang Yang-ming and his disciples to Lo Ju-fang, who was Chou's own mentor. This work, according to Huang, was flawed by its tendency to lump the different schools and thinkers together like "amalgamating gold, silver, copper, and iron into one vessel." It was an articulation of Chou's own "purpose" and failed to clarify the "purpose of each school." As an alternative to Chou's *Sheng-hsüeh tsung-chuan*, Huang compiled the *Ming-ju hsüeh-an*, which even included what Huang judged to be "one-sided views and mutually opposed doctrines." Huang was aware that the divergent views of Ming Neo-Confucians were not all equally valid. Some were "profound" and "pure" while others were "shallow" and "imperfect." But they each embodied what a school or thinker had attained. The attainment of each school or thinker constituted the "purpose" of that school or thinker and was, in Huang's terms, "a gate whereby students might gain entrance [into the Tao]." Students, Huang emphasized, should pay particular attention to the differences between the many schools and thinkers. They should not try to seek confirmation from thoughts or doctrines which were of the same kind as their own. "Learning," Huang said, cannot be a matter of "aiding water with water."[259]

Like Huang, Chang Hsüeh-ch'eng also considered diversity in thought to be desirable and inevitable. As Nivison has observed, he condemned "partisanship" and "self-serving" but affirmed "self-expression." He advocated the individualization of writers and scholars and proposed to revitalize the concept of *chia* ("school/family") or *chia-hsüeh* ("the learning of a school/ family") as a category in the classification of writers and scholars so that a writer or scholar could be saved from "character-lessness" and be identified in his uniqueness as a "specialist" in a special "school."[260] He also regarded the difference between Chu Hsi and Lu Hsiang-shan as a difference which "shall always exist" and "can never be made to coincide." He thus dismissed both the "squabbles" among the followers of Chu and Lu and the attempts at "mediation" as alike in being "superfluous" (*to-shih*).[261] "Paths of learning" are necessarily divergent. They reflect the complexity of mankind in "nature" and embody what individuals could each claim as their "singular attainment" (*tu-te*).[262] "The Tao," Chang said, "is public, but the study of it is private"; and "words are rooted in the mind and differ [from person to person] as much as faces do."[263]

As noted before, Chiao Hung's pluralist conception of textuality as the thematizable expression of the "self-attainment" of a school or thinker involves a certain linguistic skepticism which, though intersecting the Buddhist and Taoist varieties, differs from them in that it does not just advocate the use of language for the sake of undoing language. It states the asymmetry between language and the Tao not only as a thesis on the ineffability of the Tao but also as a reminder that language is intrinsically devoid of meaning and must not be allowed to become a self-possessing system of self-referential signification. This means that, in writing, language cannot be legitimately used other than as a "vehicle" of the Tao and that, in reading, one must go beyond the language of what one reads to reenact in one's experience the Tao embodied therein. What, according to Chiao Hung, is problematical is not language per se as a system of signs but its use by man who is ultimately responsible for whether or not language can function to represent the Tao as truth and to ensure the survival of the Tao as a linguistic presence. He thus refused to attribute the decline of the Confucian Tao to the burning of the books by the First Emperor of Ch'in (r. 221–209 B.C.) and maintained that it was not the First Emperor of Ch'in but the scholars themselves who should assume the blame for the loss of the books. Pointing out that vast numbers of books disappeared both before and after the Ch'in, he said, "The state of Ch'in [literally, "the people of Ch'in"] burned the books, but books survived; while the Han Confucians studied the Classics exhaustively, but [the Tao] in the Classics was interrupted."[264]

The thrust of Chiao Hung's linguistic skepticism thus consists not so much in reducing speech to silence as in stressing the need to transcend language to realize in practice the Tao as truth, the reality of which as experience provides language with meaning as representation. It is the kind of linguistic skepticism which also prevailed among the "intellectual genealogists" and the "evidential" scholars whose valuation of self-attainment as an ideal implies the belief in the necessity of going beyond language to apprehend the Tao through experiential realization. Thus, T'ang Pin cautioned against reading Sun Ch'i-feng's *Li-hsüeh tsung-chuan* "merely as a book." What Sun described in the book, he said, should be "truly realized in experience" (*shih-shih t'i-yen*) so that "this mind [of mine] will be full of Heavenly Principle" and "the 'great foundation' and the 'universal path' will reside in myself."[265] Huang Tsung-hsi also stated that the many doctrines presented in the *Ming-ju hsüeh-an* were not meant to be a substitution for "actual effort" (*ch'ieh-shih kung-fu*) and should not be read "merely to enhance [one's] views" (*t'u-tseng chien-chieh*). Learning, Huang said, would not be "authentic" unless it could be "of use to one's self."[266] Similarly, Chang Hsüeh-ch'eng condemned scholars of his time for pursuing "evidential research" as a matter of "following fashion" (*ch'ü feng-ch'i*) with no regard for "mental attainment (*hsin-te*). "To study," he said, "is to seek mental attainment" which entails "self-knowledge" (*tzu-chih*). One must choose "what is close to one's mind and nature."[267] Even Tai Chen, who was a towering figure in the Ch'ing world of "evidential research" and who proclaimed that "when the language of the past is made clear, the old Classics will become clear and the meaning of the principles of the sages and worthies will become clear," did not consider the "hearing of the Tao" to be simply a matter of mastering language. Rather, he said that one "must empty" one's "dependence" on language and "experientially comprehend" (*t'i-hui*) the Classics as texts. He compared reading to eating and said that one should study to "strengthen one's wisdom and courage" just as one eats to "nurture one's stamina." "Books," Tai Chen claimed, "cannot fully encompass words and words cannot fully encompass meaning." Therefore, "a student should engage in deep reflection for self-attainment" so that "the Tao will reside in man and not in words."[268]

This type of linguistic skepticism which Chiao Hung articulated through concepts derived from Buddhism and Taoism but which was an integral part of the idea of "self-attainment" is not unique to the thinkers of the late Ming and early Ch'ing. In fact, it may be understood as a characteristically Neo-Confucian reformulation in terms of experiential self-realization of the

classical Confucian theory of language as propounded by
Confucius, Mencius, and Hsün Tzu who, as noted before, though
confident of the power of language to represent the Tao,
nevertheless preferred doing to speaking and advocated silence as
transcendence of speech in action. Already among the Sung Neo-
Confucians, "self-attainment" was a cherished ideal[269] and
entailed an instrumental view of language as both continuous and
asymmetrical with the Tao. It informed their indictment of purely
literary and textual pursuits as extraneous or even contrary to the
cultivation of the Tao, which was as much a matter of experience
beyond language for them as it was for their counterparts in the
late Ming and early Ch'ing. Therefore, in discussing the *Odes*,
Ch'eng Hao "would not utter a word of literal explanation (*hsün-
ku*)." "He would only brood over the odes leisurely to get the real
taste of them, softly chanting them in a rising and falling voice. In
that way he enabled one to achieve something."[270] Ch'eng I, who
was most vocal in his condemnation of "literary composition"
and "textual criticism" (*hsün-ku*)[271] also rejected "literal explanation" in favor of "real tasting." He said, "If one reads the *Analects*
and the *Book of Mencius* many times, he will fully understand
their meaning. If he tries to explain them literally, he will never get
the full meaning. Some time ago I annotated the two books, but
when I came to think of it, I felt my annotation was superfluous.
So I merely corrected some misunderstandings on the part of
certain former scholars and put the books in shape."[272] He also
said, "In reading the *Analects*, simply consider Confucius' pupils'
questions as your own and the Sage's answers as what you have
personally heard today. Then you will get something. If you can
look into the *Analects* and the *Book of Mencius* deeply and
explore them and get the real taste of them, eventually your
cultivation will reach the point of maturity at which your physical
nature will become excellent."[273] Likewise, Chu Hsi considered
reading to be a matter of "experiential examination" (*t'i-ch'a*) and
suggested that what one reads be "verified" (*yin-cheng*) against
one's mind/heart. He said, "One should read the Six Classics as if
they had never existed. If one would only seek the principles of the
Way in one's self, one will find [the Six Classics] easy to
understand."[274]

Thus viewed as a Neo-Confucian reformulation of the classical Confucian theory of language, however, linguistic skepticism in the late Ming and early Ch'ing is nevertheless different from its antecedent in the Sung. This difference relates to a difference in the structure of self as a concept, and is part of the ongoing debate between Ch'eng-Chu and Lu-Wang, as the two major persuasions of Neo-Confucianism, involving the metaphysics of the universe, the ontology of man, and the problem of intersubjectivity in the epistemological relationship between the reader and the read.

CHAPTER FIVE

A Synthetic Neo-Confucianism as Restructured Neo-Confucianism

Heaven, Nature, and the Way

LIKE MANY OTHER thinkers in Chinese history, Chiao Hung advocated the idea of man forming one body with heaven, earth, and the myriad things. He conceived of this cosmic identity of man in both physical and metaphysical terms. Physically, "heaven, earth, man, and things are nothing but this one ether (*ch'i*)."[1] Man is thus no different from heaven, earth, and things in being made of *ch'i* as the primal stuff and is governed by the same cosmological forces of *yin*, *yang*, and the Five Agents (*wu-hsing*) that also regulate the physical universe.[2] Metaphysically, man is endowed with Nature (*hsing*), which unites within itself heaven, earth, and things. Thus Chiao Hung said, "Above lies heaven, beneath lies earth, and in between are the ten thousand things. All are my Nature."[3] This view of human nature postulates man as a creature who is existentially inseparable from heaven, earth, and things and who can be considered genuine or fulfilled only if he realizes his intrinsic oneness with the universe.

That man is endowed with such Nature is, according to Chiao Hung, a matter of "Heavenly Destiny" or *t'ien-ming* which is sometimes rendered as "Mandate of Heaven" and which is well known in the West as a concept in Chinese political philosophy. In Neo-Confucianism, however, *t'ien-ming* is much more than a political concept. It is first and foremost a concept in what Mou Tsung-san calls "moral metaphysics"[4] and has broad significance for man not only as a social and political animal but, to use a Chinese expression, as a "transparent and luminous" (*ling*) being who is inherently able to transcend the immediacy of his existence as an individual and to become identified with the entirety of the universe as a cosmic being.

The term *t'ien* was used by Chiao Hung in two related but clearly distinguishable senses which I will call respectively "heaven" and "Heaven." *T'ien* as "heaven" is simply a designation for the physical sky and is used in contexts where, for instance, Chiao Hung juxtaposed it with man and earth as one of the Three Powers (*san-ts'ai*).[5] It is a material existence consisting of *ch'i* with a distinct form. It is not, however, what the eyes can see as the "blue sky" (*ts'ang-ts'ang*). The sky, according to Chiao Hung, only appears to be blue because of the vast distance and "ether" (*ch'i*) which lie between man and the sky. He pointed out that the P'eng bird in the *Chuang Tzu* saw the earth as blue when it looked down from 90,000 *li* above and said that things, when looked at from afar and through "ether," always seemed to be blue.[6]

Rather than the "blue sky" which the eyes can see, *t'ien* as heaven is envisioned by Chiao Hung as a huge sphere in which are contained the earth and twenty-eight other constellations. Basing himself on the "eliptical theory" (*hun-t'ien shuo*)[7] and on the calculations of such texts as the *Chou-pi suan-ching*,[8] Chiao Hung reckoned this heaven to be 365¼ degrees in circumference, with a radius of 193,500 *li*. The earth, on the other hand, was said to have a diameter of 30,000 *li* and to be fluctuating upwards and downwards at the center of heaven according to the season of the year. Beginning with the spring equinox, the earth rests at the precise center of heaven so that the two centers of heaven and earth coincide with one another. From the time of the spring equinox to the summer solstice, however, the earth gradually descends a distance of 15,000 *li* so that the top edge of the earth is on the same level as the center of heaven at the time of the summer solstice. Thereafter, the earth begins to ascend until the autumn equinox, when the two centers of heaven and earth again conicide with one another. As autumn turns to winter, the earth continues to ascend until the winter solstice, when the bottom edge of the earth hits the center of heaven, thus completing the cycle of descension and ascension. The entire course of this cycle covers a distance of 30,000 *li*, which also happens to be the exact "thickness" of the earth.[9]

In thus containing the fluctuating earth at its center, *t'ien* as heaven not only "embraces" and "illuminates" the myriad things on earth[10] but, through the "circulation" of its *ch'i* and in cooperation with earth, "activates" (*yün-tung*) them as well.[11] In doing so, however, heaven, or for that matter earth also, does not ever become aloof from or seek dominance over the myriad things. Instead, it partakes of their being and bears to them a relationship of interdependence and interaction. Thus, Chiao Hung said, "heaven and earth share in the being of man and things, while things share in the being of man who in turn shares in the being of things."[12] Following the terminology of the *Yin-fu ching*, Chiao Hung characterized this relationship of interdependence and interaction as one of "plundering" (*tao*) and said that heaven, earth, man, and things might be regarded as "mutually stealing" (*hsiang-ch'ieh*) because they "shared" in each other's being.[13] "Plundering" and "mutual stealing" are rather extreme metaphors. They suggest a sense of violence and are characteristic of the kind of language used in the *Yin-fu ching*. For Chiao Hung, however, they describe the creative mechanism of "change" in the universe, which, he said, "is generation and regeneration without cease and is never exhausted in spite of being continually used."[14]

The totality of heaven, earth, man, and things in their creative relationship of "mutual stealing" is what Chiao Hung means by *t'ien* as Heaven which he defined variously as "a collective name for the myriad things" and as "the creation and transformation of the cosmos."[15] In other words, *t'ien* as

"Heaven" refers to the universe in its entirety both as a state of being and as a process of "change." It implies *t'ien* as heaven, but is different in that it exists only metaphysically or "above form" and is beyond sensory perception. In Chiao Hung's terms, it is "without sound and smell"[16] and is equated with man's Nature (*hsing*). He said, "Heaven is nothing but Nature which is pure, tranquil, and originally so."[17]

The conceptual basis upon which Chiao Hung established this equation between Heaven and Nature is the idea of Heavenly Destiny which he derived from the *Doctrine of the Mean*.[18] The *Doctrine of the Mean* began with the statement that "what Heaven confers on man as Destiny is called his Nature."[19] This statement suggested to Chiao Hung a view of human nature which is Heavenly not only in origin but also in quality, for Heaven in bestowing Destiny on man as Nature is not merely engaged in an act of constituting Nature for man. Heaven gives itself over to man and becomes embodied in man as Nature. This concept of Heavenly Destiny entails a certain creator-creation relationship between Heaven and man's Nature. It does not, however, imply that Heaven and man's Nature form a duality, because Heaven in creating Nature for man recreates itself in man as Nature. Man's Nature is thus identical with Heaven and unites within itself heaven, earth, and the myriad things just as Heaven does. Moreover, such virtues as "sincerity" (*ch'eng*), "impartiality" (*kung*), "humanity" (*jen*), and "generation and regeneration" (*sheng-sheng*), etc. characterize Heaven as well as man;[20] and man "in choosing what is good and holding it firmly"[21] is simply "choosing" and "holding the Way of Heaven" which is not distinct from "the Way of man."[22]

In viewing man's Nature as being conferred by Heaven and in characterizing it in terms of Heaven's virtues of "sincerity" and "humanity," etc., Chiao Hung is unexceptionally Neo-Confucian. In this regard, he merely followed a standard Neo-Confucian doctrine which was begun by Chou Tun-i and Chang Tsai and which was further articulated by the Ch'eng brothers and Chu Hsi.[23] On the other hand, Chiao Hung did not just equate his Nature as a concept with Neo-Confucian Heaven. He also identified his Nature as Heaven with the Way (*Tao*) which he understood not only in Neo-Confucian terms as the Way of Heaven infused with "sincerity" and "humanity," etc. but also in Buddhist and Taoist terms as "Emptiness" (*k'ung*) and "Nothing-ness" (*wu*).

"Nature and the Way," Chiao Hung said, "are one."[24] They are different only as names but designate the same "original substance" (*pen-t'i*), which is "crisp and pure" (*kan-ching*) and which is "not in the slightest muddied or stained" (*wu i-hao t'o-ni tai-shui*).[25] Alluding to a passage in the *Mencius*, Chiao Hung described it as "being immaculate and incomparably so" (*hao-hao hu pu-k'o shang-i*) as if it had been "washed in the Rivers Chiang and Han" and had been "bleached by the autumn sun."[26] As such, the "original substance" has no fixed name and was, according to Chiao Hung, known in ancient China by a variety of terms all of which meant "this." During the time of Yao and Shun, it was called *shih* as, for instance, in such passages from the *Book of History* as: "Alas! Who is in accord with *this* (*shih*) that I may raise up and employ?" (*ch'ou-tzu jo-shih teng-yung*); and "Being charged with the Mandate of Heaven, we only take *this* (*shih*) to be the affair of our administration" (*ch'ih t'ien-chih-ming wei-shih wei-chi*).[27] In these instances, the character *shih* is simply an "archaic expression" for its homonym *shih* and refers to nothing other than the "original substance" which, Chiao Hung maintain-ed, is often spoken of in the *Book of Changes* as *tz'u* and among Confucius' disciples as *ssu*. Ch'i-tiao K'ai, according to Chiao Hung, used the word *ssu* in precisely such a way when he said to Confucius: "I am not yet able to rest in the assurance of *this* (*ssu*)."[28] In later times, however, because of its suggestive value as a metaphor symbolizing the "original substance" as a path leading and penetrating everywhere, the term *Tao* came to be used in place of the ancient designations *shih*, *tz'u*, and *ssu*.[29]

As a metaphor for the "original substance," the term *Tao* invokes a concrete image and is for this reason regarded by Chiao Hung as less preferable than *shih*, *tz'u*, and *ssu*, which are "not restricted by the signification of words" (*pu-chih yen-i*) and are therefore most suited for what in later times is known as the Way which "does not have a shape or body" and "cannot be named by words that signify." Not having a shape or body, the

Way does not occupy any space or, as Chiao Hung put it, "is without location" (*wu-fang*). It is neither in the "front" nor in the "back" and cannot be measured in terms of either "size" (*ta-hsiao*) or "quantity" (*to-shao*).[30] It transcends thought and sensory perception and is in this sense considered by Chiao Hung to be "tranquil" (*chi*) and "vacuous" (*hsü*).[31] Morally, the Way is viewed by Chiao Hung in the same fashion that the "original substance" of *liang-chih* is viewed by Wang Yang-ming. Wang Yang-ming's "Four Dicta" (*ssu-chü*), especially as they were interpreted by Wang Chi (1498–1583), postulate the "original substance" of *liang-chih* both as the source of ordinary goodness and as a transcendental being which is beyond good and evil.[32] Following in the wake of Wang Yang-ming and Wang Chi, Chiao Hung also maintained that the Way as the source of moral goodness was in itself "without right and wrong" or "good and evil."[33] Speaking in terms of Nature, which Chiao Hung equated with the Way, he said that "although those who do good are different from [those who do] evil, they are just the same in deviating from Nature" which is "originally without good [and evil]."[34]

As that which is devoid of moral and physical attributes, the Way is not a thing or being and is regarded by Chiao Hung in Taoistic terms as "Nothingness."[35] Moreover, as "Nothingness," the Way is also viewed as being "without self-nature" (*wu tzu-hsing*) and is therefore spoken of further in Buddhistic terms as "Emptiness" which he understood to be the same as the "Buddha-nature," "True Suchness," and "Perfect Enlightenment."[36] As "Nothingness" and "Emptiness," however, the Way exists as reality, and its existence is eternal and unconditioned. In Chiao Hung's terms, it "comes from nowhere" and "does not have a beginning or end." It is simply "self-so" (*tzu-jan*) and has no other reason than itself for it to be "so."[37]

Being thus eternally self-existent, the Way is also creative, both morally and cosmologically. I have noted that Chiao Hung denied that the "Nothingness" of Lao Tzu and Chuang Tzu was morally nihilistic and claimed that it was the basis upon which "social and moral teachings were established."[38] His Way as "Nothingness" is thus transmoral but not amoral.

Therefore, although he said that the Way was in itself "without good and evil," he nonetheless regarded it as the source of moral goodness. "Goodness," he said, "comes from Nature"[39] and "is the function of Nature."[40] Cosmologically, the Way as "Nothingness" and "Emptiness" produces Being, and Being produces heaven and earth, which in turn interact and produce the myriad things.[41] Following the *Lao Tzu*,[42] Chiao Hung said, "Things under Heaven are born of Being, and that is why it is said that the named is the mother of the myriad things. Being is born of Nothingness, and that is why it is said that the nameless is the beginning of heaven and earth."[43] "Nothingness" or "Emptiness" is thus the "root" (*ken*) of all things[44] and is considered by Chiao Hung to be necessarily so because, he said, "Nothingness necessarily produces Being"[45] and "the Way must be carried in vessels."[46] This being the case, the phenomenal world of Being and "vessels" is nothing but the manifestation of the Way's necessary creativity as Nothingness and Emptiness.

In its existence as reality which is necessarily creative, the Way is prior to, and transcends the limit of, the phenomenal world which is its creation. In Chiao Hung's terms, the Way "cannot be confined by heaven and earth" or "harmed by *yin* and *yang*" and is "lustrously beyond forms or images."[47] But transcendental as the Way is, it "does not exist above things"[48] and is immanent in things. Chiao Hung spoke of it in Buddhistic terms as "devoid of all characteristics but existing in the midst of all *dharmas*."[49] Therefore, although the Way is not a thing with a definable "form" and cannot be measured in terms of "size" or "quantity," it "embraces all forms" and "is involved in the multitude of numbers."[50] Similarly, although the Way is said to be "without a location" and to be neither in "front" nor in "back," it may also be said to be either on the "right" or on the "left."[51] It is omnipresent and all pervasive. There is not a thing that can remain apart from it even "for a moment";[52] and "there is nowhere that one puts one's foot that is not the field of the Way"[53] which, Chiao Hung said, "is the same as the daily uses of the people."[54] Thus, during an "intellectual discussion" when a student complained that Chiao Hung engaged only in "ordinary conversation" without ever referring to the Way, Chiao Hung replied that "ordinary conversation" concerned itself with nothing but the Way.[55]

In creating the phenomenal world which it embraces and pervades, the Way operates according to the waxing and waning of *yin* and *yang*, which Chiao Hung understood in standard Chinese terms as mutually producing and succeeding. He said, "*Yin* in its turn produces *yang*. *Yang* in its turn produces *yin*. *Yin* and *yang* alternate, and so change and transformation are of themselves orderly. This is what is called things being produced as a result of orderliness."[56] The alternation of *yin* and *yang* is thus the mechanism of the Way's creative activity, which merely creates and does not appropriate its creation. Quoting the *Lao Tzu*, Chiao Hung described this activity as "producing without claiming possession, benefitting without exacting gratitude, and being the steward without exercising authority."[57] He also followed the *Lao Tzu* in terming it "nonactivity" (*wu-wei* or *wu-tung*) and thereby distinguished it from activity in the ordinary sense as the opposite of "quiescence" (*ching*). The Way's activity and quiescence are, according to Chiao Hung, not mutually opposed. They coexist for each other and extend into each other. Activity grows out of quiescence and always returns to quiescence. In this sense, activity is "controlled" (*chih*) by quiescence and has quiescence as its "lord" (*chün*). On the other hand, however, quiescence also leads to activity and is "the reason for there being activity." It is "a quiescence which is not quiescent" (*wu-ching erh ching*) and which cannot be obtained if one seeks it apart from activity.[58]

That the Way's quiescence is not quiescent but leads to activity is why the Way as Nothingness is creative of heaven, earth, and the myriad things, which, Chiao Hung said, "are all produced from Vacuity and Nothingness."[59] To "complete" its task as the creator, however, the Way must return to quiescence. Thus, echoing Lao Tzu, who characterized the "movement of the Way" as "reversal,"[60] Chiao Hung said that "the Way completes its creation by means of returning."[61] Activity and quiescence are therefore the two phases of a cycle whereby the Way as creativity achieves its realization as a creative process. In this process, Being is born of Nothingness when the Way proceeds from quiescence to activity. Conversely, when the Way proceeds from activity to quiescence, Being is transformed into Nothingness. Hence, like activity and quiescence, Being and Nothingness are also not mutually opposed. Rather, they form a continuum and are mutually transformable. Nothingness can become Being, and Being can also become Nothingness. The process of Nothingness becoming Being and Being again becoming Nothingness is, according to Chiao Hung, nothing but the myriad things "arising out of" and "returning to" the Way.[62]

Ultimately, activity and quiescence, Being and Nothingness are considered by Chiao Hung to be identical. For this reason, he was critical of those who tried to observe quiescence but failed to recognize activity to be the same as quiescence, saying that their quiescence lacked what Lao Tzu had called "firmness" (*tu*).[63] Similarly, he criticized Yen Tzu for falling short of becoming a sage because Yen Tzu only understood Being "as though" (*jo*) it were Nothingness and did not see it as Nothingness.[64] This identification of activity with quiescence and Being with Nothingness implies an existentialist view, according to which the Way as creator and the phenomenal world as creation are different merely as modes of existence but are indistinguishable ontologically. Therefore, alluding to the *Book of Changes*, Chiao Hung said, "'What exists above form is called the Way. What exists below form is called the vessels.' But [the Way and the vessels] are not two things."[65] Specifically, this existentialist view of creator and creation as identical means that the Way as Nothingness/Emptiness is embodied in the phenomenal world of "vessels" as nothingness/emptiness, which only seems to possess being and activity but which in reality is without being and activity. Speaking in Buddhistic terms, Chiao Hung said that "all *dharmas* in their original nature are without being" and that they "have no self-characteristics" and should be regarded as "empty."[66] He also said, "If you try to watch the myriad things at the moment of their arising, they seem to be active and to have being. In reality, however, they are without the slightest being or activity."[67]

For Chiao Hung, therefore, the Way as a creative process is also a process of the Way's self-creation. It involves the generation from and return to Nothingness/Emptiness of a world which has only apparent being and is actually nothingness/emptiness. Such a conception of the Way may properly be characterized as Buddho-Taoist. It posits a Taoist process of creation, especially as was advocated by Lao Tzu, who envisioned the Way as the creator engaged in a cyclical movement beginning with the generation of Being by Nothingness and ending with Being's reversion to Nothingness.[68] As a Taoist process of creation, however, Chiao Hung's Way also has a distinctly Buddhist dimension since it is informed by the Buddhist concept of "Emptiness." Thus his Way as Nothingness has no "body or shape," is beyond words and intellection and is "empty" and "without self-nature." Moreover, as a concept, Buddhist Emptiness is not simply a designation for the Ultimate Realtity or the Absolute as Taoist Nothingness is; it also refers to the true nature of all *dharmas* and is the ground of being of the phenomenal world. Thus, from the Buddhist point of view, the Absolute and the phenomenal are both "empty" and are ontologically identical. *Nirvāṇa* is *saṁsāra* and *saṁsāra* is *nirvāṇa*. This ontological identity which the concept of Emptiness entails between the Absolute and the phenomenal does not prevail in Lao Tzu's vision of the universe. Lao Tzu considered *te* or "virtue" to be the "Tao 'dwelling' in objects" and to be "what individual objects obtain from the Tao."[69] He did not, however, proceed to say that *te* is Tao or that the phenomenal world of being is ultimately the same as the absolute world of Nothingness. In fact, as noted before, Lao Tzu distinguished *Tao* and *te* and contrasted them, viewing the realms of being and Nothingness as continuous but not identical. Chiao Hung, however, equated the Taoist idea of Nothingness with the Buddhist concept of Emptiness, an equation which compelled him to expand Lao Tzu's view of the phenomenal world. For Chiao Hung, "contemplation on return" (*kuan-fu*) is not simply a matter of concentrating on the idea that all things will return to the "root" of Nothingness, as it was for Lao Tzu.[70] It is also a matter of achieving the mystical insight into the ontological oneness of being and Nothingness, both of which are "empty" and devoid of "self-nature."[71]

Thus, in terms of his vision of the Way as Emptiness and his consequent identification of being with Nothingness, Chiao Hung went much beyond Lao Tzu. Nevertheless, he remained true to Lao Tzu in seeing the Way as the creator which Buddhist Emptiness is not. As will be shown later, Emptiness is not the direct generative cause of the phenomenal world and is in this regard quite different from Nothingness. By retaining the creative aspect of Taoist Nothingness and by coupling it with Buddhist Emptiness, Chiao Hung developed a concept of the Way which cannot be wholly assimilated into either and must be understood as a synthesis of the two.

As a Buddho-Taoist synthesis, however, Chiao Hung's concept of the Way is not exclusively Buddho-Taoist. It contains elements which the vast majority of Neo-Confucians, including those of the orthodox Ch'eng-Chu persuasion, would not reject as being necessarily un-Confucian. For instance, his idea that the alternation of *yin* and *yang* constitutes the mechanism of the Way's creativity is standard among the Neo-Confucians and has been an integral part of Neo-Confucian cosmology since Chou Tun-i's "An Explanation of the Diagram of the Great Ultimate" (*T'ai-chi t'u shuo*) and "Penetrating the Book of Changes" (*T'ung-shu*).[72] Moreover, his existentialist identification of activity with quiescence is a view which Wang Yang-ming had strongly advocated.[73] This view differs somewhat from Chu Hsi's understanding of the problem. Chu never went so far as to identify activity with quiescence as being ontologically one and the same. He merely considered that the Great Ultimate or Principle was the common source for activity and quiescence and that it was involved in both activity and quiescence. Thus, he said, "Activity is the Principle in circulation, and that is the Great Ultimate in the midst of activity. Quiescence is the Principle in preservation, and that is the Great Ultimate in the midst of quiescence."[74] Nevertheless, Chu Hsi did not regard activity and quiescence as being mutually opposed, but saw them as bearing a relationship of mutual implication and would no doubt have approved of Chiao Hung's position that activity and quiescence coexist for each other and extend into each other.[75] Chu Hsi, and other Neo-Confucians as well, would also have no difficulty in accepting Chiao Hung's vision of ultimate reality as being both transcendent and immanent, even though they would have disputed his characterization of the Way as Nothingness and Emptiness. In fact, the following quotation from Chu Hsi on the Great Ultimate could just as readily have come from Chiao Hung:

> Master Chou refers to [*T'ai-chi* as] *Wu-chi* precisely because it occupies no position, has no shape or appearance, and because he considers it to be prior to physical things, and yet has never ceased to be after these things came to be. He considers that it is outside *yin* and *yang* and yet operates within them, that it permeates all form and is everywhere contained, and yet did not have in the beginning any sound, smell, shadow, or resonance that could have been ascribed to it.[76]

To be sure, these elements which Chiao Hung shared with other Neo-Confucians are not uniquely Confucian. They do not therefore necessarily suggest that Chiao Hung's concept of the Way is still Confucian. Certainly, the theory that ultimate reality is both transcendent and immanent cuts across the systemic boundaries of the Three Teachings, which, in spite of their disagreements on the precise relationship between the Absolute and the phenomenal, all maintain that the Absolute goes beyond and permeates the phenomenal. The ideas of *yin* and *yang* are not particularly important to the *Lao Tzu*, where they appeared only once, and there is uncertainty as to whether they were intended as cosmological concepts.[77] In the *Chuang Tzu*, however, they were used a number of times with unmistakable cosmological significance. Thus it is said in the *Chuang Tzu*:

> Perfect *Yin* is stern and frigid; Perfect *Yang* is bright and glittering. The sternness and frigidity come forth form heaven, the brightness and glitter emerge from earth; the two mingle, penetrate, come together, harmonize, and all things are born therefrom. Perhaps someone manipulates the cords that draw it all together, but no one has ever seen his form.[78]

It may further be pointed out that the view of activity and quiescence as organically related or ontologically identical could very well be Buddhist as it was expounded with great eloquence by Seng-chao (374–414), even though primarily from a logical and epistemological point of view.[79]

Nevertheless, there is a truly Confucian dimension to Chiao Hung's concept of the Way. It comes from his identification of the Way as Nothingness and Emptiness with Heaven or Nature, understood in standard Neo-Confucian terms as "sincerity," "impartiality," "humanity," and "generation and regeneration." Thus, as creativity, Chiao Hung's Way is not only morally creative but creative of morals which are characteristically Confucian. This grafting of Confucian morals onto a Buddho-Taoist Way would have been inconceivable to many Neo-Confucians, especially those of the orthodox Ch'eng-Chu school. Chiao Hung, however, felt no sense of contradiction. For him, Confucian morals can spontaneously and effusively "flow" from the Way precisely because the Way is Nothingness and Emptiness and, as such, is not "obstructed" by "emotional entanglements" and the "multitude of uncertainties."[80]

Chiao Hung did not particularly elaborate on the meaning of "sincerity" except for saying that it is "existential" (*hsien-hsien ch'eng-ch'eng*)[81] and that it is the Way or Nature of Heaven.[82] As for the concept of "impartiality," Chiao Hung equated it with "humanity," which he defined variously as "awareness" or "enlightenment" (*chüeh*),[83] as "penetrating the beginning and end,"[84] as "the mind of the humane man . . . in being able to self-establish and self-penetrate,"[85] and, above all, as "generation and regeneration."[86] The idea of "generation and regeneration" can be traced back to the *Book of Changes*.[87] Its identification with "humanity," however, is a distinctly Neo-Confucian innovation.[88] As such, the concept of "generation and regeneration" not only exalts "humanity" from what to earlier Confucians was an ontological virtue of man to a cosmic life force but distinguishes the Neo-Confucian mode of creation from that of the Buddhists and Taoists. As T'ang Chün-i has pointed out with regard to the *Lao Tzu*, the Taoist Way as creativity operates as a series of repeating cycles and is not a process of growth. It does not imply newness or progress and is fundamentally different from the Neo-Confucian Way as creativity which, being a process of "generation and regeneration," is engaged in "daily reno-vation" (*jih-hsin*).[89] In this regard, Chiao Hung is still Neo-Confucian because he retained the concept of generation and regeneration, within which he subsumed such cyclical movements as the alternation of *yin* and *yang*, activity and quiescence, and being and Nothingness in a spiral process involving the continual replacement of the old by the new. For Chiao Hung, therefore, "Nature [the Way] in itself is daily renovated."[90] It constantly goes beyond itself and is intrinsically self-transcending.

    The concept of generation and regeneration is also absent from Buddhism, whose idea of creativity is of an entirely different kind. In Buddhism, creativity is a result of "dependent co-origination" (*yüan-ch'i*) and is not an inherent power of the Way as Emptiness.[91] In Mou Tsung-san's terms, the Buddhist Way as Emptiness is not the "direct generative cause" (*chih-chieh sheng-yin*) of the phenomenal world as the Neo-Confucian Way is.[92] The Neo-Confucian Way, whether conceived of as Principle (*li*), Heaven, or Nature, is comprised of both *t'i* or "substance" and *yung* or "function." *T'i* exists ontologically as the being of the Way and generates *yung* in the phenomenal world as the activity of the Way. *T'i* and *yung* thus form a pair of ontogenetically conjoined correlates as the necessary content of the Neo-Confucian Way and set this Way apart as a concept from Buddhist Emptines.

    In its basic meaning, the term "emptiness" is "depen-dent co-origination." As such, "emptiness" is not a metaphysical concept but a mere description of dependent co-origination and cannot be analyzed in terms of the categories of *t'i* and *yung*. It would not make sense if we spoke of "emptiness" in this usage as the *t'i* of dependent co-origination or of dependent co-origination as the *yung* of emptiness. The *t'i-yung* analysis simply does not apply to emptiness as dependent co-origination. On the other hand, however, emptiness can become a metaphysical concept when it is realized as the Ultimate Emptiness (*pi-ching k'ung*) through the Eightfold Negation and mystical contemplation. The

Ultimate Emptiness thus realized is called the "correct principle" (*cheng-li*) and is equivalent to the Realm of Dharma (*fa-chieh* or *Dharmadhātu*), True Suchness (*chen-ju* or *Bhūtatathatā*), the Law-body (*fa-shen* or *Dharmakāya*) or any such terms[93] which can be and have been analyzed in terms of *t'i* and *yung*. As an example, we may turn to the Sung dynasty monk Ch'eng-ch'ien. In his commentary on Fa-tsang's (643–712) "Treatise on the Golden Lion" (*Chin-shih-tzu chang*), Ch'eng-ch'ien referred to the "gold" of the "golden lion" as the *t'i* of *Dharmadhātu* and to the "lion" as the *yung* of *Dharmadhātu*.[94] Similarly, the *Awakening of Faith* (*Ch'i-hsin lun*) also speaks of *Dharmakāya* as the *t'i* of True Suchness and of *Nirmāṇakāya* and *Sambhogakāya* as the *yung* of True Suchness. *Dharmakāya* as the *t'i* of True Suchness is, according to the *Awakening of Faith*, "undifferentiated" and "devoid of all characteristics" but is "complete and not lacking in anything," whereas *Nirmāṇakāya* and *Sambhogakāya* as the *yung* of True Suchness can "extinguish ignorance and reveal the original *Dharmakāya*."[95]

In point of fact, therefore, the *t'i-yung* analysis has been used in both Buddhist and Neo-Confucian metaphysics. This similarity of usage, however, is only apparent and not real, since the relationship between *t'i* and *yung* as implied in the Neo-Confucian concept of the Way is of a totally different kind from the *t'i-yung* relationship as it appears in the Buddhist ideas of True Suchness and *Dharmadhātu*. As Mou Tsung-san has pointed out, *Dharmakāya* as the *t'i* of True Suchness does not of itself generate *Nirmāṇakāya* and *Sambhogakāya* as the *yung* of True Suchness. It is only in response to the Bodhisattvas, Śrāvakas, Pratyekabuddhas, and sentient beings that *Dharmakāya* becomes manifest as *Nirmāṇakāya* and *Sambhogakāya*. Therefore, although *Nirmāṇakāya* and *Sambhogakāya* are manifestations of *Dharmakāya*, *Dharmakāya* is not their "direct generative cause," and the immediate responsibility for their coming-into-existence lies with the Bodhisattvas, Śrāvakas, Pratyekabuddhas, and sentient beings.[96] The same may also be said of the relationship between the gold and the lion of the "golden lion" as it is stated in Ch'eng-ch'ien's commentary on the *Treatise on the Golden Lion*. As the *t'i* of *Dharmadhātu*, the gold is certainly necessary for the existence of the lion. But the lion as the *yung* of *Dharmadhātu* is not a necessary outgrowth of the gold because the gold does not of itself transform into the lion without the conditioning of the skillful goldsmith. Therefore, as in the *t'i-yung* relationship of the three bodies of the Buddha, it is not the gold as *t'i* but the craftsmanship of the goldsmith that provides the "direct generative cause" for the lion to come into being as the *yung* of *Dharmadhātu*.[97]

When we turn to Neo-Confucianism, the relationship between *t'i* and *yung* is very different. In the Neo-Confucian concept of the Way, *t'i* not only exists as the being of the Way but is necessarily creative of *yung* as the activity of the Way. Neo-Confucian *t'i* is thus both the ground of being and the "direct generative cause" of Neo-Confucian *yung*. It is true that Neo-Confucian *t'i* does not materialize as *yung* without the mediation of *ch'i* or "ether" as the third party. *Ch'i* thus performs a function which may seem comparable to that which is assumed by, for instance, the Bodhisattvas, Śrāvakas, Pratyekabuddhas, and sentient beings in the *Dharmakāya's* manifestations as *Nirmāṇakāya*. This resemblance in function, however, is superficial. Unlike the Bodhisattvas, etc., who are the "direct generative cause" of *Nirmāṇakāya* and *Sambhogakāya*, *ch'i* does not give rise to any kind of *yung*. In the Neo-Confucian frame of reference, *t'i* remains the sole creative agent responsible for the generation of *yung*, while *ch'i* is merely the medium through which *t'i* materializes as *yung*. Moreover, *ch'i*, though a mere medium, is nonetheless necessary and real, whereas the Bodhisattvas, Śrāvakas, Pratyekabuddhas, and sentient beings are only conditional and illusory. These differences imply that there is an essential distinction in the conception of *yung* between the Buddhists and the Neo-Confucians. Neo-Confucian *yung*, because it is created by the necessary and real *t'i* through the equally necessary and real *ch'i*, cannot but also be necessary and real. By contrast, Buddhist *yung* is conditional and illusory because it has as its "direct generative cause" beings who have only conditional and illusory existence. Furthermore, according to Buddhism, what is conditional and illusory must be made necessary and real.

Nirmāṇakāya and *Sambhogakāya*, for instance, are ultimately to be absorbed into *Dharmakāya*, just as the Bodhisattvas, Śrāvakas, Pratyekabuddhas, and sentient beings are eventually to be transformed into enlightened Buddhas. Therefore, while Neo-Confucian *t'i* brings forth *yung* through the never-ending process of generation and regeneration, Buddhist *t'i* assimilates *yung* by converting *yung* into *t'i* which alone has real and necessary existence.

As noted before, orthodox Neo-Confucians often contrasted their Way as Principle with Buddhist Emptiness, which they rejected as nihilistic. In doing so, they were accused by Chiao Hung of being "entangled with names without investigating facts."[98] Chiao Hung's accusation has a certain plausibility, for, as Charles Fu has pointed out, in Mahāyāna Buddhism, especially in its Chinese articulations as T'ien-t'ai, Hua-yen, and Ch'an, there is "transcendence-in-immanence" and "Nāgārjuna's 'negativistic' logico-ontological analysis of the epistemological duality of the mind, the truth, and the reality constructed by men as well as of the ontological nondifferentiation of nirvāṇa/saṃsāra, absolute/relative, etc., is finally transformed into a direct, positive, and dynamic affirmation of the reality of the phenomenal world and everyday life."[99]

However, plausible as Chiao Hung's accusation is, it is also beside the point. It overlooks the context in which orthodox Neo-Confucians rejected Buddhist Emptiness as nihilistic. Structurally speaking, the issue involved is not one of immanence versus transcendence or this-worldliness versus other-worldliness. Rather, in the orthodox Neo-Confucian confrontation with Buddhism, the issue of immanence versus transcendence or this-worldliness versus other-worldliness constitutes what in Michel Foucault's terms is an "object" of discourse.[100] As such, it has a certain specificity of meaning and can become intelligible only in terms of its deployment in the context of orthodox Neo-Confucianism as a "discursive formation,"[101] which is metaphysically constituted by the conception of the Way as the "direct generative cause" of the phenomenal world. To the extent that Buddhist Emptiness entails a *t'i* which does not of itself generate *yung*, it is not a "creative reality"[102] and may meaningfully be rejected by orthodox Neo-Confucians as nihilistic.

In purely abstract terms, this rejection is not indisputable, for Buddhism in fact affirms a *t'i* which does not happen to be of the Neo-Confucian kind. Nevertheless, it makes sense as a statement on Emptiness as the antithesis of the Neo-Confucian Way. As such, Emptiness articulates a characteristically Buddhist universe to which even Ch'an is not an exception. Ch'an has often been claimed to be "a happy combination of Buddhist transcendentalism and Taoist naturalism,"[103] into which "the Chinese feeling for life has been assimilated."[104] But in terms of the *t'i-yung* relationship that it maintains, Ch'an is still recognizably Buddhist. For examples, I will turn to Ta-chu Hui-hai, who was an eighth-century monk and a disciple of Ma-tsu Tao-i (709–788). Ta-chu used the *t'i-yung* analysis on a number of occasions to clarify the apparently paradoxical nature of ultimate reality, which he designated variously as "The Absolute," *Dharmakāya, Prajñā,* and *Vimala* as in Vimalakīrti. On these occasions, the ultimate reality is said to be possessed of a "substance" which "does not differentiate"; it is "formless," "immaterial," and "spotless" and is in this sense considered to be "void." At the same time, the ultimate reality as "substance" is also described by Ta-chu as "not void" because the "substance" of the ultimate reality "contains functions as numerous as the sands of the Ganges," "avails itself of the prevailing green bamboos" and "yellow flowers" to "reveal" or "manifest itself" and has the *kīrti* of Vimalakīrti as its "functional manifestation" which "proceeds from the fundamental substance." Significantly, however, Ta-chu characterized the functioning of his "substance" as "responsive functioning" (*ying-yung*) which arises in response to "circumstances" and "to the needs of living beings like the moon being reflected in the water."[105] Thus, as was the case with *The Awakening of Faith* and Ch'eng-ch'ien's commentary on Fa-tsang's *Treatise on the Golden Lion,* Ta-chu's *t'i* is still not the "direct generative cause" of *yung*; and what has been referred to as Ch'an's "dynamic and naturalistic reemphasis on the reality of the phenomenal world and everday life" actually operates in a normatively Buddhist framework and is governed by a type of *t'i-yung* relationship which, though reality-affirming in its own terms, is nihilistic in the Neo-Confucian sense.

Being thus beside the point, however, Chiao Hung's counterrejection of the orthodox Neo-Confucian rejection of Emptiness still deserves to be taken seriously. As will be shown later, this counterrejection is couched in terms which suggest an ontologically monistic affirmation of the identity of the physical and the metaphysical. As such, it is an expression of his dissatisfaction with Ch'eng-Chu orthodoxy as an ontologically dualistic philosophy of *li* and *ch'i* and is informed by his critical stand as a pluralist and by his philosophical formulation of what Irene Bloom has termed the "monism of *ch'i*,"[106] which is a restructured form of Neo-Confucianism and which entailed a change in the Neo-Confucian perception of Buddhism as a system of thought. Therefore, although his existentialist identification of the Absolute with the phenomenal was articulated in Buddhist terms, it did not oblige him to accept the Buddhist logic of *t'i* and *yung*. His way remained inherently and necessarily creative in the Neo-Confucian sense of "generation and regeneration." He regarded *t'i* and *yung* or their equivalent categories such as the "One" (*i*) and the "many" (*to*) and the "root" (*pen*) and the "branch" (*mo*) as ultimately identical[107] and ontogenetically conjoined. He spoke of Nature as *t'i* and "emotions" (*ch'ing*) as *yung* and said, "Emotions are born of Nature."[108]

Mind and Emotions

Chiao Hung uses the term Mind in two contrasting senses. On the one hand, he calls it "Original Mind" (*pen-hsin*),[109] "True Mind" (*chen-hsin*),[110] "Correct Mind" (*cheng-hsin*),[111] and the "Mind of purity, brightness, and wonder" (*ching-ming-miao hsin*).[112] On the other hand, when speaking of Mind in the second sense he refers to it in Mencius' terms as the "lost mind" (*fang-hsin*),[113] in Chuang Tzu's terms as the "closed mind" (*ch'eng-hsin*),[114] and in Buddhistic terms as the "discriminating" (*fen-pieh hsin*)[115] or "clinging mind" (*p'an-yüan hsin*).[116]

Mind in the first sense as "Original Mind" is simply Nature or the Tao and is "not differentiated from Nature" or the Tao.[117] Just like Nature or the Tao, it "has neither a body nor a location" and is "not a thing which can be held or pointed to."[118] It is also "without sound and smell" and is thus beyond sensory perception and "cognitive comprehension" (*chih-chieh*).[119] Also like Nature or the Tao which is all-pervasive and which exists eternally, the Original Mind "suffuses Heaven and earth,"[120] "does not regard anything as external" (*wu-wai*),[121] and is "without past or present."[122] It is "universally illuminating" (*p'ien-chao*)[123] and is what everyone possesses.[124] It "does not exist because of Yao" the sage-ruler, nor does it "become extinguished because of Chieh" the wicked tyrant.[125]

The Original Mind is viewed by Chiao Hung as nothing but Nature or the *Tao* understood in psychological terms of consciousness, knowing, and perceiving. Thus Chiao Hung said, "The human mind is the Tao .... The world calls it mind because there is nothing of which it is not conscious."[126] Thus understood, the Original Mind is "self-luminous and self-spiritual." It "knows without deliberation and possesses ability without study."[127] For this reason, it is described as "spontaneous knowing" and "perceiving."[128] In its knowing and perceiving, however, the Original Mind does not discriminate between the knower and the known or the perceiver and the perceived. It is like the mind of a newborn babe who is still in the "primal state of undifferentiated purity and simplicity" and does not know the distinction between self and others because his "discriminating consciousness has not yet arisen."[129] In this sense, the knowing and perceiving of the Original Mind are thoroughly identified with the objects known and perceived.

On the other hand, however, the Original Mind is also detached from and transcends what it knows and perceives. Like King Prasenajit's Ganges River in the *Śūraṅgama Sūtra*, which remained the same while the king's body changed in every moment of thought,[130] the Original Mind is "indestructible" and is not transformed with the transformation of things which it knows and perceives.[131] Therefore, a man possessed of the Original Mind, while seeing and hearing, may have his "eyes filled with form" (*rūpa, se*) and his "ears filled with sound." He is never-theless indifferent to the "form" as a "blind man" and treats the "sound" as though it were an "echo"; he does not "follow the gate of sound and form."[132] In this sense, the knowing and perceiving of the Original Mind do not "rest" (*i*) anywhere[133] or "dwell" (*chi*) in anything.[134] They are "vacuous and profound" (*hsü-hsüan*) and are referred to by Chiao Hung as "no knowing" (*wu-chih*) and "no perceiving" (*wu-chien*).[135]

The basis of "no knowing" and "no perceiving" lies in the ontology of the Original Mind which, like Nature or the Tao, is regarded by Chiao Hung as Emptiness and Nothingness[136] and is often spoken of by him as "no mind" (*wu-hsin*).[137] The Original Mind understands that both the mind itself as the knower and perceiver and the things which it knows and perceives are "empty" and devoid of selfhood.[138] It "does not possess a self internally, nor does it possess things externally."[139] Consequently, it does not "abide in" (*chu*) or "cling to" (*chih*) either things or views.[140] Like a "raft floating about on the sea,"[141] it is "un-attached" (*wu-hsi*)[142] and "unmoored" (*wu-ch'i-p'o*).[143] It "exhi-bits the unadorned, embraces the uncarved block, and has few desires and little thought of self."[144] It does not "grasp" (*ch'ü*) and as a result does not "hold to one thing or reject another" (*p'an-yüan*). Rather, it forms one body with all things and is free from the error of "instituting one matter while abandoning a hundred others."[145] For this reason, it is said to be "possessed of all principles and inexhaustible in its use."[146] Nothing, however, can become "an obstacle to its vacuity"[147] as it remains undisturbed by the "flow of successive thoughts" (*nien-nien ch'ien-liu*) which rise and fall as things come and go.[148] It "abides in the *dharma* of no thought"[149] and is "imperturbable" and "unobstructed."[150]

Being unattached and unclinging, the Original Mind "does not incline to either side" (*wu p'ien-i*) and is described by Chiao Hung as being in the state of "centrality" or "equilibrium" (*chung*).[151] Being imperturbable and without the flow of succes-sive thoughts, it is said to be "quiescent" (*ching*) or "tranquil" (*chi*).[152] However, like the quiescence of Nature or the Tao, the quiescence of the Original Mind is not opposed to activity, but is the basis for activity. Therefore, in addition to being able to know and perceive, the Original Mind is also able to be "affected" (*kan*) by things and to respond to things with "emotions" (*ch'ing*) whereby the Original Mind "penetrates" (*t'ung*) things.[153] "Emotions," according to Chiao Hung, "are the activity of quiescence"[154] whereas "affections penetrate because of tranquillity."[155] That the Original Mind in its quiescence should lead to activity and become affected with emotions is a necessary development. Therefore, emotions, though stimulated by external things, are nonetheless intrinsic to the Original Mind or Nature. "[The Original] Mind," Chiao Hung said, "is not separate from emotions" and "the quiescence of Nature does not prevail by remaining apart from emotions."[156] He also compared the relationship between emotions on the one hand and the Original Mind or Nature on the other to that between a child and its mother or a branch and its root,[157] suggesting that emotions are a direct and organic outgrowth of the Original Mind or Nature. As such, emotions are viewed by Chiao Hung as ontologically identical with the Original Mind or Nature. He said that "grief, anxiety, indignation, resentment, love, hate, distress, and sympathy are all Mind" and that "happiness, anger, sorrow, and joy are all Nature."[158] He further used the familiar water/waves analogy in which the Original Mind or Nature is held to be water and emotions to be the waves, saying, "Waves never cease to be water."[159] He was thus critical of Li Ao (fl. 798) for advocating the "elimination of emotions" for the purpose of "restoring Nature" and said that in doing so Li deviated from Mencius who "discoursed on Nature on the basis of emotions" and who maintained that "it you let people follow their emotions, they will be able to do good."[160]

As the activity of the Original Mind, emotions not only originate in but never become separated from quiescence. In fact, the activity and quiescence of the Original Mind are just like those of Nature or the Tao in being mutually penetrating and permeating and in being existentially identical. Thus, speaking of the Mind in its affective state as the activity of Nature, Chiao Hung said, "quiescence is called Nature, but in it there is Mind. Activity is called Mind, but in it there is Nature."[161] Because quiescence implies activity, the Mind is necessarily dynamic.

Conversely, because activity implies quiescence, the Mind always stops after being active. This stopping does not occur as a result of some external force, but develops from within the Mind which stops of itself, is "self-stopping" (*tzu-chih*).[162] Following a tradition which was already well established among the Sung Neo-Confucians and which continued to be popular among such Ming Neo-Confucians as Huang Wan (1480–1554) and Wang Chi,[163] Chiao Hung spoke of the Mind's "self-stopping" in terms of the hexagram *ken*. On the basis of the commentary on this hexagram, where it is stated that "when one stops as the back does, one loses all consciousness of self and is able to walk in the courtyard without seeing anybody in it,"[164] Chiao Hung compared the Original Mind to the back of a man's body, which, he said, "is [active with many] functions, but never fails to be fixed."[165]

For Chiao Hung, therefore, the Original Mind is contemporaneously active and quiescent. It "thinks" (*ssu*), but its thinking always "stops at the right place" (*chih ch'i-so*) and "does not exceed proper limits" (*pu-ch'u ch'i wei*).[166] It also emotes, but its emotions are neither "excessive" (*kuo*) nor "insufficient" (*pu-chi*), and are always "regulated" (*chieh*) and "harmonious" (*ho*).[167] This "regulation," however, does not involve repression and is simply the "stopping" of the Original Mind.[168] It sets in naturally after an emotion has run full course and has become fulfilled. This, according to Chiao Hung, is the meaning of Tzu-yu's saying that "in mourning one's emotion stops when it reaches sorrow."[169] In Chiao Hung's view, therefore, the emotions of the Original Mind are properly proportionate to external stimuli. They "follow" (*sui-shun*) things or situations to which they spontaneously "respond" (*ying*).[170] But they do not ever become attached to things or situations and are not plagued by subjective desires.[171] They are without "willfulness" (*i*), "insistence" (*pi*), "obstinacy" (*ku*), or "egotism" (*wo*).[172] The Original Mind which generates emotions of this kind is like "a bird flying through the sky or a shadow dancing on water." It expresses emotions as they are called for by the occasion, but is not entangled with them. It leaves no emotional trace behind after the expression of emotions and is not emotionally tangled.[173] It "experiences happiness, anger, sorrow, and joy but is in itself not happy, angry, sorrowful, joyous" (*yu-hsi fei-hsi yu-nu fei-nu* . . .).[174]

In contrast to the Original Mind which is identical with Nature and is aware of all things, the lost mind is "alienated from Nature" (*li-yü-hsing*)[175] and is "deluded and unaware" (*mi erh pu-chüeh*).[176] It does not have the self-awareness that it is spontaneously knowing and perceiving and is sufficient in all things. As a result, it lacks self-confidence, is haunted by doubts, and abandons itself to the quest of knowing and perceiving through the sense organs.[177] It is like the mind of a man who, though sitting before a candle in the middle of the night, is unable to find fire to rekindle his cold cook stove and has therefore to go hungry because he does not realize that the flame of the candle is fire.[178] It is also like the mind of a man who is engaged in the contemplation of water. He begins with the water in his own pond, but finds it not to be sufficiently watery. Thereupon, he searches the wide world over, looking for better water in streams and rivers and even in the ocean without realizing that his own tears and saliva are also water.[179]

In thus abandoning its original self and seeking knowledge via the sense organs, the lost mind chases after things and situations[180] and is not able to see "that which is beyond forms or images."[181] It is hyperactive, "forgets" to return to quiescence,[182] and is afflicted by an endless flow of "thoughts" (*nien*).[183] Clinging to things and scampering about, it is restless and ill at ease like a monkey without a tree.[184] It has also lost its spontaneity and has become unable to respond actively to things and situations with properly balanced emotions. As a result, its emotions are no longer self-regulated and are entirely "dominated" (*chu*) by external things and situations.[185] Paradoxically, however, the lost mind in its emotions, though dominated by external things and situations, has strong subjective desires and is obsessed with them. It is discriminating and exclusive, "following" (*shun*) certain things but "going against" (*ni*) others.[186] It "has that which it likes and that which it fears" with no particular regard for objective circumstances.[187]

Intellectually, the lost mind is "obstructed" by "habitual views" (*hsi-chien*)[188] and is full of what in Lao Tzu's terms are "preconceived ideas" (*ch'ien-shih*).[189] Consequently, it cannot see things as they are. It "mistakes the east for the west"[190] and attributes such characteristics as "height," "solidity," and "location" (lit. "front and back" *ch'ien-hou*) to the Tao which in itself is without these characteristics.[191] In spite of its being mistaken, however, the lost mind "is stubbornly attached to its views" and "contends with all under Heaven."[192] In sum, the lost mind is "submerged" in both "lustful desires" (*shih-yü*) and "willful views" (*i-chien*), the latter of which Chiao Hung considers to be the more difficult to eradicate and thus the more pernicious.[193] Having already abandoned itself, the lost mind is nevertheless "in love with itself" (*tzu-lien*).[194] It is egotistical without an ego and is alienated from the world because it is alienated from itself. Chiao Hung described it as a mind which, he said, "being at odds with itself regards all under heaven as external to itself."[195]

The distinction which Chiao Hung made between the Original Mind and the lost mind is reminiscent of the twofold concept of the mind as the "human mind" (*jen-hsin*) and the "Mind of the Tao" (*tao-hsin*),[196] which the Ch'eng brothers had advocated and with which Chu Hsi had also been concerned. Chu Hsi's views on the problem regarding the human mind and the Mind of the Tao changed a number of times during the course of his life.[197] In the beginning, he considered the human mind to be "fettered by the selfishness of the physical body" and the Mind of the Tao to be "obtained from the correctness of Heaven and earth."[198] Thus, in his "Essay on the Contemplation of the Mind" (*Kuan-hsin shuo*), he stated, "The reason why the human mind is said to be precarious is that human desire sprouts, and the reason why the Mind of the Tao is said to be subtle is that Heavenly Principle is profound."[199] Chu Hsi's stand in this essay is essentially the same as that of the Ch'eng brothers. Ch'eng Hao, for instance, had said, "The human mind is precarious because of human desire, whereas the Mind of the Tao is subtle because of Heavenly Principle."[200] Ch'eng I had also said, "The human mind is selfish desire, whereas the Mind of the Tao is the correct Mind."[201] Thus, like the Ch'eng brothers, Chu Hsi in the beginning posed the human mind in diametrical opposition to the Mind of the Tao and identified it with selfish desire.

However, Chu Hsi's views on this point shifted somewhat in his later years. Toward the end of his life, he moderated his early stance and arrived at a position which no longer equated the human mind with selfish desire but postulated it as standing between the Mind of the Tao and selfish desire. Therefore, in what may be called the settled view of his later life, Chu Hsi divided the mind three ways into the Mind of the Tao, the human mind, and the mind of selfish desire. The Mind of the Tao stands at one extreme and is purely good and totally without evil. It is the Mind which fully manifests and realizes Heavenly Principle or Tao. Lying in the middle is the human mind, which is mind in its natural state with all its drives and instincts. By itself, the human mind is neutral in moral value. At the other extreme, there is the mind of selfish desire, which is evil and runs contrary to the Heavenly Principle or Tao.[202]

However, though different as a conceptual scheme, Chu Hsi's three-way division is not a repudiation of his earlier dichotomous view. As T'ang Chün-i has pointed out,[203] the human mind in the three-way division cannot actually stand alone or remain neutral. It must either follow the dictates of, and thereby become transformed into, the Mind of the Tao; or it must descend to the level of selfish desires and become indistinguishable from them as evil. Therefore, Chu Hsi said,

Man has only Heavenly Principle and human desires. When this one advances, the other retreats; and when the other advances, this one retreats. There is no such thing as being neutral without either advancing or retreating. If a man does not advance [into Heavenly Principle], he necessarily retreats [into human desires]. Like Liu Pang [247–195 B.C.] and Hsiang Yü [232–202 B.C.] confronting each other from their positions at Jung-yang and Ch'eng-kao [both in modern Honan], when one of them advanced a pace, the other retreated a pace and vice versa.[204]

Thus, in the final analysis, Chu Hsi's later concept of a threefold mind is reducible to his early concept of a twofold mind which the Ch'eng brothers had advocated and which may be regarded as the Neo-Confucian precedent for Chiao Hung's distinction between the Original Mind and the lost mind.

There are, however, important differences between
Chu Hsi's twofold concept and that of Chiao Hung. Chu Hsi
bifurcated the human mind from the Mind of the Tao on the basis
of *ch'i*, which is a central concept in Chang Tsai's Neo-
Confucianism. As conceived by Chang Tsai, *ch'i* is the underlying reality of the universe. It permeates all existence and
phenomena. In its original state, this *ch'i* is undifferentiated and
formless and is designated by Chang Tsai as the "Great Vacuity"
(*t'ai-hsü*), which he in turn identifies with the Great Ultimate. As
such, this *ch'i* "prehends"[205] heaven, earth, and the myriad things,
which are nothing but *ch'i's* particularization as a result of its con-
densation and dispersion or contraction and expansion. As the
undifferentiated Great Vacuity, *ch'i* is utmost good. In its
differentiation into individual things, however, *ch'i* often exhibits
onesidedness or imbalance, which in turn leads to enmity and thus
evil.[206] For Chang Tsai, therefore, *ch'i*, though not necessarily or
intrinsically evil, is nevertheless the source of evil because, as
Wing-tsit Chan has said, it provides "the occasion for evil."[207]

Chang Tsai's concept of *ch'i* was inherited by Chu
Hsi. It was, however, an inheritance mediated by Ch'eng I, who
did not simply follow Chang Tsai in considering *ch'i* to be the
source of evil but further contrasted it with Principle (*li*).[208]
Consequently, Chu Hsi made acknowledgment to both Chang
Tsai and Ch'eng I for the concept of physical nature which is a
corollary of the idea of *ch'i* as the source of evil. He said,

> The doctrine of physical nature originated with Chang and Ch'eng
> (Ch'eng I). It made a tremendous contribution to the Confucian
> School and is a great help to us students. None before them had
> enunciated such a doctrine. Hence with the establishment of the
> doctrine of Chang and Ch'eng, the theories [of human nature] of
> all previous philosophers collapse.[209]

Doctrinally, Chu Hsi rejected Chang Tsai's identification of *ch'i*
with the Great Ultimate. Rather, like Ch'eng I, he contrasted *ch'i*
with *li*, which he in turn equated with the Great Ultimate.[210]
Nevertheless, he, and Ch'eng I as well, derived from Chang Tsai
the idea of *ch'i* as the source of evil. He also showed indebtedness
to Chang Tsai in that he placed considerably greater emphasis on

ch'i than the Ch'eng brothers had. The importance of *ch'i* in Chu Hsi's system is especially apparent in his theory of mind, which differs somewhat from that of the Ch'eng brothers. The Ch'eng brothers did not distinguish between mind and Nature ontologically but only in terms of "substance" (*t'i*) and "function" (*yung*), "quiescence" (*ching*) and "activity" (*tung*), and the "unactivated" (*wei-fa*) and the "activated" (*i-fa*). They saw mind as the function, activity, and activation of Nature which is substance, quiescence, and nonactivation.

      Chu Hsi, however, viewed mind as the "spiritual luminosity of *ch'i*" (*ch'i chih ching-shuang*) and considered it to be possessed of both substance and function, quiescence and activity, activation and nonactiviation. As such, Chu Hsi's mind is ontologically differentiated from Nature and emotions. In this regard, he was like Chang Tsai who maintained that "mind unites Nature and emotions."[211] Chu Hsi's view on the mind's relationship to Nature or *li* on the one hand and to emotions or *ch'i* on the other will be examined in detail later. What needs to be emphasized here is that he adopted from Chang Tsai the idea of *ch'i* as the source of evil and that he used it to constitute the basis for his distinction between the human mind and the Mind of the Tao. Thus, in his preface to his commentary on the *Doctrine of the Mean*, which represents the settled views of his later years, Chu Hsi said,

> The reason why there is said to be the distinction between the human mind and the Mind of the *Tao* is that it [mind] is sometimes born of the selfishness of form and *ch'i* and at other times originates in the correctness of Nature and Destiny. What the mind is aware of is thus different. As a result, sometimes it is regarded as precarious and ill at ease while at other times it is regarded as subtle, mysterious and difficult to discern . . . . The Mind of the Tao must be made the master of the self so that the human mind will listen to its dictates.[212]

      Chiao Hung differs from Chu Hsi in that he does not use the concept of *ch'i* as the basis for distinguishing between the Original Mind and the lost mind and also in that he maintains a concept of *ch'i* which differs materially from that of Chu Hsi. In a dialogue with a student who asked him about Mencius' teaching on the "nurturing of *ch'i*" (*yang-ch'i*),[213] Chiao Hung said that what Mencius had talked about as *ch'i* was what other sages and worthies had called mind or Nature and that, like Mind or Nature, *ch'i* "suffuses heaven and earth" and "is most great and most sturdy." He also praised Mencius for the use of the term *ch'i* which, he said, is a "most wonderful" word; it designates that which does not contain the slightest bit of excessive emotions or discriminating consciousness and is "vacuous and responsive to things."[214] It is, according to Chiao Hung, because of these marvelous qualities of *ch'i* that Lao Tzu advocated "concentrating on *ch'i* to achieve suppleness" and that the *Yin-fu ching* recommended the "control of the mind with *ch'i*." Also, Chiao Hung claimed, the same marvelous qualities of *ch'i* are the reason for Chuang Tzu's statement, "Do not listen with yours ears, listen with your mind. No, do not listen with your mind, but listen with your *ch'i*."[215]

For Chiao Hung, therefore, *ch'i* is not a source of evil but is synonymous with mind or Nature. Thus, unlike Chu Hsi, he could not and did not distinguish Original Mind from the lost mind on the basis of *ch'i*. Instead, he turned to such Buddhist ideas as "delusion" (*mi*) and "enlightenment" (*chüeh*) or "ignorance" (*wu-ming*) and "wisdom" (*chih-hui*) to make the distinction.[216] This means that, for Chiao Hung, whether the mind is the Original Mind or the lost mind has nothing to do with *ch'i*, but is a matter of whether the mind retains the self-awareness of the truth of "emptiness" or "nonego." According to Chiao Hung, the "self" understood as *ātman* in the Buddhist sense is the reason why there is ignorance;[217] "preconceived ideas" can exist only because "the self is not voided."[218] However, whether or not the mind retains this self-awareness of the truth of "emptiness," the mind as a whole is either "deluded" or "enlightened." Thus, Chiao Hung said, "When ignorance does not arise, that is wisdom."[219] In this sense, Chiao Hung's mind is always one and undivided; and his distinction between the Original Mind and the lost mind is not one between two kinds of mind existing simultaneously alongside each other, but is one between two mutually exclusive states of one and the same mind.

In this regard, Chiao Hung is quite different from Chu Hsi who, as noted earlier, distinguished the human mind from the Mind of *Tao* on the basis of *ch'i* as the source of evil. Chu Hsi's *ch'i*, though never apart from *li* or Nature, is nevertheless ontologically and existentially distinct. It combines with *li* or Nature to form individual beings and things, but does not become mixed up with *li* or Nature. Thus, Chu Hsi said, "Although it [Nature, which Chu Hsi identifies with *li* or the Tao] is implanted in material force, yet material force is still material force and Nature is still Nature, the two not being confused. . . . It is incorrect to regard the more refined part of material force as Nature and the coarser part of Nature as material force."[220] This duality of *li* and *ch'i* means that, for Chu Hsi, the mind which stands between *li* and *ch'i* can be one and undivided but is not always so, as it is for Chiao Hung. The human mind, according to Chu Hsi, can ascend to conform to the dictates of the Mind of the Tao and thereby become transformed into the Mind of the Tao. When this transformation takes place, there is only one mind. For this reason, Chu Hsi sometimes spoke of the mind as being one and undifferentiated—as, for instance, when he said in the beginning of his preface to his commentary on the *Doctrine of the Mean*, "Mind in its vacuous spirituality and intelligent awareness is simply one." Also, when asked about Lu Hsiang-shan's idea of the Mind as being without the distinction between the human mind and the Mind of the Tao, Chu Hsi said, "That doctrine is also all right."[222] On the other hand, when the human mind descends and becomes submerged in material desires, the Mind of the Tao does not go down with the human mind or become similarly submerged in material desires. Rather, the Mind of the Tao remains identified with *li* and coexists with the now corrupt human mind. In this sense, Chu Hsi's distinction between the human mind and the Mind of the Tao postulates not two mutually exclusive states of the same mind but two kinds of mind which are separated from each other by *ch'i* as the source of evil.

Chiao Hung's differences from Chu Hsi in the twofold concept of mind are not to be wholly explained as a result of the Buddho-Taoist influence, which is readily discernible. They reflect a basic, qualitative discrepancy in the concept of mind between

Chu Hsi as the great synthesizer of Sung Neo-Confucianism and Chiao Hung as a late Ming proponent of the Lu-Wang school of Neo-Confucianism. Chu Hsi, as noted earlier, considered mind to be standing between *li* or Nature and *ch'i* or emotions. As such, the mind is defined by him in terms of both. Therefore, he said,

> In comparison with Nature, mind is just as subtle but has traces. In comparison with *ch'i*, mind is just as natural but is more spiritual.[224]

He also said,

> Nature is that which has not yet become active. Emotion is that which is already active. Mind includes both activity and inactivity. When mind is inactive, it is Nature; when it is active it becomes emotions. This is what is called mind uniting Nature and emotions.

Thus defined in terms of both Nature and emotions, Chu Hsi's mind is nevertheless not fully identified with either. It has a distinct identity of its own not only conceptually but existentially. Thus, he said, "Although mind unites and commands Nature and emotions, that is not to say that mind is mixed together with Nature and emotions and is not differentiated from them."[226]

Like Chu Hsi, Chiao Hung also maintained the logical distinctions between mind, Nature, and emotions. Thus, as noted earlier, he considered mind in its state as the Original Mind to be Nature or the *Tao* understood in specifically psychological terms. He also considered emotions to be the outgrowth of Nature or the Original Mind, comparing Nature or the Original Mind to water and emotions to waves in the water. He was, however, unlike Chu Hsi in that he ultimately obliterated these differences by viewing mind, Nature, and emotions as ontologically identical. Therefore, while Chu Hsi generally differentiated "humanity," "righteousness," "propriety," and "wisdom" from the "seven emotions" (*ch'i-ch'ing*) and paired these four ontological virtues of man with the "Origination" (*yüan*), "Flourishing" (*heng*), "Advantage" (*li*), and "Firmness" (*chen*) of Heaven,[227] Chiao Hung, as noted earlier, maintained the position that "grief, anxiety, indignation . . .

and sympathy are all Mind" and that "happiness, anger, sorrow, and joy are all Nature." In doing so, Chiao Hung not only anticipated Liu Tsung-chou (1578–1645), who matched the four ontological virtues of Nature with the four emotions of "happiness, anger, sorrow, and joy";[228] he was also fully in tune with the Neo-Confucian tradition as it had been constituted by Lu Hsiang-shan and Wang Yang-ming.

Lu Hsiang-shan, as is well known, took mind to be identical with Nature or Principle and was generally reluctant to distinguish between mind, Nature, capacity, and emotions. Therefore, when asked about "how to differentiate between Nature, capacity, mind, and emotions," Lu replied, "In raising a question of this kind, my friend, you are being trivial like branches and leaves. . . . As for emotions, Nature, mind, and capacity, they are simply one and the same thing."[229] Lu also rejected the distinction between the human mind and the Mind of the Tao and the contrast between Heavenly Principle and human desire. He said

> To say that the human mind is human artifice and the Mind of the Tao is Heavenly Principle is incorrect. The term "human mind" is nothing but talk [with no validity behind it]. . . . To speak of human desire in contrast to Heavenly Principle is incorrect. Man has both good and evil while Heaven also has both good and evil. How can all goodness be ascribed only to Heaven and all evil only to man?[230]

He also said,

> What is said about [the difference between] Heavenly Principle and human desire is not the best doctrine. For if Heaven alone is possessed of Principle, while man is possessed only of desire, then Heaven and man are different in category. This theory [of distinguishing between Heaven and man] originated with Lao Tzu. . . . It is said in the *Book of History*: "The human mind is precarious; the Mind of the Tao is subtle." Interpreters have frequently explained the human mind as being equivalent to human desire, and the Mind of the Tao as being equivalent to Heavenly Principle. This explanation is incorrect, for Mind is one; how, then, can man have two Minds?[231]

Thus, for Lu, as for Chiao Hung, mind is identical with both Nature and emotions. It is also one and undivided; the mind as a whole either exists as the Original Mind or becomes submerged in material desires and egotistical ideas. There is no occasion when the two states of the mind can coexist side by side as they do for Chu Hsi.[232] As for Wang Yang-ming, although he accepted the conceptual distinction between the human mind and the Mind of the Tao and also acknowledged in psychological terms the differences between mind, Nature, capacity, and emotion, he nevertheless considered them all to be "existentially identical and ontologically one."[233]

As the above analysis indicates, Chiao Hung fits squarely in the Lu-Wang tradition. Being in the Lu-Wang tradition, however, Chiao Hung also differs from both Lu and Wang, partly as a result of the influence of Buddhism and Taoism. Therefore, for instance, although Lu Hsiang-shan equated mind with Nature or Principle and did not as a rule speak of mind in terms of *ch'i*, he still considered *ch'i* to be the source of evil and individual inequality. Thus, he said,

When a man is born in the midst of heaven and earth, his *ch'i* may be pure or turbid, his mind may be intelligent or stupid, and his behavior may be worthy or unworthy .... It is only natural that the worthy man is necessarily intelligent in mind and necessarily pure in *ch'i*, whereas the unworthy man is necessarily stupid in mind and necessarily turbid in *ch'i*[234]

At birth all people are possessed of this Ultimate. However, their endowment of *ch'i* may be pure or turbid. As a result, their intelligence and consciousness may be open or closed. In giving birth to people, Heaven causes those who know first to enlighten those who know later .... Ancient sages and worthies are the same kind of people as common men. They are, however, among the first enlightened of "Heaven's people."[235]

Depending on the quality of *ch'i*, the defects of the students differ in a thousand or even ten thousand ways. How can they be exhaustively enumerated?[236]

For Lu, therefore, *ch'i* is still a negative concept, as it was for Chu Hsi and other Sung Neo-Confucians. It imposes a limitation on what otherwise is a perfectly egalitarian view of man. In this regard, Chiao Hung is fundamentally different from Lu, since for Chiao Hung, men are not born different or unequal in the sense that they are endowed with different kinds of *ch'i* at birth.They only become different in their later development as a result of whether or not they realize their inborn Nature, which is "constant" and the "same" in all men. This, according to Chiao Hung, is what Confucius meant when he said that "men are alike by Nature and become far apart through practice."[237]

Chiao Hung was obviously influenced by Taoism in his idea of *ch'i* which, as noted earlier, he derived from such Taoist texts as the *Lao Tzu*, the *Chuang Tzu* and the *Yin-fu ching*. On the other hand, however, his positive concept of *ch'i* may not be regarded entirely as a result of Taoist influence, not only because he also cited Mencius as his authority but because his thought in this regard typifies a widely held view of *ch'i* which was common during the late Ming, especially in the left-wing Wang Yang-ming School of Mind. This school, of which Chiao Hung was a member, promoted what in de Bary's terms was an "optimistic and liberal view" of man characterized by emphasis on *ch'i* and "recognition of the passionate and appetitive nature of the individual."[238] It may also be noted that this late Ming trend toward a positive appreciation of *ch'i*, and therefore emotions and human desires, actually began in mid-Ming with Wang Yang-ming, Wang T'ing-hsiang (1474–1544), and Lo Ch'in-shun (1465–1547). As Yamashita Ryūji has pointed out, these three Neo-Confucians all advocated the identity of *li* and *ch'i*; and Wang Yang-ming and Lo Ch'in-shun in particular further propounded an affirmative view of emotions as an inherent part of man's Nature.[239] Therefore, with regard to the concept of *ch'i*, although Chiao Hung is radically different from Lu Hsiang-shan, the difference represents a general difference in the tenor of thought between Sung and Ming Neo-Confucianism.

Another notable difference between Lu Hsiang-shan and Chiao Hung lies in Chiao Hung's greater emphasis on knowing as a faculty of the mind. The tremendous emphasis which Chiao Hung placed on knowing is reflected in the fact that he distinguished between the Original Mind and the lost mind in terms of "wisdom" and "ignorance." It is also evident in his idea of knowing, which he considered both the key to the recovery of Nature and the precondition for the exercise of such virtues as "humanity" and "propriety."[240] In this regard, Chiao Hung is again closer to Wang Yang-ming than to Lu Hsiang-shan. Wang, as Hsü Fu-kuan has observed,[241] emphasized knowing much more than Lu Hsiang-shan; Wang designated the mind as "original-good-knowing" (*liang-chih*), as Lu did not, and also regarded "knowing as the substance of mind" and the four cardinal virtues of humanity, righteousness, propriety, and wisdom as mere "manifestations" (*piao-te*).[242] However, while both Wang and Chiao Hung emphasize the importance of knowing, they differ somewhat in their understanding of knowing as an activity. Wang's knowing is first and foremost concerned with the mind's volitional ideas as its direct object.[243] It does not entail knowing things or situations as Nothingness or Emptiness. Although Wang described mind or *liang-chih* as "vacuity" (*hsü*) and Nothingness (*wu*),[244] such descriptions apply only to the mind or *liang-chih* as the knowing subject and not to things or situations as objects to be known. Thus he said,

> The eye has no substance of its own. Its substance consists of the colors of all things. The ear has no substance of its own. Its substance consists of the sounds of all things. The nose has no substance of its own. Its substance consists of the smells of all things. The mouth has no substance of its own. Its substance consists of the tastes of all things. The mind has no substance of its own. Its substance consists of the right or wrong of the influence and responses of Heaven, Earth, and all things.[245]

For Wang, therefore, "vacuity" and "Nothingness" are a part of the language of Neo-Confucian mysticism. They constitute the typical Neo-Confucian theory of "no mind" which, as de Bary has pointed out, requires the mind to be emptied of its egotistical self and to be simultaneously filled with the mind of Heaven and earth.[246]

By contrast, Chiao Hung's knowing is not simply a function of Wang's Neo-Confucian "no mind." It is also knowing in the Buddhist sense (i.e., knowing the truth of Emptiness) which, as a concept, describes not only the ontological reality of the mind but the metaphysical existence of the entire universe. Thus, for Chiao Hung, knowing involves the Mind's knowing things or situations as being Empty. His idea of "nonabiding" of the Original Mind refers to both the Mind which does not abide and to things or situations which do not have an enduring identity or selfhood for the Mind to abide by.[247] There is therefore a distinctly Buddhist dimension to Chiao Hung's concept of knowing as a faculty of the mind. The significance of this Buddhist dimension, however, though not to be denied, must not be exaggerated. Like his concept of *ch'i*, which was Taoist influenced but which also typified a general trend in Ming Neo-Confucianism, the Buddhist dimension of his concept of knowing should also be appreciated in the broad framework of the Neo-Confucian theories of mind. In fact, the Buddhist idea of Emptiness is but one of the many concepts which Chiao Hung used in his analysis of mind. It operates as an addition to a large repertoire of characteristically Neo-Confucian conceptual categories such as "equilibrium," "harmony," "stopping," "activation," and "nonactivation," "emotions," and "stimulus" (*kan*) and "response" (*ying*), which can all be traced to classical works of Confucianism such as the *Mencius*, the *Doctrine of the Mean*, and the *Book of Changes*.

Learning and the Sage

"Learning" (*hsüeh*) for Chiao Hung is a goal-oriented process. It must be firmly focused on "seeing into Mind" and "knowing Nature," which, as we have seen, constitute the purpose of learning without which the expenditure in effort in learning would most likely be "labor in vain." For Chiao Hung, the pursuit of learning begins with "establishing the will by which one determines to become a sage."[248] Sagehood is inherent in the Nature which everyone possesses and which "is the same in every person regardless of whether he is a Shun or a Chih or whether he lives in the past or the present."[249] Nevertheless, the realization of sagehood depends upon learning because man's Nature, in which sagehood inheres, though "self-illuminating" and "self-sufficient," cannot remain so if the person involved does not learn; for "the brightness [of Nature] would then be mistaken for obscurity and its sufficiency for inadequacy," with the result that the "authenticity of Nature" (*hsing-chen*) becomes lost in "falsehood" (*wang*).[250] To learn to become a sage is thus to "eliminate falsehood" and to "restore Nature."[251] It involves nothing more than the realization in consciousness of one's innate moral Nature and is simply a matter of "self-awakening" (*tzu-chüeh*).[252] As such, learning is viewed by Chiao Hung as an "easy" task which requires no "exertion."[253] A person "merely stops seeking greedily" and "returns the light" of his Mind or Nature "to shine back upon" himself (*hui-kuang fan-chao*); then all of a sudden he is restored in his Nature, his "original homeland."[254]

On the other hand, however, learning is also considered by Chiao Hung to be "difficult" and, paradoxically, its difficulty lies precisely in its being "easy"; the fact that it does not require "exertion" also means that "there is nowhere one can make the exertion."[255] Moreover, although restoration of Nature takes place all of a sudden, it has to be preceded by a process of cultivation. Thus, Chiao Hung said, "One must be enlightened to the Principle suddenly, but must cultivate affairs gradually. Sudden enlightenment is easy whereas gradual cultivation is difficult."[256] The gradual cultivation of affairs can also be a rather long process. It requires constant "effort" (*kung-fu*) which is to be maintained in the midst of daily activity and not to be neglected even "in moments of haste" or "in seasons of danger."[257] It also involves "knowing," which alone can establish the kind of "self-confidence" (*tzu-hsin*) necessary for a person to recover his "lost" mind. Lack of self-confidence is considered by Chiao Hung to be the root cause of a person's abandoning himself to search for truth from without.[258] For this reason, Chiao Hung maintains that learning can only proceed when there is self-confidence and that self-confidence is "the mother of the Way."[259] But, necessary as it is for the pursuit of learning, self-confidence is not false pride and cannot be asserted as a mere article of faith. It develops naturally as a result of knowing Nature or the Way.[260] For Chiao Hung, therefore, if a person is not self-confident, it is only because his knowing is imperfect.[261] As soon as he comes to know Nature or the Way and thus has his "eyes opened," he will be able to see himself as an equal of Yao, Shun, and King Wen. He will also be like Yen Hui, who "was the son of a poor man living in a mean narrow lane" but who was able to proclaim, "What kind of man was Shun? What kind of man am I? Anyone who makes something of himself will become just like that."[262]

The "knowing" referred to above is conceived as a process of deconditioning. It consists in the "knowing of errors" (*chih-fei*)[263] and is the kind of "knowing" which, according to Chiao Hung, was practiced by Confucius and his disciple Ch'ü Po-yü. Confucius, as is well known, set his mind on learning at the age of fifteen and described his progress thereafter in terms of five stages. Thus, it is said in the *Analects* that he "established himself in the pursuit of learning by the age of thirty, had no perplexities by forty, knew the will of Heaven by fifty, and was ready to listen to it by sixty, and could follow his heart's desire without transgressing by seventy."[264] This progress is characterized by Chiao Hung as "retreat" or "relinquishment" (*t'ui*) and not as "advancement" or "gain" (*chin*). It is a result of Confucius being able to "transform" (*hua*) with advancing years by perceiving and rejecting as wrong what he had previously considered to be right.[265] Following in the footsteps of his master, Ch'ü Po-yü also "transformed" as he grew older and saw as wrong at the age of fifty what he had held to be right at forty-nine.[266] Characteristically, the "transformation" is understood by Chiao Hung as the "dissolving and melting away" (*hsiao-jung*) of errors. As such, it is indistinguishable from the "knowing of errors." Speaking metaphorically in the language of a physician, Chiao Hung said that a person "would not suffer from illness if he would only recognize illness as illness."[267] For Chiao Hung, therefore, "knowing" is not only cognitive but also therapeutic. It carries within itself the mechanism of self-rectification and is the "knowing" of Wang Yang-ming's "original-good-knowing" which unites knowledge with action.

Chiao Hung further elaborated this idea by equating "knowing" with a number of technical concepts which he appropriated from a variety of classical sources. For instance, he spoke of it as the "fasting of the mind" (hsin-chai), which is an important concept in the *Chuang Tzu*,[268] and as "cleansing" (ti-ch'u) and "daily decrease" (jih-sun), which he derived from the *Lao Tzu*.[269] He also discussed his "knowing" in terms of the two hexagrams of "Peeling Off" (po) and "Restoration" (fu).[270] The fact that the hexagram "Restoration" appears in the *Book of Changes* right after the hexagram "Peeling Off" is, according to Chiao Hung, not accidental, since what is attempted by "Restoration" cannot be accomplished without what is required by "Peeling Off." The central image of the hexagram "Peeling Off" is the "bed." According to Chiao Hung, the "bed" is employed by the *Book of Changes* as a symbol for "emotional desires" and "willful views" because it suggests sexual desire, which is most susceptible to overindulgence. Just as the bed in the hexagram "Peeling Off" has to be stripped of its "legs," "frame," and "skin" before the "large uneaten fruit" can finally be revealed, so the restoration of Nature, which is the purpose of the hexagram "Restoration," cannot be achieved unless "emotional desires" and "willful views" are thoroughly gotten rid of. "Without the process of peeling off," Chiao Hung asked, "how can there be restoration?"[271]

What Chiao Hung's "knowing" has to know and rectify are "emotional desires" and "willful views", the two types of "errors" characteristic of the lost mind. Of these two, "emotional desires," at least in the form of sexual desire, may become overindulged more easily. Nevertheless, "willful views" are the more pernicious, because, as we have seen, they are more difficult to eradicate, especially if they happen to be the "profound" (hsüan) and "subtle" (miao) kind which scholars are apt to grasp at and cling to. They are compared by Chiao Hung to "tiny bits of gold" which have gotten into the eye; they obstruct the vision, but are nonetheless valued by the suffering person, who is reluctant to remove them.[272] Ultimately, however, the two types of errors are of the same kind. They both are manifestations of "willfulness" (i). "Willfulness," Chiao Hung said, "is what insistence, obstinacy, and egotism depend upon." It is also responsible for a person's "excess of emotions and alienation from Nature" (*ch'ing-chih-jao hsing-chih-li*). As such, it must be "conquered" if Nature is to be restored.[273]

The effort to "conquer willfulness" is, according to Chiao Hung, "the sage's pursuit of learning by 'washing the mind so as to withdraw and hide in secret.'"[274] In pursuing learning of this kind, however, the sage does not become isolated from the world; for "withdrawing and hiding in secret" also entails the "concern for good fortune and misfortune in common with other men."[275] Nor does the sage ever become without emotions; his mind may become "refined, pure, and self-collected," but it "does not depart from emotions,"[276] which are intrinsic to the Original Mind. It is only that the sage has "forgotten emotions" in the sense that his emotions no longer have a "root"[277] in "willfulness." As a result, he is able to respond emotionally to things or situations, but is never carried away in his emotions by them.[278] This sagely state of mind is to be achieved by inner mind cultivation which, however, does not deprive the mind of contact with the external world. "A man of wisdom," Chiao Hung said, "eliminates the [willful] mind, but not affairs."[279] Purifying the mind of its "willfulness" and thus its "wild emotions" and "thoughts of desire" is, according to Chiao Hung, what Mencius advocated as *chin-hsin*, which is usually read as "fulfilling the mind" but which Chiao Hung interpreted as "voiding the mind."[280] This "voiding," however, is also realization of Nature.[281] For, just as the rectification of an error occurs simultaneously with the "knowing" of the error, so the realization of Nature is concomitant with "voiding the mind." Again using the language of a physician, Chiao Hung said, "There is only medicine to remove impediments to vision. There is no medicine to bestow vision."[282] For Chiao Hung, the mind is originally self-illuminating. Hence, there can be no question of its acquiring illumination from without. There can only be the question of removing obscurations so that the mind can shine again in its original luminosity. To learn is simply to learn to know where one has erred.

In his idea of learning and knowing as a process of deconditioning, Chiao Hung was obviously influenced by Taoism, especially the Taoism of Lao Tzu and Chuang Tzu, who, as noted, provided him with such key concepts as "cleansing," "daily decrease," and the "fasting of the mind." By comparison, the influence of Buddhism on him in this regard seems much less visible. Nevertheless, it must have been equally real and significant if we take into account the fact that Chiao Hung was deeply involved in the study of Buddhism, which, especially in its Ch'an form, also "demands a thorough process of intellectual demolition and cultural deconditioning."[283]

But, for a number of reasons, this Buddho-Taoist influence does not necessarily preclude Chiao Hung's being a good Confucian. First, the idea of learning as deconditioning is not uniquely or exclusively Buddhist and Taoist. It can be traced back, as it was by Chiao Hung, to the *Book of Changes* and is prevalent among the followers of the Lu-Wang school. In fact, both Lu Hsiang-shan and Wang Yang-ming propounded just such a view of learning. Lu, for instance, said that "the Original Mind is immediately restored if one knows one's errors."[284] He also said that "this old man is not capable of anything except recognizing illness."[285] He was critical of his fellow scholars for "trying to increase" their learning and said, "I merely decrease and am thus different."[286] Wang Yang-ming also defined "learning to become a sage" as a matter of "getting rid of selfish human desires and preserving the Principle of Nature"; it is, he said, "like refining gold and achieving perfection in quality."[287]

Second, in terms of actual practice, Chiao Hung's learning does not entail retreating into the mountains or forests as is often the case with Taoism. Nor does it require monastic discipline as in Buddhism. I have already discussed Chiao Hung's concept of the *sangha*, which is considered by him to be different from the lay world only as a vocational community and not as a special path of cultivation necessary for enlightenment. As a rule, Chiao Hung's learning is a lifelong process of constant effort. As such, it is to be pursued in an ordinary social context amid such daily activities as "coming and going," "arising and retiring," and "eating and drinking," and is not to be interrupted even in times of "illness" or moments involving "life and death."[288] For this reason, Chiao Hung advocated practicing "experiential realization wherever one happens to be."[289] For the same reason, he criticized Tzu-yu for dismissing Tzu-hsia's students as being ignorant of the "root" (*pen*) of learning because they were only taught such "branches" (*mo*) as "sprinkling and sweeping," "answering and replying" and "advancing and receding."[290] He said, "The root and the branches are one .... There should be no seeking for the root apart from the branches. Can a gentlemen in teaching others abandon affairs and still talk about the Principle?"[291]

This emphasis on ordinary daily existence as the context for learning is well exemplified in Chiao Hung's concern for social consensus as a basis of truth. For Chiao Hung, as for Wang Yang-ming,[292] truth can never be private and is necessarily public. It must be personally and experientially realized; in Chiao Hung's terms, it has to be "checked against and found to be in accord with one's Mind" (*ts'an-ho yü-hsin*).[293] But the personally realized truth has to be confirmed in a public dialogue, whether formally through the institution of "intellectual discussion," which, as we have seen, Chiao Hung much favored, or informally by being open to the views of others. Subjectivity must be transformed into intersubjectivity; the fact that a person holds a view alone without being able to make it prevail among others is a sure indication that the person has yet to overcome his "egoism" (*chi*).[294]

For Chiao Hung, therefore, learning cannot be a lonely quest. It is a journey which one takes in the company of teachers and friends, both of whom have a vital role to play in Chiao Hung's concept of learning. Teachers provide guidance which can be instrumental in one's sudden awakening to the truth.[295] Friends are as necessary to one's learning as the "props" (*fu*) are to the ancient cart, which could not move without overturning if deprived of their support.[296] This, according to Chiao Hung, is the reason for Tseng Tzu's statement that "the gentlement promotes his humanity through friends."[297] Thus, when a student confessed that he was without "wild thoughts" when surrounded by friends at a discussion meeting but "wild thoughts" often returned to plague him as soon as he left the meeting, Chiao Hung replied, "Who asked you to leave?" Then, quoting an alleged saying by Matteo Ricci (1552–1610), Chiao Hung said, "'Friends are my second self.' These words are both wonderful and appropriate."[298] To be sure, the mere emphasis on teachers and friends is not necessarily Confucian. The monks in a Buddhist monastery also value their masters and fellow monks. Nevertheless, Chiao Hung's valuation of teachers and friends is different from that of the Buddhists. In Chiao Hung's frame of reference, the teacher does not command as much authority as would, say, a Ch'an master. He does not put the "seal of approval" (yin-k'o) on the student's attainment in learning. Moreover, he bears to the student a relationship which, though highly personal, may or may not be formal. In fact, according to Chiao Hung, the teacher need not be any person in particular, but can be anybody anywhere. He said, "The passersby in the streets are all my teachers."[299] Such a conception of the teacher contains a strong element of egalitarianism which had been growing in the Wang Yang-ming School of Mind, especially among Chiao Hung's fellow members of the T'ai-chou school.[300] It can also be traced to Confucius, who, as Han Yü said of him, had "no constant teacher"[301] and declared in the Analects, 7:2, "When I walk along with two others, they may serve me as my teachers." As for friends, their function in the Buddhist cultivation of enlightenment does not seem to have been clearly defined, whereas in Confucianism it was articulated as early as the time of Tseng Tzu. This perhaps is not surprising, since friendship is one of the five basic human relationships which, doctrinally speaking, have been a Confucian preoccupation. Chiao Hung's emphasis on the role of friends in learning embodies both the traditional Confucian concern for friendship and the enhanced inportance that it received in the T'ai-chou school.[302]

The third reason for which Chiao Hung must still be considered Confucian in his concept of learning is his affirmation of the necessity of "thinking" or "intellection" (ssu). For him, although Nature as the ultimate reality is in itself "without thoughts," it cannot be penetrated without "thinking."[303] Thus, quoting a passage from the Book of History where it is stated that "the virtue of thinking is perspicaciousness" and "perspicaciousness becomes manifest in sageliness,"[304] Chiao Hung said that "thinking is the path to becoming a sage" and that "we all enter enlightenment via this [thinking]."[305] "Thinking" also provides the context for the occasion of "sudden enlightenment," which, according to Chiao Hung, takes place only after a long process of "thinking" and "rethinking" (*ch'ung-ssu*) involving "anxiety" (*chün-p'o*) and "distress" (*k'un*).[306] During this process, one feels as if one were being closed in on all sides by straight solid walls which one could not penetrate. All of a sudden, however, the walls crack and crumble and one achieves enlightenment.[307] "Distress" in connection with learning is thus considered the distinguishing mark of a "man of great wisdom" and not as the trait of a "lowly man" (*hsia-min*). A man is regarded as "lowly" only if he gives up his effort after he has encountered "distress." Such a man fails in his learning and is indistinguishable from those who simply do not bother to learn. This, according to Chiao Hung, is the significance of Confucius' remark that "as to those who are distressed but do not learn—they are the lowest of the people."[308] For Chiao Hung, a student in pursuit of learning must become engaged in "thinking" and "rethinking" and experience psychological agony which goes with this kind of hard "thinking." Otherwise, Chiao Hung said, "even [a teacher] as stimulating as the sage will not be able to do anything about him."[309]

The fourth and final reason for regarding Chiao Hung's concept of learning as Confucian is the emphasis which it places on scholarship and culture as values. He interpreted the *tao* in *tao-wen-hsüeh* as *yu* or "via" and thereby miantained that "a gentlemen honors the moral Nature *via* intellectual inquiry."[310] The two categories of "moral Nature" and "intellectual inquiry" were thus considered by Chiao Hung to form a unitary process in which "intellectual inquiry" bears a necessary relationship to and is constitutive of "moral Nature." He said, "Intellectual inquiry is that whereby there is the honoring of moral Nature. It is not that the honoring of moral Nature is an additional effort lying outside of intellectual inquiry."[311] Specifically, "intellectual inquiry" involves "extensive study of culture" (*po-wen*) and cultivation of "broad hearing and seeing" (*to-wen to-chien*),[312] without which one cannot hope to achieve "oneness" or the "simplicity" (*yüeh*) of the rites as an ideal.[313]

This high regard for scholarship and culture would seem to make Chiao Hung a champion of "comprehensive knowledge" (*po-hsüeh*) in the tradition of the Sung school. Such a view of Chiao Hung, however, does not correspond to his image of himself. As we have seen, he criticized Ch'eng I and Chu Hsi for misinterpreting the "investigation of things" and "extension of knowledge" and held them responsible for the practice of seeking Principle from without in disregard for the cultivation of the mind. He also condemned the followers of Chu Hsi for being pre-occupied with "vulgar learning" (*su-hsüeh*) because, he said, they pursued only "extensive study of culture" and "intellectual inquiry" but showed no concern for the "simplicity" of the rites and the "honoring of moral Nature."[314]

These criticisms of the Ch'eng-Chu school are standard among the followers of Lu and Wang. They are perhaps a little too extreme, and certainly cannot be applied to Chu Hsi himself. Chu was obviously aware of the "onesidedness" of some of his followers and was concerned for maintaining the balance between "intellectual inquiry" and "honoring the moral Nature." Therefore, after the Goose Lake Debate in a letter to Hsiang An-shih he said, "What Tzu-ching [Lu Hsiang-shan] talks about are matters of honoring the moral Nature. What I, Hsi, usually discuss pertains mostly to intellectual inquiry. From now on, I ought to turn back to myself and thereby make the effort. Hopefully, by eliminating my shortcomings and acquiring strengths of others, I will not fall into onesidedness."[315]

On the other hand, Chiao Hung's "extensive study of culture" and "intellectual inquiry" were meant to be carried out in a conceptual framework of learning or cultivation which is markedly different from that of Chu Hsi. Chu Hsi, as T'ang Chün-i has noted, distinguishes between the "expressed" mind and the "unexpressed" mind, which require two mutually complementary but qualitatively different types of cultivation. For the "unexpressed" mind, the cultivation known as "perserving and nurturing" (*han-yang* or *ts'un-yang*) is prescribed, whereas for the "expressed" mind, the cultivation is comprised of a number of forms such as "reflection and examination" (*hsing-ch'a*) and "thorough investigation of Principle" (*ch'iung-li*).[316] Moreover,

Chu Hsi does not explicitly identify cultivation as the "function" of the mind's "substance." In fact, because of his tendency to speak of mind as the "spiritual luminosity of *ch'i*" distinguished from *li*, Chu Hsi is inclined to see cultivation as a matter of *a posteriori* effort.[317] By comparison, Chiao Hung does not distinguish two types of cultivation but recognizes only one, which is deconditioning. Thus, he said that "perserving and nurturing" is not different from "voiding the Mind" and involves nothing but the constant "voiding of the Mind."[318] He also does not consider cultivation as an *a posteriori* effort, but as the self-functioning of the substance of the Mind which, he said, "is of itself alert" (*yüan-tzu hsing-hsing*).[319] Therefore, when a student asked him whether or not "caution, care, dread, and fear" (*chieh-shen k'ung-chü*) constituted the proper effort for the cultivation of Nature and Destiny, he said, "Caution, care, dread, and fear are manifestations of the vitality of Nature and Destiny."[320] His identification of cultivation with the self-functioning of the substance of the Mind is part of the context for his thesis that cultivation requires no effort.[321] In these regards, Chiao Hung is just like Lu Hsiang-shan and Wang Yang-ming, who viewed Chu Hsi's different types of cultivation simply as "different modes or moments of man's self-awakening" or as "different expressions of . . . *liang-chih's* substance in its functions."[322]

CHAPTER SIX

The Restructuring of Neo-Confucianism

THROUGHOUT THIS BOOK, I have specified the Buddhist and Taoist elements in Chiao Hung's thought, but emphasized the need to consider him still as a Neo-Confucian. In doing so, my purpose has been not to minimize the reality of Buddhist and Taoist influence on Chiao Hung but to underline the Neo-Confucian impulse of his syncretism. It is worth noting that the presence of Buddhist and Taoist ideas in Chiao Hung's thought did not disrupt his outlook as a Neo-Confucian. He continued to view the metaphysical reality of the universe in vitalistic terms as an intrinsically creative process of "daily renewal" and to affirm the necessity of "thinking" or "intellection" as a precondition for enlightenment. He also advocated a form of linguistic skepticism which required not so much the reduction of speech to silence as the transcendence of language in the "self-attainment" of the Tao as experience.

The ideas that Chiao Hung derived from Buddhism and Taoism were consistently deployed to establish the oneness of the physical with the metaphysical, function with substance, mind with Nature, cultivation with enlightenment, etc. which he regarded not only as genetically conjoined but also as existentially and ontologically identical. We have seen how this was the case with his use of the Buddhist idea of "Emptiness" as a metaphysical principle which is creative of, but does not form a duality with, the phenomenal world of being as creation because, in creating the phenomenal world of being, "Emptiness" recreates itself in the phenomenal world of being as "emptiness." He also used the Buddhist idea of "ignorance" and the Taoist conceptions of "preconceived idea" and "closed mind" to underscore the empirical reality of evil and the necessity of cultivation so that he could do away with the conception of *ch'i* as a source of evil and see mind as an undivided whole which is capable of rectifying itself through the self-functioning of its substance. What Chiao Hung thus did with Buddhist and Taoist ideas in terms of metaphysics and conceptions of mind and cultivation has a parallel in his linguistic theory, in which Buddhist and Taoist symbols were used to constitute the view of language as a unity of both *semeion* and *eikon* and of both representation and therapy. Like his "Emptiness" as the reality principle which is an intrinsically creative process of self-creation and like his undivided mind which is innately self-rectifying, his language is inherently efficacious in representing the Tao as *eikon* because of its origin as *semeion* and in providing therapy for the redemption of the Tao because of its representativeness as *eikon*.

Chiao Hung's use of Buddhist and Taoist ideas is thus governed by a systematicity which coheres with the discursive regularity of his thought as a holistically monistic formation. It is a formation which fits squarely into the Lu-Wang framework and which is self-consciously pro-Lu-Wang as it is frankly anti-Ch'eng-Chu. As such, it is part of the ongoing debate during the Ming between the Ch'eng-Chu and Lu-Wang schools of Neo-Confucianism and exemplifies what I have called the "monism of *ch'i*," which prevailed in both the late Ming and the early Ch'ing as an attempt to restructure the dualistic Neo-Confucianism of *li* and *ch'i* as a Ch'eng-Chu heritage from the Sung. The metaphysical and ontological implications of the monism of *ch'i* as a new form of Neo-Confucianism are fairly well known; they have been the focus of much of our recent literature on Chinese philosophy. I will therefore confine myself to a discussion of its significance for the relationship between the Lu-Wang school of Neo-Confucianism in the Ming and the Han Learning of "evidential research" in the Ch'ing in terms of Neo-Confucian perspectives on Buddhism and theories of knowledge.

   I have already made a detailed examination of Chiao Hung's refutations of the orthodox Sung Neo-Confucian criticisms of Buddhism. These refutations were in a sense beside the point but nonetheless significant because they embodied a monistic logic which followed as a concomitant from Chiao Hung's orientation as a *ch'i* monist. For Chiao Hung, it would not be valid to charge Buddhism, as Ch'eng Hao did, with having "only seriousness to straighten the internal life, but no righteousness to square the external life" because the "internal" and the "external" could not be bifurcated as a duality and the granting of "seriousness" to the Buddhist "internal life" necessarily entailed the granting of "righteousness" to the Buddhist "external life." In thus refuting the orthodox Sung Neo-Confucian criticisms of Buddhism according to a monistic logic, Chiao Hung spoke not only as a syncretist but for a whole group of late Ming and early Ch'ing Neo-Confucians who were not always so sympathetic toward Buddhism as Chiao Hung was but whose statements on Buddhism witnessed a change in perspective corresponding to the change in the infrastructure of Neo-Confucianism from Ch'eng-Chu's dualistic philosophy of *li* and *ch'i* to the restructured monism of *ch'i*. A case in point is Hunag Tsung-hsi, who rejected the orthodox Sung Neo-Confucian criticisms of Buddhism as "superficial." He said in his "Notes on Organization" of the *Ming-ju hsüeh-an*,

> It is often said that in literary and practical accomplishments the Ming did not measure up to former dynasties. Yet in the philosophy of Principle it attained what other dynasties had not. In everything Ming scholars made the finest distinctions and classifications, as if they were sorting the hairs on an oxen or picking silk threads from a cocoon. They thereby discovered what other scholars had failed to discover. Though the Ch'engs and Chu Hsi spent many words in refuting the Buddhists, they never got beneath the surface. Buddhism's specious reasonableness and confounding of truth they failed to point out. But Ming scholars were so precise in their analysis that the Buddhists were completely exposed and trapped.[1]

Huang did not specify in this passage how the orthodox Sung Neo-Confucian criticisms of Buddhism might be considered as "superficial." A clue, however, can be gained from the *Ming-ju hsüeh-an*, where he criticized a number of Ming Neo-Confucian anti-Buddhist statements which had been standard among the orthodox Neo-Confucians of the Sung. For instance, he denied the charge that Buddhism was necessarily nihilistic.[2] He pointed out that the Buddhists "regard True Emptiness as wonderful being"[3] and that they did not really intend to negate things and emotions. "The Buddhists consider happiness, anger, sorrow, joy, Heaven, earth, and the ten thousand things to be coming into and going out of existence in the midst of Emptiness. [These emotions and things and the universe] do not obstruct the circulation [of the Way]. What need is there for them to be annihilated?"[4] He also maintained that Buddhism could not be distinguished from Confucianism and therefore refuted as un-Confucian simply by characterizing it as a doctrine which "transcends the world" (*ch'u-shih*), is "selfish" or "self-interested," and is solely concerned with the "inner" or "mind" but not with the "outer" or "Nature."[5] These orthodox Sung-style criticisms missed the crux of the real problem which, according to Huang, lay in Buddhism's "seeing function as Nature" (*tso-yung chien-hsing*). In Huang's terms, this means that the Buddhists saw only "substance in [its state of] circulation" and that, as a result, they perceived only change, not constancy in the midst of change.[6]

As conceived by Huang, the universe had two aspects: the active and the tranquil. In its active aspect, the universe appeared as the "circulation of great transformation which does not cease day or night." This aspect of the universe was "change" (*pien*), which, however, was not random, but contained within itself a certain regularity. Therefore, Huang said,

After spring, there is necessarily summer; and after autumn, there is necessarily winter. Men do not transform into things; and things do not transform into men. Grass does not change into plants; and plants do not change into grass.[7]

This order represents the tranquil aspect of the universe. It has "remained as it is since antiquity" and is referred to by Huang as "true constancy" (*chen-ch'ang*). These two aspects of the physical universe also prevail in the life of man. In man, the active and therefore changing aspect manifests itself as the circular movement of emotions between the two states of "being aroused" (*i-fa*) and "not yet aroused" (*wei-fa*). The "true constancy" of man exists in the midst of the changing emotional states as the four Mencian "beginnings" of goodness, i.e., the four fundamental feelings of commiseration, shame, deference, and the sense of right and wrong.[8]

The Confucians, according to Huang, saw both "change" and "constancy" in man and the universe whereas the Buddhists saw "change," which they viewed in absolute terms as "uncreated and inextinguishable." In this sense, what the Buddhists actually saw was not really wrong; it only fell short of the Ultimate Truth because they did not probe deeply enough to see the "unchanging" in the midst of change. Being thus without the "true constancy" to rely on, the Buddhists could not but drift with the flow of events and were unable to maintain a firm sense of good and evil or right and wrong. For the same reason, the Buddhists had to accept an "adverse" situation and "abide by it as if it were fate." The Confucians, on the other hand, recognized only "righteousness" (*i*). They did not concern therselves with "life and death" or "propitiousness and adversity." They "lived if it were righteous to live and died if it were righteous to die."[9]

The "true constancey" which the Confucians perceived but which the Buddhists missed was identified by Huang as Principle,[10] which he, like the Ch'eng brothers and Chu Hsi, considered to be the same as Nature. He said, "What pertains to Heaven is Principle and what pertains to man is Nature."[11] Moreover, Principle bears to *ch'i* the same kind of relationship that prevails between Nature and mind.[12] Unlike Ch'eng I and Chu Hsi, however, Huang regarded this relationship as one of identity. He said that Principle and material force or Nature and mind were merely "concepts" (*ming*) created by man to describe two different aspects of the same thing. When viewed in terms of its change, the universe is called material force. But the same universe is also called Principle because its change as material force conforms to a pattern of "regularity." Principle and material force or Nature and mind are thus "two concepts for the same thing" (*i-wu erh liang-ming*). They do not designate "two things which are of the same substance" (*liang-wu erh i-t'i*).[13] *Ch'i* or mind, from this point of view, refers not only to change but to intrinsically "regular" change, wheras *li* or Nature is not only "regularity" but the intrinsic "regularity" of *ch'i* or mind as change.

Because Huang identifies *li* and *ch'i* or Nature and mind as one, he denies that "*ch'i* must be governed by *li*," saying that to say so is to see "*ch'i* as a dead matter."[14] For the same reason, he denies that *li* is able to generate *ch'i*[15] and that it has to be attached to *ch'i* in order to circulate in the phenomenal world.[16] He thus criticized Hsüeh Hsüan for suggesting through the simile of "sunlight" and "flying bird" that "*li* became involved in activity by riding on the occasion of *ch'i* just as rays of sunlight got into flight by riding on the back of a flying bird."[17] Huang insisted that both *li* and *ch'i* be viewed as both active and tranquil. In their active aspect, both are "daily renewed." They both go through the continual process of "coagulation and dispersion"; and neither the *li* nor the *ch'i* from the past can be the *li* or the *ch'i* of the future. In their tranquil aspect, however, both *li* and *ch'i* are "infinite and eternal" (*wu ch'iung-chin*) and are without "coagulation and dispersion."[18] Similarly, Huang denies the primacy of Nature over mind, maintaining that Nature cannot be solely identified with the tranquil state "before emotions are aroused" or mind be solely identified with the active state "after emotions are aroused." He regarded distinctions of this kind between mind and Nature as fallacies of the Sung Neo-Confucians, particularly Chu Hsi, who, though considering mind as "the commander of Nature and emotions," never actually overcame the view of mind and Nature as a duality.[19]

Closely related to Huang's rejection of what he considered to be the dualistic views of *li* and *ch'i* and Nature and mind is his condemnation of the characteristically Sung Neo-Confucian concept of *ch'i* or *ch'i-chih* ("physical endowment") as a source of evil. He said that *ch'i* or *ch'i-chih* is never evil and that what Chang Tsai called the "nature of physical endowment" (*ch'i-chih chih-hsing*) is nothing but Nature, which is intrinsically and always good. Huang allows that in the process of change, irregularities or evil may occur in the form of "excess" (*kuo*) or "insufficiency" (*pu-chi*). Such irregularitites, however, have nothing to do with *ch'i*. They only occur because *ch'i* has lost its "original so-ness" (*pen-jan*). But the *ch'i* that has lost its original so-ness is no longer really *ch'i*, which, being identified with *li*, is inherently regular and can never be a source of evil.[20] Huang pointed out that Mencius only spoke of evil as a result of mind becoming "submerged" (*hsien-ni*), but never attributed this "submergence" to *ch'i* or *ch'i-chih* as a source of evil.[21] For Huang, therefore, there is no *ch'i* that is not "spiritual" (*ling*) because *ch'i* is *li*.[22] Likewise, there is no mind that is not "self-regulating" and "self-regulated" (*tzu-yu chu-tsai*) because mind is Nature.[23] The reason why *ch'i* is *ch'i* and mind is mind is precisely that *ch'i* or mind contains within itself the ordering principle of *li* or Nature.[24]

Huang's monistic conceptualization of *li* and *ch'i* underlies his rejection of the Sung-style criticism of Buddhism as a doctrine concerned only with mind but not with Nature. This Sung position is, according to Huang, untenable because it presupposes a dualistic view of mind and Nature and regards Nature or *li* as external to mind. Therefore, instead of criticizing Buddhism for being concerned only with mind, Huang maintained that the Buddhists did not understand either mind or Nature and that they did not underestand Nature precisely because they did not understand mind.[25] To regard this issue otherwise was to commit the same kind of fallacy that the Buddhists had committed. Huang observed that although the Sung-style Neo-Confucians regarded *li* or Nature as something to be integrated with mind whereas the Buddhists considered *li* as an "obstacle" to the mind, they were the same in maintaining a dualistic view and in seeing Nature as external to mind.[26]

We will not be concerned with the question of whether or not Huang was justified in his criticisms. The point to be emphasized is that his criticisms of Buddhism are fully consistent with his refutations of the Sung-style Neo-Confucianism and that they both embody a restructured Neo-Confucian outlook which holds a monistic view of *li* and *ch'i*. As Neo-Confucianism changed as a system of signification, its perspective on Buddhism also changed to express an altered Neo-Confucian vision. Huang, though not an advocate of the "oneness of the Three Teachings," had a certain sympathy for Buddhism as a non-Confucian teaching and was different from Tai Chen, who was as uncompromisingly anti-Buddhist as the orthodox Neo-Confucians of the Sung school. Significantly, however, Tai rejected the Sung-style criticisms of Buddhism as much as and according to the same logic as Chiao Hung and Huang Tsung-hsi did. He disputed the contrast that Ch'eng I had drawn between Confucianism as a doctrine "based on Heaven" and Buddhism as a doctrine "based on mind."[27] This contrast, according to Tai, indicated an awareness on the part of the Ch'eng brothers and Chu Hsi that Buddhism was somehow different from Confucianism in "purpose" (*chih-kuei*). But, "blinded" as they were by their early studies of and "attainment" in Buddhism, they did not quite understand what this difference consisted of. As a result, they mistakenly characterized it as a difference between "Heaven" and "mind," which Tai viewed as inseparable. "Which man or thing," Tai asked, "is not based on Heaven. How can it be said that mind must remain apart from Heaven?"[28] For Tai, as it was for Huang Tsung-hsi, the difference between Buddhism and Confucianism lay entirely somewhere else; it came from the failure of the Buddhists (or, for that matter, the Taoists also) to perceive "great constancy" (*ta-ch'ang*) in the midst of "change." Tai said,

> It is said in the *Book of Changes*, "The rarefied *ch'i* constitutes things. The wandering away of spirit constitutes change. From this we know the characteristics and conditions of spiritual beings."[29] [The reason why] the rarefied *ch'i* constitutes things is that *ch'i* in its rarefaction coagulates. That is the constancy of changing things and varying forms. [The reason why] the wandering away of spirit constitutes change is that spirit still exists while wandering away. [Therefore,] although its form decays, the rarefied *ch'i* does not scatter right away, but undergoes changes that are infinite beyond inquiry. Lao Tzu, Chuang Tzu, and the Buddhists see only change

constituted by the wandering away of spirit and are ignorant of the great constancy. [As a result,] when they see the gathering of the rarefied *ch'i*, they judge it to be of a different origin [from that of the wandering away of spirit].[30]

That Chiao Hung, Huang Tsung-hsi, and Tai Chen, in spite of their different judgments on the truth value of Buddhism as a teaching, should all have rejected the Sung-style critique of Buddhism according to the same logic and viewed Buddhism from a unified perspective is noteworthy but not surprising; they were all advocates of monism of *ch'i*. Tai Chen, as Ch'eng Chung-ying's study of his *Inquiry into Goodness* has shown,[31] was as committed as Chiao Hung and Huang Tsung-hsi were to desubstantializing and desacralizing the *li* in Ch'eng-Chu's dualistic system of *li* and *ch'i* and to reconceptualizing *li* as the *li* of *ch'i*. He denied that *li* was an external endowment "contained in the mind" (*chü-yü-hsin*) and said that mind was intrinsically capable of "knowing the unchanging regularities of events and things" because it was inherently "spiritual and luminous" and its "spirituality and luminosity" were not what it had to "acquire" from without and "store" within.[32] He also diputed Chu Hsi's characterization of the two forces of *yin* and *yang* as *ch'i* pertaining to the realm "within form" (*hsing-erh-hsia*) and of the "reason" (*so-i*) for the alternation of *yin* and *yang* during the "transformation of *ch'i*" (*ch'i-hua*) as *li* or Tao pertaining to the realm "above form," saying that the distinction between *li* and *ch'i* could not be found in the Six Classics, Confucius, and Mencius and that what this distinction articulated as the Tao was not in accord with the Tao propounded by the *Book of Changes*. He pointed out that the two expressions "is called" (*chih-wei*) and "is spoken of as" (*wei-chih*) differed in meaning and usage in ancient Chinese. Whenever the expression "is called" is used in a statement in ancient Chinese, what follows the expression, i.e., the grammatical predicate, is the topic or epistemological subject of the statement, whereas what precedes the expression, the grammatical subject, functions as a comment or epistemological predicate whereby the grammatical predicate is "explicated" (*chieh*) as the epistemological subject. Therefore, when the

Doctrine of the Mean states in the first chapter that "what is mandated by Heaven is called Nature, to follow Nature is called the Way, and cultivating the Way is called teaching," the topics that the *Doctrine of the Mean* is concerned with in these three statements are "Nature," "Way," and "teaching," which the expression "is called" has enunciated as epistemological subjects. To say that "what is mandated by Heaven is called Nature" is, according to Tai Chen, the same as to say that "Nature is that by which what is mandated by Heaven is called."

By contrast, when the expression "is spoken of as" is used in a statement in ancient Chinese, the grammatical subject is the same as the epistemological subject and is "distinguished" (*pien*) as such in its "concreteness" (*shih*) by a grammatical predicate which is also the epistemological predicate. Therefore, when the *Doctrine of the Mean* states in chapter 21 that "luminosity resulting from sincerity is spoken of as Nature, and sincerity resulting from luminosity is spoken of as teaching," the topics of these two statements are "luminosity resulting from sincerity" and "sincerity resulting from luminosity" and not "Nature" and "teaching," which function as predicates both grammatically and epistemologically to provide "concreteness" for the two grammatical subjects so that the latter can be "differentiated" (*ch'ü-pieh*) from one another as epistemological subjects.

Similarly, when the *Book of Changes* states in the fifth chapter of the "Appended Remarks" (*Hsi-tz'u*) that "the alternation of *yin* and *yang* is called the Tao," it is making a statement on the Tao as the "the alternation of *yin* and *yang*." However, when the *Book of Changes* states in the twelfth chapter of the "Appended Remarks" that "that which is above form is spoken of as the Tao and that which is within form is spoken of as things," the statement is not to be taken to mean that only the Tao and not the *ch'i* of *yin* and *yang* may be considered as "that which is above form." For, in making this latter statement, the *Book of Changes* is making a statement on "that which is above form" and "that which is within form" and not on the Tao and "things," which are enlisted by the *Book of Changes* on this occasion as predicates to "distinguish" between "that which is above form" and "that

which is within form" as the two phases in the "transformation of
ch'i"; "that which is above form" refers to the phase when ch'i has
yet to assume a form and "that which is within form" to the phase
when ch'i has come to be possessed of a form. But, whether as
"that which is above form" or as "that which is within form," it is
the same ch'i in transformation. The distinction between the two
does not imply the priority or superiority of one over the other
and is not a good reason for bifurcating ch'i from li or the Tao,
which, according to Tai Chen, is simply the intrinsically creative
operation of ch'i in the "ceaseless flow" as "the alternation of yin
and yang."[33]

As a mode of thought, monism of ch'i in the Ming was
not confined to the Lu-Wang school. For, as noted before, one of
its early proponents in mid-Ming was Lo Ch'in-shun, who, though
critical of Ch'eng I and Chu Hsi for viewing li and ch'i as a
duality, was an avowed member of the Ch'eng-Chu school and
considered his own work to be an attempt to continue the
program of Ch'eng I and Chu Hsi and to "integrate" what they
had not integrated. He said,

It has long been true that those who are committed to the learning
of the Way have always honored and trusted the Ch'eng brothers
and Chu Hsi. Recently, however, those who talk about the learning
of the Way calmly place themselves above the Ch'eng brothers and
Chu Hsi. But when their attainment is examined, it turns out to be
what the Ch'eng brothers and Chu Hsi studied in early years and
discarded in the end. Isn't it a mistake if a person, after devoting his
whole life to seeking the Way, merely picks up what the former
worthies have discarded, considering it a personal treasure and
then turning around and criticizing them? . . . I have taken up all
the writings of the Ch'eng brothers and Chu Hsi, immersing myself
in the study of them and thinking carefully about them over and
over again without cease. It is only in the case of the words of
Ch'eng Hao that I feel not the slightest doubt. The writings and
conversations of Ch'eng I and Chu Hsi are indeed voluminous.
They often probe the furthest depths and attain the utmost
subtlety, exploring both sides of an argument to the fullest. The
reason why I have doubts is simply that I have yet to see that they
achieve a final integration . . . . To search their statements for what

is not yet integrated can only be done by one who genuinely honors and trusts them. This is why I devote all my mind to them and dare not be neglectful.[34]

On the other hand, though not unique to the Lu-Wang school, monism of *ch'i* prevailed in the Ming largely among thinkers who more or less adhered to Wang Yang-ming's theory of *liang-chih*[35] or, as the case of Chiao Hung indicates, who professed allegiance to both Lu Hsiang-shan and Wang Yang-ming. To be sure, Lu himself never spoke of *li* as the *li* of *ch'i*. In fact, he did not speak much of *ch'i*, and the few statements that he made suggested that he shared with Chu Hsi the view of *ch'i* as a source of evil. Nevertheless, Lu did not oppose *ch'i* with *li*. Accordingly, the negative conception that he held of *ch'i* did not entail for him a cosmological dualism, as it did for Chu Hsi. As his exchange with Chu Hsi on Chou Tun-i's *Explanation of the Diagram of the Great Ultimate* testifies, Lu's cosmology is unequivocally monistic; it identifies the physical with the metaphysical and does not make the ontological bifurcation between the Great Ultimate and the forces of *yin* and *yang*.[36]

Moreover, Lu equated *li* with mind and advocated a theory of man, according to which man leads a monistic existence not only in the sense that man's being is indivisible into Chu Hsi's dichotomous categories of mind and Nature, Heavenly Principle and human desire, the mind of man and the mind of the Tao, etc., but also in the sense that man as a knowing subject is indistinguishable from the object to be known. Lu conceived of knowledge in dynamic terms as the existential activity of the mind as knowing, which bears a reflexive relationship to what is known not because the mind never errs in what it knows but because, as noted before, the mind in its being as *li* is inherently capable of rectifying the errors in its knowing. He said,

When this mind is preserved, this Principle is naturally clear. [As a result,] when you ought to be compassionate, you will naturally be compassionate . . . ; and when you are confronted with right and wrong, you will naturally be able to distinguish them . . . . This is what it means to say that "all embracing and extensive, and deep and unceasingly springing, these virtues come forth at all times."[37]

He also said,

> Your hearing is by nature distinct and your vision is by nature
> clear. By natural endowment you are capable of serving your
> father with filial piety and your elder brother with brotherly
> respect. There is nothing intrinsically wanting in you. There is no
> need to seek elsewhere. All depends on your establishing your self
> in life.[38]

In these regards, Lu is both different from Chu Hsi and in accord
with Wang Yang-ming and could indeed be meaningfully claimed
by Chiao Hung and his like as a symbolic resource alongside
Wang Yang-ming for the articulation of monism of *ch'i*, even
though Lu's own monistic outlook is established through the idea
of *li* and not through the idea of *ch'i* and constitutes what in
Yamashita Ryūji's terms is a form of "monism of *li*" (*ri ichigen
ron*).[39]

Lu's equation, which Wang shared, of mind with *li* is
central to the Chu-Lu controversy which is partly focused on the
problem of "book learning" or, more literally, "book reading" (*tu-
shu*). Repeatedly, Chu Hsi criticized Lu for neglecting book
learning and viewed Lu in this regard as a "heretic" who deviated
from "the Way of the sages" and "corrupted" the minds of the
students. Chu said,

> Chin-hsi [Lu, who was a native of Chin-hsi in Kiangsi] merely
> wants self-attainment. It is certainly nice if what is self-attained is
> right. However, what happens if what is self-attained is wrong? It
> is better if a person is humble about himself and engages in the
> reading of books.[40]

Chu also said,

> In his learning, Mr. Lu merely wants to find this one piece of
> thread. But he does not know that he has nothing to string together
> [with the thread]. Moreover, in expounding his doctrine, he is most
> unwilling to teach others to read books. [For Mr. Lu,] a person
> simply gropes for enlightenment in such a way that it seems as
> though there were a barrier in front of him. This person is supposed
> to have done his job as soon as he is able to jump over the barrier.

This [neglect of book learning] has badly corrupted the students. I am old and have not much time left. I was not going to expose [Mr. Lu]. But I am afraid that later people might mistakenly consider my learning to be similar to his. [As a result,] I now feel compelled to talk earnestly to expose him. I would say that he is definitely a heretic and that his learning is definitely crooked learning and is definitely not the Way of the sages.[41]

What Chu Hsi spoke of here as "this one piece of thread" refers to what Chan has rendered as the "one thread" in *Analects* 4:15,[42] where Confucius said to Tseng Tzu, "There is oneness that strings my Way together." In response, Tseng Tzu said, "Yes." Confucius, according to Chu Hsi, saw that Tseng Tzu had understood the individual principles in things and events, but was concerned that Tseng Tzu might not have known that all these individual principles formed a unity as the "oneness" of Principle. Consequently, Confucius said what he said as a reminder to Tseng Tzu who was able to concur with Confucius because Tseng Tzu was already accomplished in self-cultivation and had the "ability" to comprehend Confucius' Way as a unity. Through their neglect of "book learning," Lu Hsiang-shan and his followers missed "the many principles" that the sages in the past had experienced and recorded in books.[43] They did not therefore possess Tseng Tzu's "ability" and had no notion of what "oneness" (*i*) was supposed to "string together" (*kuan*). Comparing the "oneness" of Confucius' Way to "a piece of thread" and the principles that Tseng Tzu perceived in things and events to traditional Chinese coins which had a hole in the center, Chu Hsi said, "One must first accumulate a bunch of loose coins before one can proceed to string them together with a piece of thread."[44]

In the above-quoted statement, in which Chu Hsi rejected Lu as a "heretic," he did not specify what he meant by "heresy." Most likely, however, he had Buddhism and Taoism in mind. For, on a different occasion when he was again talking about the problem of "one thread," he made a statement which indicates that his well-known condemnation of Lu as a Ch'anist is closely related to his perception of Lu as a person against "book learning." He said, "Don't worry about not being able to grasp the oneness. Worry only about not being able to grasp what is to be strung together. If the oneness is talked about before what is to be strung together is grasped, those whose natural endowment is lofty will degenerate into Buddhism and Taoism, while those whose natural endowment is low will simply become confused and unable to distinguish things and events.[45]

These charges by Chu Hsi against Lu Hsiang-shan lend credence to the view of Lu as an "anti-intellectualist" who did "not repudiate 'inquiry and study' altogether" but who considered "knowledge accumulated through *tao wen-hsüeh*" to be "at most morally irrelevant."[46] Significantly, however, they were denied by both Lu himself and Wang Yang-ming later. Lu said, "People say that I do not teach others to read books. But, for instance, when Min-ch'iu [Li Po-min] came the day before yesterday to ask me where to put his hand [to begin cultivation], I told him to read the Lü-ao and T'ai-chia [chapters of the *Book of History*] and the parts which begin with the passage on the 'trees on the Ox Mountain' in the Kao-tzu [chapter of the *Mencius*]. When have I ever opposed the reading of books? It is only that I differ from others in the way I read."[47] Wang Yang-ming said, "As I now look through what is recorded in Hsiang-shan's collected works, [I find it to be] untrue that he never taught his followers to read books or investigate principles."[48] Indeed, Lu Hsiang-shan cannot be said to have overlooked book learning either as a value or as an undertaking. Though cherishing the spirit of independence and advocating "self-establishment" (*tzu-li*) and "self-valuation" (*tzu-chung*) so that his students would "not follow upon someone else's heels" or "depend on teachers, friends, and books,"[49] Lu was nonetheless a devoted reader and considered his own accomplishments to be a result of his "diligence" in making "inquiries" (*k'ao-chiu*) and doing reading. He once said of himself to his students,

I have been inquiring into and drilling myself on one thing after another and one event after another day after day and month after month [without interruption] to this day. I was not born with understanding. Nor do I have a special trick. . . . I have always been diligent in trying to gain understanding. My eldest brother usually gets up at the first stroke of the fourth watch and finds me doing nothing but reading, checking in a book, or sitting in silence. He has often talked about this to his children and nephews and is of the view that others are not as diligent [as I am]. It is rather funny, though, that people today talk about me as being lazy and not trying to gain understanding.[50]

      Moreover, Lu condemned those who "bundled up books without reading" as "ramblers without root"[51] and said that one should not only "study comprehensively the words and deeds" of the past sages but "peruse extensively" and "examine thoroughly" the records of the "rise and fall [of dynasties], order and disorder, right and wrong and gain and loss."[52] It is true that Lu's emphasis on "book learning" has strong moral overtones. He did not consider "intellectual inquiry" (*tao wen-hsüeh*) to be possible without the "honoring of moral Nature" (*tsun te-hsing*).[53] He was also supremely concerned with the cultivation of a morally discriminating will (*chih*) which, according to his disciple Fu Meng-ch'üan (*chin-shih* of 1175), was what Lu taught people "first":

Fu Tzu-yüan [Fu Meng-ch'üan] returned from here [the shool] to his home and Ch'en Cheng-chi [Ch'en Kang] asked him, "What is it that teacher Lu teaches people first?" He replied, "To exercise discrimination in one's will." [Chen-chi] asked again, "What discrimination is to be made?" He replied, "The discrimination between Righteousness (*i*) and Profit (*li*)."[54]

Nevertheless, in spite of his reputation for assigning priority to "moral faith" over "inquiry and study,"[55] Lu did not regard the cultivation of will as a purely moral endeavor. Rather, he maintained that the success in the cultivation of will depended on "knowledge" (*chih-shih*). Alluding to Confucius' statement that he "established the will for learning at the age of fifteen" (*Analects* 2:4), Lu said, "At a time like this, there will not be a single person with will in a hundred or even a thousand years. This is because people [today] do not understand what to will for. There must be knowledge before there can be will."[56] Lu further said, "People must have great will. Ordinary people are sunk in sound, color, wealth, and power. Their good mind and good Nature are obscured. What shall today's people do in order to gain understanding of having will? They must first have knowledge."[57] Also, Lu criticized a student of his for having a fixation on the practice of "doing what one ought to do," saying, "[In the statement in the *Doctrine of the Mean* on] 'extensive study,' 'accurate inquiry,' 'careful thinking,' 'clear sifting,' and 'earnest practice,' 'extensive study' comes first whereas 'earnest practice' comes last. My friend, you have yet to become extensive in your study. How would you know that what you practice is what you ought to be doing?"[59]

Lu, it may be noted further, talked a great deal about how to read. Reading, according to Lu, should be an active "search" for the vital "arteries" (*hsüeh-mai*). It should not simply be a matter of "understanding words" or "comprehending literal meaning." To try to "comprehend literal meaning only" is, in Lu's terms, "having no will."[60] In order to find the vital "arteries," the reader must have a "pure" mind or will. Otherwise, he will not only be wanting in the resolve for the pursuit of book learning but be actually harmed by what he reads. Lu said,

> The student must tidy up the field [of his mind] until it is pure. Then, he may arouse himself to become established [in his will]. If the field [of his mind] is not pure, he will not be able to arouse himself to become established [in his will]. In doing learning, the ancients read books. It is through the reading of books that they became accomplished in learning. However, if the field [of a person's mind] is not pure, he will not be able to read books; and if he does read books, it would be like loaning troops to the rebel army or helping the robbers with provisions.[61]

In addition to a pure mind, the "search" for the vital arteries also requires the total, experiential involvement of the reader's self. "Words," said Lu, must not be allowed to remain as "words unto themselves."[62] This means that one does not read books just to talk about them. Rather, one reads them in the living context of one's "daily activity" (*jih-yung*)[63] so that one will be able to "think" about them in the "immediacy of one's self" (*ch'ieh-shen*).[64] In particular, one reads with the view to "curing" oneself of "illness." The books that one reads need not be large in number or "extraordinary" in content. But they must be relevant to one's "illness." Lu said,

> The words of the sages and men of wisdom are spread out in books. What is it that is not contained in [these words]? The commentaries and subcommentaries are so numerous that they fill a room to the ceiling and make an ox sweat to carry. They may be compared to the prescriptions in a medicine basket. [These prescriptions] have been collected in a process of thorough search which did not overlook a single thing. However, [the prescription that] a good doctor uses need not be extraordinary. It need only be good enough to cure an illness.[65]

The prescription analogy suggests that, for Lu, reading is not a passive performance of reception, but entails the active exercise of critical judgement. Just as a "good doctor" has to select a proper prescription from among a whole collection of prescriptions, so the reader must "judge" (*tuan*) for himself the truth value of what he reads. Lu said,

> [What is stated in] a book can be falsified while the Principle (*li*) cannot be falsified. If what a book talks about pertains to the Principle, I can certainly evaluate it according to the Principle. But if what a book talks about pertains to affairs, affairs have their principles [and the book can still be evaluated according to the Principle]. If we read the books of the people from the past and judge them according to the Principle, how can truth and falsehood ever escape us?[66]

The ideal attitude recommended by Lu toward books is one of neither "disbelief" nor "necessary belief."[67]

Being thus totally and experientially involved in his reading, however, the reader must not beome belabored. Genuine understanding, according to Lu, is the spontaneous outgrowth of a process of "maturation" (*ching-shu*) during which the reader "muses" over what he reads in "an easy-going manner" (*yu-erh-jou-chih*) and "savors it to his heart's content" (*yen-erh-yü-chih*).[68] If he encounters something which he does not understand, he should not resort to "laborious thinking" (*k'u-ssu*) or "forced probing and strenuous seeking" (*ch'iang-t'an li-so*) which would only make the mind "confused." Instead, he should put it aside and focus on what he can undestand. For, according to Lu, the fact that the reader has something which he does not understand means that his mind "has yet to become full and luminous." By concentrating on what is "easy to understand," his mind will become "increasingly full and luminous" with the result that he will eventually understand what he does not understand. Otherwise, the reader will "lose his self" in what he reads and be "obstructed by words and phrases."[69] In reading, Lu said, one "must not neglect what is easy to understand or depend on what is already understood."[70]

In view of Lu's discourse on book learning, Chu Hsi's charges against Lu as a person against book learning appear rather perplexing, especially so because Chu sounds remarkably like Lu in much of what he himself had to say about book learning. Notwithstanding his erudition and prodigious activity as a scholar and commentator, Chu Hsi considered book learning to be of only "secondary importance" (*ti-erh-i*) because, like Lu, he believed that the Principle apprehended through the cultivation of learning was fully embodied in one's self. He said, "In learning, one must try to comprehend what is relevant and essential to one's self. [By this standard,] book learning is already [a matter of] secondary importance. One's self embodies all the principles which are not additional acquistions from the outside."[71] Also, like Lu, Chu regarded reading as a morally involved pursuit which could be undertaken only by a person with a "firm" will or "clean" mind. He said, "How can a person read books if his will is not made firm?"[72] He also said, "There is a method in reading books. It is simply that one does not begin to read books until one has scrubbed one's mind clean."[73] Or, again, he said, "Students must collect this very mind and make it concentrated, tranquil, and pure so that it will not be running wild or scattered in the daily round of activity and repose. Only then will they be able to read books."[74] He further compared reading to "handling affairs" (*tso-shih*) and said that one should "discriminate between right and wrong" in reading as well as in handling affairs.[75]

In addition to viewing the purity of will or mind as a prerequisite for reading, Chu is also like Lu in emphasizing the necessity of going beyond the "following of texts and chasing after literal meaning" (*sui-wen chu-i*) to strive for experiential realization. He said, "The books we read and the principles we thoroughly investigate must be experientially realized in ourselves. I wonder whether or not what we discuss and investigate each day is being daily realized in your minds or seen by your eyes. If not, what you do is no more than following texts and chasing after literal meaning. If you rush along in your reading to beat the deadline without seeing where [Yen Hui's] delight lies, I am afraid you will gain no benefit in the end."[76] Specifically, as in the case of Lu, experiential realization of what one reads entails for Chu understanding in the "immediacy of one's self" (*ch'ieh-chi*).[77] This means that "when one reads the Six Classics, one does so by seeking the Principle of the Way in one's self as if there were no Six Classics"[78] and that "when one puts down a book, nothing whatsoever of the book's meaning is left in one's bosom."[79] Chu Hsi criticized the scholars since the Ch'in and Han dynasties for not advocating "return to one's self" in reading:

> In reading, one must not seek the meaning of the Principle entirely from what is written on paper. Instead, one must return to one's self (note-taker's note: using his hand, [Chu] pointed to himself) and do the seeking in one's self. No one since the Ch'in and Han dynasties has talked about this . . . . The sages have only pointed out what we have yet to see in ourselves. We will succeed only if we merely avail ourselves of the sages' words and do the seeking in ourselves.[80]

Again, as in the case of Lu, the search in what one reads for what is "relevant and essential to one's self" is conceived by Chu in therapeutic terms as "curing illness." He said,

Now, in reading, it is important to focus on what the sages have taught others as the places to make effort. This is like using medicine to cure illness. One must find out how an illness is caused and what prescription is to be used in order to cure it. [One need also ask about] what medicines to use, how many grams or milligrams for each, how to roast them, how to broil them, how to mix them, how to cut them, how to simmer them, and how to take them. [Reading] is only like this.[81]

Finally, like Lu, Chu was also opposed to belaboring oneself while reading. He warned against "going after what is obscure" and said that one should concentrate on "what is clear and comprehensible."[82] He also said, "In reading, one must be calm in mind and relaxed in intent. Immersing oneself [in what one reads] and going over it again and again, one will naturally understand it after a while."[83] He further said, "One must not spend the whole day thinking about a piece of reading. Otherwise, I am afraid one would succeed only in forcing the mind to run wild after [the externals]. One should take a short break to nurture the spirit and then come back to the reading."[84] For this reason, Chu Hsi cautioned against being "greedy for quantity" (*t'an-to*) and considered the "greed for quantity" to be the "worst disease" in reading.[85] He said,

In the past, there was a bunch of scholars who were greedy for quantity. They tried to read the *Chou-li*, the various histories, and the documents of the current dynasty, all of which they wanted to comprehend. They spent a lot of effort on what is inessential. Before long, they became terribly confused and did not know what to do with themselves.[86]

Instead of being "greedy for quantity," one should always "measure one's strength" and try not only to avoid being overburdened by what one reads but actually to have "strength left over." Chu Hsi compared reading to shooting with a bow and arrow and said that if a person could handle a five-pound bow, he should use only a four-pound bow.[87] The extra strength is to be used for review, which, according to Chu Hsi, is the key to "maturation" (*ching-shu*) in understanding. Therefore, if a person is capable of reading a whole page a day, he should only try to read half a page so that he will have the energy to reread the half page that he has read before.[88] In a statement reminiscent of Lu Hsiang-shan's injunction against "neglecting what is easy to understand or depending on what is already understood," Chu Hsi said,

> In reading, one must be meticulous. Even when reviewing what one has already read, one must still be meticulous. It is enough to read two or three paragraphs a day. It is not the places where one has doubts that one should try to look at. It is precisely the places where one has no doubts that one should try to look at. Herein lies all the effort [for reading].[89]

I have quoted rather extensively from both Chu Hsi and Lu Hsiang-shan on reading, even at the risk of documentary overskill. I have done so, however, because they highlight a problem area which needs be examined critically if we are to understand the tension between Chu and Lu as a dynamic in the development of Neo-Confucianism. If, as I have tried to demonstrate, Chu sounds much like Lu in his theory of reading, then what sense does it make for Chu to have accused Lu of being a person against book learning? Did Chu misrepresent Lu? I should think not. Or, rather, if he did, the misrepresentation is not fortuitous but programmatic in the sense that it is made possible by the systemic differences between Chu and Lu as proponents of two divergent forms of Neo-Confucianism. Like the question of transcendence in the Neo-Confucian confrontation with Buddhism, the problem of reading is an "object" of discourse in Chu's contention with Lu and has for each a specificity of meaning which is related to the distinct conception that they each held of self as a reading subject. On this score, Lu seems to have been the more perceptive of the two. He indicated an awareness of the issue involved when he said, "When have I ever opposed the reading of books? It is only that I differ from others in the way I read."

As a dualist, Chu Hsi conceived of man's self as being

composed of mind and Nature which, like their correlative categories of *ch'i* and *li* and the mind of man and the mind of the Tao, exist as a unity only in the ideal state of sagely perfection, but are otherwise separate from one another both existentially and ontologically. To overcome the separation between mind and Nature, one must engage in moral and intellectual cultivation, such as reading, which will transform the mind and bring it into conformity with Nature. This transformation of the mind, however, is not the mind's self-transformation unless the mind thus involved as the agent of transformation is the mind of the Tao, which, of course, is not the mind to be transformed because it is equated by Chu Hsi with Nature or *li*. Therefore, when Chu Hsi said that in reading, "one must return to one's self," he was speaking not of mind but of Nature or *li* embodied in one's self. Like the word "mind" used by Chu Hsi to mean either the mind of man or the mind of the Tao, the word "self" in Chu Hsi can also designate either mind or Nature. When "self" is used as a designation for Nature, then reading as a form of cultivation for the transformation of the mind is the self-activity of the Nature of one's self. As such, it requires no point of reference beyond one's self and is spoken of by Chu Hsi as the "return to one's self." On the other hand, when "self" is used to mean mind as opposed to Nature, then reading becomes an activity which is no longer intrinsic to one's self; it must go beyond one's self as the reading subject to appropriate what is objectively embodied in the reading as Nature or *li* so that the appropriated Nature can act upon the self as mind and transform it into the self as Nature. For this reason, Chu Hsi often spoke of Nature or *li* in seemingly contradictory terms both as that which one inherently possesses and as that which one comes to possess as a result of "comprehension (*li-hui*) through "experience" (*ching-li*). He said, for instance,

A person at birth possesses all the principles of the Way. The reason why he needs to read books is that he has yet to experience the many [principles of the Way]. The sages have experienced the many [principles of the Way] and have written down [their experience] in books for people to read. In reading books today, our purpose is to see the many principles of the Way. Once we are able to comprehend [the principles], they will all turn out to be what we ourselves originally possess.[90]

By contrast, Lu Hsiang-shan was a monist for whom man's self consisted of mind, which he equated with Nature or *li*. He also rejected the distinction between the mind of man and the mind of the Tao and considered mind to be always one and indivisible. It is true that mind for Lu can and often does become corrupt and is thus in need of transformation. This transformation, however, was understood by Lu as the mind's self-transformation because, as noted before, mind as Nature or *li* is inherently self-rectifying. Therefore, when Lu advocated the total and experiential invlovment of one's self in what one reads, he was referring to mind as Nature or *li* and not to Nature or *li* as opposed to mind. This means that reading as a form of cultivation for the transformation of mind is and always remains for Lu the self-activity of one's self as mind. It does not ever require and cannot in fact have a point of reference beyond one's mind as the reading subject. For Lu, reading is not a passive performance in which the mind simply receives Nature from what it reads. Rather, reading is a dynamic activity of the mind which is constitutive of what it reads while it reads. For this reason, Lu was opposed to subjecting one's self as a "guest" (*k'o*) to the "external doctrines" as the "host" and insisted that one's self retain the initiative as the host.[91] The guest/host analogy suggests that, for Lu, there is interaction between the reader and the read in reading. It is, however, an interaction which takes place within the horizon of the reader who directs the activity of reading from his position as the host. Reading or understanding is, according to Lu, necessarily positional. Therefore, when Lu pronounced that "the Six Classics are my footnotes and I am a footnote to the Six Classics,"[92] he was not exactly proposing the view that "I" as the reading subject and the Classics as the object to be read were mutually explanatory with the "I" playing the alternate roles as the "host" to be "footnoted" by the Classics and as the "guest" to "footnote" the Classics. Rather, he was saying that "I" as the reading subject should assume the position as the "host" and read the Classics in the light of myself as "my footnotes" because "I" would not be able to understand the Classics and provide them with an explanatory "footnote" unless "I" positioned myself as the "host."

What is thus in dispute between Chu Hsi and Lu Hsiang-shan is not a question of who is for or against reading but a question of what transpires in the activity of reading. It arose as a point of contention between Chu and Lu because they each had a different conception of what should prevail as the proper epistemological relationship between the mind as the reading subject and what is read as the object. For Chu Hsi, who sees reading as a procedure which entails the appropriation by the mind as subject of Nature or *li* embodied in what is read as object, what Lu advocates as reading cannot but be dismissed as nonreading because it does not even distinguish the mind as subject from what is read as object. From Lu's point of view, reading cannot be other than the constitutive activity of the mind's self-apprehension because his thesis that "mind is Principle" requires him to deny the separability of subject and object as a duality. For Lu, as it was later for Wang, what is read or perceived does not have an existence independent of the mind as the reader or perceiver. Both Lu and Wang maintained a unitary view of the mind as subject and Principle as object and did not consider nonpositional understanding to be a possibility. In a statement which is reminiscent of Lu, Wang characterized the Six Classics as "a record of my mind" and suggested that "the reality of the Six Classics" be sought in the reader's "own mind." He said,

> The Classics are [an account of] of the constant Way. In terms of its locus in Heaven, the Way is called Mandate (*ming*). When it is bestowed on man, it is called Nature. As that with which a person is born, it is called mind. Mind, Nature, and Mandate are one . . . . With regard to the constant Way, that which speaks of it as the circulation of the waxing and waning of *yin* and *yang* is called the *Book of Changes*; that which speaks of it as the execution of laws, regulations, and affairs of government is called the *Book of*

History; that which speaks of it as the musical and lyrical expression of Nature and feelings is called the *Book of Odes*. . . . The Six Classics are nothing other than the constant Way of my mind. Therefore, the *Book of Changes* is a record of the waxing and waning of *yin* and *yang* of my mind; the *Book of History* is a record of the laws, regulations, and affairs of government of my mind; the *Book of Odes* is a record of the musical and lyrical expression of Nature and feelings of my mind. . . . In his relationship to the Six Classics, the superior man honors the *Book of Changes* by seeking the waxing and waning of *yin* and *yang* in his own mind and acting [according to this rhythm] constantly; he honors the *Book of History* by seeking the laws, regulations, and affairs of government in his own mind and practicing them constantly . . . . In their concern for posterity, the sages of the past wrote the Six Classics to uphold the ultimate standard of man (*jen-chi*). [In doing so, the sages] are like the ancestors of a wealthy family. [These ancestors] were afraid that the descendants might forget and lose the amassed property and treasure and become poor and destitute. As a result, they made a record of what the family owned and left it to the descendants so that the descendants would be able to keep and enjoy the amassed property and treasure generation after generation without the affliction of poverty. The Six Classics are thus a record of my mind; and the reality of the Six Classics lies in my mind . . . . Not knowing to seek the reality of the Six Classics in their mind, the scholars of the world look for it vainly in shadows and echoes and become entangled in the trivia of words and meanings . . . . They are like the descendants of the wealthy family, who, not attending to the keeping and enjoyment of the property and treasure actually amassed, gradually forgot and lost them and who would still point to the inventory record, saying clamorously, "Here is our amassed property and treasure."[93]

In their denial of Principle as an objective existence independent of the mind as subject, Lu and Wang resemble phenomenologically oriented philosophers of the modern West such as Martin Heidegger and Hans-Georg Gadamer, who also conceive of reality as perceived reality and of objects as intended objects and regard knowing or understanding as necessarily positional in nature. For such a conception of reality, Lu and Wang, as noted before, have often been characterized as "subjective/idealist." Strictly speaking, however, this characterization is no more applicable to Lu and Wang than to Heidegger and Gadamer, who reject the subject/object polarity and are critical of the notion of the objectivity of an object precisely because this notion is conceived on the condition of the human ego as the presentational subject and is incapable of allowing an object to disclose itself in the power of its own being. For, according to Heidegger and Gadamer, what prevails in the subject/object framework of much of European philosophy is a certain rationalist and "technological" mode of thinking which is exemplified by the Cartesian sense of certainty in the rationality of man as subject and the modern scientistic attempts to restructure the world for control or mastery, in which the human subject reigns supreme as the ultimate point of reference for what is known or seen; an object is such only insofar as it exists as that which the conscious subject presents to itself, i.e., as an object of the subject's consciousness. What is alleged to be the objectivity of an object, therefore, is nothing but an objectification established by human subjectivity. It operates as a conception in what Heidegger condemned as "subjectivism" through which man has become hopelessly entangled in the circle of his own projection. Far from being "subjectivist/idealist," Lu and Wang in traditional China and Heidegger and Gadamer in the modern West are all involved in an effort to go beyond the subject/object dichotomy so that reality would not be viewed as an acquired possession but as the "facticity" of the "lifeworld" to which the human subject belongs and which man as subject will allow to emerge in its lived concreteness through experiential participation.[94]

On the other hand, in their attempt to transcend the subject/object schema, Lu and Wang are also notably different from Heidegger and Gadamer. These differences are significant because, in a Heideggerian manner of speaking, they reveal the "placedness" of Lu and Wang as traditional Chinese Neo-Confucians and of Heidegger and Gadamer as modern European phenomenologists. For Heidegger and Gadamer, to see reality as perceived reality is not just to deny the possibility of nonpositional understanding. It is also to affirm understanding as interpretation which does not take place outside the interpreter's horizon of meaning but always in the context of his situatedness in a particular time and place. For this reason, both Heidegger and Gadamer conceive of understanding in hermeneutical terms, as an intrinsically problematical undertaking in which the interpreter can never fully transcend his finitude as a historically and linguistically determinate being to comprehend what he encounters as it really is in itself. Understanding as interpretation is thus necessarily circular, and the interpreter is forever enclosed in a hermeneutical circle which discloses what he interprets only to the extent that his being-in-the-world allows. This hermeneutical circle is different from the circle of "subjectivism" in that it is free from the rationalist and "technological" certainty in the rationality of man as subject and does not disguise objectification as objectivity. It recognizes circularity in understanding as a human limitation which, though unavoidable, is to be confronted and countered with a "wakeful responsiveness" so that man will be in a position to respect things for their intrinsic worth and to interact dialogically with them in their living autonomy and not to treat them as inert objects to be controlled or manipulated through science and technology. Insofar as the hermeneutical circle of Heidegger and Gadamer is a critique of the circle of "subjectivism" in European rationalism, it promises to displace the human ego from the privileged status as the focal point of reference and to deliver things from the domination of anthropocentrism for disclosure. In doing so, however, it also puts the full disclosure of things in themselves perennially beyond human reach. Understanding, according to Heidegger and Gadamer, is not only necessarily positional but can never be truly free of presupposition.[95]

There is much in the philosophy of Lu and Wang that can be applied as a critique of the kind of "subjectivism" that Heidegger and Gadamer find deplorable in European rationalist and "technological" thinking. Both Lu and Wang, as noted before, attempted to transcend the subject/object polarity and insisted on experiential participation as the basis of understanding. They were also keenly aware that human understanding was

highly problematical. Repeatedly, they warned against the dis-
guising of objectification as objectivity and condemned what in
their terms was the "self-centeredness" (*ssu*) of an egotistical man.
Lu, for instance, contrasted the "impartiality" (*kung*) of the Tao
with the "self-imposed self-centeredness" of a "self-limiting" (*tzu-
hsiao*) and "self-confining" (*tzu-hsia*) man[96] and said that if the
slightest amount of "self-centeredness" were allowed to "mix in"
with a person's "learning," this person would cease to be able to
"approximate" the Tao.[97] He also advocated "self-forgetfulness"
(*wang-chi*) as a value and said that the Principle should be "left
alone" without the interference of the self.[98] The ideal attitude,
according to Lu, to maintain toward the Principle entails the
religiosity of King Wen's "reverential watchfulness" (*hsiao-hsin i-
i*) toward the Lord-on-High. "This Principle," said Lu, "suffuses
the universe. How can it be fabricated by man?"[99] Similarly,
Wang considered "arrogance" (*ao*) to be "a great illness in a
man's life" and said that "all the good points of the ancient sages
consisted in being egoless (*wu-wo*)."[100] He also condemned "self-
centered willfulness" (*ssu-i*) as "selfish exercise in intelligence" and
contrasted it with the "learning of a superior man" who, being
"broad and impartial," was always able to "follow and respond to
things as they come."[101]

    However, for all their awareness of the problematical
nature of human understanding, Lu and Wang never conceived of
the idea of a hermeneutical circle. For, according to Lu and Wang,
mind, though likely to err, also has the innate ability to rectify
itself. Human understanding or perception is thus problematical,
but not intrinsically so. Man's "self-centeredness," which is
responsible for preventing things from full disclosure, is not
ontologically rooted in man's being and is instead a corruption of
man's originally luminous mind, which is inherently devoid of an
egotistical self and is in principle capable of self-decentering to
constitute things as they really are. Therefore, Lu said, "The Tao
suffuses Heaven and Earth. Man cannot enter the Tao because of
his self-centered ego. However, if a person would step back [from
himself] and become aware of this [self-centeredness], he will
naturally enter [the Tao]."[102] Likewise, Wang said, "There is only
the need to eliminate self-centered willfulness. What [need] is there

to worry further about not understanding the principles."[103] In this regard, Lu and Wang are radically different from Heidegger and Gadamer. As traditional Chinese Neo-Confucians, Lu and Wang did not have the egocentric rationalism of a Descartes to contend with. Instead, they were engaged in a dispute with Chu Hsi, who, in spite of his dualism of Nature and mind, was no less forceful than Lu and Wang in affirming the intrinsic oneness of man as subject with things as objects. He also believed as much as Lu and Wang did in the necessity of experiential participation as the principle for understanding. The issue thus confronting Lu and Wang ultimately in the transcendence of the subject/object polarity is not, as it is for Heidegger and Gadamer, to establish the continuity in being between man as subject and things as objects through experience as an epistemological principle. Rather, it is a question of articulating a monistic theory of man so that experience would be assured of an ontologically unitary foundation in man's being and be able to function as an existentially self-transcending activity to effect the Neo-Confucian mystical vision of man forming one body with Heaven, earth, and the myriad things.

In terms of the situation since the mid-Ming, the significance of the restructured Neo-Confucianism as monism of *ch'i* lies not only in the reconceptualization of *li* as the *li* of *ch'i* but, even more important, in the identification of mind with Nature or *li* and the concomitant denial of *li* as an existence independent of the mind. As noted before, the idea of *li* as the *li* of *ch'i* was not confined to the Lu-Wang school in the Ming. Lo Ch'in-shun regarded himself as a follower of the Ch'eng-Chu school, but he criticized Ch'eng I and Chu Hsi for dichotomizing *li* and *ch'i* and was an early advocate of *li* as the *li* of *ch'i*. Lo, it may be noted further, also rejected Chang Tsai's distinction between the ideal Nature of Heaven and Earth (*t'ien-ti chih-hsing*) and the indivildualized nature of physical endowment (*ch'i-chih chih-hsing*) and affirmed feelings and desires naturalistically.[104] Nevertheless, Lo insisted that mind be differentiated from Nature or *li* and that mind as the knowing subject refer beyond itself to *li* as the object of its knowing.[105] In this regard, Lo still remained in the mold of Ch'eng I and Chu Hsi and was justified in his claim to being an adherent of the Ch'eng-Chu school. Not surprisingly, Lo, though not dismissing the insight attained through Ch'an meditation as necessarily invalid, reiterated the Sung-style criticism of Buddhism as a doctine based on mind in contrast with Confucianism as a doctrine based on Nature.[106] He said,

> Illuminating the mind and seeing into Nature in Buddhism and realizing the mind and knowing Nature in our Confucianism seem similar but are actually different. For vacuous spirituality and intelligent awareness are the wonders of the mind whereas perfect subtlety and total unity are the reality of Nature. Buddhism generally has insight into the mind but lacks insight into Nature.[107]

In the mid-Ming, therefore, when the idea of *li* as the *li* of *ch'i* ceased to be a uniquely Lu-Wang articulation of a monistic universe, the epistemological and ontological equation of mind with Nature continued as an issue to divide the Lu-Wang school from the Ch'eng-Chu school. It is noteworthy that the debate between Lo Ch'in-shun and Wang Yang-ming in the mid-Ming concerned not the question of *li* as the *li* of *ch'i* but the question of Nature as the Nature of the mind.[108]

In thus viewing *li* monistically as the *li* of *ch'i* but maintaining the dualistic distinction between mind and Nature, Lo Ch'in-shun was criticized by Huang Tsung-hsi as "self-contradictory" (*tzu-hsiang mao-tun*).[109] Huang said,

> That which is *ch'i* in Heaven is mind in man. That which is *li* in Heaven is Nature in man. What is true of *li* and *ch'i* is also true of mind and Nature. There is absolutely no difference [between *li* and *ch'i* on the one hand and mind and Nature on the other]. When man is born on receiving *ch'i* from Heaven, he has only one mind. However, through the alternation of activity and tranquillity, [the feelings of] pleasure, anger, sorrow, and joy follow one another in endless succession. [Therefore,] when a man ought to be compassionate, he is naturally compassionate; when he ought to have a sense of shame and dislike, he naturally has a sense of shame and

dislike; when he ought to be reverential, he is naturally reverential; and when he ought to have a sense of right and wrong, he naturally has a sense of right and wrong. What is called Nature is that which remains orderly and cannot be obscured regardless of the complexity and confusion [of a situation]. It is not a separate entity that exists prior to the mind and is attached to the mind. But Master [Lo] is of the view that Heavenly Nature is established in correctness when life is first engendered whereas luminous consciousness arises after one is born. He regards luminous consciousness as mind and not as Nature . . . . Clearly, he took Nature to be prior [to the mind] and considered it to be the master of the mind. [This doctrine of mind and Nature] is no different from the theory that *li* is capable of generating *ch'i*. Dosen't it seriously contravene the Master's discourse on *li* and *ch'i*? How could it be that *li* and *ch'i* are *li* and *ch'i* whereas mind and Nature are mind and Nature with the result that these two [sets of categories] divide man from Heaven and render the mutual penetration [of man and Heaven] impossible?[110]

Huang's criticism is not incontrovertible. For, as Irene Bloom has pointed out, Lo's Nature was not "a 'thing' or an 'entity' which gave rise to the mind" but the "developmental tendency in all living beings." As such, its distinction from mind as consciousness was required by Lo's epistemological theory that Nature, though to be apprehended as a whole in its aspect of unity, had to be enacted in its particularity as the "creative potential" by individuals according to their different capacities.[111] Nevertheless, Huang made a point which, though not strictly fair to Lo, is nonetheless revealing of the difference between Lo and Huang as *ch'i*-monists. Huang who regarded *li/ch'i* and Nature/ mind as paired correlates was a monist of the Lu-Wang persuasion and advocated a form of monism of *ch'i* which entailed the view of both *li* as the *li* of *ch'i* and Nature as the Nature of mind. Therefore, when Huang, as noted before, stated that "mind has no substance in and of itself" and that "wherever the effort extends is its substance," he was not saying that mind was devoid of "substance" as Nature or *li*. Rather, he was suggesting that Nature or *li* as the "substance" of the mind be understood functionally and dynamically as the regularity of the mind's activity of self-regulation.

Huang's type of monism of *ch'i* exemplifies a widespread formation which prevailed not only in Chiao Hung in the late Ming but also in Tai Chen and Chang Hsüeh-ch'eng in the Ch'ing. Tai, as noted before, also denied *li* to be an external endowment "contained in the mind" and maintained a monistic outlook which affirmed the oneness of *li* and *ch'i* and of Nature and mind. Chang Hsüeh-ch'eng, on the other hand, did not engage in a sustained discourse on the metaphysics of *li* and *ch'i* or the ontology of Nature and mind. But, as Nivison has noted, his "celebrated identification of the Classics as 'history' implies a far-reaching modification of the basis of Ch'eng-Chu metaphysics, the dualism of the *tao* and 'matter,' of principles and things."[112] It is also noteworthy that Chang, in a series of three essays on "Comprehensiveness and Simplicity" (*po-yüeh*), defended Wang Yang-ming's doctrine of *liang-chih* as a "legacy from Mencius" and considered his own conception of learning to be a continuation of the "heritage of Mr. Wang's *liang-chih*."[113] To be sure, Chang in these three essays was primarily concerned with the problem of learning and did not envision *liang-chih* to be more than an epistemological category, as Wang did. Nevertheless, the theory of learning that he conceived of through *liang-chih* as an epistemological category conforms to Wang's idea of learning in discursive regularity. Therefore, for Chang as it was for Wang (or, for that matter, for Lu Hsiang-shun), learning is to be undertaken for the sake of "self-establishment" (*tzu-li*), which he understood in monistic terms as the self-realization of an individual's "personal disposition" (*hsing-ch'ing*) and not in dualistic terms as the mind's internalization of the external Nature or *li*. For this reason, Chang was opposed to the following of a definite "norm" (*kuei-chü*). The student, according to Chang, should "make the effort" on what "he himself perceives to be close to his endowment." He need not be "ashamed" of not being able to do what others are capable of doing, but only be "concerned about not being able to become a specialist in his own right" (*huan-chi pu-neng tzu-ch'eng-chia erh*).[114] In a statement which is reminiscent of a passage in which Wang Yang-ming discussed sagehood as a qualitative individual achievement in terms of the purity of gold as an analogy,[115] Chang said,

> In learning, people today cannot be the same as the ancients. It is not because they do not measure up to the ancients in capacity. Rather, circumstances have made them so .... Nevertheless, the cardinal meaning of the Six Classics is as bright as the sun and the stars and what happens in a hundred generations in the future can be inferred from the gain and loss of the Three Dynasties. Those who are lofty and luminous are sharp about what they seek because they are broad but unconcerned with detail, whereas those who are deep and contemplative take one step at a time and reach their destination gradually. Everyone has that which is close to his endowment and which he is able to accomplish. Self-attainment is thus what everyone is capable of. How can one hold on to a fixed formula and impose it on others?[116]

It is true that Chiao Hung, Tai Chen, and Chang Hsüeh-ch'eng differed considerably in attitude toward Neo-Confucianism in general and its Lu-Wang persuasion in particular. While Chiao Hung was an avowed partisan of the Lu-Wang school, Chang Hsüeh-ch'eng favored the coexistence of both Ch'eng-Chu and Lu-Wang even though his personal sympathy rested largely with Lu-Wang. He, as noted before, advocated the acceptance of both Chu Hsi and Lu Hsiang-shan in their difference which he regarded as a reflection of the uniqueness of what they each had realized as their "singular attainment." Significantly, however, his reason for accommodating both Chu and Lu implies a characteristically Lu-Wang principle according to which knowing is necessarily positional knowing. He, as noted before, considered "paths of learning" to be inevitably divergent because "the Tao is public, but the study of it is private."

In the case of Tai Chen, it is well known that he was critical of both Ch'eng-Chu and Lu-Wang and rejected them both as Buddhistic and Taoistic. However, he did not lump Ch'eng-Chu and Lu-Wang together without differentiation. The Ch'eng brothers and Chu Hsi, according to Tai, talked about *li* in terms of "what the Buddhists and Taoists referred to" as the "True Emptiness" and the "True Lord" (*chen-tsai*). In doing so, they "mixed Buddhist [and Taoist] doctrines in with Confucianism" with the result that they "could not but dichotomize *li* and *ch'i* as a duality and hold the corporeal *ch'i* responsible" as a source of evil. Like the Buddhists and Taoists for whom the "True Emptiness" or "True Lord" was that which was "attached" to the "corporeal body," the Ch'eng brothers and Chu Hsi postulated *li* "in addition to" *ch'i* as a "thing" to be "attached" to *ch'i*. Lu Hsiang-shan and Wang Yang-ming also mixed the textualities of Buddhism, Taoism, and Confucianism. But they did so in an entirely different manner. Instead of talking about *li* in terms of the Buddhist and Taoist concepts of "True Emptiness" and "True Lord," Lu and Wang "substantialized them with *li*" (*i-li shih-chih*) with the result that the "True Emptiness" of the Buddhists and the "True Lord" of the Taoists came to be possessed of "sagely wisdom, humanity, and righteousness." Rather than "mixing Buddhist [and Taoist] doctrines in with Confucianism," Lu and Wang, according to Tai, "interjected Confucianism into Buddhism [and Taoism]" (*yüan-ju i-ju yü-shih*).[117]

The differentiated attack that Tai Chen made on Ch'eng-Chu and Lu-Wang is noteworthy for both what it said about Ch'eng-Chu and what it did not say about Lu-Wang. It charged Ch'eng-Chu with dualism, which was pointedly missing as an accusation against Lu-Wang. Obviously, dualism of the Ch'eng-Chu kind was not what Tai found problematical about Lu and Wang, who were in fact monistic as Tai himself was. In this regard, Tai was consistent. He repeatedly criticized the Ch'eng brothers and Chu Hsi for bifurcating *li* from *ch'i*, Nature from mind, and the metaphysical from the physical[118] but did not apply the same criticisms to Lu and Wang. There was, of course, one criticism which Tai directed against both Ch'eng-Chu and Lu-Wang. This criticism concerned the idea of "recovering the original Nature" (*fu-ch'i-ch'u*), which both Ch'eng-Chu and Lu-Wang accepted as an accurate description of what transpired in learning but which Tai rejected as Buddhistic and Taoistic because of its similarity to what Tai perceived to be the Buddhist and Taoist conceptualization of "True Emptiness" and "True

Lord" as "total self-sufficiency" (*wan-ch'üan tzu-tsu*). In place of
the idea of "recovering the original Nature," Tai proposed the
notion of "broadening" (*k'uo-ch'ung*) which would require learning to be understood as a process of growth sustained by "inquiry
and study" (*wen-hsüeh*). He compared "man's virtuous Nature"
to the physical body and said, "The physical body is small in the
beginning, but grows to be big in the end. Virtuous Nature is dull
and obscure in the beginning, but becomes sagely wisdom in the
end. The growth of the physical body depends on the nurturing of
food and drink. It is a matter of increase over a long period of time
and not a matter of recovering the original Nature. [From this,] it
is clear that virtuous Nature advances toward sagely wisdom by
depending on inquiry and study and not as a result of recovering
the original Nature."[119]

On this issue, Tai is indeed different from both Ch'eng-
Chu and Lu-Wang. There is, however, a difference between Tai's
difference from Ch'eng-Chu and his difference from Lu-Wang on
"recovering the original Nature" because the "original Nature" to
be "recovered" in "recovering the original Nature" is not the same
in Ch'eng-Chu as in Lu-Wang. Therefore, when Tai rejected
"recovering the original Nature" in Ch'eng-Chu, he was rejecting
both the idea of return or restoration implied in "recovering" and
Ch'eng-Chu's dualistic conception of the "original Nature" as the
Nature opposed to mind. By contrast, when Tai rejected "recovering the original Nature" in Lu-Wang, he was only rejecting
the restorative view of learning as "recovering," not Lu-Wang's
monistic identification of the "original Nature" as the Nature of
mind. Tai's Nature or *li*, as Cheng Chung-ying has observed, is
not only the "pattern of things" but also the "discerning and
guiding ability of the mind for achieving comprehensiveness in
oneself, society and the universe as a whole."[120] For Tai, knowing,
though not restorative, is still as it is for Lu and Wang the
constitutive activity of the mind's self-transformation. The mind
needs be "nurtured" through "inquiry and study" in order to
achieve growth. But this growth is the mind's self-growth, the
"nurturing" of which does not entail the mind's appropriation of
that which is extrinsic to itself. For this reason, Tai said,

"Concerning human relationships and daily activity, the knowing of man's mind, wherever it happens to be, knows compassion, shame, reverence, and yielding and the distinction between right and wrong. Its incipient orderliness can be observed. This is what is called the goodness of Nature. When what it knows as compassion is broadened, humanity is fully realized. . . . This being the case, what is called compassion or humanity is not something which lies outside the mind's knowing as if it were an additional thing stored in the mind."[121]

The difference between Tai's view of learning as "broadening" and Lu-Wang's view of learning as "recovering the original Nature" is by no means trivial; one is developmental in orientation while the other is restorative. But in so far as both views are predicated on the same epistemological relationship between the knower and the known and are deployed in the same discursive space which is constituted by the monistic identification of both *li* as the *li* of *ch'i* and Nature as the Nature of mind, their difference is intrasystemic and not intersystemic. As such, Tai's difference from Lu and Wang on "recovering the original Nature" is to be appreciated not as a sign of Tai's radical departure from Lu and Wang but for what it reveals of the dynamic complexities of the Lu-Wang formation as a historical dispersion which prevailed in the mid-Ming but persisted into the early Ch'ing and which unified an otherwise diverse group of thinkers, including Chiao Hung, Tai Chen, and Chang Hsüeh-ch'eng. Chiao, Tai, and Chang certainly had their differences, not only in attitude toward Sung and Ming Neo-Confucianism but in other matters as well. Chang fought a lifelong battle with Tai over the value of philological scholarship, while Tai, though he did not actually do so, would no doubt have faulted Chiao as he did Lu and Wang for mixing the textualities of Buddhism, Taoism, and Confucianism and for holding a restorative view of learning. Nevertheless, different as they were as individuals, they all participated in a monistic discursive practice, the regularities of which as a Lu-Wang heritage informed their shared outlook as monists and actually governed their differences as the rules of their differentiation. For this reason, I have argued in this book for the placing in the Lu-Wang tradition of the obvious Chiao Hung and the not so obvious Tai Chen and Chang Hsüeh-ch'eng. To use the chess game as a metaphor, the tension between Chiao Hung as a "wild Ch'anist" and Tai Chen as a spokesman for "evidential research" and between Tai Chen as a reputed philological "fox" and Chang Hsüeh-ch'eng as a philosophical "hedgehog"[122] is like the rivalry in a chess game in which the two contenders play against one another, but nonetheless play the same game.

Works Written, Compiled, or Edited by and Attributed to Chiao Hung

1. *Chang Yü-hu chi* (Collected Works of Chang Yü-hu [Chang Hsiao-hsiang, 1132–1169]) in eight *chüan* plus one *chüan* of "Appendix" (*fu-lu*). It was originally published in the Sung with two prefaces dated 1201. Chiao Hung edited it for republication in the Ming. A rare copy printed in 1644 is preserved in the National Central Library in Taipei.

2. *Ch'i-yen lü-hsi* (An Anthology of Finely Crafted Seven-Character Regulated Poetry) in one *chüan*. It was compiled by Chiao Hung. A copy of the Wan-li edition is preserved in the Palace Museum in Taipei.

3. *Chiao Jo-hou wen-ta* (Chiao Jo-hou's [Chiao Hung's] Dialogue) in one *chüan*. The *Imperial Catalogue* took notice of this work and condemned it as "wild and reckless" because it attacked Mencius and exalted Mo Ti and Yang Chu.[1] I have not been able to locate a copy of this work, which may no longer be extant.

4. *Chiao-shih lei-hsüan man-chin-t'ai* (Extraordinary Sayings Selected and Classified by Chiao Hung) in four *chüan*. The term *man-chin-t'ai* in the title is a name for an extraordinary kind of "moss" (*t'ai*) which, when thrown into water, "spreads like a creeper plant" (*man*) and "glitters like gold" (*chin*).[2] The Naikaku Bunko in Tokyo holds a copy of this work in the Wan-li edition, from which the Far Eastern Library at the University of Chicago has made a xerox copy.

5. *Chiao-shih lei-lin* (A Collection of Chiao Hung's Classified Reading Notes) in eight *chüan*. It consists of Chiao Hung's reading notes from 1580 to 1582. It was first published in the Wan-li period with Chiao Hung's postface dated 1585 and was later incorporated into the *Yüeh-ya t'ang ts'ung-shu*, from which the Commercial Press in Shanghai has made a reproduction as nos. 189–193 of the first series of the *Ts'ung-shu chi-ch'eng* (1936). Copies of the Wan-li edition are preserved in the National Central Library, National Taiwan University, and Academia Sinica in Taiwan, the Gest Collection at Princeton University, and the Naikaku Bunko and the Seikadō Bunko in Tokyo.

6. *Chiao-shih pi-ch'eng* (Chiao Hung's Notebook) in six *chüan* plus eight *chüan* of "Continuation" (*hsü-chi*). It consists of Chiao Hung's notes on a variety of subjects ranging from such technial matters as the end-rhymes in ancient poetry and the attempts of the Han court to transplant lichee nuts from Cochin-China to philosophically intricate issues regarding mind, Nature, and knowledge. It was published twice in the Wan-li period, first in parts in 1580 and then in its entirety in 1606.[3] The work in its entirety has also been incorporated into the *Chin-ling ts'ung-shu* and the *Yüeh-ya t'ang ts'ung-shu*. The *Yüeh-ya t'ang ts'ung-shu* edition was reproduced by the Commercial Press in Shanghai in 1935 as nos. 2924–2927 of the first series of the *Ts'ung-shu chi-ch'eng*, and by the Commercial Press in Taipei in 1971 as Special no. 125 of the *Jen-jen wen-k'u* series. Copies of the 1606 edition are preserved in the Naikaku Bunko, the Seikadō Bunko, and the Sonkeikaku Bunko in Tokyo and the Gest Collection at Princeton University. There is also a Japanese edition of this work (1649), a copy of which is preserved in the Naikaku Bunko.

7. *Chih-shen lu* (A Record of Devotion) in one *chüan*. It is a personal account of the overthrow of Emperor Chien-wen as experienced by Shih Chung-pin (1366–1427), who was a partisan of Emperor Chien-wen. The work had apparently been out of print and circulation for many years when Chiao Hung found a copy of it in 1586 in a Taoist temple. Concerned as he was about the paucity of material for Emperor Chien-wen's period, Chiao Hung edited the work and had it republished.[4] Chiao Hung's preface was dated 1619.

8. *Chih-t'an* (Extraneous Talk) in three *chüan*. It was published as an independent work in the Wan-li period in Ch'en Chi-ju's (1558–1639) *Pao-yen t'ang pi-chi*. The *Imperial Catalogue* also took notice of it as a separate publication.[5] However, the *Yüeh-ya t'ang ts'ung-shu* and the *Chin-ling ts'ung-shu* have included it in the *hsü-chi* of the *Chiao-*

shih pi-ch'eng. It is both an analysis of a number of concepts in Buddhism, Confucianism and Taoism and a discourse on the oneness of the Three Teachings. A copy of the Wan-li edition is preserved in the National Central Library in Taipei.

9. *Chin-hsüeh chih* (A Record of the Prefectural School in the Southern Capital) in eight *chüan* which Chiao Hung coauthored with some of the students at the Prefectural School. It was first published in the Wan-li period with Chiao Hung's preface dated 1603. A copy of the original Wan-li edition is preserved in the National Central Library in Taipei and has been reproduced by the Kuo-feng ch'u-pan she in Taipei (1965).

10. *Chuang-tzu i* (A Wing to the *Chuang Tzu*) in eight *chüan* plus two additional *chüan* as "Appendix" (*fu-lu*) and "Corrections" (*ch'üeh-wu*). It was compiled by Chiao Hung from the commentaries of forty-nine scholars, including himself, and was first published in the Wan-li period with Chiao Hung's preface dated 1588. It has been incorporated into the *Hsü tao-tsang* and the *Chin-ling ts'ung-shu.* It received a somewhat negative review from the *Imperial Catalogue,*[6] but was printed into the Ssu-ku Manuscript Library. Copies of the Wan-li edition are preserved in the National Central Library in Taipei, the Gest Collection at Princeton University, and the Naikaku Bunko. The Naikaku Bunko also has a copy of a Japanese edition published in 1653 in eleven *chüan.* This work was also printed together with Chiao Hung's *Lao-tzu i* (see below) in the Wan-li period as a combined publication entitled *Lao-Chuang i,* consisting of the *Lao-tzu i* in three *chüan* and the *Chuang-tzu i* in eight *chüan.* A copy of the *Lao-Chuang i* in the Wan-li edition is preserved in the Sonkeikaku Bunko.

11. *Chuang-yüan ts'e* (The Palace Examination Papers of the *Chuang-yüan*). It is a collection of palace examination papers by *chuang-yüan* since 1478. The date of its first publication and the number of *chüan* in its original form are uncertain. There is an eight-*chüan* edition published in the K'ang-hsi period (1661–1722) with an undated preface by Wu Tao-nan, who was the *pang-yen* ("second palace graduate") of 1589. This eight-*chüan* edition contains the *chuang-yüan* papers of the early Ch'ing dynasty up to the year 1667. There is also a late Ming edition in seven *chüan,* a copy of which is preserved in the National Central Library in Taipei. This seven-*chüan* edition of the late Ming, however, is already an expansion of Chiao Hung's original version.

12. *Chung-yüan wen-hsien* (Literary Documents of the Central Domain) in twenty-four *chüan*. It was first published in the Wan-li period. The prefaces by Chiao Hung and T'ao Wang-ling were not dated. It consists of excerpts from the Classics and other works in history, philosophy, and literature. According to the *Imperial Catalogue*, this work was probably compiled as a manual for the civil service examination students, since Chiao Hung was alleged to have said in the preface that he had excluded from this work whatever was not relevant to the examinations. The *Imperial Catalogue* condemned it for its exclusive concern with the examinations and also for the textual alterations which occurred in its selections from the Classics. On the other hand, however, the *Imperial Catalogue* suspected that the work was actually put together by some book dealer and was only attributed to Chiao Hung because Chiao Hung, though daring and unorthodox, was nevertheless "erudite" and would not have been so "perverse" as to have altered the texts of the Classics.[7] I am inclined to concur with the *Imperial Catalogue* on this issue of authorship because Chiao Hung, though not necessarily opposed to the examination system, would most likely find the exclusive examination orientation of this work deplorable. As noted in the text, study for Chiao Hung was pursued in order to know one's Nature, not for the sake of advancing a career. Moreover, notwithstanding his involvement in the reinterpretation of the Classics, altering the texts would be contrary to his stance as a pioneer of "evidential research." The National Central Library in Taipei has a fragment (seven *chüan*) of this work in the Wan-li edition, a complete set of which is preserved in the Gest Collection at Princeton University.

13. *Erh-shih-chiu tzu p'in-hui shih-p'ing* (An Annotated Anthology of Twenty-Nine Philosophers) in twenty *chüan* which Chiao Hung coedited with Weng Cheng-ch'un (*chuang-yüan* of 1592) and Chu Chih-fan (*chuang-yüan* of 1595). In addition to the eighteen philosophers in the *Hsin-ch'i erh T'ai-shih hui-hsüan chu-shih chiu-tzu ch'üan-shu p'ing-lin* (see below), this anthology incorporates eleven other philosophers, including Wei-liao Tzu, Mo Tzu, Yen Tzu, Yin-wen Tzu, Kuei-ku Tzu, and Sun-wu Tzu. It was first published in the Wan-li period with a preface by Li T'ing-chi (*chin-shih* of 1583) dated 1616. Copies of this work in the Wan-li edition are preserved in the National Central Library in Taipei, the Naikaku Bunko, the Son-keikaku Bunko, and the Gest Collection at Princeton University.

14. *Fa-hua ching ching-chieh p'ing-lin* (A Collection of Critical Com-

mentaries on the Essentials of the *Lotus Sūtra*) in two *chüan*. The date of its original publication is not certain. It has been incorporated into the *Dai Nihon zoku zōkyō*.

15. *Hsi-ch'ao ming-ch'eng shih-lu* (A Veritable Record of the Renowned Officials of the Glorious [Ming] Dynasty) in twenty-seven *chüan*. I have not been able to locate a copy of this work. According to the *Imperial Catalogue*, however, it is a set of biographies written with the aim of supplementing the *Ming shih-lu*, which departed from the practice of the *Sung shih-lu* by not giving a detailed biographical account when the death of an official was reported. In writing this work, Chiao Hung made use of private works of the "unofficial" kind and thereby preserved a host of information which is valuable for checking the official accounts. He was also said to be fair and detached in treating the officials who were involved in the Ching-nan Incident (i.e., Yung-lo's overthrow of Chien-wen).[8]

16. *Hsin-ch'i erh T'ai-shih hui-hsüan chu-shih chiu-tzu ch'üan-shu p'ing-lin* (A Newly Published Anthology of the Complete Works of Nine Philosophers with Critical Commentaries Compiled by Two Grand Historians). This work which Chiao Hung coedited with Weng Cheng-ch'un is divided into two parts: the "Original Collection" (*cheng-chi*) in fourteen *chüan* and the "Continuation" (*hsü-chi*) in ten *chüan*. The "Original Collection" consists of the texts of nine philosophers, including Lao Tzu, Chuang Tzu, Huai-nan Tzu, Hsün Tzu, Han-fei Tzu, and Wen-chung Tzu. The "Continuation" also consists of the texts of nine philosophers, including Ho-kuan Tzu, Pao-p'u Tzu, Kuan Tzu, and Kuan-yin Tzu. A copy of the Wan-li edition is preserved in the Gest Collection at Princeton University.

17. *Hsin-k'an Chiao T'ai-shih hsü-hsüan pai-chia p'ing-lin Ming-wen chu-chi* (Continuation of a Newly Published Treasury of Ming Dynasty Essays with Critical Commentaries Compiled by the Grand Historian Chiao Hung) in ten *chüan*. A copy of the Wan-li edition is preserved in the Sonkeikaku Bunko.

18. *Hsin-k'an Chiao T'ai-shih hui-hsüan pai-chia p'ing-lin Ming-wen chu-chi* (A Newly Published Treasury of Ming Dynasty Essays with Critical Commentaries Compiled by the Grand Historian Chiao Hung) in ten *chüan*. A copy of the Wan-li edition is preserved at National Normal University in Taipei.

19. *Hsin-chien Chiao T'ai-shih hui-hsüan pai-chia p'ing-lin ming-wen chu-chi* (A Newly Published Treasury of Famous Essays with Critical Commentaries Compiled by the Grand Historian Chiao Hung) in four

chüan. A copy of the Wan-li edition is preserved in the Gest Collection at Princeton University.

20. *Huang-Ming jen-wu k'ao* (An Inquiry into the Dignitaries of the Ming Empire). I have not been able to locate a copy of the original edition and have instead used Shu Ch'eng-hsi's reprint, which has six *chüan* plus one "opening *chüan*" (*shou-chüan*) with two prefaces dated 1594 and 1595, respectively. The "opening *chüan*" consists of treatises by a certain Chang Fu on the Yellow River, the "Southern Dwarfs" (*nan-wo*), and the "Northern Barbarians" (*pei-lu*). The remaining six *chüan* cover the Ming dynasty from the beginning to the reign of Emperor Mu-tsung (1567–1573). Original copies of Shu Ch'eng-hsi's reprint are preserved in the National Central Library in Taipei, the East Asian Library at Columbia University, and the Naikaku Bunko.

21. *I-ch'üan* (An Aid to the *Book of Changes*) in six *chüan* plus one *chüan* of "Appended Discussions" (*fu-lun*). It was first published in the Wan-li period with Chiao Hung's preface dated 1612. The Naikaku Bunko holds a copy of this work in the rare Ming edition, from which the Far Eastern Library at the Univiersity of Chicago has made a xerox copy.

22. *Kuo-ch'ao hsien-cheng-lu* (A Record of Worthies of the Reigning [Ming] Dynasty) in one hundred and twenty *chüan*. It was first published in the Wan-li period with prefaces by Huang Ju-heng (1558–1626) and Ku Ch'i-yüan (1565–1628) dated 1616. Copies of the original Wan-li edition are preserved in the National Central Library in Taipei, the Naikaku Bunko, the Library of Congress, and the East Asian Library at Columbia University. A facsimile reproduction of the original Wan-li edition has been made by T'ai-wan hsüeh-sheng shu-chü in Taipei as no. 6 of Wu Hsiang-hsiang, ed., *Chung-kuo shih-hsüeh ts'ung-shu* (1965).

23. *Kuo-shih ching-chi chih* (Bibliographical Treatise of the [Ming] State History) in five *chüan* plus one supplementary *chüan* of "Corrections" (*chiu-miu*). It was published twice in the Wan-li period: the original Wan-li edition and the edition collated and published by Hsü Hsiang-yün's Man-shan kuan in Ch'ien-t'ang. A copy of each is preserved in the National Central Library in Taipei. The work has also been printed into the *Yüeh-ya t'ang ts'ung-shu*, from which the Commercial Press in Shanghai has made a reprint in four volumes as nos. 25–28 of the first series of the *Ts'ung-shu chi-ch'eng* (1939). The *Yüeh-ya t'ang ts'ung-shu* edition has also been reproduced by the Kuang-wen shu-chü in Taipei (1972). The Wan-li edition by Hsü Hsiang-yün's Man-

shan kuan is the basis of a Japanese edition which was printed with Japanese punctuation in Kyoto by Noda Shōuemon. The publication date of the Japanese edition is uncertain. Copies of it, however, are preserved in the Naikaku Bunko and the East Asian Collection of the Hoover Institution at Stanford University.

24. *Lao-tzu i* (A Wing to the *Lao Tzu*) which Chiao Hung compiled from the commentaries of sixty-five scholars, including himself. It was copied into the Ssu-k'u Manuscript Library, and the *Imperial Catalogue* gave it a very favorable review, saying that Chiao Hung, though often misrepresenting Confucianism, nevertheless had original insights into Buddhism and Taoism.[9] Several editions of this work now exist:

(a) The Wan-li edition collated and published by Wang Yüan-chen in two *chüan* plus one *chüan* of "Appendix" (*fu-lu*) with Wang's preface dated 1587. Copies of it are preserved in the Palace Museum and Tung-hai University in Taiwan, the Naikaku Bunko, and the Gest Collection at Princeton University. It has been reproduced by the I-wen yin-shu kuan in Taipei (1965) as no. 77 of the first series of Yen Ling-feng, ed., *Wu-ch'iu-pei chai Lao-tzu chi-ch'eng*. This 1965 reproduction does not have Chiao Hung's preface, but contains not only the *fu-lu* but also the *k'ao-i* ("Examination of Textual Variations"), which noted the differences in wording in more than ten editions of the *Lao Tzu* and which Chiao Hung derived from Hsüeh Chün-ts'ai's *Lao-tzu chi-chieh*.

(b) The Ssu-k'u Manuscript Library edition in two *chüan* plus one *chüan* of *k'ao-i*.

(c) A six-*chüan* edition in the *Hsü tao-tsang*.

(d) An 1895 Nanking edition by the Chin-ling k'o-ching ch'u in eight *chüan* including both the *fu-lu* and the *k'ao-i*. It has been reproduced by the Kuang-wen shu-chü in Taipei (1962).

(e) The *Chin-ling ts'ung-shu* edition of 1916 in eight *chüan* including both the *fu-lu* and the *k'ao-i*.

(f) A Japanese edition in four *chüan* published in Kyoto by Kojima Ichirōuemon (1653), which has been reproduced in Taipei by the I-wen yin-shu kuan (1965) as no. 78 of the first series of Yen Ling-feng, ed., *Wu-ch'iu-pei chai Lao-tzu chi-ch'eng*. This 1965 reproduction is complete with the prefaces by both Chiao Hung and Wang Yüan-chen but does not have the *fu-lu* or the *k'ao-i*.

25. *Leng-chia ching ching-chieh p'ing-lin* (A Collection of Critical Commentaries on the Essentials of the *Lankāvatāra Sūtra*) in one

chüan. The date of its original publication is uncertain. It has been incorporated into the *Dai Nihon zoku zōkyō*.

26. *Leng-yen ching ching-chieh p'ing-lin* (A Collection of Critical Commentaries on the Essentials of the *Śūraṅgama Sūtra*) in three *chüan*. The date of its original publication is uncertain. It has been incorporated into the *Dai Nihon zoku zōkyō*.

27. *Liang-Han ts'ui-pao p'ing-lin* (An Anthology of Treasured Selections from the Two Han Histories with Collected Critical Commentaries) in three *chüan*. It was compiled by Chiao Hung in collaboration with Li T'ing-chi and Li Kuang-chin. The first two *chüan* consist of selections from the *Han Shu* and the third *chüan* of selections from the *Hou-Han Shu*. A copy of the Wan-li edition is preserved in the National Central Library in Taipei.

28. *Liang-Su ching-chieh* (The Two Su Brothers' Commentaries on the Classics) in sixty-four *chüan*. It consists of Su Shih's commentaries on the *Book of Changes* and the *Book of History* and Su Ch'e's commentaries on the *Book of Odes*, the *Spring and Autumn Annals*, the *Analects*, the *Mencius*, and the *Lao Tzu*. It was first published in the Wan-li period. Copies of the Wan-li edition are preserved in the National Central Library in Taipei and the Seikadō Bunko.

29. *Sheng-an wai-chi* (The Outer Collection of Yang Sheng-an [Yang Shen]) in one hundred *chüan*, which Chiao Hung compiled in cooperation with Yeh Tsun and Wang Ssu-ching. It incorporates thirty-eight works by Yang Shen on the Classics, history, philology, phonology, geography, calligraphy, painting, foods and utensils, etc. It was first published in the Wan-li period with a preface by Ku Ch'i-yüan dated 1616 and a postface by Chiao Hung dated 1617. Copies of the Wan-li edition are preserved in the National Central Library in Taipei, the Naikaku Bunko, and the Gest Collection at Princeton University.

30. *Shih-Han ho-ch'ao* (Excerpts from the *Shih Chi* and the *Han Shu*) in ten *chüan*. It consists primarily of selections from the biographies of the *Shih Chi* and the *Han Shu*, but also certains a number of excerpts from the various treatises of these two works on economics, water works, the "barbarians," etc. It was printed in the Wan-li period with Chiao Hung's preface dated 1619. A copy of the Wan-li edition is preserved in the Far Eastern Library at the University of Chicago.

31. *Su-shu k'an-wu* (Common Mistakes in Printed Characters) in twelve *chüan*. The *Imperial Catalogue* spoke highly of it as a work which is thorough and comprehensive without, however, falling into the

trivialities of technical etymology.[10] It was printed into the Ssu-k'u Manuscript Library, from which the Commercial Press in Shanghai has made a photolithographic reprint (1935). Chiao Hung's preface was dated 1610.

32. *Tan-yüan chi* (Collected Works of Chiao Tan-yüan [Chiao Hung]) in forty-nine *chüan*. It was first published in the Wan-li period with a preface by Keng Ting-li dated 1606. Copies of the Wan-li edition are preserved in the National Central Library in Taipei, the Naikaku Bunko, and the Sonkeikaku Bunko. It has been printed into the *Chin-ling ts'ung-shu*.

33. *Tan-yüan hsü-chi* (Continuation of the Collected Works of Chiao Tan-yüan) in twenty-seven *chüan*. It was first published in the Wan-li period with a preface by Hsü Kuang-ch'i (1562–1633) dated 1611. Copies of the Wan-li edition are preserved in the Naikaku Bunko and the Sonkeikaku Bunko. It has been printed into the *Chin-ling ts'ung-shu*.

34. *Tung-po chih-lin* (A Collection of Su Tung-po's Jottings) in five *chüan* with a critical commentary by Chiao Hung. A copy of the rare Ming edition is preserved in the National Central Library in Taipei.

35. *Tz'u-lin li-kuan piao* (A Chronological Table of Hanlin Officials) in three *chüan*. It is listed in the Bibliographical Treatise of the *Ming Shih*. I have not been able to locate a copy of this work, which may no longer be extant.

36. *Wu-yen lü-hsi* (An Anthology of Finely Crafted Five-Character Regulated Poetry) in one *chüan*. It was compiled by Chiao Hung. A copy of the Wan-li edition is preserved in the Palace Museum in Taiwan.

37. *Yang-cheng t'u-chieh* (An Illustrated Thesaurus of Morally Edifying Sayings and Deeds). This work was not divided into *chüan* when it was first published in the Wan-li period. It was, however, reorganized into three *chüan* when it was republished by Ts'ao Pin in 1669. Copies of the Wan-li edition are preserved in the National Central Library in Taipei and in the Naikaku Bunko.

38. *Yin-fu ching chieh* (An Explanation of the *Yin-fu ching*) in one *chüan*. It was first published in the Wan-li period in Ch'en Chi-ju's *Pao-yen t'ang pi-chi*. Chiao Hung's postface was dated 1586.

39. *Yü-kung chieh* (An Elucidation of the Yü-kung Chapter of the *Book of History*) in one *chüan*. It is listed in the Bibliographical Treatise of the *Ming Shih*. I have not been able to locate a copy of this work, which may no longer be extant.

40. *Yü-t'ang ts'ung-yü* (A Collection of Notes on the Hanlin Academy) in eight *chüan*. It is a record of the words and deeds of the Hanlin officials since the beginning of the Ming dynasty. It was first published in the Wan-li period with Chiao Hung's preface dated 1618. Copies of the Wan-li edition are preserved in the National Central Library in Taipei, the Sonkeikaku Bunko, and the Seikadō Bunko.

41. *Yüan-chüeh ching ching-chieh p'ing-lin* (A Collection of Critical Commentaries on the Essentials of the *Sūtra of Perfect Enlightenment*). The date of its original publication is uncertain. It may no longer be extant except for its first *chüan*, which has been printed into the *Dai Nihon zoku zōkyō*.

Notes

1. The Problem

1. Helmer Ringgren, "The Problem of Syncretism," in Sven S. Hartman, ed., *Syncretism*, p. 7.

2. *Ibid.*, p. 12.

3. Ake Hultkrantz, "Pagan and Christian Elements in the Religious Syncretism among the Shoshoni Indians of Wyoming," in Hartman, ed., *Syncretism*, p. 15.

4. *Ibid.*

5. T'ang Yung-t'ung, *Han Wei liang-Chin Nan-Pei-Ch'ao Fo-chiao-shih*, 1:39–42.

6. Nakamura Hajime, *Ways of Thinking of Eastern Peoples* (Honolulu: East-West Center Press, 1964), pp. 293-94.

7. For the origin and development of this legend and its role in Chinese history, wee Wang Wei-ch'eng, "Lao-tzu hua-hu shuo k'ao-cheng."

8. *Chou I*, 8:3b–4a; see James Legge, trans., *The I Ching*, p. 389; Richard Wilhelm and Cary F. Baynes, trans., *The I Ching*, 1:362-63.

9. Hui-yüan, "San-pao lun," in Seng-yu, ed., *Hung-ming chi*, in *Taishō shinshū daizōkyō* (hereafter cited as *Taishō*) 52(2102):34.

10. The Six Perfections are: giving, keeping the precepts, patience, vigor, meditation, and wisdom. See W.E. Soothill, *A Dictionary of Chinese Buddhist Terms* (Taipei: Ch'eng-wen ch'u-pan she, 1969), pp. 134-35.

11. The five virtues are (1) being righteous (*i*) as a father; (2) being kindly (*tz'u*) as a mother; (3) being fraternal (*yu*) as an elder brother; (4) being respectful (*kung*) as a younger brother; and (5) being filial (*hsiao*) as a son. See *Tz'u Hai* (Taipei: Chung-hua shu-chü, 1965), 1:140.

12. The essay in its original form is no longer extant. Parts of it were quoted by Tsung Ping (375–443) in a letter to Ho Ch'eng-t'ien (370–447) in which Tsung Ping staged a rebuttal of Hui-lin's "On Black and White." Tsung Ping's letter to Ho Ch'eng-t'ien was included in the *Hung-ming chi* and served as the main source of Tokiwa Daijō's discussion of Hui-lin in his *Shina ni okeru Bukkyō to Jukyō Dōkyō*, pp. 74-77. Tokiwa Daijō's use of this letter by Tsung Ping explains his somewhat one-sided presentation of Hui-lin as a Buddhist renegade. This part of my analysis of Hui-lin is based on a long

quotation from "On Black and White" preserved in Hui-lin's biography in the *Sung Shu* (Po-na-pen edition), 97:14b–19b. See also Walter Liebenthal, "The Immortality of the Soul in Chinese Thought," pp. 365-73.

13. Yen Yen-chih, "T'ing-kao erh-chang," in *Hung-ming chi*, p. 89.

14. Liu Ts'un-yan, "The Penetration of Taoism into the Ming Neo-Confucian Elite."

15. Liu Ts'un-yan, "Taoist Self-Cultivation in Ming Thought," in Wm. Theodore de Bary and the Conference on Ming Thought, *Self and Society in Ming Thought*, p. 308.

16. For Kuan Chih-tao, Yang Ch'i-yüan, and Chou Ju-teng as syncretists, see Araki Kengo, *Mindai shisō kenkyū*, pp. 130–39, 237–43. For Li Chih's syncretism, see Wm. Theodore de Bary, "Individualism and Humanitarianism in Late Ming Thought," in *Self and Society*, pp. 209-13.

17. See Araki Kengo, "Confucianism and Buddhism in the Late Ming," in Wm. Theodore de Bary and the conference on Seventeenth Century Chinese Thought, *The Unfolding of Neo-Confucianism*, pp. 53-54.

18. E. Zürcher, *The Buddhist Conquest of China*, p. 12.

19. Wm. Theodore de Bary et al., eds., *Sources of Chinese Tradition*, 1:278–79.

20. I.e., after Kumārajīva's arrival in 401. See Kenneth Ch'en, *Buddhism in China*, p. 69.

21. I.e., the first five of the ten Buddhist commandments, against killing, stealing, adultery, lying, and drinking intoxicating liquors. See Soothill, *Dictionary*, p. 118.

22. Yen Chih-t'ui, "Chia-hsün kuei-hsin p'ien," in Tao-hsüan ed., *Kuang hung-ming chi*, in *Taishō* 52 (2103):107.

23. Leon Hurvitz, "Wei Shou, Treatise on Buddhism and Taoism," *Yün Kang* (Kyoto University, 1965), 16:33n2.

24. Albert E. Dien, "Yen Chih-t'ui (531–591+): A Buddho-Confucian."

25. See Leon Hurvitz, *Chih I*, pp. 233-51.

26. The so-called scheme of "Five Periods and Eight Teachings"; see *ibid.*, pp. 252–301.

27. Chih-i, *Mo-ho chih-kuan*, in *Taishō* 46 (1911):77. The Triple Refuge refers to the Buddha, the *Dharma*, and the *saṅgha* (Soothill, *Dictionary*, p. 69). The Ten Good Deeds are defined as refraining from the ten evils of killing, stealing, adultery, lying, speaking with a double tongue, coarse language, filthy language, covetousness, anger, and perverted views (Soothill, *Dictionary*, pp. 47, 50). The Four *Dhyānas* are the four types of meditation which lead to the four *dhyāna* heavenly regions (Soothill, *Dictionary*, p. 179).

28. Chih-i's detailed exposition of the "Ten Dharma-Gates of Contemplating the Mind" is contained in his *Mo-ho chih-kuan*, pp. 52-100. See also Hurvitz, *Chih I*, pp. 367-68.

29. Chih-i, *Mo-ho chih-kuan*, p. 78.

30. This text is printed in the *Dai Nihon zoku zōkyō* (ser. 1, pt. 2, case 15, 5:433b–38a) as the *Chart of the Master-Disciple Succession of the Ch'an School Which Transmitted the Mind-Ground in China* (*Chung-hua ch'uan-hsin-ti Ch'an-men shih-tzu ch'eng-hsi t'u*).

31. This text is printed in *Taishō* 45 (1886): 707-10. It is noteworthy that

whereas the earlier *p'an-chiao* texts such as the *T'i-wei po-li ching* began with the "Doctrine Concerning Man and God," Tsung-mi's *Yüan-jen lun* preceded the discussion of the "Doctrine Concerning Man and God" with a section on Confucianism and Taoism.

32. *Taishō* 45 (1886): 708. Translations in the quotation are taken with minor modifications from Wm. Theodore de Bary, ed., *The Buddhist Tradition*, p. 181.

33. Chih-i, *Mo-ho chih-kuan*, p. 77.

34. *Taishō* 45 (1886): 708. Translations taken with minor modifications from de Bary, ed., *The Buddhist Tradition*, p. 181.

35. Chih-yüan, "Ssu-shih-erh chang ching hsü," in *Hsien-chü p'ien*, 1:32a–32b.

36. Ch'i-sung, "Fu-chiao p'ien (a)," *T'an-ching wen-chi*, in *Taishō* 52 (2115): 649.

37. Ch'i-sung, "Fu-chiao p'ien (b)," *T'an-ching wen-chi*, in *Taishō* 52 (2115): 657.

38. *Ibid.*, p. 660.

39. These essays are collected in *T'an-ching wen-chi*, in *Taishō* 52 (2115): 660–83.

40. Allusion to *Analects* 1:9.

41. Ch'i-sung, "Fu-chiao p'ien (c)," *T'an-ching wen-chi*, in *Taishō* 52 (2115): 660–61.

42. *Ibid.*, p. 660.

43. Ch'i-sung, "Fu-chiao p'ien (a)," p. 651.

44. Ch'i-sung, "Fu-chiao p'ien (c)," p. 660.

45. Zürcher, *The Buddhist Conquest of China*, p. 12.

46. Liu Mi, *San-chiao p'ing-hsin lun* (preface dated 1324), in *Taishō* 52 (2117): 781-94; Shen Shih-jung, *Hsü yüan-chiao lun* (preface dated 1385).

47. *Pei Shih* (Po-na-pen edition), 33:31b, 33a; *Sui Shu* (Po-na-pen edition), 77:2a–2b, 4a.

48. T'ao Tsung-i, *Nan-ch'un ch'o-keng lu*, pp. 376-77. See also F. W. Mote, "Notes on the Life of T'ao Tsung-i."

49. Igor de Rachewiltz, "Yeh-lü Ch'u-ts'ai (1189–1234): Buddhist Idealist and Confucian Statesman," p. 210.

50. Liu, *San-chiao p'ing-hsin lun*, p. 781.

51. See chapter 4.

52. For a comprehensive treatment of Lin Chao-en, see Judith Berling, *The Syncretic Religion of Lin Chao-en*.

53. *Ibid.*, pp. 81-82, 213–19. Translation differs slightly from Berling's.

54. Quoted in Sakai Tadao, *Chūgoku zensho no kenkyū*, p. 285. The concluding statement is derived from *Analects* 3:1. I have modified some of Sakai's punctuation according to David Roy's suggestion.

55. Ku Yen-wu, *Jih-chih lu*, 7:7a–b.

56. Wm. Theodore de Bary, "Neo-Confucian Cultivation and the Seventeenth Century 'Enlightenment'" (hereafter cited as "Cultivation and Enlightenment"), in *Unfolding*, pp. 161-62.

57. See Jen Yu-wen, "Ch'en Hsien-chang's Philosophy of the Natural," in de Bary, *Self and Society*, pp. 53-92.

58. See Ch'en's poems on Chuang Tzu in *Po-sha Tzu ch'üan-chi*, 6:59a, 9:6b.

59. *Ibid.*, 5:43a.
60. See Wei-ming Tu, *Neo-Confucian Thought in Action*, pp. 43, 63-66, 72-74.
61. *Ibid.*, pp. 69, 73, 79, 114.
62. *Ibid.*, pp. 62-72, 114-15, 124, 128-29.
63. Huang Tsung-hsi and Ch'üan Tsu-wang, *Sung-Yüan hsüeh-an*, p. 548.
64. *Ibid.*, p. 554. The other disciple was Hsieh Liang-tso.
65. *Ibid.*, p. 551.
66. *Ibid.*, pp. 551-52.
67. *Ibid.*, p. 552; *Mencius* 2A:2:16.
68. *Sung-Yüan hsüeh-an*, pp. 551, 552; *Mencius* 7A:38.
69. *Sung-Yüan hsüeh-an*, p. 552.
70. *Ibid.*, p. 742.
71. *Ibid.*, p. 750.
72. *Ibid.*, pp. 573, 575.
73. *Ibid.*, pp. 691–92.
74. *Ibid.*, p. 693.
75. See the sections on *Anuttara-samyak-sambodhi* in the *Dimond Sūtra*, in *Taishō* 8 (235): 749, 750-51, 752.
76. *Doctrine of the Mean*, 25:2.
77. *Sung-Yüan hsüeh-an*, p. 694.
78. *Ibid.*, p. 1394.
79. *Ibid.*, p. 1404.
80. See the statement by *Ssu-k'u ch'üan-shu chien-ming mu-lu* in *Tz'u-hu i-shu* (Ssu-ming ts'ung-shu edition), p. la.
81. *Sung-Yüan hsüeh-an*, pp. 1402–4.
82. *Analects* 9:4; Wing-tsit Chan, *A Source Book in Chinese Philosophy*, p. 35.
83. *Tz'u-hu i-shu*, 17:25b. For the metaphor of "accepting a thief as one's son," see *Ta-fo-ting ju-lai mi-yin hsiu-cheng liao-i chu p'u-sa wan-hsing shou-leng-yen ching* (hereafter cited as *Shou-leng-yen ching*), in *Taishō* 19 (945): 108, and *Ta-fang-kuang yüan-chüeh hsiu-to-lo liao-i ching*, in *Taishō* 17 (842): 919.
84. Berling, *The Syncretic Religion of Lin Chao-en*, pp. 81–89, 220–28.
85. Kristin Yü Greenblatt, "Chu-hung and Lay Buddhism in the Late Ming," in de Bary, *Unfolding*, pp. 104, 110-11.
86. Ogawa Kan'ichi, "Koji Bukkyō no kinsei teki hatten, " pp. 51-52.
87. Nakamura, *Ways of Thinking of Eastern Peoples*, p. 291.
88. De Bary, "Individualism and Humanitarianism," pp. 175–76. See also Tadao Sakai, "Confucianism and Popular Eucational Works," in de Bary, *Self and Society*, pp. 331-64.
89. Philip B. Yampolsky, trans., *The Platform Sutra of the Sixth Patriarch*, p. 159.
90. See chapter 3.
91. Greenblatt, "Chu-hung," pp. 122-23, 129.
92. *Ibid.*, p. 111.
93. Takao Giken, "Unsei Daishi Shukō ni tsuite," pp. 260-62.
94. Greenblatt, "Chu-hung," pp. 100-2.
95. *Ibid.*, pp. 95-96, 112; see also Chu-hung, "Chieh-sha fang-sheng wen," in *Yün-ch'i fa-hui*, 22:5a, 10a.

96. Wing-tsit Chan, "The Evolution of the Confucian Concept of *Jen*," pp. 313–15; see also Chan, *Source Book*, p. 530.

97. See Hu Cheng-fu's essay on "Nonkilling" and Chiao Hung's comments on it in *Chiao-shih pi-ch'eng* (hereafter cited as *Pi-ch'eng*) in *Chiao-shih pi-ch'eng cheng-hsü*, 2:52–55 and T'ao Wang-ling's "Fang-sheng pien-huo," 30:la–5a.

98. Sakai, "Confucianism and Popular Educational Works," p. 338.

99. Ku, *Jih-chih lu*, 18:23b–25a.

100. See chapter 2.

101. See Yang Ch'i-ch'iao, "Ming-tai chu-ti chih ch'ung-shang fang-shu chi ch'i ying-hsiang."

102. Sakai, *Chūgoku zensho no kenkyū*, pp. 227-33. See also Araki, *Mindai shisō kenkyū*, pp. 265-66 and Mano Senryū, "Mindai ni okeru sankyō shisō: toku ni Rin Chōon o chūshin to shite."

103. See Li Chih, "Sheng-chiao hsiao-yin," *Hsü fen-shu* in *Fen-shu hsü fenshu*, pp. 66–67.

104. Araki, *Mindai shisō kenkyū*, p. 266.

105. See my article "Chiao Hung and the Revolt Against Ch'eng-Chu Orthodoxy" (hereafter cited as "Revolt Against Ch'eng-Chu"), in de Bary, *Unfolding*, pp. 271–303.

106. Araki, "Confucianism and Buddhism," p. 44. See also Julia Ching, *To Acquire Wisdom: The Way of Wang Yang-ming*, pp. 162-65.

107. Wang Yang-ming, *Wang Yang-ming ch'üan-chi* (hereafter cited as *Yang-ming ch'üan-chi*), 31:603.

108. See Araki, *Mindai shisō kenkyū*, pp. 265-91.

109. See Tu, *Neo-Confucian Thought in Action*, pp. 49-50.

110. See Araki, "Confucianism and Buddhism," p. 43.

111. Christian Murck, "Chu Yun-ming" (paper presented to the Columbia University Regional Seminar on Neo-Confucian Studies, May 5, 1978, pp. 17-22).

112. Wing-tsit Chan, "Chu Hsi and Yüan Neo-Confucianism," in Hok-lam Chan and Wm. Theodore de Bary, eds., *Yüan Thought: Chinese Thought and Religion Under the Mongols* (New York: Columbia University Press, 1982), pp. 197 and 218.

113. See Irene Bloom, "On the 'Abstraction' of Ming Thought: Some Concrete Evidence from the Philosophy of Lo Ch'in-shun," in Wm. Theodore de Bary and Irene Bloom, eds., *Principle and Practicality*, pp. 76-91.

114. See my "Revolt Against Ch'eng-Chu," pp. 271–76.

2. The Man

1. *Ming Shih*, 288:7393.

2. Huang Tsung-hsi, *Ming-ju hsüeh-an*, p. 361

3. Shen I-kuan, *Ming chuang-yüan t'u-k'ao*, B:61b.

4. Keng Ting-hsiang, *Keng T'ien-t'ai hsien-sheng wen-chi*, 1:3:22b. Allusion is to *Analects* 2:4 where Confucius said that at fifty he "knew Heaven's will."

5. De Bary, "Introduction," *Self and Society*, p. 23.

6. See my "Revolt Against Ch'eng-Chu," pp. 271-76, 289-96; also chapter 2.

7. *Ming Shih*, 288:7392.
8. Chiao Hung, *Tan-yüan chi*, 13:1b. See also Chiao Jui's biographies in Chiao Hung, *Kuo-ch'ao hsien-cheng lu* (hereafter cited as *Hsien-cheng lu*) (Taipei: T'ai-wan hsüeh-sheng shu-chü, 1965), 100:61a, and Kuo T'ing-hsün, *Pen-ch'ao fen-sheng jen-wu k'ao* (hereafter cited as *Fen-sheng jen-wu*), 13:27a.
9. *Tan-yüan chi*, 13:1b.
10. Li, *Hsü fen-shu*, p. 56; Ch'en Tso-lin, *Shang-yüan Chiang-ning hsiang-t'u ho-chih* (hereafter cited as *Hsiang-t'u ho-chih*), 4:4b.
11. Li, *Hsü fen-shu*, p. 56.
12. Ch'en, *Hsiang-t'u ho-chih*, 4:4b.
13. This was the title with which Chiao Hung referred to his father. See *Tan-yüan chi*, 13:1b.
14. Li, *Hsü fen-shu*, pp. 56-57.
15. Chiao Hung, *Tan-yüan hsü-chi*, 15:10a.
16. Li, *Hsü fen-shu*, p. 56. Here Li Chih was quoting Chiao Hung's own account of his father.
17. *Hsien-cheng lu*, 100:61a–62a; Kuo, *Fen-sheng jen-wu*, 13:27a–28b.
18. The other two were Huang Shang-chih (T. Tsung-shang, H. Lung-kang, 1504–1577) and Li Wei-ming (dates unknown). *Tan-yüan chi*, 30:1a.
19. *Tan-yüan hsü* 1:2a–b.
20. *Tan-yüan chi*, 28:12a.
21. *Ibid.*, 15:7b.
22. *Tan-yüan hsü*, 15:9a–b.
23. *Ibid.*, 15:9b.
24. The other two were Sun K'uang (T. Wen-jung, H. Yüeh-feng, 1542–1613) and Li T'ing-chi (T. Erh-chang, H. Chiu-wo, *chin-shih* of 1583). *Ming-ju hsüeh-an*, p. 362.
25. Title of wives of sixth-grade officials. It was bestowed on Chiao Hung's wives in 1592. *Tan-yüan hsü*, 15:9a.
26. *Ibid.*, 15:9b–11b.
27. *Ibid.*, 15:9a–b.
28. *Ming Shih*, 295:7572–3; Hsü Tzu, *Hsiao-tien chi-chuan*, 51:679, and *Hsiao-tien chi-nien*, 4:670.
29. *Tan-yüan chi*, 28:12a.
30. Jung Chao-tsu, "Chiao Hung chi ch'i ssu-hsiang," pp. 5, 6, 7, 10, 14. He took the examination in 1565, 1568, 1571, 1577, 1583.
31. *Ming shih-lu*, 105:209:8b, 10b.
32. Chiao Hung, *Lao-tzu i*, preface:2b; *Tan-yüan chi*, 16:6b, 15:17b, 37:8b, 16:17b.
33. *Lao-tzu i*, preface:2b.
34. *Ibid.*, preface:2b–3a; *Tan-yüan chi*, 47:7a.
35. Keng Ting-hsiang, *Keng T'ien-t'ai hsien-sheng ch'üan-shu*, 8:11b, 15a.
36. *Tan-yüan chi*, 20:11b–12a.
37. Ch'en, *Hsiang-t'u ho-chih*, 5:2a
38. *Tan-yüan chi*, 20:10b.
39. *Ibid.*, 47:1a.
40. *Ibid.*, 20:11a; *Keng T'ien-t'ai hsien-sheng ch'üan-shu*, 8:14b.
41. *Tan-yüan chi*, 20:11a.

42. See *Keng T'ien-t'ai hsien-sheng ch'üan-shu*, 8:14a, 15a–b. To distinguish the names of the two younger brothers in romanization, the elder of the two appears in this book as Ting-lii and the younger one as Ting-li.

43. *Ibid.*, 8:14b; *Tan-yüan chi*, 33:5b.

44. *Keng t'ien-t'ai hsien-sheng ch'üan-shu*, 8:14b.

45. *Ming-ju hsüeh-an*, 32:319.

46. *Ibid.*, 35:362.

47. *Ming Shih*, 288:7393; *Ming-ju hsüeh-an*, 35:361.

48. *Tan-yüan chi*, 20:12a.

49. *Ibid.*, 27:5b; Jung, "Chiao Hung," p.15.

50. *Tan-yüan chi*, 20:12a.

51. *Ibid.*, 31:18a–b. Lu, being Confucius' native state, stands for the realm of Confucianism.

52. *Ibid.*, 31:18a–20b, 37:la–b, 41:2b.

53. *Ibid.*, 24:la-2a, 35:2a.

54. *Tan-yüan hsü*, 14:10a.

55. De Bary, "Individualism and Humanitarianism," p. 191.

56. Li, *Hsü fen-shu*, 2:56; Jung Chao-tsu, *Li Chih nien-p'u*, pp. 22–23, 30–31.

57. Li, *Hsü fen-shu*, 2:56.

58. *Ibid.* This paragraph is built around an allusion to *Tso Chuan*, 24th year of Duke Hsiang, according to which accomplishments in virtue, meritorious service, and words are the three ways of gaining immortality. See James Legge, *The Ch'un Ts'ew with the Tso Chuen*, in the *Chinese Classics*, 5:507.

59. Li, *Hsü fen-shu*, 2:56.

60. Jung, *Li Chih nien-p'u*, pp. 69, 45–64.

61. See Li Chih's letter to Chiao Hung in *Hsü fen-shu*, 1:28–30.

62. *Ibid.*, 4:104.

63. See Li's biography by Yüan Chung-tao (1570–1624) reprinted in *Fen-shu*, in *Fen-shu hsü fen-shu*, p. 4.

64. Li Chih, *Ts'ang-shu*, preface by Chiao Hung.

65. Jung, *Li Chih nien-p'u*, pp. 54-55, 63-64.

66. P'an Tseng-hung, *Li Wen-ling wai-chi*, pp. 189–90. For a detailed account of Kalingarāja's mutilation of the Buddha, see the *Mahāparinirvāna Sūtra* (*Ta pan-nieh-p'an ching*), in *Taishō* 7(374):551. For the Diamond Sūtra's interpretation of this story, see Edward Conze, *Buddhist Wisdom Books, Containing the Diamond Sutra and the Heart Sutra*, p. 54. Except for some variation in detail, this story seems to be a *Jataka* tale, one version of which has been translated into English by Conze, *Buddhist Scriptures*, pp. 26-30.

67. Shen Te-fu, *Yeh-huo pien* (1827 edition), 27:18a.

68. *Ming-ju hsüeh-an*, 35:361.

69. P'eng Shao-sheng, *Chü-shih chuan* (1878), 44:10a.

70. Li, *Ts'ang-shu*, Chiao Hung's preface.

71. *Ming Shih*, 288:7393.

72. *Tan-yüan chi*, 16:6b, 15:17b, 37:8b.

73. *Ibid.*, 13:18b.

74. As discussed earlier in this chapter.

75. *Pi-ch'eng*, 4:103.

76. *Tan-yüan chi*, 17:12b.
77. For an English translation of this text, see Charles Luk, trans., *The Śūraṅgama Sūtra*.
78. See Pei-yi Wu, "The Spiritual Autobiography of Te-ch'ing," in de Bary, *Unfolding*, p. 80.
79. Araki, *Mindai shisō kenkyū*, pp. 271–73.
80. *Tan-yüan chi*, 17:12b.
81. *Ibid.*
82. *Ibid.*
83. *Ibid.*; Chiao Hung, *Chiao-shih pi-ch'eng hsü-chi* (hereafter cited as *Pi-ch'eng hsü*), in *Chiao-shih pi-ch'eng cheng-hsü*, 2:170.
84. *Tan-yüan chi*, 12:2a-4a.
85. *Ming-ju hsüeh-an*, 35:355.
86. *Keng T'ien-t'ai hsien-sheng wen-chi*, 3:31b.
87. *Tan-yüan chi*, 37:5b and 8a–b, 39:1b, 3a, 4b, 5a–6a, 11a 11b, 12b, 13b, 41:2a, 4a, 5b–6a, 9a, 12b, 14a, 17a, 42:3a, 13a–b, 44:1b-2a, 45:4a; *Tan-yüan hsü*, 24:1b.
88. *Tan-yüan chi*, 42:10b, 13:2b, 17:13a–14a.
89. *Ibid.*, 8:2b–3a, 3b-4a, 15:17b–18a, 16:18a–19a, 19:1a-2b, 3a-4b, 21:14a–16a, 22:2b, 13b–14a, 18b, 19b; *Tan-yüan hsü*, 2:17a–18a, 4:18a–19b, 20a–21b, 24a-25a, 8:1a-5b, 7b-12b, 9:9b-10a. Chiao Hung compiled four commentaries on the *Lotus*, the *Laṅkāvatāra*, the *Śūraṅgama*, and the *Sūtra of Perfect Enlightenment* (see the appendix).
90. *Analects* 13:21; see also Ching, *To Acquire Wisdom*, pp. 25–27.
91. An example is Liang Ch'i-ch'ao, *Intellectual Trends in the Ch'ing Period*, p. 28. See also Liang's *Chung-kuo chin-san-pai nien hsüeh-shu shih*, pp. 5-7.
92. See my "Revolt Against Ch'eng-Chu," pp. 271-76, 292-96.
93. De Bary, "Introduction," *Self and Society*, pp. 1-27, and "Individualism and Humanitarianism," pp. 145–245.
94. *Tan-yüan chi*, 14:2a–3a; *Tan-yüan hsü*, 1:1a–2a, 9:17b, 10:36b–39a.
95. Ch'ien Mu, *Chung-kuo chin-san-pai-nien hsüeh-shu shih* (hereafter cited as *Hsüeh-shu shih*), 1:135–38.
96. Shen, *Ming Chuang-yüan t'u k'ao*, B:61b.
97. *Keng T'ien-t'ai hsien-sheng wen-chi*, 1:3:22b.
98. *Ibid.*, 1:3:23a.
99. *Tan-yüan chi*, 13:1b.
100. *Ibid.*, 13:5a, 15b.
101. *Ming Shih*, 288:7392.
102. *Ibid.*, 304:7766.
103. *Ibid.*, 304:7777.
104. Liu Jo-yü, *Cho-chung chih*, 16:100; Hsia Hsieh, *Ming T'ung-chien*, 1:19:803.
105. *Ming Shih*, 288:7393.
106. *Tan-yüan chi*, 13:10a.
107. *Ibid.*
108. *Ibid*, 15:15b.
109. *Ming shih-lu*, 107:247:10a.
110. *Tan-yüan hsü*, 1:2b–3a.
111. For Han Yü and the *ku-wen* movement, see Liu Wu-chi, *An Introduction*

to Chinese Literature (Bloomington: Indiana University Press, 1966), pp. 125-40, and Stephen Owen, *The Poetry of Meng Chiao and Han Yü* (New Haven: Yale University Press, 1975), pp. 1-23.

112. Arthur W. Hummel, *Eminent Chinese of the Ch'ing Period*, p. 176; L. Carrington Goodrich and Chaoying Fang, *Dictionary of Ming Biography*, 1:209-10.

113. *Tan-yüan hsü*, 5:2a; *Tan-yüan chi*, 3:2a–3a.

114. *Dictionary of Ming Biography*, 1:338.

115. *Ming shih-lu*, 108:269:1b–2a.

116. *Ming Shih*, 228:7393.

117. *Tan-yüan chi*, 3:3a-4a, 15:1a-b.

118. *Ming shih-lu*, 110:314:4a.

119. *Ming Shih*, 288:7393.

120. *Ibid.*, 288:7392; *Ming shih-lu*, 108:271:5b, 8a–b and 108:264:1b–4a.

121 See Li Tsung-t'ung, *Chung-kuo shih-hsüeh shih*, pp. 71-73, 34-35; Chin Yü-fu, *Chung-kuo shih-hsüeh shih*, pp. 108-9.

122. Yang Lien-sheng, "The Organization of Chinese Official Historiography: Principles and Methods of the Standard Histories from the T'ang through the Ming Dynasty" (hereafter cited as "Chinese Official Historiography"), in W. G. Beasley and E. G. Pulleyblank, eds., *Historians of China and Japan*, pp. 45–46.

123. See Wolfgang Franke, "The Veritable Records of the Ming Dynasty," in Beasley and Pulleyblank, *Historians of China and Japen*, pp. 70–71.

124. *Tan-yüan chi*, 5:5b–6a.

125. *Ibid.*

126. *Ibid.*, 5:6a–b.

127. *Ibid.*, 5:6b-7a.

128. *Ibid.*, 5:7a-b.

129. *Ibid.*, 4:2b-4a.

130. Yang, "Chinese Official Historiography," p. 52.

131. E. G. Pulleyblank, "Chinese Historical Criticism: Liu Chih-chi and Ssu-ma Kuang," in Beasley and Pulleyblank, *Historians of China and Japan*, pp. 139-40.

132. *Tan-yüan chi*, 4:3a-4a.

133. Yang, "Chinese Official Historiography," p. 53.

134. De Bary, "Introduction," *Self and Society*, pp. 22-23, and "Individualism and Humanitarianism," pp. 171-74; see also P. T. Ho, *The Ladder of Success in Imperial China*.

135. Officially the project was suspended only temporarily. But it was never resumed. *Ming shih-lu*, 110:311:7a. See also Sun Ch'eng-tse, *Ch'un-ming meng-yü lu*, 13:4a.

136. *Ming Shih*, 288:7392.

137. *Ch'ing-ting ssu-k'u ch'üan-shu tsung-mu* (hereafter cited as *Imperial Catalogue*), 87:1b-2a.

138. Hsü Sze-in, *Chung-kuo mu-lu-hsüeh shih*, p. 153.

139. Naitō Torajirō, *Shina shigaku shi*, p. 368.

140. *Ibid.*, p. 369.

141. *Hsien-cheng lu*, Huang Ju-heng's preface, pp. 6–7.

142. *Ibid.*, p. 6 and Ku Ch'i-yüan's preface, pp.1–2.

143. This term was used by Ku Ch'i-yüan in his preface to the *Hsien-cheng lu*, p. 2. Huang Ju-heng, however, used the term "fiction" (*hsiao-shuo*), p. 6.

144. See Herbert Franke, "Some Aspects of Chinese Private Historiography in

the Thirteenth and Fourteenth Centuries," in Beasley and Pulleyblank, *Historians of China and Japan*, p. 116.

145. *Imperial Catalogue*, 63:3b.

146. *Hsien-cheng lu*, Huang Chang-chien's preface, p. 5.

147. A branch of learning that deals with historical precedents, anecdotes, and ceremonial matters.

148. Naitō, *Shina shigaku shi*, pp. 343-47.

149. *Hsien-cheng lu*, Huang Chang-chien's preface, pp. 1-3.

150. Wan Ssu-t'ung, *Shih-yüan wen-chi*, 7:3a-b.

151. *Ming shih-lu*, 110:313:2a.

152. *Ming Shih*, 288:7393; *Ming-ju hsüeh-an*, 35:361.

153. *Tan-yüan chi*, 3:4a-6a.

154. *Tan-yüan hsü*, 5:2a.

155. *Ming Shih*, 288:7393; *Fu-ning fu-chih*, 15:16a; *Ming shih-lu*, 100:316:4b.

156. See Jung, "Chiao Hung," pp. 26–32.

157. *Tan-yüan chi*, 13:25a.

158. *Ibid.*, 13:22b.

159. Yeh Ch'ang-chih, *Ts'ang-shu chi-shih shih*, 3:157; Yang Li-ch'eng and Chin Pu-ying, *Chung-kuo ts'ang-shu-chia k'ao-lüeh*, p. 105a.

160. I.e., (1) *Chin-hsüeh chih*, (2) *Erh-shih-chiu tzu p'in-hui shih-p'ing*, (3) *Hsien-cheng lu*, (4) *I-ch'üan*, (5) *Sheng-an wai-chi*, (6) *Su-shu k'an-wu*, (7) *Tan-yüan chi*, (8) *Tan-yüan hsü*, (9) *Chih-shen lu*, (10) *Shih-Han ho-ch'ao*, and (11) *Yü-t'ang ts'ung-yü*. See the appendix for details.

161. *Tan-yüan chi*, 14:2a-3a.

162. *Ibid.*; *Pi-ch'eng*, 3:63-64.

163. Ch'en Ti, *Mao-shih ku-yin k'ao*, Ch'en Ti's postface, p. 1a.

164. E.g., by Hu Shih. See his "The Scientific Spirit and Method in Chinese Philosophy," p. 124.

165. *Mao-shih ku-yin k'ao*, Ch'en Ti's postface, p. 1a.

166. Ōkubo Eiko, *Min Shin jidai shoin no kenkyū*, pp. 141-47; *Hsiu-ning hsien-chih*, 2:15b. Both these works maintain that the Huan-ku Academy was founded by Chu Shih-lu in 1589 when Chu became the county magistrate of Hsiu-ning. However, according to the *Tan-yüan chi* (48:1a), both Chan Jo-shui and Tsou Shou-i taught at the academy. Chan and Tsou died (1560 and 1562, respectively) long before Chu's arrival as magistrate. The discrepancy between Ōkubo and the *Hsiu-ning hsien-chih* on the one hand and the *Tan-yüan chi* on the other can be resolved on the basis of the account in the *Huan-ku shu-yüan chih* (13:1b), which states that while the academy existed as an institution before 1589, it was housed in either a local monastery or a shrine and did not have a definite physical site until Chu mobilized the local populace and constructed a cluster of buildings.

167. *Tan-yüan chi*, 48:1a–b.

168. *Ibid.*, 49:1a.

169. *Ibid.*, chüan 48-49.

170. De Bary, "Individualism and Humanitarianism," p. 154.

171. *Ibid.*

172. *Ibid.* For examples, see Wing-tsit Chan, trans., *Instructions for Practical Living and Other Neo-Confucian Writings by Wang Yang-ming*, pp. 81-82 (#124), 216-17 (#262), and 249 (#319).

173. *Tan-yüan chi*, 49:4b.

174. *Ibid.*, 47:8a-b. This exchange between Hsia Yü-feng and a friend was also recorded by Huang Tsung-hsi in his biography of Hsia T'ing-mei, who was an uneducated peasant from Fan-ch'ang and whom Keng Ting-hsiang sent to study with Chiao Hung. Hsia Yün-feng and Hsia T'ing-mei are most likely the same person. See *Ming-ju hsüeh-an*, 32:319–20.

175. *Tan-yüan chi*, 47:1b–2a.

176. See Hsü Ai's (1478–1517) preface to the *Ch'uan-hsi lu* in *Yang-ming ch'üan-chi*, "Old Prefaces" (*chiu-hsü*), p. 2.

177. Translation adapted from Chan, *Instructions*, p. 255 (#330).

178. *Ming Shih*, 288:7393.

179. Hummel, *Eminent Chinese of the Ch'ing Period*, p. 195.

3. A Syncretist's Critique of Ch'eng-Chu Orthodoxy

1. *Pi-ch'eng*, 4:103.

2. The "piping of Heaven " is an allusion derived from the *Chuang Tzu*. See Burton Watson, trans., *The Complete Works of Chuang Tzu*, p. 37.

3. *Pi-ch'eng*, 4:104–5.

4. Not an exact quotation from Tzu Ssu. Translation adapted from James Legge, trans., *The Doctrine of the Mean* in *The Chinese Classics*, 1:428 (31:1).

5. Translation adapted from James Legge, trans., *The I Ching* (New York: Dover, 1963), appendix 3, sec. 1, 11:67, p. 372.

6. *Pi-ch'eng*, 4:103–5.

7. These prefaces have been printed collectively as one piece in *Tan-yüan chi*, 23:14a–21a.

8. Watson, *Complete Chuang Tzu*, pp. 296-97.

9. *Pi-ch'eng*, 4:103–4.

10. *Mencius* 2B:4. My translation follows Legge.

11. *Pi-ch'eng*, 4:103–4

12. Ch'ien Ta-hsin, *Shih-chia chai yang-hsin lu*, 19:457.

13. Chiao Hung, *Chuang-tzu i*, appendix:5b–7b, bibliography:1a.

14. Chang Ping-lin, *Ch'ung-ting ch'i-wu lun shih*, p. 1a.

15. *Chuang-tzu i*, 1:18a.

16. See Watson, *Complete Chuang Tzu*, pp. 36–37.

17. *Pi-ch'eng*, 4:104.

18. *New Catholic Encyclopedia*, 6:1069.

19. Walter Bauer, *Orthodoxy and Heresy in Earliest Christianity*, p. xxiii.

20. Geffrey B. Russel, *Dissent and Reform in the Early Middle Ages*, pp. 136–43.

21. *Ibid.*, pp. 134-35; *The Catholic Encyclopedia*, 7:256.

22. *The Catholic Encyclopedia*, 7:256-75.

23. Wing-tsit Chan, trans., *Reflections on Things at Hand*, pp. 279-88.

24. Hu Chü-jen, *Chü-yeh lu*, *chüan* 7.

25. Quoted in Ch'ien Mu, *Hsüeh-shu shih*, pp. 159-60.

26. Paul A. Cohen, *China and Christianity*, p. 19. Strictly speaking, Cohen's concern is not heresy but heterodoxy, which denotes a deviation not serious enough to be punished as heresy. However, in terms of my consideration here, the difference in the degree of seriousness between heresy and heterodoxy is not relevant. Insofar as heterodoxy is a mild form of heresy, it is still an intrasystemic concept to be understood both as the antithesis of orthodoxy and in contradistinction to paganism, schism, and apostasy.

27. *Ibid.*

28. Bauer, *Orthodoxy and Heresy*, p. xxiii.

29. *Ibid.*, p. xxiiinl.

30. See chapter 4.

31. *Pi-ch'eng hsü*, 1:161.

32. *Ibid.*, 1:161, 2:169.

33. *Ibid.*

34. Quoted in Hou Wai-lu, et al., *Chung-kuo ssu-hsiang t'ung-shih* (hereafter cited as *T'ung-shih*), 4B:979.

35. Wilhelm/Baynes, *The I Ching*, 1:321.

36. *Ibid.*

37. De Bary, "Individualism and Humanitarianism," p. 168.

38. Hou, *T'ung-shih*, 4B:974–95. See also de Bary's discussion of the problem in "Individualism and Humanitarianism," pp. 165-66, 168-69.

39. De Bary, "Individualism and Humanitarianism," pp. 165-66, 168.

40. Hou, *T'ung-shih*, 4B:963.

41. De Bary, "Individualism and Humanitarianism," p. 169.

42. *Pi-ch'eng hsü*, 2:169.

43. *Tan-yüan chi*, 12:7b.

44. *Ibid.*, 12:7b-8a, 14:5b.

45. *Ibid.*, 12:8a.

46. *Ibid.*, 12:6b, 8a.

47. *Chou I*, 9:1a.

48. *Tan-yüan chi*, 12:9a, 13b.

49. See *Analects* 15:41.

50. *Tan-yüan chi*, 13:17b, 48:11a-b

51. *Ibid.*, 12:7a, 14:4a.

52. *Analects* 14:34.

53. An allusion to the *Han Shu* (Po-na-pen edition), 65:2b.

54. *Pi-ch'eng hsü*, 1:150, 162.

55. *Tan-yüan chi*, 14:4a–b.

56. *Ibid.*, 14:4a.

57. See Joseph Levenson, *Confucian China and Its Modern Fate*, 1:3-4; Ying-shih Yü, "Some Preliminary Observations on the Rise of Ch'ing Confucian Intellectualism" (hereafter cited as "Ch'ing Confucian Intellectualism"), pp. 108-9.

58. Levenson, *Confucian China and Its Modern Fate*, p. 4.

59. *Mencius* 4B:19. Translation adapted from James Legge, *The Works of Mencius*, in *The Chinese Classics*, 2:325.

60. *Tan-yüan chi*, 13:21b.

61. *Ibid.*, 14:4a and 4b–5a.

62. *Ibid.*, 12:5a, 13:21b.

63. *Ibid.*, 12:10a. "Straightening the inside by being reverent" is an allusion to

the *I Ching*, "Wen-yen chuan," commentary on the K'un hexagram; see Legge, *The I Ching*, p. 420.

64. I.e., "Look not at what is contrary to propriety; listen not to what is contrary to propriety; speak not what is contrary to propriety; make no movement which is contrary to propriety." *Analects* 12:1.

65. See *Analects* 17:13 and *Mencius* 7B:37.

66. *Tan-yüan chi*, 12:4b-5a, 12:10a, 14:4b.

67. *Ibid.*, 12:5a–b, 8a, 14:4b–5a.

68. *Pi-ch'eng hsü*, 2:169.

69. *Tan-yüan chi*, 12:7b–8b.

70. Cohen, *China and Christianity*, p. 15.

71. Ch'en, *Buddhism in China*, pp. 136-37.

72. Cohen, *China and Christianity*, p. 15.

73. *Pi-ch'eng hsü*, 2:169-70.

74. *Analects* 6:19.

75. *Pi-ch'eng hsü*, 2:169-71.

76. For a discussion of such "Sinomania," see Cohen, *China and Christianity*, pp. 30-33.

77. *Pi-ch'eng hsü*, 2:170.

78. *Ibid.*, 4:104.

79. *Tan-yüan chi*, 12:13a.

80. *Pi'ch'eng hsü*, 2:169.

81. *Pi-ch'eng*, 4:130.

82. For Han Yü's letter to Meng Chien, see *Han Ch'ang-li chi* (Taipei: Commercial Press, 1953), 4:83-86. This translation of the quotation is adapted from Derk Bodde, trans., *A History of Chinese Philosophy*, 2:411.

83. I have followed Philip B. Yampolsky in the translation of this term. As he has explained, the term implies that "by good works in this world a person prepares the ground (*t'ien*) which will produce the fruits and flowers (*fu*) of the next world." See Yampolsky, *Platform Sutra*, p. 128*n*22.

84. *Tan-yüan chi*, 47:9a-b.

85. *Ibid.*, 12:3b.

86. This advice is usually attributed to Ch'eng I. It appears in *Ho-nan Ch'eng-shih i-shu* (hereafter cited as *Ch'eng-shih i-shu*) (Shanghai: Commercial Press, 1935), *chüan* 15 and has been ascribed by some to Ch'eng Hao. See A. C. Graham, *Two Chinese Philosophers: Ch'eng Ming-tao and Ch'eng Yi-ch'üan*, p. 141.

87. *Tan-yüan chi*, 12:13b.

88. An occurrence described in *Ho-nan Ch'eng-shih wai-shu* (in *Erh-Ch'eng ch'üan-shu*, Ssu-pu pei-yao edition), 12:18a; see Chan, *Source Book*, p. 542.

89. *Tan-yüan chi*, 12:13a.

90. Graham, *Two Chinese Philosophers*, p. 85.

91. Chiang Yung, *Chin-ssu lu chi-chu* (hereafter cited as *Chin-ssu lu*), 13:3b; see also Chan, *Reflections*, pp. 285-86.

92. Graham, *Two Chinese Philosophers*, p. 88.

93. *Chin-ssu lu*, 13:3a; Chan, *Reflections*, p. 285.

94. *Chin-ssu lu*, 13:4a; Chan, *Reflections*, p. 286.

95. Wing-tsit Chan, "Chu Hsi's Completion of Neo-Confucianism," p. 67.

96. Chan, *Source Book*, p. 637.

97. *Ibid.*
98. Chan, "Chu Hsi's Completion of Neo-Confucianism," p. 66.
99. Chu Hsi, *Chu-tzu ch'üan-shu*, 60:20b.
100. *Chin-ssu lu*, 13:4a. Translation adapted from Chan, *Reflections*, p. 286.
101. Chan, *Source Book*, p. 646; *Chu-tzu ch'üan-shu*, 60:12b. Allusion is to *Lao Tzu*, chapter 1.
102. *Chu-tzu ch'üan-shu*, 60:12b; translation adapted from Chan, *Source Book*, p. 646.
103. *Ibid.*
104. *Chu-tzu ch'üan-shu*, 60:14b. Translation adapted from Chan, *Source Book*, p. 648.
105. *Chu-tzu ch'üan-shu*, 60:15b–16b; Chan, *Source Book*, p. 649.
106. *Chu-tzu ch'üan-shu*, 60:14b. Translation adapted from Chan, *Source Book*, p. 648.
107. Chu Hsi, *Chu-tzu yü-lei*, 124:8b.
108. Chang Tsai, *Chang-tzu ch'üan-shu*, 2:47. Translation adapted from Chan, *Reflections*, p. 286.
109. *Ch'eng-shih i-shu*, pp. 24, 34-35, 80, 153: see also Chan, *Source Book*, 533-34, 535-36.
110. Chan, *Source Book*, p. 565.
111. *Ch'eng-shih i-shu*, pp. 216, 300; Chan, *Source Book*, p. 564.
112. An allusion derived from *Chuang Tzu*, chapter 33; see Watson, *Complete Chuang Tzu*, pp. 370-71.
113. See *Lao Tzu*, chapter 16; Wing-tsit Chan, trans., *The Way of Lao Tzu*, p. 128.
114. An allusion to the *Lao Tzu*, chapter 16.
115. *Tan-yüan chi*, 14:10a–b.
116. *Ibid.*, 14:12a.
117. *Ibid.*, 14:10a.
118. *Ibid.*, 12:12a.
119. *Ibid.*, 16:18a.
120. *Ibid.*
121. Mou tsung-san, *Hsin-t'i yü hsing-t'i*, 1:115-89.
122. *Ch'eng-shih i-shu*, p. 80; Chan, *Source Book*, pp. 535-36.
123. *Ch'eng-shih i-shu*, p. 289.
124. *Chu-tzu ch'üan-shu*, 60:12a-19a.
125. *Ch'eng-shih i-shu*, pp. 24, 80, 166, 216; Chan, *Source Book*, pp. 535, 554, 564.
126. *Ch'eng-shih i-shu*, pp. 166, 168; see also Chan, *Source Book*, p. 555.
127. *Ch'eng-shih i-shu*, p. 3; translation adapted from Graham, *Two Chinese Philosophers*, p. 85.
128. Chan, *Source Book*, p. 577.
129. Lu Hsiang-shan, *Lu Hsiang-shan ch'üan-chi* (hereafter cited as *Hsiang-shan ch'üan-chi*), p. 11. Translation adapted from Chan, *Source Book*, pp. 575-76.
130. *Chu-tzu ch'üan-shu*, 58:11b-13a, 61:12b-13b; see also Chan, *Source Book*, pp. 646-47.
131. *Chu-tzu ch'üan-shu*, 61:12b.

132. *Ch'eng-shih i-shu*, p. 40.
133. *Ibid.*, p. 153; Chan, *Reflections*, p. 185. Shen Tzu refers to Shen Pu-hai (d. B.C. 337) and Han Tzu to Han Fei Tzu (d. B.C. 233).
134. *Ch'eng-shih i-shu*, pp. 168, 216; Chan, *Source Book*, p. 555; Chan, *Reflections*, p. 285.
135. *Ch'eng-shih i-shu*, p. 356; *Lao Tzu*, chapter 38.
136. *Lao-tzu i*, preface:2a.
137. *Ibid.*
138. *Tan-yüan chi*, 22:21a.
139. *Lao-tzu i*, preface:2a–b.
140. *Pi-ch'eng hsü*, 1:158.
141. Paraphrase of *Chuang Tzu*, chapter 11. Translation adapted from Watson, *Complete Chuang Tzu*, p. 124.
142. *Tan-yüan chi*, 22:21a.
143. *Chuang Tzu*, chapter 15; Watson, *Complete Chuang Tzu*, p. 169.
144. *Tan-yüan chi*, 22:21b.
145. *Ibid.*, 12:1b, 12a-b.
146. *Ibid.*, 12:8b, 12a; *Pi-ch'eng hsü*, 2:170.
147. *Analects* 8:4.
148. *Pi-ch'eng hsü*, 2:170.
149. *Ibid.*
150. *Ibid.*
151. *Tan-yüan chi*, 12:10b.
152. See Yoshito Hakeda, trans., *The Awakening of Faith Attributed to Aśvaghosha*, pp. 31, 36-46.
153. *Tan-yüan chi*, 12:3a.
154. *Ibid.*, 12:10b–11a, 11b–12a; *Pi-ch'eng hsü*, 2:187.
155. *Tan-yüan chi*, 12:11a–b, 16:17b.
156. James Legge, *The Confucian Analects*, in *The Confucian Classics*, 1:168.
157. *Ibid.*, p. 168*n*8.
158. *Ibid.*
159. *Tan-yüan chi*, 12:10b–11a; see also *Pi-ch'eng hsü*, 1:151.
160. Ho Yen, *Ku-pen Lun-yü chi-chieh* in Yen Ling-feng, ed., *Wu-ch'iu-pei chai Lun-yü chi-ch'eng*, case 2, 1:2:14b; Huang K'an, *Lun-yü i-shu* in *Wu-ch'iu-pei Lun-yü*, case 3, 1:2:28b–29a.
161. *Chou I*, "Hsi Tz'u (A)," 7:3a.
162. Chan, *Source Book*, p. 498.
163. Ch'en Hsiang-tao, *Lun-yü ch'üan chieh*, in *Wu-ch'iu-pei Lun-yü*, case 6, 1:2:6b.
164. See de Bary, "Cultivation and Enlightenment," pp. 163-64.
165. *Chang-tzu ch'üan-shu*, p. 8.
166. Chen Te-hsiu, *Lun-yü chi-pien* in *Wu-ch'iu-pei Lun-yü*, case 6, 1:2:9b–10a; Chang Shih, *Nan-hsüan Lun-yü chieh* in *Wu-ch'iu-pei Lun-yü*, case 2, 1:2:13a-b.
167. *Tan-yüan chi*, 12:10b–11a.
168. *Pi-ch'eng*, 1:1; *Pi-ch'eng hsü*, 1:163.
169. Legge, *Confucian Analects*, 9:8.

170. Arthur Waley, trans., *The Analects of Confucius*, p. 140; James Ware, trans., *The Sayings of Confucius*, p. 61.
171. E.g., Hsing Ping (932–1010), *Lun-yü chu-shu* in *Wu-ch'iu-pei Lun-yü*, case 5, 1:2:12a.
172. Chih-hsü, *Lun-yü tien-ching pu-chu* in *Wu-ch'iu-pei Lun-yü*, case 10, 1:68.
173. *Ibid.*

4. Mysticism and Pluralism

1. Nakamura, *Ways of Thinking of Eastern Peoples*, pp. 288, 294.
2. *Ibid.*, pp. 291, 292, 293.
3. Nakamura's terms, *ibid.*
4. *Ibid.*, p. 292.
5. My thinking on this matter is indebted to Michel Foucault. See his *The Archaeology of Knowledge*, pp. 31–39.
6. Berling, *The Syncretic Religion of Lin Chao-en*, pp. 200-19.
7. *Tan-yüan chi*, 17:13a.
8. This statement appears in chapter 1 of the *Doctrine of the Mean*, which was originally a part of the *Li Chi* or *Book of Rites*.
9. *Tan-yüan chi*, 16:18a–b.
10. *Ibid.*, 17:12a-b.
11. *Ibid.*, 17:12b.
12. *Pi-ch'eng hsü*, 2:171. "Interpreting a dream while in a dream" is an allusion derived from the *Chuang Tzu*, chapter 2 (see Watson, *Complete Chuang Tzu*, p. 47), and *Ta-pan-jo po-lo-mi-to ching*, in *Taishō* 7(220):1084.
13. See Hans-Georg Gadamer, *Truth and Method*, pp. 378-89; Bernard Lonegan, "The Concept of Verbum in the Writings of St. Thomas Aquinas."
14. Reading *hsiang* as the *hsiang* in "Hsiao-hsiang chuan" and therefore "component lines" (*yao*).
15. *Pi-ch'eng hsü*, 2:169.
16. *Tan-yüan chi*, 14:2b.
17. See *Pi-ch'eng*, 6:123-42.
18. *Ibid.*, 6:133.
19. *Ibid.*, 6:123.
20. *Ibid.*, 6:132-33.
21. *Ibid.*, 6:124.
22. *Pi-ch'eng hsü*, 3:200.
23. *Tan-yüan chi*, 14:2b.
24. Gadamer, *Truth and Method*, p. 385.
25. *Pi-ch'eng hsü*, 1:156, 5:248-49.
26. *Pi-ch'eng*, 6:123.
27. *Ibid.*, 4:103.
28. *Pi-ch'eng hsü*, 1:163; *Tan-yüan hsü*, 22:2b.

29. *Ibid.*; *Wei-mo-chieh so-shuo ching* (hereafter cited as *Wei-mo ching*), *Taishō* 14(475):548: see also Charles Luk, trans., *The Vimalakīrti Nirdeśa Sūtra*, p. 75.

30. *Pi-ch'eng hsü*, 1:156, 170, 2:185, 5:249.

31. *Ibid.*, 1:154–55.

32. *Ibid.*, 1:168.

33. *Chuang-tzu i*, "On Reading the *Chuang-tzu*," p. 1a

34. *Pi-ch'eng hsü*, 1:154-55.

35. *Ibid.*, 1:147, 148-49, 153.

36. *Ibid.*, 1:150.

37. *Pi-ch'eng*, 1:7-8.

38. See Watson, *Complete Chuang Tzu*, p. 302.

39. *Tan-yüan chi*, 22:2b. The "horse" analogy will be discussed later in this chapter.

40. *Tan-yüan chi*, 12:5b.

41. *Analects* 7:2; Chan, *Source Book*, p. 31.

42. *Analects* 17:19; Chan, *Source Book*, p. 47.

43. *Mencius* 5A:5; Chan, *Source Book*, p. 77.

44. See my "Revolt against Ch'eng-Chu," pp. 271-72.

45. *Ibid.*, pp. 271-76, 292-96. See also de Bary, "Introduction," *Self and Society*, pp. 1-27.

46. *Pi-ch'eng hsü*, 1:147.

47. Bernard P. Dauenhauer, *Silence*, pp. 16–24, esp. pp. 19-21.

48. *Pi-ch'eng hsü*, 1:149.

49. *Ibid.*, 1:147.

50. Chu Hsi, *Ssu-shu chi-chu*, 2:4:1a.

51. Legge, *Confucian Analects*, 7:2.

52. Waley, *Analects*, pp. 104, 123.

53. Following Legge's translation except for the concluding sentence (Legge, *Confucian Analects*, 9:15).

54. *Pi-ch'eng hsü*, 1:148-49.

55. See chapter 3.

56. Chu, *Ssu-shu chi-chu*, 2:4:1a and 3:9:5a–b.

57. See *Analects* 11:2 and *Mencius* 2A:2:18.

58. *Mencius* 3B:9 (Legge's translation, p. 279).

59. *Mencius* 4A:22 (Legge's translation, p. 311).

60. *Analects* 2:13.

61. *Ibid.*, 4:24.

62. *Ibid.*, 14:29.

63. *Ibid.*, 8:27.

64. *Ibid.*, 5:24.

65. *Ibid.*, 1:3, 17:17.

66. *Ibid.*, 7:3.

67. *Mencius* 4A:16.

68. *Analects* 8:20.

69. *Mencius* 4B:11.

70. Gadamer, *Truth and Method*, p. 16.

71. *Ibid.*, p. 17.

72. *Analects* 14:21 (Legge's translation, p. 284).

73. *Analects* 14:4.

74. *Ibid.*, 15:7 (translation adapted from Waley, pp. 194–95).

75. *Analects* 16:6 (translation adapted from Waley, p. 205).

76. *Analects* 10:1 (translation adapted from Waley, p. 146).

77. *Analects* 10:2 (translation adapted from Waley, p. 146).

78. *Mencius* 7B:31 (translation adapted from D. C. Lau, *Mencius*, p. 200).

79. *Mencius* 4A:8, 10 (translation adapted from D. C. Lau, pp. 121, 122).

80. *Mencius* 7A:43 (translation adapted from D. C. Lau, p. 192).

81. Chung-ying Cheng, "On *Yi* as a Universal Principle of Specific Application in Confucian Morality."

82. *Mencius* 4B:11.

83. *Ibid.*, 3B:9.

84. *Ibid.*, 2A:9.

85. *Ibid.*, 7B:23 (translation adapted from Lau, p. 193, and W. A. C. H. Dobson, trans., *Mencius*, pp. 50-51).

86. A similar observation has been made by Lik Kuen Tong. Tong, however, approaches the problem of speech and silence in terms of speech and action and not in terms of "advance" and "retreat." See his "The Meaning of Philosophical Silence: Some Reflections on the Use of Language in Confucian Thought," pp. 175–77.

87. T'ang Chün-i, *Chung-kuo che-hsüeh yüan-lun: tao-lun p'ien* (hereafter cited as *Yüan-lun: tao-lun*), pp. 207–8, 273-75.

88. *Chou I*, "Hsi Tz'u (A)," 7:6a.

89. *Analects* 8:3; Chan, *Source Book*, p. 40.

90. *Mencius* 2A:2; see Chan, *Source Book*, p. 62.

91. *Mencius* 5A:4 (translation adapted from Lau, p. 142).

92. See T'ang Yung-t'ung, *Wei-Chin hsüan-hsüeh lun-kao*, pp. 26-47.

93. *Analects* 20:3.

94. *Mencius* 2A:2 (translation adapted from Lau, pp. 77, 78).

95. Wang Hsien-ch'ien, ed., *Hsün-tzu chi-chieh*, 22:280-81. Translation taken with modification from Burton Watson, trans., *Hsün Tzu*, pp. 146-47.

96. *Hsün-tzu chi-chieh*, 22:201; see Watson, *Hsün Tzu*, p. 147.

97. *Hsün-tzu chi-chieh*, 5:53.

98. *Ibid.*, 6:66. I have followed Yeh Shao-chün in taking "Tzu-hsia shih chih chien-ju" as the "contemptible Confucians in Tzu-hsia's school." See Yeh, *Hsün Tzu*, p. 32.

99. *Hsün-tzu chi-chieh*, 5:53, 55.

100. *Ibid.*, 6:61.

101. *Ibid.*, 5:55.

102. *Ibid.*, 6:61.

103. *Ibid.*, 5:56.

104. *Ibid.*, 6:61.

105. T'ang, *Yüan-lun*: tao-lun, p. 209.

106. *Analects* 17:21 (translation adapted from Waley, p. 215).

107. T'ang, *Yüan-lun*: tao-lun, pp. 263-64, 267-68.

108. *Mencius* 6A:7 (translation modified from Lau, p. 164, and Chan, *Source Book*, pp. 55-56).

109. *Mencius* 3A:1 (translation modified from Lau, p. 95, and Chan, *Source*

Book, p. 66). See also Chan, *Source Book*, p. 66 for the allusions to Ch'eng Chien, the *Book of History*, etc.

110. *Mencius* 4B:26. The point of this passage is fairly clear. However, the language involved is rather problematical. I have followed Chiang Po-ch'ien's commentary in taking the *ku* to be the same in use as the *ku* in Hsün Tzu's "ch'ih-chih yu-ku yen-chih ch'eng-li" in *Hsün Tzu*, chapter 6. For Chiang's commentary, see *Meng Tzu*, vol. 1 in Shen Chih-fang, ed., *Yü-i kuang-chieh ssu-shu* (Taipei: Ch'i-ming shu-chü, 1952). For other interpretations, see Chan, *Source Book*, p. 76; Lau, *Mencius*, p. 133; and A. C. Graham, "The Background of Mencius' Theory of Human Nature," pp. 251-54.

111. *Mencius* 2A:6 (translation modified from Chan, *Source Book*, p. 65).

112. *Mencius* 2A:6.

113. *Mencius* 6A:6 (translation modified from Chan, *Source Book*, pp. 53-54).

114. *Mencius* 2A:6 (translation adapted from Chan, *Source Book*, pp. 65-66).

115. *Mencius* 3A:5 (translation modified from Chan, *Source Book*, pp. 70-71, and Dobson, *Mencius*, pp. 106-7).

116. *Mencius* 2B:7. According to Ch'ao Ch'i, "middle antiquity" refers to the time of the Duke of Chou. See his *Meng Tzu*, 4:8b.

117. *Mencius* 4A:27 (translation modified from Chan, *Source Book*, p. 76).

118. *Hsün-tzu chi-chieh*, 22:284.

119. *Ibid.*, 19:231 (translation modified from Bodde, *A History of Chinese Philosophy*, 1:297).

120. See *Hsün-tzu chi-chieh*, 11:131–50, 19:231-51, 20:252-57, 23:289-300.

121. *Ibid.*, 21:263-64 (translation modified from Watson, *Hsün Tzu*, pp. 127-28).

122. *Hsün-tzu chi-chieh*, 21:263; see Watson, *Hsün Tzu*, p. 127.

123. *Hsün-tzu chi-chieh*, 22:281; see Watson, *Hsün Tzu*, p. 147.

124. *Hsün-tzu chi-chieh*, 22:274-75; see Watson, *Hsün Tzu*, pp. 139-40.

125. *Hsün-tzu chi-chieh*, 23:289; see Watson, *Hsün Tzu*, p. 157.

126. *Hsün-tzu chi-chieh*, 22:283-84; translation partly based on Watson, *Hsün Tzu*, pp. 150-51.

127. See *Hsün-tzu chi-chieh*, chapters 19, 20, 23.

128. *Ibid.*, 23:294-96.

129. *Ibid.*, 23:294 (translation modified from Watson, *Hsün Tzu*, p. 160).

130. *Hsün-tzu chi-chieh*, 23:295 (translation partly based on Watson, *Hsün Tzu*, pp. 165-66).

131. *Mencius* 7A:1.

132. *Hsün-tzu chi-chieh*, 17:205; see Watson, *Hsün Tzu*, pp. 79–80.

133. *Hsün-tzu chi-chieh*, 17:205 (translation modified from Chan, *Source Book*, pp. 116).

134. *Hsün-tzu chi-chieh*, 17:208; see Watson, *Hsün Tzu*, p. 82.

135. Vincent Y. C. Shih, "Hsün Tzu's Positivism."

136. *Hsün-tzu chi-chieh*, 17:207-8; see Watson, *Hsün Tzu*, p. 82.

137. *Hsün-tzu chi-chieh*, 17:209-11; see Watson, *Hsün Tzu*, pp. 83–85.

138. *Hsün-tzu chi-chieh*, 17:206 and 211; see Watson, *Hsün Tzu*, pp. 80, 86.

139. *Hsün-tzu chi-chieh*, 17:207-8 (translation modified from Chan, *Source Book*, p. 120).

140. *Hsün-tzu chi-chieh*, 17:206 (translation from Chan, *Source Book*, p. 117, with slight modification).

141. *Hsün-tzu chi-chieh*, 9:103-4 (translation modified from Watson, *Hsün Tzu*, p. 144).

142. *Hsün-tzu chi-chieh*, 22:279 (translation modified from Watson, *Hsün Tzu*, p. 44).

143. Two highly problematical clauses of which various interpretations have been made by both traditional commentators and modern translators (see *Hsün-tzu chi-chieh*, p. 276; H. H. Dubs, *The Works of Hsüntzu*, p. 283; Watson, *Hsün Tzu*, p. 141; Chan, *Source Book*, p. 125). My translation is based on the interpretation suggested by T'ang Chün-i, who took the word for "form" (*hsiang*) to mean "shape" (*chuang*) and interpreted these two clauses in light of Hsün Tzu's distinction between *chuang* and *shih* ("reality") (see T'ang, *Yüan-lun: tao-lun*, pp. 137-41).

144. *Hsün-tzu chi-chieh*, 22:276.

145. *Ibid.*, 22:279 (translation partly based on Watson, *Hsün Tzu*, pp. 144-45).

147. *Hsün-tzu chi-chieh*, 22:276-78 (translation partly based on Watson, *Hsün Tzu*, pp. 142-43).

148. *Hsün-tzu chi-chieh*, 22:279; see Watson, *Hsün Tzu*, p. 144. My understanding of *pu-fu* follows the interpretation suggested by T'ang Chün-i in his *Yüan-lun: tao-lun*, pp. 160-61.

149. *Hsün-tzu chi-chieh*, 22:281; see Watson, *Hsün Tzu*, p. 147.

150. *Lao Tzu*, chapter 14.

151. *Ibid.*, chapter 32. Translation modified from D. C. Lau, *Lao Tzu: Tao Te Ching*, p. 91.

152. Wang Hsien-ch'ien, *Chuang-tzu chi-chieh*, 2:14.

153. *Ibid.*, 25:173.

154. *Wei-mo ching*, pp. 550–51; Luk, *Vimalakīrti*, pp. 92–100.

155. *Wei-mo ching*, p. 555; Luk, *Vimalakīrti*, p. 122.

156. T'ang, *Yüan-lun: tao-lun*, pp. 348–98, esp. pp. 350–70. However, some of the statements cited from the *Lao Tzu* to exemplify each of the six types are my own selections and not provided by T'ang.

157. Translation by Chan, *Source Book*, p. 174.

158. Translation adapted from *ibid.*, p. 152, and Lau, *Lao Tzu*, p. 82.

159. Translation adapted from Chan, *Source Book*, p. 146.

160. Translation adapted from *ibid.*, p. 150.

161. *Chuang-tzu chi-chieh*, 13:85.

162. Translation by Chan, *Source Book*, pp. 168-69.

163. Translation adapted from Lau, *Lao Tzu*, p. 99.

164. Translation derived from Chan, *Source Book*, p. 170, with minor modifications.

165. Translation from *ibid.*, p. 147.

166. *Ibid.*, pp. 154-55.

167. *Ibid.*, p. 158.

168. Translation derived from *ibid.*, pp. 143, 146-48, with minor modifications.

169. *Chuang-tzu chi-chieh*, 25:175; Watson, *Complete Chuang Tzu*, p. 293.

170. *Chuang-tzu chi-chieh*, 24:159; Watson, *Complete Chuang Tzu*, p. 269.

171. *Chuang-tzu chi-chieh*, 2:14 (translation derived from Watson, *Complete Chuang Tzu*, p. 44, with minor modifications).

172. *Chuang-tzu chi-chieh*, 2:9.

173. *Ibid.*, 2:11; Watson, *Complete Chuang Tzu*, p. 41.

174. *Chuang-tzu chi-chieh*, 2:12 (translation by Watson, *Complete Chuang Tzu*, pp. 42-43, with minor modifications).

175. *Chuang-tzu chi-chieh* 2:9-10; Watson, *Complete Chuang Tzu*, pp. 39-40.

176. *Chuang-tzu chi-chieh*, 2:11; Watson, *Complete Chuang Tzu*, p. 41.

177. Jacques Derrida, *Writing and Difference*, pp. 292-93.

178. Edward W. Said, *Beginnings*, p. 342.

179. Jacques Derrida, *Of Grammatology*, trans. by Gayatri Chakravorty Spivak, "Translator's Preface," p. xix.

180. *Chuang-tzu chi-chieh*, 2:12–13 (translation derived from Watson, *Complete Chuang Tzu*, p. 43, with slight modification).

181. *Chuang-tzu chi-chieh*, 27:182; Watson *Complete Chuang Tzu*, p. 304. My reading of Chuang Tzu and Derrida differs somewhat from that of Michelle Yeh, who sees Chuang Tzu's *Tao* as devoid of "any onto-theological implications" and views the difference between Chuang Tzu and Derrida as "one in emphasis rather than in essence" (see her "The Deconstructivist Way: A Comparative Study of Derrida and Chuang Tzu," p. 114). I have, however, argued that Chuang Tzu's Tao, though not "onto-theological," is nonetheless ontological. For this reason, I regard Chuang Tzu and Derrida as traveling on two entirely different paths, even though their paths cross at certain points.

182. *Chuang-tzu chi-chieh*, 2:13; Watson, *Complete Chuang Tzu*, p. 43.

183. See *Vimalakīrti*, chapter 2 and *Lotus Sūtra*, chapter 2.

184. Walter Liebenthal, *Chao Lun: The Treatises of Seng-chao*, p. 47.

185. Translation adapted from Liebenthal, *Chao Lun*, p. 41. For *Chao Lun* in the Chinese original, see *Taishō* 45(1858):150-61.

186. Translation adapted from Liebenthal, *Chao Lun*, p. 48.

187. I.e., *Mādhyamika Śāstra* and *Dvādaśa-dvāra* by Nāgārjuna and *Śata Śāstra* by Āryadeva.

188. Liebenthal, *Chao Lun*, p. 46.

189. See Junjirō Takakusu, *The Essentials of Buddhist Philosophy*, p. 163.

190. Yampolsky, *Platform Sutra*, p. 173.

191. Yanagida Seizan, *Rinzai roku*, p. 158; see Irmgard Schloegl, trans., *The Zen Teaching of Rinzai*, pp. 53–54.

192. E. g., Yanagida, *Rinzai roku*, pp. 127, 145, 175.

193. Translation by Yampolsky with slight modification, *Platform Sutra*, pp. 150-51.

194. Yanagida, *Rinzai roku*, p. 167.

195. *Ibid.*, pp. 119-20.

196. *Ibid.*, pp. 169–70.

197. *Ibid.*, p. 140.

198. The trigger or *chi* in the expression *chi-feng* is the trigger of a crossbow, while *feng*, strictly speaking, refers to the sharpness of the edge of an arrowhead and not of a razor (see *Chung-wen ta tz'u-tien* [Taipei: Chung-kuo wen-hua ta-hsüeh ch'u-pan pu, 1982, popular edition], 5:485).

199. See Yampolsky, *Platform Sutra*, pp. 170-73.

200. Yanagida, *Rinzai roku*, pp. 139-40.

201. Chih-i, *Miao-fa lien-hua ching hsüan-i* (hereafter cited as *Fa-hua hsüan-i*), *Taishō* 33(1716):704. See also *ibid.*, pp. 682, 684, 770 and Hurvitz, *Chih I*, p. 333.

202. Chih-i, *Fa-hua hsüan-i*, pp. 683, 685, 690, 696-97, 702-4, 712-13, 764-65, 768-70, 773, 797-800.

203. See Hurvitz, *Chih I*, pp. 252-301; Ch'en, *Buddhism in China*, pp. 305-11.

204. For an English translation of this parable, see Hurvitz, *Chih I*, pp. 235-36.

205. Chih-i, *Fa-hua hsüan-i*, pp. 682, 688-89, 690, 696-97, 703-4, 705, 713, 714, 770. For an analysis of Chih-i's view of the *Lotus*, see Hurvitz, *Chih I*, pp. 223-32.

206. T'ang Chün-i, *Chung-kuo che-hsüeh yüan-lun: yüan-tao p'ien* (3) [hereafter cited as *Yüan-lun: yüan-tao* (3)] (Hong Kong: Hsin-ya shu-yüan yen-chiu so, 1974), pp. 1119–20.

207. See Leon Hurvitz, trans., *Scripture of the Lotus Blossom of the Fine Dharma*, p. 28.

208. Chih-i, *Fa-hua hsüan-i*, p. 697.

209. *Ibid.*, p. 773.

210. *Ibid.*

211. *Ibid.*, pp. 682–83.

212. *Ibid.*, pp. 696, 715.

213. *Ibid.*, p. 770.

214. *Ibid.*, p. 773.

215. *Ibid.*, pp. 693-94.

216. Watson, *Complete Chuang Tzu*, pp. 165-66.

217. *Chuang-tzu chi-chieh*, p. 95.

218. Tao-yüan, *Ching-te ch'uan-teng lu*, 27:13a; Yüan-wu K'o-ch'in, *Pi-yen lu*, in *Ch'an-hsüeh ta-ch'eng*, 1:7:171; Hui-k'ai, *Wu-men kuan* in *Ch'an-hsüeh ta-ch'eng*, 2:16; Hui-ming, *Wu-teng hui-yüan*, 1:6b–7a; Ch'ü Ju-chi (1590–1650), *Chih-yüeh lu*, 1:1:42b. This version is taken from the *Pi-yen lu*. The translation is adapted from Thomas and J. C. Cleary, *The Blue Cliff Record*, 2:412.

219. *Tsa a-han ching*, in *Taishō* 2(99):234.

220. *Ta pan-nieh-p'an ching*, p. 469.

221. Chih-i, *Fa-hua hsüan-i*, p. 697.

222. *Pi-yen lu*, 4:110; Cleary, *The Blue Cliff Record*, 2:279.

223. Seng-chao, *Chao Lun*, p. 157; Chih-i, *Miao-fa lien-hua ching wen-chü*, in *Taishō* 34(1718):2.

224. *Lao Tzu*, chapter 80.

225. *Ibid.*, chapter 32.

226. *Chuang-tzu chi-chieh*, 2:14.

227. *Pi-ch'eng hsü*, 2:171.

228. *Ibid.*, 2:169.

229. *Ibid.*, 1:153.

230. *Tan-yüan chi*, 48:11a.

231. *Ibid.*, 47:1a–b.

232. *Chuang-tzu chi-chieh*, 26:181; Watson, *Complete Chuang Tzu*, p. 302.

233. *Tan-yüan chi*, 22:2b.

234. *Pi-ch'eng hsü*, 2:184-85.

235. *Chuang-tzu chi-chieh*, 33:215-24, esp. pp. 216, 221-22.

236. *Pi-ch'eng hsü*, 3:202-3.

237. *Ibid.*, 3:202, 4:214.

238. Chiao Hung, *Kuo-shih ching-chi chih* (hereafter cited as *Ching-chi chih*), 2:25–26.

239. *Pi-ch'eng hsü*, 1:164.

240. *Ibid.*, 3:202.

241. *Pi-ch'eng*, 1:27-28.

242. *Ching-chi chih*, 2:20.

243. See my "Revolt Against Ch'eng-Chu," pp. 271-76, 292-96.

244. T'ang, *Yüan-lun: tao-lun*, p. 223.

245. Sun Ch'i-feng, *Li-hsüeh tsung-chuan*, Sun's preface, p. 3a.

246. *Ibid.*, T'ang's preface, pp. 2a–b.

247. *Ming-ju hsüeh-an*, p. 158.

248. *Ibid.*, pp. 8, 336.

249. Chang Hsüeh-ch'eng, *Wen-shih t'ung-i*, 1:7b–8a.

250. Yü Ying-shih, *Lun Tai Chen yü Chang Hsüeh-ch'eng* (hereafter cited as *Tai yü Chang*), pp. 46, 48.

251. *Analects* 9:4.

252. *Ibid*, 18:8; translation by Legge, *Confucian Analects*, p. 217.

253. Chiao Hsün, *Lun-yü t'ung-shih* in *Mu-hsi-hsüan ts'ung-shu*, pp. 2a–7b, esp. 4b–7b. See also his *Lun-yü pu-shu* in *Chiao-shih ts'ung-shu*, 1:5a-8a. For the allusion to Confucius' "one thread" of "truthfulness and reciprocity," see *Analects* 4:15.

254. Yü, *Tai yü Chang*, pp. 45-53. See also David Nivison, *The Life and Thought of Chang Hsüeh-ch'eng* (hereafter cited as *Chang Hsüeh-ch'eng*), pp. 139-62.

255. *Li-hsüeh tsung-chuan*, Sun's preface, pp. 1b, 2b; Sun's "Notes on Organization of the Book" (*i-li*), pp. 1b–2a; T'ang's preface, pp. 1b-2a.

256. *Mencius* 4B:14; Lau, *Mencius*, p. 130.

257. Tai Chen, *Tai Tung-yüan chi*, pp. 17-18, 24.

258. *Ibid.*, pp. 18–19; Tai Chen, *Meng-tzu tzu-i shu-cheng*, pp. 9, 12, 15, 16, 19, 23-25.

259. *Ming-ju hsüeh-an*, Huang's preface, p. 1, and his "Notes on Organization of the Book" (*fan-li*), p. 1.

260. Nivison, *Chang Hsüeh-ch'eng*, pp. 69-76, 171-76.

261. Chang, *Wen-shih t'ung-i*, 2:25b.

262. Chang Hsüeh-ch'eng, *Wen-chi* in *Chang-shih i-shu*, 22:37b.

263. Chang, *Wen-shih t'ung-i*, 4:19a, 32a-b; Nivison, *Chang Hsüeh-ch'eng*, pp. 176, 178.

264. *Pi-ch'eng hsü*, 3:197.

265. *Li-hsüeh tsung-chuan*, T'ang's preface, pp. 3a-b. The "great foundation" and the "universal path" are allusions to the *Doctrine of the Mean* (see Chan, *Source Book*, p. 98).

266. *Ming-ju hsüeh-an*, "Notes on Organization of the Book," pp. 1, 2.

267. Chang, *Wen-shih t'ung-i*, 9:34b-39b, esp. pp. 35a-b, 39a.

268. *Tai Tung-yüan chi*, 2:31-32, 33, 51. The statement that "books cannot fully encompass words and words cannot fully encompass meaning" is derived from the *Book of Changes* (see *Chou I*, 7:10a).

269. T'ang, *Yüan-lun: tao-lun*, pp. 221-22.

270. Chan, *Reflections*, pp. 105-6.
271. *Ibid.*, pp. 63-65.
272. *Ibid.*, p. 104.
273. *Ibid.*, p. 103.
274. *Chu-tzu yü-lei*, 11:12a.

5. A Synthetic Neo-Confucianism as Restructured Neo-Confucianism

1. Chiao Hung, *Yin-fu ching chieh*, p. 1b.
2. See Chiao Hung's defense of Liu Hsiang's "Treatise on the Five Agents" in *Pi-ch'eng*, 1:10.
3. *Pi-ch'eng hsü*, 1:165.
4. Mou, *Hsin-t'i yü hsing-t'i*, 1:115–89, esp. pp. 135–36.
5. *Yin-fu ching chieh*, p. 1b.
6. *Pi-ch'eng hsü*, 3:209. For the P'eng bird, see Watson, *Complete Chuang Tzu*, p. 29.
7. See de Bary et al., *Sources of Chinese Tradition*, 1:193-94; Joseph Needham, *Science and Civilization in China*, (Cambridge: Cambridge University Press, 1958), 3:216-19.
8. For the *Chou-pi suan-ching* and its astronomical theories, see Needham, *Science and Civilization in China*, 3:19–24, 210-16.
9. *Pi-ch'eng hsü*, 3:208-9.
10. *Pi-ch'eng*, 3:58.
11. *Chuang-tzu i*, 5:41b.
12. *Yin-fu ching chieh*, p. 1b.
13. *Ibid.*
14. *Ibid.*
15. *Tan-yüan chi*, 4:5b–6b.
16. *Ibid.*, 47:6b.
17. *Pi-ch'eng hsü*, 1:167.
18. *Ibid.*, 1:164-65, 4:213; *Tan-yüan chi*, 47:6b.
19. *Doctrine of the Mean* 1:1.
20. *Pi-ch'eng*, 4:106; *Pi-ch'eng hsü* 1:164, 4:213; *Tan-yüan chi*, 4:6b.
21. An allusion to the *Doctrine of the Mean* 20:18.
22. *Tan-yüan chi*, 47:6b–7a.
23. T'ang, *Yüan-lun: tao-lun*, pp. 583-89. See also his *Chung-kuo che-hsüeh yüan-lun: yüan-hsing p'ien* (hereafter cited as *Yüan lun: yüan-hsing*), pp. 321–411.
24. *Pi-ch'eng hsü*, 1:152.
25. *Tan-yüan chi*, 47:17a.
26. *Ibid.* Allusion is to *Mencius* 3A:4:13 (translation adapted from Lau, *Mencius*, p. 103)
27. See James Legge, trans., *The Book of Historical Documents*, in *The Chinese Classics*, pp. 23, 89. My translation, however, is based on Chiao Hung's interpretation, which appears in *Pi-ch'eng hsü*, 5:248-49.
28. *Analects* 5:5.

29. *Pi-ch'eng hsü*, 1:158, 5:248-49, 1:156.

30. *Ibid.*, 1:149, 156 and 5:249; *Lao-tzu i*, 5:37a.

31. *Tan-yüan chi*, 23:15a–b.

32. T'ang Chün-i, "The Development of the Concept of Moral Mind from Wang Yang-ming to Wang Chi" (hereafter cited as "Moral Mind"), in de Bary, *Self and Society*, pp. 108-16.

33. *Pi-ch'eng hsü*, 1:153.

34. *Lao-tzu i*, 2:29a.

35. *Ibid.*, 2:33b-34a, 4:13b.

36. *Ibid.*, 2:33b-34a; *Pi-ch'eng hsü*, 2:174-75.

37. *Lao-tzu i*, 2:39b–40a; *Pi-ch'eng hsü*, 1:156.

38. See chapter 3.

39. *Tan-yüan chi*, 48:12b.

40. *Pi-ch'eng hsü*, 4:214.

41. *Yin-fu ching chieh*, p. 3a.

42. *Lao Tzu*, chapters 1 and 40.

43. *Lao-tzu i*, 4:13b.

44. *Pi-ch'eng*, 1:2.

45. *Lao-tzu i*, 4:13b

46. *Pi-ch'eng hsü*, 1:153.

47. *Yin-fu ching chieh*, p. 3a. The expression "lustrously beyond forms or images" is derived from the *Ying-fu ching* (concluding sentence).

48. *Lao-tzu i*, 2:40a.

49. *Ibid.*

50. *Yin-fu ching chieh*, p. 3a.

51. *Lao-tzu i*, 3:31a.

52. *Pi-ch'eng hsü*, 1:154; *Tan-yüan chi*, 22:16b.

53. *Tan-yüan chi*, 48:6b.

54. *Yin-fu ching chieh*, p. 2b.

55. *Tan-yüan chi*, 47:6a.

56. *Yin-fu ching chieh*, p. 3a.

57. *Lao Tzu*, chapter 10. Translation adapted from Lau, *Lao Tzu*, p. 66. See also *Lao-tzu i*, 1:33a-b.

58. *Lao-tzu i*, 3:26b; *Yin-fu ching chieh*, pp. 1a-b, 3a.

59. *Chuang-tzu i*, 4:4a.

60. *Lao Tzu*, chapter 40.

61. *Yin-fu ching chieh*, p. 3a.

62. *Ibid.*, p. 1b; *Lao-tzu i*, 3:27a.

63. *Lao-tzu i*, 2:15a–b; allusion is to *Lao Tzu,* chapter 16.

64. *Pi-ch'eng*, 1:2; allusion is to *Analects* 8:5.

65. *Pi-ch'eng hsü*, 1:155; allusion is to the *Book of Changes*, "Hsi Tz'u (A)," chapter 12 (see *Chou I*, 7:10b).

66. *Pi-ch'eng hsü*, 2:176.

67. *Lao-tzu i*, 2:15b.

68. My understanding of the *Lao Tzu* in this regard follows the somewhat traditional interpretation as formulated by, for instance, T'ang Chün-i (see his *Yüan-lun: tao-lun*, pp. 352–53, 378-93, 397-98). For three reasons, I have decided not ot adopt D. C. Lau's revisionist thesis that Lao Tzu did not propound a "circular" theory of change (see D. C. Lau, "The Treatment of Opposites in Lao Tzu"): (1) the idea of "circular" movement

is not absent from the *Lao Tzu*, where, for instance, the Way is said to be "revolving without cease and without fail" (chapter 25); (2) I cannot overlook what in Lau's terms is the language of "generation" and explain away (as Lau does) Lao Tzu's statement that "Being and Nothingness produce each other" (chapter 2) as a statement which makes only a "logical" point and "has nothing to do with production either as a historical, or even as a metaphysical, concept" (Lau, "The Treatment of Opposites," p. 347); and (3) the idea of "circular" change need not be incompatible with Lao Tzu's valuation of the "soft," as Lau has supposed, because although the "circular" process of growth and decline is ultimately inevitable, the span of this process is not predetermined and can be prolonged if one abides by the "soft."

69. Bodde, tr., *A History of Chinese Philosophy*, 1:180.

70. *Lao Tzu*, chapter 16; see T'ang, *Yüan-lun: tao-lun*, pp. 370–76.

71. *Lao-tzu i*, 2:15a–b, 33b–34a.

72. For an English translation of these two essays, see Chan, *Source Book*, pp. 463-80.

73. Ching, *To Acquire Wisdom*, pp. 112-40.

74. *Chu-tzu yü-lei*, 94:7a-b.

75. For a discussion of Chu Hsi in this regard, see T'ang, *Yüan-lun: tao-lun*, pp. 451-58.

76. Chu Hsi, *Chu Wen-kung wen-chi*, 36:10a-b. Translation by Julia Ching in *To Acquire Wisdom*, p. 12.

77. See Lau, *Lao Tzu*, pp. 44, 47.

78. Watson, *Complete Chuang Tzu*, p. 225; see also pp. 114, 118, 120, 144, 267, 291, 294-95.

79. See his *Chao Lun*. See also Liebenthal, *Chao Lun*, pp. 46-145, and Richard H. Robinson, *Early Mādhyamika in India and China*, pp. 123-55.

80. *Tan-yüan chi*, 48:4a-b.

81. *Ibid.*, 49:6b.

82. *Pi-ch'eng hsü*, 1:164.

83. *Tan-yüan chi*, 47:1b.

84. *Pi-ch'eng hsü*, 1:155.

85. *Ibid.*, 1:163.

86. *Pi-ch'eng*, 4:106.

87. See Legge, *The I Ching*, p. 356.

88. See Chan, "The Evolution of the Confucian Concept of *Jen*," pp. 311–16.

89. See T'ang, *Yüan-lun: tao-lun*, pp. 397-98. The concept of "daily renovation" comes from the *Book of Changes* (see Legge, *The I Ching*, p. 356) and *The Great Learning* (see Legge, *The Great Leaning*, in *The Confucian Classics*, 1:361).

90. *Pi-ch'eng hsü*, 1:152.

91. T'ang, *Yüan-lun: yüan-tao (3)*, pp. 1379–1401.

92. Mou, *Hsin-t'i yü hsing-t'i*, 1:612. The discussion is indebted to Mou's analysis of the problem of *t'i* and *yung* in Buddhism (see *ibid.*, pp. 571–657).

93. See Chan, *Source Book*, pp. 357, 436-37n44.

94. Ch'eng-ch'ien, *Chu chin-shih-tzu chang*, esp. pp. 75b–76a.

95. See Hakeda, *The Awakening of Faith*, pp. 65, 68, 69-70; for Chinese original, see *Taishō* 32:579.

96. Mou, *Hsin-t'i yü hsing-t'i*, 1:607-16.

97. Ch'eng-ch'ien, *Chu chin-shih-tzu chang*, pp. 75b–76a.

98. See chapter 3.

99. Charles Fu, "Morality or Beyond: The Neo-Confucian Confrontation with Mahāyāna Buddhism," pp. 390-91.

100. Foucault, *The Archaeology of Knowledge*, pp. 40-49.

101. *Ibid.*, pp. 31-39.

102. I have derived this term from Mou Tsung-san (see his *Hsin-t'i yü hsing-t'i*, 1:33-42).

103. Fu, "Morality or Beyond," p. 391.

104. Heinrich Dumoulin, *A History of Zen Buddhism*, p. 104.

105. Hui Hai, *Tun-wu ju-tao yao-men lun* and *Chu-fang men-jen ts'an-wen yü-lu* in *Dai Nihon zoko zōkyō*, ser. 1, pt. 2, case 15, 5:425b, 429a, 429b–30a; John Blofeld, *The Zen Teaching of Hui Hai*, pp. 77, 104, 111.

106. Bloom, "'Abstraction' of Ming Thought," pp. 69-125, esp. pp. 76-91.

107. *Pi-ch'eng hsü*, 1:148, 150, 160, 162, 166.

108. *Ibid.*, 1:166; *Tan-yüan chi*, 48:2a.

109. *Tan-yüan chi* 48:5b-6a; *Lao-tzu i*, opening *chüan*:3a.

110. *Tan-yüan chi*, 48:2b, 2b–3a.

111. *Ibid.*, 48:2b, 10b.

112. *Pi-ch'eng hsü*, 2:175.

113. *Tan-yüan chi*, 48:4b-5a; allusion is to *Mencius* 6A:11.

114. *Chuang-tzu chi-chieh*, 2:8-9.

115. *Tan-yüan chi*, 48:11b.

116. *Ibid.*, 48:12b; *Pi-ch'eng hsü*, 2:175.

117. *Tan-yüan chi*, 49:3a.

118. *Pi-ch'eng hsü*, 1:156.

119. *Ibid.*, 1:150, 156.

120. *Tan-yüan chi*, 48:2b.

121. *Pi-ch'eng hsü*, 4:213.

122. *Ibid.*, 1:156.

123. *Ibid.*, 2:177.

124. *Ibid.*, 1:136.

125. *Tan-yüan chi*, 48:3a. Reference to Yao and Chieh is an allusion to *Hsün Tzu* (see *Hsün-tzu chi-chieh*, 17:205).

126. *Pi-ch'eng hsü*, 1:156.

127. *Ibid.*, 1:159.

128. *Ibid.*, 1:167; *Chuang-tzu i*, 1:63a.

129. *Pi-ch'eng hsü*, 1:167.

130. *Shou leng-yen ching*, p. 110; Luk, *The Śūraṅgama Sūtra*, p. 26.

131. *Tan-yüan chi*, 49:7a.

132. *Pi-ch'eng hsü*, 2:180. The images of the blind man and the echo are derived from *Wei-mo ching*, p. 540; see also Luk, *Vimalakīrti*, p. 23.

133. *Tan-yüan chi*, 47:17a.

134. *Pi-ch'eng hsü*, 1:150; *Chuang-tzu i*, 4:48a.

135. *Chuang-tzu i*, 4:48a; *Tan-yüan chi*, 47:17a.

136. *Pi-ch'eng hsü*, 2:175; *Tan-yüan chi*, 47:10a & 48:12a.

137. For example *Tan-yüan chi*, 48:2b; *Lao-tzu i*, 2:24a.

138. *Pi-ch'eng hsü*, 2:180, 184.

139. *Ibid.*, 2:173.

140. *Lao-tzu i*, 6:42a.

141. An allusion to *Analects* 5:6.
142. *Pi-ch'eng hsü*, 1:156.
143. *Lao-tzu i*, 2:29a.
144. *Ibid.*, 2:23b-24a. The statement is quoted from the *Lao Tzu*, chapter 19; translation adapted from Lau, *Lao Tzu*, p. 75.
145. *Tan-yüan chi*, 48:9a.
146. *Ibid.*, 48:4b.
147. *Ibid.*, 47:13b.
148. *Pi-ch'eng hsü*, 2:173-74.
149. *Ibid.*, 2:177.
150. *Tan-yüan chi*, 48:6a.
151. *Ibid*, 48:3b; allusion is to *Doctrine of the Mean*, chapter 1.
152. *Tan-yüan chi*, 6:4a, 47:10b.
153. *Ibid.*, 6:4a; *Pi-ch'eng hsü*, 2:172.
154. *Chuang-tzu i*, 2:58a.
155. *Pi-ch'eng hsü*, 2:172; allusion is to the *Book of Changes* (see Legge, *The I Ching*, p. 370).
156. *Pi-ch'eng hsü*, 1:165, 2:172.
157. *Tan-yüan chi*, 4:1a.
158. *Ibid.*, 6:4a; *Pi-ch'eng hsü*, 1:166.
159. *Pi-ch'eng hsü*, 1:165.
160. *Pi-ch'eng*, 1:15. Allusion is to *Mencius* 6A:6; translation based on Chiao Hung's interpretation.
161. *Pi-ch'eng hsü*, 2:173.
162. *Ibid.*, 1:149, 2:172; *Chuang-tzu i*, 2:9a.
163. See Berling, *The Syncretic Religion of Lin Chao-en*, pp. 116-37.
164. Translation adapted from Legge, *The I Ching*, pp. 175-76.
165. *Pi-ch'eng hsü*, 1:149.
166. *Ibid.* The ideas of "stopping at the right place" and "not exceeding proper limits" are derived from the *Book of Changes* (see Legge, *The I Ching*, pp. 256, 332).
167. *Tan-yüan chi*, 47:14a-b. The concepts of "excess" and "insufficiency" are derived from *Analects* 11:15 and *Doctrine of the Mean* 4. Being "regulated" and "harmonious" are ideas from *Doctrine of the Mean* 1.
168. *Pi-ch'eng hsü*, 1:165.
169. *Ibid.*, 1:156. Allusion is to *Analects* 9:14.
170. *Pi-ch'eng hsü*, 1:167.
171. *Ibid.*, 2:178.
172. *Tan-yüan chi*, 48:10a. Confucius is said to be free from these four psychological traits (see *Analects* 9:4).
173. *Tan-yüan chi*, 6:4a.
174. *Pi-ch'eng hsü*, 1:167-68.
175. *Pi-ch'eng*, 2:29.
176. *Tan-yüan chi*, 48:4b.
177. *Ibid.*, 47:8a, 48:4a-b, 5a, 49:6b; *Pi-ch'eng hsü*, 1:162, 2:171-72, 176; *Chuang-tzu i*, 1:62b-63a.
178. *Pi-ch'eng hsü*, 1:159.
179. *Ibid.*, 2:171-72.
180. *Ibid.*, 2:172.
181. *Yin-fu ching chieh*, p. 3a.

182. *Ibid.*, p. 1a.
183. *Pi-ch'eng hsü*, 2:178.
184. *Tan-yüan chi*, 48:12b.
185. *Ibid.*, 48:3b-4a.
186. *Ibid.*, 48:11b.
187. *Ibid.*, 48:2b.
188. *Ibid.*, 47:17b.
189. *Pi-ch'eng hsü*, 1:149. See *Lao Tzu*, chapter 38, where it is stated, "Preconceived ideas are the artificiality of the Way and the beginning of folly."
190. *Pi-ch'eng hsü*, 2:174.
191. *Ibid.*, 1:149.
192. *Lao-tzu i*, 6:42a.
193. *Tan-yüan chi*, 47:13a.
194. *Pi-ch'eng hsü*, 2:172.
195. *Ibid.*, 1:152.
196. The concepts of the "human mind" and the Mind of the Tao" are derived from the *Book of History* (see Legge, *The Book of Historical Documents*, p. 61).
197. See T'ang, *Yüan-lun: yüan-hsing*, pp. 401-3.
198. *Chu-tzu ch'üan-shu*, 36:23b.
199. *Chu Wen-kung wen-chi*, 63:20b.
200. *Ch'eng-shih i-shu*, 11:139.
201. *Ibid.*, 19:280.
202. T'ang, *Yüan-lun: yüan-hsing*, pp. 402–3. See also T'ang, "Moral Mind," pp. 94–95.
203. T'ang, *Yüan-lun: yüan-hsing*, p. 407.
204. *Chu-tzu yü-lei*, 13:3a.
205. I have followed T'ang Chün-i in rendering the Chinese term *han-she* as "prehend"; see his "Chang Tsai's Theory of Mind and its Metaphysical Basis," pp. 124-25.
206. For Chang Tsai's theory of *ch'i*, see *ibid.*, pp. 113-36.
207. Chan, *Source Book*, p. 511. See also Wing-tsit Chan, "Neo-Confucian Solution of the Problem of Evil."
208. T'ang, *Yüan-lun: tao-lun*, pp. 428-32.
209. *Chu-tzu ch'üan-shu*, 2:19a; *Chu-tzu yü-lei*, 4:15a. Translation by Chan, *Source Book*, p. 511.
210. Chan, "Chu Hsi's Completion of Neo-Confucianism," pp. 65–69.
211. T'ang, *Yüan-lun: tao-lun*, pp. 478-82, 493-95; *Yüan-lun: yüan-hsing*, pp. 379-84. See also Graham, *Two Chinese Philosophers*, pp. 65-66. For Chu Hsi's characterization of mind as *ch'i chih ching-shuang*, see *Chu-tzu yü-lei*, 5:3b. For Chang Tsai's statement that "mind unites Nature and emotions," see *Chang-tzu ch'üan-shu*, p. 290.
212. Chu Hsi, *Ssu-shu chi-chu*, "Preface to the *Commentaries on the Doctrine of the Mean*," 1:1a-b.
213. See *Mencius* 2A:2.
214. *Tan-yüan chi*, 48:8b.
215. *Ibid.; Lao-tzu i*, 1:32b; *Yin-fu ching chieh*, p. 2b. Allusions are to *Lao Tzu*, chapter 10; Watson, *Complete Chuang Tzu*, pp. 57-58; *Yin-fu ching*, in *Yin-fu ching chieh*, p. 2a.
216. For examples, see *Tan-yüan chi*, 48:4b-5a, and *Pi-ch'eng hsü*, 2:177.

217. *Pi-ch'eng hsü*, 2:179.

218. *Ibid.*, 1:149.

219. *Ibid.*, 2:177.

220. Chan, *Source Book*, p. 618. The explanatory note in brackets is mine.

221. Chu Hsi, *Ssu-shu chi-chu*, "Preface to the *Commentaries on the Doctrine of the Mean*," 1:1a.

222. *Chu-tzu yü-lei*, 78:3b.

223. See T'ang, *Yüan-lun: yüan-hsing*, p. 422.

224. *Chu-tzu yü-lei*, 5:5b.

225. *Ibid.*, 5:12a.

226. *Ibid.*

227. T'ang, *Yüan-lun: yüan-hsing*, pp. 388-89. For *yüan, heng, li, chen*, see Legge, *The I Ching*, p. 57.

228. For Liu Tsung-chou in this regard, see T'ang, *Yüan-lun: yüan-hsing*, pp. 388, 475.

229. *Hsiang-shan ch'üan-chi*, 35:288.

230. *Ibid.*, 35:302. Translation adapted from Siu-chi Huang, *Lu Hsiang-shan: A Twelfth-Century Chinese Idealist Philosopher*, p. 54.

231. *Hsiang-shan ch'üan-chi*, 34:252. Translation adapted from Huang, *Lu Hsiang-shan*, p. 38.

232. T'ang, *Yüan-lun: yüan-hsing*, p. 421. See also his "Moral Mind," pp. 97-100.

233. T'ang, "Moral Mind," pp. 107-8.

234. *Hsiang-shan ch'üan-chi*, 6:52.

235. *Ibid.*, 23:181. "Heaven's people" alludes to *Mencius* 7A:19.

236. *Hsiang-shan ch'üan-chi*, 5:40.

237. *Pi-ch'eng hsü*, 1:147; *Chuang-tzu i*, 1:16b–17a. Allusion is to *Analects* 17:2.

238. De Bary, "Introduction," *Self and Society*", p. 23.

239. Yamashita Ryūji, *Yōmeigaku no kenkyū*, 2:3-4, 80-96. For Lo Ch'in-shun, see Bloom, "'Abstraction' of Ming Thought," pp. 69–125.

240. See *Pi-ch'eng hsü*, 1:155. See also the discussion later in this chapter.

241. Hsü Fu-kuan, *Chung-kuo ssu-hsiang-shih lun-chi*, pp. 46-50.

242. *Yang-ming ch'üan-chi*, 1:4, 10. See also Chan, *Instructions*, pp. 15 (#8) and 34 (#38).

243. See T'ang, "Moral Mind," pp. 103-4.

244. See Ching, *To Acquire Wisdom*, p. 139.

245. *Yang-ming ch'üan-chi*, 3:70. Translation by Chan, *Instructions*, p. 223 (#277).

246. De Bary, "Cultivation and Enlightenment," p. 165.

247. Discussed earlier in this chapter.

248. *Tan-yüan chi*, 49:4a.

249. *Ibid.*, 4:1a.

250. *Ibid.*

251. *Ibid.*

252. *Ibid.*, 47:14a.

253. *Pi-ch'eng hsü*, 2:185.

254. *Tan-yüan chi*, 47:1b, 48:6b-7a, 49:6b.

255. *Pi-ch'eng hsü*, 2:185.

256. *Tan-yüan chi*, 47:4a.

257. *Ibid.*, 49:2a–b. "Moments of haste" and "seasons of danger" allude to *Analects* 4:5:3.

258. *Tan-yüan chi*, 47:9a.

259. *Pi-ch'eng hsü*, 1:151.

160. *Ibid.*, 1:151-52.

161. *Tan-yüan chi*, 49:2b.

262. *Ibid.*, 49:1b-2a. For the allusion to Yen Hui, see *Analects* 6:9 and *Mencius* 3A:1.

263. *Tan-yüan chi*, 47:5a.

264. *Analects* 2:4.

265. *Pi-ch'eng hsü*, 1:149.

266. *Tan-yüan chi*, 47:5a. For the reference to Ch'ü Po-yü, see Watson, *Complete Chuang Tzu*, p. 288, and *Huai-nan Tzu* (Ssu-pu pei-yao ed.), 1:9a.

267. *Tan-yüan chi*, 47:5a-b.

268. *Chuang-tzu i*, 2:8b-9a; *Tan-yüan chi*, 49:7a-b. See also Watson, *Complete Chuang Tzu*, pp. 57-58.

269. *Lao-tzu i*, 1:32b-33a; *Tan-yüan chi*, 47:5a, 13:2a-b. See also *Lao Tzu*, chapters 10 and 48.

270. Hexagrams nos. 23-24. See Wilhelm/Baynes, *Book of Changes*, 1:99-106, 2:140-49.

271. *Tan-yüan chi*, 48:7b.

272. *Lao-tzu i*, 1:32b-33a.

273. *Pi-ch'eng hsü*, 1:151.

274. *Ibid.* The idea of sage's learning as "washing the mind so as to withdraw and hide in secret" is derived from the *Book of Changes*, "Hsi Tz'u (A)," chapter 11 (see Wilhelm/Baynes, *I Ching*, 1:340).

275. *Pi-ch'eng hsü*, 2:172-73. The idea that the sage is "concerned for good fortune and misfortune in common with other men" is derived from the *Book of Changes*, "Hsi Tz'u (A)," chapter 11 (see Wilhelm/Baynes, *I Ching*, 1:340).

276. *Pi-ch'eng hsü*, 2:172-73.

277. *Ibid.*, 1:164, 167-68.

278. *Ibid.*, 2:178-79.

279. *Lao-tzu i*, 1:33a.

280. *Pi-ch'eng*, 1:26. Allusion is to *Mencius* 7A:1.

281. *Tan-yüan chi*, 49:3a.

282. *Pi-ch'eng hsü*, 1:153.

283. De Bary, "Individualism and Humanitarianism," p. 196.

284. *Hsiang-shan ch'üan-chi*, 35:296.

285. *Ibid.*, 35:290.

286. *Ibid.*, 34:256.

287. *Ch'uan-hsi lu*, in *Yang-ming ch'üan-chi*, p. 19; translation by Chan, *Instructions*, p. 61.

288. *Pi-ch'eng*, 1:1.

289. *Tan-yüan chi*, 49:6a.

290. Alludes to *Analects* 19:12.

291. *Pi-ch'eng hsü*, 1:148.

292. See de Bary, "Individualism and Humanitarianism," pp. 155-56.

293. *Pi-ch'eng hsü*, 1:163.

294. *Tan-yüan chi*, 48:2b; see also *Lao-tzu i*, 1:32b–33a.
295. *Tan-yüan chi*, 47:1b.
296. Alludes to the *Shih Ching*. See James Legge, tr., *The Book of Poetry* in *The Chinese Classics*, 4:318–19.
297. *Analects* 12:24.
298. *Tan-yüan chi*, 48:9b. Ricci was referred to as "Mr. Li from the West." The alleged saying by Ricci was probably derived from Ricci's first book in Chinese, *Chiao-yu lun* ("Treatise on Making Friends") (see Goodrich and Fang, *Dictionary of Ming Biography*, 2:1139).
299. *Tan-yüan chi*, 49:7b–8a.
300. For this egalitarianism, see de Bary, "Individualism and Humanitarianism," pp. 145-247, esp. pp. 154-60, 171-78.
301. See Han Yü's "Discourse on Teachers," in de Bary et al., *Sources of Chinese Tradition*, 1:375.
302. See de Bary, "Individualism and Humanitarianism," pp. 178-79, 185-86; see also Ronald Dimberg, *The Sage and Society: The Life and Thought of Ho Hsin-yin*, pp. 85-118.
303. *Tan-yüan chi*, 4:1b.
304. Translation adapted from Legge, *The Book of Historical Documents*, p. 327.
305. *Tan-yüan chi*, 47:12b-13a.
306. *Ibid.*, 47:3b; *Pi-ch'eng hsü*, 1:155.
307. *Tan-yüan chi*, 47:3b.
308. *Ibid.* Allusion is to *Analects* 16:10.
309. *Pi-ch'eng hsü*, 1:155.
310. *Pi-ch'eng*, 4:108–9.
311. *Ibid.*
312. *Tan-yüan chi*, 48:11b-12a, 12b.
313. *Pi-ch'eng hsü*, 1:154.
314. *Pi-ch'eng*, 4:109.
315. *Chu Wen-kung wen-chi*, 54:6a.
316. T'ang, "Moral Mind," pp. 94-97.
317. T'ang, *Yüan-lun: yüan-hsing*, pp. 629-30.
318. *Tan-yüan chi*, 49:3a-b.
319. *Ibid.*, 48:10a.
320. *Ibid.*, 48:5b. *Chieh-shen k'ung-chü* alludes to *Doctrine of the Mean* 1.
321. *Pi-ch'eng hsü*, 1:165, 2:179.
322. T'ang, "Moral Mind," pp. 100, 107.

6. The Restructuring of Neo-Confucianism

1. *Ming-ju hsüeh-an*, "Notes on Organization of the Book," p. 1.
2. *Ibid.*, p. 151.
3. *Ibid.*, pp. 8, 371.
4. *Ibid.*, p. 261.

5. *Ibid.*, pp. 216-17, 336, 486.
6. *Ibid.*, pp. 7-8; see also pp. 101-2, 229, 311, 352, 357.
7. *Ibid.*, p. 8.
8. *Ibid.*, pp. 8, 126.
9. *Ibid.*, pp. 8, 132, 336, 607.
10. *Ibid.*, p. 8.
11. *Ibid.*, p. 485.
12. *Ibid.*, p. 8.
13. *Ibid.*, p. 466.
14. *Ibid.*
15. *Ibid.*, p. 524.
16. *Ibid.*, pp. 485-86.
17. *Ibid.*, p. 44.
18. *Ibid.*
19. *Ibid.*, p. 486.
20. *Ibid.*, p. 285; see also pp. 372-73, 428.
21. *Ibid.*, p. 399.
22. *Ibid.*, p. 52; see also pp. 15, 182.
23. *Ibid.*, p. 448.
24. *Ibid.*, p. 289.
25. *Ibid.*, p. 486.
26. *Ibid.*, p. 192, 448.
27. *Ch'eng-shih i-shu*, 21A:300.
28. *Tai Tung-yüan chi*, 2:8:9; see also *Meng-tzu tzu-i shu-cheng*, p. 19.
29. *Book of Changes*, "Hsi Tz'u (A)," chapter 4. Translation adapted from Chan's *Source Book* (p. 265) according to Tai's interpretation (see *Meng-tzu tzu-i shu-cheng*, p. 17).
30. *Tai Tung-yüan chi*, 2:8:21.
31. Chung-ying Cheng, *Tai Chen's Inquiry into Goodness*, pp. 17-53, esp. pp. 17-30.
32. *Meng-tzu tzu-i shu-cheng*, pp. 7-8.
33. *Ibid.*, pp. 21-22.
34. Lo ch'in-shun, *K'un-chih chi* (1622). Translation from Irene Bloom, with minor modification; see Bloom, "Notes on Knowledge Painfully Acquired: A Translation and Analysis of the *K'un-chih Chi* by Lo Ch'in-shun (1465–1547)," pp. 43–46, 181–83.
35. Bloom, "Notes on Knowledge" p. 30; Yamashita, *Yōmeigaku no kenkyū*, 2:115-25.
36. See Siu-chi Huang, *Lu Hsiang-shan*, pp. 79-86.
37. *Hsiang-shan ch'üan-chi*, 34:252. The concluding statement is a quotation from the *Doctrine of the Mean*, chapter 31.
38. *Hsiang-shan ch'üan-chi*, 34:254. Translation derived from Chan, *Source Book*, p. 582, with minor modification.
39. Yamashita, *Yōmeigaku no kenkyū*, 1:138.
40. *Chu-tzu yü-lei*, 120:32b.
41. *Ibid.*, 27:15a–b.
42. Chan, *Source Book*, p. 27.
43. For Chu Hsi's conception of books as a record of the sages' experience of the "many principles" in things and events, see his statement in *Chu-tzu yü-lei*, 10:1a.

44. *Ibid.*, 27:15a; see also 27:1b, 4b-5a.
45. *Ibid.*, 27:5a.
46. Yü, "Ch'ing Confucian Intellectualism," p. 108.
47. *Hsiang-shan ch'üan-chi*, 35:289.
48. *Yang-ming ch'üan-chi*, 21:394; see also Julia Ching, *The Philosophical Letters of Wang Yang-ming*, p. 73.
49. *Hsiang-shan ch'üan-chi*, 35:294, 301.
50. *Ibid.*, 35:302.
51. *Ibid.*, 34:269.
52. *Ibid.*, 12:103.
53. *Ibid.*, 34:255.
54. *Ibid.*, 34:254. Translation by Huang, *Lu Hsiang-shan*, p. 61.
55. Yü, "Ch'ing Confucian Intellectualism," p. 108.
56. *Hsiang-shan ch'üan-chi*, 35:293.
57. *Ibid.*
58. *The Doctrine of the Mean*, chapter 20; Chan, *Source Book*, p. 107.
59. *Hsiang-shan ch'üan-chi*, 35:287.
60. *Ibid.*, 35:279, 288.
61. *Ibid.*, 35:302. The phrase "loaning troops to the rebel army or helping the robbers with provisions" is an allusion derived from Li Ssu's biography in the *Shih Chi* (Ssu-pu pei-yao ed.), 87:4b.
62. *Hsiang-shan ch'üan-chi*, 35:287.
63. *Ibid.*, 11:91.
64. *Ibid.*, 34:261.
65. *Ibid.*, 7:60.
66. *Ibid.*, 32:242.
67. *Ibid.*
68. *Ibid.*, 14:119, 35:279.
69. *Ibid.*, 3:22-23, 11:91.
70. *Ibid.*, 10:89.
71. *Chu-tzu yü-lei*, 10:1a.
72. *Ibid.*, 11:2a.
73. *Ibid.*
74. *Ibid.*, 11:1b.
75. *Ibid.*, 11:7b.
76. *Ibid.*, 11:1a. For "Yen Hui's delight," see Ch'eng I's essay on "What Yen Tzu Loved to Learn" in Chan, *Source Book*, pp. 547–50.
77. *Chu-tzu yü-lei*, 11:5b.
78. *Ibid.*, 11:12a.
79. *Ibid.*, 10:10b.
80. *Ibid.*, 11:5b.
81. *Ibid.*, 10:1b–2a.
82. *Ibid.*, 11:5a.
83. *Ibid.*, 11:5b.
84. *Ibid.*, 11:3a.
85. *Ibid.*, 104:4b.
86. *Ibid.*, 11:14a.
87. *Ibid.*, 10:5b.
88. *Ibid.*, 10:5a-b.

89. *Ibid.*, 10:11a.
90. *Ibid.*, 10:1a.
91. *Hsiang-shan ch'üan-chi*, 1:3.
92. *Ibid.*, 34:254.
93. *Yang-ming ch'üan-chi*, 7:65-66.
94. For a synoptic overview of Heidegger and Gadamer on the subject/object schema, see Richard E. Palmer, *Hermeneutics*, pp.142–52, 164–65, 171-80.
95. *Ibid.*, pp. 134-39, 171-84, 186-201; see also Josef Bleicher, *Contemporary Hermeneutics*, pp. 101-3, 108-16.
96. *Hsiang-shan ch'üan-chi*, 35:291.
97. *Ibid.*, 35:313.
98. *Ibid.*, 35:310.
99. *Ibid.*, 35:301. The reference to King Wen is an allusion derived from the *Book of Odes*; see Legge, *The Book of Poetry*, p. 433.
100. *Yang-ming ch'üan-chi*, 3:81-82.
101. *Ibid.*, 2:38.
102. *Hsiang-shan ch'üan-chi*, 35:301.
103. *Yang-ming ch'üan-chi*, 1:18.
104. See Bloom, "Notes on Knowledge," pp. 63-81.
105. See *ibid.*, pp. 86-135.
106. See *ibid.*, pp. 87, 100-2.
107. Lo, *K'un-chih chi*, 1:2b.
108. *For details of this debate, see Bloom, "Notes on Knowledge," pp. 110–35.*
109. *Ming-ju hsüeh-an*, 47:485.
110. *Ibid.*, 47:485-86.
111. Bloom, "Notes on Knowledge," pp. 97-100.
112. Nivison, *Chang Hsüeh-ch'eng*, p. 276.
113. Chang, *Wen-shih t'ung-i*, 2:21b-22a.
114. *Ibid.*, 2:18a, 21b-22a.
115. *Yang-ming ch'üan-chi*, 1:18–19. For an English translation of this passage, see Chan, *Instructions*, pp. 60-62.
116. Chang, *Wen-shih t'ung-i*, 2:21b-22a. There is an obvious disagreement between Ying-shih Yü and myself concerning the significance of Chang's *Liang-chih*. This disagreement reflects a rather basic difference in interpretive position. Yü contrasts Chang's *liang-chih* as an "intellectualist" concept with Wang Yang-ming's *liang-chih* as an "antiintellectualist" concept in terms of what he perceives to be the tension between *tsun te-hsing* and *tao wen-hsüeh* (see his *Tai yü Chang*, pp. 73-75). I, However, recognize Chang's *liang-chih* as distinct in being primarily an epistemological category, but consider it to be still in the mold of Wang's conception of *liang-chih* because I do not believe the issue between Ch'eng-Chu and Lu-Wang in the area of knowledge to be one of "intellectualism" versus "antiintellectualism" but one concerning the relationship between mind as the knowing subject and *li* or Nature as the object to be known.
117. *Meng-tzu tzu-i shu-cheng*, pp. 14-15.
118. See for instance, *ibid.*, pp. 9, 17-19, 21-22, 24-25, 33-36, 45-46, 53-54.
119. *Ibid.*, pp. 14-15.
120. Ch'eng, *Tai Chen's Inquiry into Goodness*, p. 20.
121. *Meng-tzu tzu-i shu-cheng*, p. 29.
122. This characterization of Tai and Chang is derived from Ying-shih Yü's *Tai yü Chang*, pp. 69-73 83-87.

Appendix

1. *Imperial Catalogue*, 125:4b-5a.
2. See *Chung-wen ta tz'u-tien*, 8:27.
3. Ch'ü Wan-li, *A Catalogue of the Chinese Rare Books in the Gest Collection of the Princeton University* (Taipei: Yee-wen Publishing, 1974), p. 289.
4. *Chih-shen lu* (1679), Chiao Hung's preface, pp. 1a-b.
5. *Imperial Catalogue*, 125:4b.
6. *Ibid.*, 146:7a.
7. *Ibid.*, 193:3b.
8. *Ibid.*, 62:3b.
9. *Ibid.*, 146:3b.
10. *Ibid.*, 41:11b.

Glossary

(Excludes authors' names and book titles which appear in the bibliography)

ai 隘
An-feng 安豐
an-jen 安人
ao 傲
Chan Jo-shui 湛若水
Ch'an 禪
ch'an-jao 纏繞
Chang Chiu-ch'eng 張九成
Chang Fu 張復
Chang Hsiao-hsiang 張孝祥
chang-ku 掌故
Chang Shih 張栻
Chang Yü-hu chi 張于湖集
Ch'ang-hsün 常洵
Ch'ang-lo 常洛
ch'ang-sheng 長生
ch'ang wu-yu 常無有
chao (illuminate) 照
Chao (surname) 趙
Che-tung hsüeh-shu 浙東學術

chen (firmness) 貞
chen (genuine, truth) 眞
chen-ch'ang 眞常
chen-ho 眞和
chen-hsin 眞心
chen-ju 眞如
Chen Te-hsiu 眞德秀
chen-tsai 眞宰
Chen-wu ying 振武營
Ch'en Ch'ien-shih 陳乾室
Ch'en Hsiang-tao 陳祥道
Ch'en Kang 陳剛
Ch'en Kuan 陳瓘
Ch'en Shan 陳山
Ch'en Yü-pi 陳于陛
Cheng (surname) 鄭
cheng (uprightness) 正
cheng-chi 正集
Cheng-chi (Ch'en Kang's courtesy
    name) 正己

Cheng Ch'iao 鄭樵
cheng-hsin 正心
Cheng Hsüan 鄭玄
cheng-hsüeh 正學
cheng-li 正理
cheng-ming 正名
cheng-shih 正史
Cheng-te 正德
cheng-yen jo-fan 正言若反
ch'eng 誠
Ch'eng Chien 成覸
Ch'eng-Chu 程朱
ch'eng-hsin 成心
Ch'eng-kao 成皐
ch'eng-li 撑犁
Ch'eng-tsu 成祖
Ch'eng-wen ch'u-pan she 成文出
版社
chi (dwell) 寄
chi (egoism) 己
chi (occasion) 機
chi (practice, trace) 迹
chi (tranquil) 寂
chi-feng 機鋒
chi-shih chung 給事中
Chi-tsang 吉藏
chi-tse 極則
ch'i (material force, ether) 氣
ch'i (open up) 啟
Ch'i (state) 齊
ch'i-chih 氣質
ch'i-chih chih hsing 氣質之性
ch'i chih ching-shuang 氣之精爽
ch'i-ch'ing 七情
ch'i-chü chu 起居注
ch'i-chung erh-ti 七種二諦
Ch'i-hsia ssu 棲霞寺
Ch'i-hsin lun 起信論
ch'i-hua 氣化
ch'i-ming pu-ch'ü 其名不去

ch'i nan-tzu 奇男子
Ch'i-shou wei 旗手衞
Ch'i-tiao K'ai 漆雕開
Ch'i-tu wei 騎都尉
Ch'i-wu lun 齊物論
Ch'i-yen lü-hsi 七言律細
chia 家
chia-ch'eng yeh-shih 家乘野史
chia-chieh 假借
Chia-ching 嘉靖
chia-fa 家法
chia-hsüeh 家學
Chia-hsün kuei-hsin p'ien 家訓
歸心篇
chia-kuan 假觀
Chiang (river) 江
Chiang Ch'ien 江謙
chiang-hsüeh 講學
chiang-kuan 講官
Chiang-ning 江寧
chiang-yu 講友
ch'iang-chih 强制
ch'iang-t'an li-so 强探力索
chiao 教
Chiao-ch'ou lüeh 校讎略
Chiao Jo-hou wen-ta 焦弱侯問答
chiao-li che 校理者
Chiao-shih lei-hsüan man-chin-t'ai
焦氏類選蔓金苔
Chiao-shih lei-lin 焦氏類林
Chiao-yu lun 交友論
ch'iao 巧
ch'iao-yen 巧言
chieh (control, regulated) 節
chieh (explicate) 解
chieh (*śīla*) 戒
Chieh (tyrant) 桀
Chieh-min 節愍
Chieh-sha fang-sheng wen 戒殺放
生文

chieh-shen k'ung-chü 戒愼恐懼
chieh-t'o 解脫
chieh-yin 接引
ch'ieh-chi 切己
ch'ieh-shen 切身
ch'ieh-shih kung-fu 切實功夫
chien 見
chien-hsin 見心
chien-ju 賤儒
Chien-wen 建文
Ch'ien-fu chang 千夫長
ch'ien-hou 前後
Ch'ien-hu 千戶
ch'ien-shih 前識
Ch'ien-t'ang 錢塘
chih (control) 制
chih (grasp, cling to) 執
chih (intended meaning, morally discriminating will) 志
chih (obstruction) 滯
chih (order) 治
chih (point to) 指
Chih (robber) 跖
chih (stop) 止
chih ch'i-so 止其所
chih-chieh 智解
chih-chieh sheng-yin 直接生因
chih-chih 致知
chih chih ching-li 治之經理
chih-chih hun-yü 滯窒昏愚
chih-chih jen-hsin 直指人心
chih-fei 知非
Chih-fu 知府
chih hsiao-t'i chih wei jen 知孝弟之為仁
chih-hsing 知性
Chih-hsü 智旭
chih-hui 智慧
chih-jen 至人
chih-kuei 指歸

chih-li 支離
chih-ming 致命
Chih-shen lu 致身錄
chih-shih (denotation of events) 指事
chih-shih (knowledge) 知識
Chih-t'an 支談
chih-tao 致道
chih-wei 之謂
chih-yen 知言
ch'ih-chih yu-ku yen-chih ch'eng-li 持之有故言之成理
ch'ih t'ien-chih-ming wei-shih wei-chi 救天之命惟時惟幾
chin (advance, gain) 進
Chin (state) 晉
Chin-hsi 金溪
chin-hsin 盡心
chin-hsing 盡性
chin-hsing chih-ming 盡性致命
Chin-hsüeh chih 京學志
Chin-ling k'o-ching ch'u 金陵刻經處
Chin-ling ts'ung-shu 金陵叢書
chin-shih 進士
Chin-shih-tzu chang 金師子章
Chin-ssu lu 近思錄
Chin-su ju-lai 金粟如來
Ch'in 秦
Ching (Duke of Ch'i) 齊景公
ching (situation) 境
ching (tranquillity, quiescence) 靜
ching-chao hsüeh 京兆學
ching-fu 敬父
ching-i chih-nei 敬以直內
ching-ming-miao hsin 淨明妙心
ching-li 經歷
Ching-nan 靖難
ching-shu 精熟
Ching-ti 景帝

ching-tso 靜坐
Ching-tz'u 淨慈
ching-wen 敬文
ch'ing 情
ch'ing-chih-jao hsing-chih-li 情之
　饒性之離
ch'ing-chih-ying 情之應
ch'ing-fang yüan-ch'ih 清方愿勅
Ch'ing-liang shan 清涼山
ch'ing-t'an 清談
chiu-hsü 舊序
chiu-miu 糾繆
Chiu T'ang-shu 舊唐書
ch'iung-li 窮理
Chou (Duke) 周公
Chou Ju-teng 周汝登
Chou Li 周禮
Chou-pi suan-ching 周髀算經
Chou Tun-i 周敦頤
ch'ou-tzu jo-shih teng-yung 疇咨
　若時登庸
chu (abide) 住
chu (host, dominate) 主
chu-chang 助長
Chu Chih-fan 朱之蕃
Chu Ch'üan-tsai 朱荃宰
chu-k'ao 主考
Chu Shih-en 朱時恩
Chu Shih-lu 祝世祿
Chu Ting 朱鼎
Chu Yün-ming 祝允明
ch'u (going forth) 出
Ch'u (state) 楚
ch'u (staying put) 處
ch'u-chia 出家
ch'u-shih 出世
ch'u-shih pen-huai 出世本懷
chü 局
chü-jen 舉人
Chü-shih feng-teng lu 居士分燈錄

chü-yü-hsin 具於心
ch'ü (grasp) 取
ch'ü (yield) 詘
Ch'ü-ching 曲靖
ch'ü feng-ch'i 趣風氣
ch'ü-pieh 區別
Ch'ü Po-yü 蘧伯玉
Ch'ü Wan-li 屈萬里
chuan-chu 轉注
Ch'uan-hsi lu 傳習錄
chüan 卷
ch'üan (authority, provisional) 權
ch'üan (fish trap) 筌
ch'üan-cha 權詐
Ch'üan-fu 權扶
chuang 狀
Chuang Tzu 莊子
chuang-yüan 狀元
Chuang-yüan ts'e 狀元策
chüeh 覺
chüeh-ssu 絕思
Chüeh-ssu chi 絕四記
chüeh-tai miao 絕待妙
chüeh-yen 絕言
ch'üeh-wu 闕誤
chui-chien 追荐
ch'ui-shih 垂示
chün 君
chün-p'o 窘迫
Chün-shan lun 均善論
chung (end) 終
chung (middle, centrality, equilib-
　rium) 中
chung-ch'iao chih hao 眾竅之號
Chung-kuo shih-hsüeh ts'ung-shu
　中國史學叢書
Chung-kuo wen-hua ta-hsüeh
　ch'u-pan pu 中國文化大學
　出版部
Chung-sheng (Yün Jih-ch'u's cour-

tesy name) 仲昇
chung-shu 忠恕
Chung-wen ta-tz'u-tien 中文大辭典
Chung-yüan wen-hsien 中原文獻
Ch'ung-cheng (academy) 崇正
Ch'ung-cheng (reign) 崇禎
ch'ung-shih 充實
ch'ung-ssu 重思
Ch'ung Yü 充虞
Erh-shih-chiu tzu p'in-hui shih-p'ing 二十九子品彙釋評
Erh Ya 爾雅
Esen Tügel 也先土干
fa 法
fa-chieh 法界
fa-men 法門
fa-shen 法身
Fa-tsang 法藏
Fan-ch'ang 繁昌
Fan Ch'ih 樊遲
Fan Hung 范弘
fan-li 凡例
Fan-wang ching 梵王經
Fang Hsiao-ju 方孝孺
fang-hsin 放心
fang-pien 方便
fang-sheng 放生
fang-shih 方士
fang-te erh-hsing 放德而行
fei-chi 廢迹
fei-ch'üan fei-shih 非權非實
fen-pieh hsin 分別心
Feng Fu 馮婦
feng-su 風俗
fu (hexagram) 復
Fu (prince) 福
fu (props) 輔
fu-ch'i-ch'u 復其初
Fu-chiao p'ien 輔教篇
fu-chu-k'ao 副主考

Fu Hsi 伏羲
Fu-hsi t'u-tsan 伏羲圖贊
fu-hsing 復性
fu-hui 附會
fu-lu 附錄
fu-lun 附論
Fu Meng-ch'üan 傅夢泉
Fu-ning 福寧
Fu Pi 富弼
fu-t'ien 福田
fu-t'ung 符同
Han (river) 漢
Han Ch'ang-li chi 韓昌黎集
Han Fei Tzu 韓非子
Han-lin yüan pien-hsiu 翰林院編修
han-she 涵攝
Han Shu 漢書
Han Tzu 韓子
han-yang 涵養
Han Yü 韓愈
hao-hao hu pu-k'o shang-i 皜皜乎不可尚已
hao-jan chih-ch'i 浩然之氣
hao-sheng 好生
heng 亨
heng-fa chih-chih 橫發直指
Heng-p'u (Chang Chiu-ch'eng's courtesy name) 橫浦
ho 和
ho-che neng-yu yü-wo 何者能有於我
Ho Ch'eng-t'ien 何承天
Ho Hsin-yin 何心隱
Ho-kuan Tzu 鶡冠子
Ho Yen 何晏
ho-yu yü-wo tsai 何有於我哉
hsi 系
Hsi-ch'ao ming-ch'eng shih-lu 熙朝名臣實錄

hsi-chien 習見

Hsi Chuan 繫傳

Hsi-jung 西戎

Hsi-ming 西銘

Hsi-tsung 熹宗

Hsi Tz'u 繫辭

hsia-min 下民

Hsia T'ing-mei 夏廷美

Hsia Yün-feng 夏雲峯

Hsiang (Duke) 襄公

hsiang (image, concrete phenomenon, thing, form) 象

Hsiang An-shih 項安世

hsiang-ch'eng 相稱

hsiang-ch'ieh 相竊

hsiang-hsing 象形

hsiang-kua 象卦

hsiang-p'ing 鄉評

Hsiang Ying-hsiang 項應祥

Hsiang Yü 項羽

hsiang-yüan 鄉愿

hsiao 孝

hsiao-chü 孝具

Hsiao-hsiang chuan 小象傳

hsiao-hsin i-i 小心翼翼

Hsiao I 孝已

hsiao-jen 小人

hsiao-jung 消融

hsiao-kung 孝恭

hsiao-shun 孝順

hsiao-shuo 小說

Hsiao-tsung 孝宗

hsiao-tsung 小宗

hsiao-yu 孝友

Hsieh Liang-tso 謝良佐

hsieh-sheng 諧聲

hsieh-yin 叶音

hsien (hexagram) 咸

hsien (immortal) 仙

hsien-hsien ch'eng-ch'eng 現現
成成

hsien-ni 陷溺

hsin (mind) 心

hsin (truthfulness) 信

Hsin-an 新安

hsin-chai 心齋

Hsin-ch'i erh T'ai-shih hui-hsüan chu-shih chiu-tzu ch'üan-shu p'ing-lin 新鍥二太史彙選注釋
九子全書評林

Hsin-chien Chiao T'ai-shih hui-hsüan pai-chia p'ing-lin ming-wen chu-chi 新鍥焦太史彙選百家
評林名文珠璣

Hsin-ch'uan lu 心傳錄

Hsin-k'an Chiao T'ai-shih hsü-hsüan pai-chia p'ing-lin Ming-wen chu-chi 新刊焦太史續選
百家評林明文珠璣

Hsin-k'an Chiao T'ai-shih hui-hsüan pai-chia p'ing-lin Ming-wen chu-chi 新刊焦太史彙選
百家評林明文珠璣

hsin-shou nien-lai t'ou-t'ou shih-tao 信手拈來頭頭是道

hsin-shuo ch'ü-i 新說曲議

hsin-te 心得

hsing (enlightenment) 省

hsing (form) 形

hsing (Nature) 性

hsing-ch'a 省察

hsing-chen 性眞

hsing-ch'ing 性情

hsing-erh-hsia 形而下

hsing-erh-shang 形而上

hsing-jen 行人

Hsing Ping 刑昺

hsing-pu chu-shih 刑部主事

hsiu-yeh 修業

Hsiung-nu 匈奴

hsü 虛
Hsü Ai 徐愛
hsü-chi 續集
Hsü Hsiang-yün 徐象檺
hsü-hsüan 虛玄
Hsü Kuang-ch'i 徐光啟
hsü-li 虛理
Hsü Shen 許慎
Hsü tao-tsang 續道藏
hsüan 玄
hsüan-kung 選貢
Hsüan-ni 宣尼
hsüan-te 玄德
Hsüan-tsang 玄奘
Hsüan-tsung 宣宗
hsüeh 學
Hsüeh Chün-ts'ai 薛君采
Hsüeh Hsüan 薛瑄
Hsüeh Hui 薛蕙
hsüeh-mai 血脈
hsün-ku 訓詁
hsün-tao erh-ch'ü 循道而趣
Hsün Tzu 荀子
Hu Cheng-fu 胡正甫
hua 化
hua-fa ssu-chiao 化法四教
hua-t'a 化他
hua-t'a ch'üan-shih 化他權實
Hua-yen 華嚴
Huai-an 淮安
Huai-nan Tzu 淮南子
huan (afflication) 患
Huan (emperor) 桓
huan-chi pu-neng tzu-ch'eng-chia
  erh 患己不能自成家耳
Huan-ku (Academy) 還古書院
Huang Chang-chien 黃彰健
Huang Ju-heng 黃汝亨
Huang K'an 皇侃
Huang-Ming jen-wu k'ao
  皇明人物考
huang-pai nan-nü chih shuo
  黃白男女之說
Huang Shang-chih (T. Tsung-
  shang, H. Lung-kang) 黃尙質
  (宗商, 龍岡)
Huang Wan 黃綰
hui-i 會意
hui-kuang fan-chao 迴光返照
Hui-lin 慧琳
Hui-neng 慧能
Hui Shih 惠施
Hui-ti 惠帝
Hui-yüan 慧遠
hun-lun 渾淪
hun-t'ien shuo 渾天說
Hung-fu (Li Chih's courtesy name)
  宏甫
huo-jan yu-ch'i 豁然有契
i (arbitrariness of opinion, intended
  meaning, willfulness) 意
i (benefit) 益
i (conjecture) 億
i (rest) 倚
i (righteousness) 義
i (unified, one, oneness) 一
i (wing) 翼
i-chiao 異教
i-chien 意見
i-chien shu-ch'ang 易簡疏暢
I Chih 夷之
i-chih (meaning and reference)
  義指
i-chih (one-track mind) 一志
I Ching 易經
i-ching chih-nei 以敬直內
i-ch'ü chih-shih 一曲之士
I-ch'uan (Ch'eng I's courtesy
  name) 伊川
i-fa 已發

I-hsia lun 夷夏論
i-hsin ch'uan-hsin 以心傳心
i-jen 義人
i-kuan 一貫
i-kuei 依歸
i-li (notes on organization of a book) 義例
i-li (philosophical principles) 義理
i-li shih-chih 以理實之
i-tuan 異端
I-wen yin-shu kuan 藝文印書館
i-wu 一物
i-wu erh liang-ming 一物而兩名
I-ya 易牙
i-yüan 藝苑
jen (chary) 訒
jen (humanity) 仁
jen (letting it be) 任
jen-chi 人極
jen-hsin 人心
Jen-jen wen-k'u 人人文庫
jen-ju 忍辱
jen-min hsing 人民性
jen-t'ien chiao 人天敎
Jih-chao 日照
jih-hsin 日新
jih-sun 日損
jih-yung 日用
jo 若
Jo-hou (Chiao Hung's courtesy name) 弱侯
jou 柔
ju 乳
ju-men 入門
Juan An 阮安
Jui (Chiao Hung's elder brother) 瑞
Jun-sheng (Chiao Hung's son) 潤生
Jung-yang 滎陽

k'ai-chi hsien-pen i-tsai yü-chi 開迹顯本意在於迹
k'ai-ch'üan hsien-shih 開權顯實
k'ai-ch'üan hsien-shih i-hsü yü-ch'üan 開權顯實意須於權
K'ai-feng 開封
kan 感
kan-ching 乾淨
kang 剛
k'ang-chih 伉直
K'ang-hsi 康熙
Kao P'an-lung 高攀龍
Kao Tzu 告子
k'ao-cheng 考證
k'ao-chiu 考究
k'ao-chü 考攄
k'ao-i 考異
ken (hexagram) 艮
ken (root) 根
Keng Ting-li 耿定力
Keng Ting-lii 耿定理
ko-chih 格制
ko-i 格義
ko-wu 格物
k'o 客
kōan 公案
Kojima Ichirōuemon 小嶋市郎右衞門
ku (obstinacy) 固
ku (therefore) 故
Ku Ch'i-yüan 顧起元
Ku Huan 顧歡
ku-jen 古人
Ku-pen Lun-yü chi-chieh 古本論語集解
ku-shan 固善
ku-wen 古文
Ku-yüan 固原
k'u-ssu 苦思
kuan (contemplation) 觀

kuan (string together) 貫
Kuan Chih-tao 管志道
kuan-fu 觀復
kuan-hsin 觀心
Kuan-hsin shuo 觀心說
Kuan Tzu 管子
Kuan-yin Tzu 關尹子
Kuang-wen shu-chü 廣文書局
k'uang 狂
k'uang-Ch'an 狂禪
kuei-chü 規矩
kuei-ken 歸根
Kuei-ku Tzu 鬼谷子
Kuei Yu-kuang 歸有光
k'un (distress) 困
k'un (hexagram) 坤
kung (impartiality) 公
kung (respectful) 恭
kung-an 公案
kung-fu 工夫
kung-hu i-tuan ssu-hai yeh-i 攻乎
　異端斯害也已
kung-lun 公論
Kung-ming I 公明儀
kung-tao 公道
Kung-tu Tzu 公都子
k'ung 空
K'ung An-kuo 孔安國
k'ung-k'ung 悾悾
k'ung-k'ung ju-yeh 空空如也
K'ung Ying-ta 孔穎達
kuo 過
Kuo Cheng-yü 郭正域
Kuo-feng ch'u-pan she 國風出版社
Kuo Hsiang 郭象
kuo-shih 國史
Kuo-tzu chien 國子監
k'uo-ch'ung 擴充
Lang-mu 朗目
Lao-Chuang i 老莊翼

Lao Tzu 老子
Lao-tzu chi-chieh 老子集解
lei 類
Lei-yang 雷陽
li (Chinese mile) 里
li (gain, advantage, profit, Ricci's
　Chinese surname) 利
Li (king) 厲
li (principle) 理
li (rites, propriety) 禮
Li Ao 李翱
li-hui 理會
Li-huo lun 理惑論
Li Kuang-chin 李光縉
li-pen 立本
Li Po-min 李伯敏
Li Shih-ch'ien 李士謙
Li Ssu 李斯
Li T'ing-chi (T. Erh-chang, H.
　Chiu-wo) 李廷機 (爾張, 九我)
Li Wei-ming 李維明
li-yü-hsing 離於性
liang-chih 良知
Liang-Han ts'ui-pao p'ing-lin 兩漢
　萃寶評林
liang-hsing 兩行
Liang-Su ching-chieh 兩蘇經解
liang-wu erh i-t'i 兩物而一體
lien-hsing 練形
lien-she 蓮社
Lin Chao-en 林兆恩
Lin-chi 臨濟
ling 靈
Ling-shan 靈山
liu 流
Liu Chih-chi 劉知幾
Liu Ch'ung 劉翀
Liu Hsiang 劉向
Liu Pang 劉邦
Liu Tsung-chou 劉宗周

liu-tu 六度
lo 酪
Lo-hsüeh pien 洛學編
Lo Hung-hsien 羅洪先
Lo Ju-fang 羅汝芳
lou 陋
Lou Liang 婁諒
Lu 魯
Lu-an 魯庵
Lu-Wang 陸王
lü (concern) 慮
lü (shoe) 履
lü (*vinaya*) 律
Lü-ao 旅獒
Lü Hui-ch'ing 呂惠卿
Lü Tsu-ch'ien 呂祖謙
luan 亂
lun-hsin che 論心者
Lun-shih 論史
Lun-yü chi-pien 論語集編
Lun-yü chu-shu 論語注疏
Lun-yü ch'üan-chieh 論語全解
Lun-yü i-shu 論語義疏
Lun-yü tien-ching pu-chu 論語點睛
　補注
Lung-tzu 龍子
Ma-tsu Tao-i 馬祖道一
Man-shan kuan 曼山舘
Mao Ch'ang 毛萇
mei 昧
meng 萌
Meng Chien 孟簡
mi 迷
mi-erh pu-chüeh 迷而不覺
miao 妙
mieh 滅
mien 沔
Mien (music master) 晃
Min-ch'iu (Li Po-min's courtesy
　name) 敏求

Min Tzu-ch'ien 閔子騫
ming (destiny, mandate) 命
ming (name, concept) 名
ming-mu 名目
ming-shih 名士
ming-tao 明道
mo (branch) 末
mo (silent) 默
mo-erh chih-chih 默而識之
Mo Ti 墨翟
Mo Tzu 墨子
Mou Tzu 牟子
mu (mother) 母
mu (tend as a shepherd) 牧
Mu K'ung-hui 穆孔暉
Mu Po-ch'ien 穆伯潛
Mu-tsung 穆宗
na 呐
Naikaku Bunko 內閣文庫
Nakamura Hajime 中村元
Nan-hsüan Lun-yü chieh 南軒論
　語解
Nan-wo 南倭
nei 內
Nei-shu t'ang 內書堂
ni 逆
nien 念
nien-fo san-mei 念佛三昧
nien-nien ch'ien-liu 念念遷流
no 訥
Noda Shōuemon 野田庄右衞門
nü 女
Ou-yang Hsiu 歐陽修
Pai-ch'uan hsüeh-hai 百川學海
Pai-hei lun 白黑論
pai-hsing jih-yung 百姓日用
Pan Ku 班固
p'an-chiao 判教
P'an-shan yü-lu 盤山語錄
P'an Shih-tsao 潘士藻

P'an Ssu 潘絲
p'an-yüan 畔援
p'an-yüan hsin 攀緣心
pang-yen 榜眼
P'ang Yün 龐蘊
Pao-p'u Tzu 抱朴子
pei (commiseration) 悲
pei (perverse) 悖
Pei-chuan chi 碑傳集
Pei-lu 北虜
Pei Shih 北史
pen 本
pen-chi 本紀
pen-chih 本旨
pen-hsin 本心
pen-jan 本然
pen-ling 本領
pen-t'i 本體
P'eng (bird) 鵬
P'eng Tung-o 彭東峨
pi (blind) 蔽
pi (dogmatism, insistence) 必
pi-ching chih 畢竟治
pi-ching k'ung 畢竟空
pi-fei ch'eng-shih yeh 必非誠士也
pi-pien 必辯
piao-te 表德
pieh-chiao 別教
pien (change) 變
pien (discourse, distinguish) 辨
p'ien 偏
p'ien-chao 偏照
p'ien-ch'üan 偏全
pin 賓
po 剝
po-hsüeh 博學
Po-i 伯夷
po-na-pen 百衲本
po-shih 博士
po-ta 博大

po-wen 博文
Po-yüeh 博約
p'o 破
p'o-fa p'ien 破法遍
pu-chi 不及
pu-chih yen-i 不滯言意
pu-ch'u ch'i-wei 不出其位
pu-erh fa-men 不二法門
pu-fu 不拂
pu-jen che 不仁者
pu-kai pu-p'ien 不該不偏
pu-li wen-tzu 不立文字
pu-mieh 不滅
pu-sheng pu-mieh 不生不滅
pu-ssu 不私
pu-yen 不言
pu-yen erh hsin-chieh 不言而心解
pu-yen erh ts'un-chu hsin 不言而存
　諸心
pu yün-miao 不耘苗
P'u-t'ien 莆田
ri ichigen ron 理一元論
san-chiao ho-i 三教合一
san-chiao hsien-sheng 三教先生
san-chiao i-yüan 三教一源
San-chiao i-yüan t'u 三教一源圖
san-chiao tz'u 三教祠
San-i chiao 三一教
san-kuei 三歸
San-pao lun 三報論
san-ts'ai 三才
se 色
Seikadō Bunko 靜嘉堂文庫
shan 善
shan hui-jen 善誨人
shan-shu 善書
Shang-jao 上饒
Shang Shu 尚書
Shang-shu shu-yen 尚書疏衍
shang-te 上德

Shang-ts'ai (i.e., Hsieh Liang-tso) 上蔡

shao-yen 少言

Shao Yung 邵雍

she 射

she fu-yü 射覆盂

shen-ch'ien 深淺

Shen-ch'iu 沈邱

shen-chung chui-yüan 愼終追遠

Shen Pu-hai 申不害

Shen Tao 愼到

Shen Te-fu 沈德符

Shen-tsung 神宗

Shen Tzu 申子

Sheng-an wai-chi 升菴外集

Sheng-chiao hsiao-yin 聖敎小引

Sheng-hsüeh tsung-chuan 聖學宗傳

sheng-sheng 生生

sheng-sheng pu-k'o ming 繩繩不可名

sheng-su 生蘇

sheng-yüan 生員

shih (affairs) 事

shih (beginning) 始

shih (concreteness, real, reality) 實

shih (homonym of *shih* meaning "this") 時

shih (perception) 識

shih (this) 是

shih (transgression) 失

Shih Chi 史記

shih-chien fa-yao 世間法藥

Shih Ching 詩經

Shih Chung-pin 史仲彬

Shih-Han ho-ch'ao 史漢合鈔

Shih-i 十翼

shih-ju 世儒

Shih-k'uang 師曠

shih-lu 實錄

shih-lun 時論

shih shan-tao 十善道

shih-shih t'i-yen 實實體驗

shih-yü 嗜欲

shou-chüan 首卷

shu 疏

Shu Ch'eng-hsi 舒承溪

shu-su 熟蘇

shu-t'u t'ung-kuei 殊塗同歸

shu-yao 樞要

shun (obedience, following) 順

Shun (sage-ruler) 舜

Shun-t'ien 順天

shuo 說

so-i 所以

so kuei-yü che ch'ün-yen chih-chung che 所貴於折羣言之衷者

Sonkeikaku Bunko 尊經閣文庫

ssu (self-centeredness) 私

ssu (think, intellection) 思

ssu (this) 斯

ssu-ch'an 四禪

ssu-chü 四句

ssu-i 私意

Ssu-k'u 四庫

Ssu-k'u ch'üan-shu chien-ming mu-lu 四庫全書簡明目錄

ssu-lu 思路

Ssu-ma T'an 司馬談

Ssu-ming ts'ung-shu 四明叢書

ssu-ping 四病

Ssu-shih-erh chang ching hsü 四十二章經序

ssu-wu 四勿

su 俗

Su Ch'e 蘇轍

su-hsüeh 俗學

Su-shen 肅愼

Su Shih 蘇軾

Su-shu k'an-wu 俗書刊誤

Su Tung-p'o 蘇東坡

sui-chi chih-tien 隨機指點
sui-chih 隨智
sui-ch'ing 隨情
Sui Shu 隋書
sui-shun 隨順
sui-t'a-i yü 隨他意語
sui-wen chu-i 隨文逐義
Sun K'o-wang 孫可望
Sun K'uang (T. Wen-jung, H. Yüeh-feng) 孫鑛(文融, 月峯)
Sun-wu Tzu 孫武子
Sung (state) 宋
Sung-hsüeh yüan-yüan chi 宋學淵源記
Sung Shih 宋史
Sung shih-lu 宋實錄
Sung Shu 宋書
ta-ch'ang 大常
ta-cheng 大政
ta-chih 大旨
Ta-chu Hui-hai 大球慧海
ta-hsiao 大小
Ta-hui Tsung-kao 大慧宗杲
ta-jen 大人
ta-li ssu ch'eng 大理寺丞
Ta-liang 大梁
ta-tao pu-ch'eng 大道不稱
Ta-tien 大顛
ta-tsung 大宗
t'ai-chi 太極
T'ai-chi t'u 太極圖
T'ai-chi-t'u shuo 太極圖說
T'ai-chia 太甲
T'ai-chou 泰州
t'ai-hsü 太虛
T'ai-tsu 太祖
T'ai-wan hsüeh-sheng shu-chü 台灣學生書局
t'ai-yen 太嚴
t'an-to 貪多

T'ang 棠
T'ang Pin 湯斌
T'ang Shu 唐書
T'ang Shun-chih 唐順之
tao (guide) 道
tao (plundering) 盜
Tao (Way) 道
Tao-an 道安
tao-chih kung-tsai 道之工宰
Tao-hsin 道心
tao-te ti hsing-shang hsüeh 道德的形上學
Tao-t'i 道體
tao wen-hsüeh 道問學
te 德
te-ch'i-i 得其一
Te-ch'ing 德清
T'eng 滕
ti-ch'u 滌除
ti-erh-i 第二義
t'i (rabbit snare) 蹄
t'i (substance) 體
t'i-ch'a 體察
t'i-hu 醍醐
t'i-hui 體會
t'i-t'ang fu ch'i-ch'i 倜儻負奇氣
T'i-wei po-li ching 提謂波利經
t'ien 天
t'ien-hsin 天心
t'ien-kuan 天官
t'ien-lai 天籟
t'ien-li 天理
t'ien-ming 天命
T'ien-t'ai 天台
t'ien-ti chih-hsing 天地之性
t'ien-tse 天則
T'ing-kao erh-chang 庭誥二章
to 多
to-shao 多少
to-shao wu-fa 多少無法

to-shih 多事
to-wen to-chien 多聞多見
to-yen 多言
Tsai-wo 宰我
ts'an-ho yü-hsin 參合於心
tsang-chiao 藏教
ts'ang-ts'ang 蒼蒼
Ts'ao Pin 曹鈖
Ts'ao Ta-hsien 曹大咸
ts'e 册
Tseng Tzu 曾子
tso (forced reasoning) 鑿
tso (work) 作
Tso Chuan 左傳
Tso Kuei 左奎
tso-shih 做事
tso-yung chien-hsing 作用見性
Tsou Shou-i 鄒守益
Tsou Te-han 鄒德涵
Tsou Te-p'u 鄒德溥
Tsu-hsin 祖心
ts'u 麁
tsuan-hsiu-kuan 纂修官
tsun te-hsing 尊德性
ts'un-yang 存養
tsung 宗
tsung-chih 宗旨
Tsung-kao 宗杲
Tsung Ping 宗炳
Ts'ung-shu chi-ch'eng 叢書集成
tu 篤
tu-shu 讀書
tu-te 獨得
t'u-lao 徒勞
t'u-tseng chien-chieh 徒增見解
tuan (beginning) 端
tuan (judge) 斷
Tuan Yü-ts'ai 段玉裁
t'ui 退
Tung-hai 東海

Tung-kuan Han-chi 東觀漢紀
Tung-p'o chih-lin 東坡志林
tung-ta 洞達
t'ung (penetrate) 通
t'ung (same) 同
t'ung-chiao 通教
t'ung-chih 同知
t'ung-i 統一
t'ung-k'ao-kuan 同考官
T'ung-shu 通書
tzu (diligent) 孜
tzu (philosopher, child) 子
Tzu-chang 子張
tzu-chih (self-knowledge) 自知
tzu-chih (self-stopping) 自止
Tzu-ching (Lu Hsiang-shan's courtesy name) 子靜
tzu-chüeh 自覺
tzu-chung 自重
Tzu-hsia 子夏
tzu-hsia 自狹
Tzu-hsia shih chih chien-ju 子夏氏之賤儒
tzu-hsiang mao-tun 自相矛盾
tzu-hsiao 自小
tzu-hsin 自信
tzu-hsing 自行
tzu-hsing ch'üan-shih 自行權實
tzu-i yüan 自意語
tzu-jan 自然
Tzu-kung 子貢
tzu-li 自立
tzu-lien 自戀
tzu-pao che 自暴者
Tzu-ssu 子思
tzu-te 自得
tzu-tsu 自足
Tzu-tu 子都
Tzu-yu 子游
tzu-yu chu-tsai 自有主宰

Tzu-yüan (Fu Meng-ch'üan's courtesy name) 子淵
Tzu-yung (Keng Ting-lii's courtesy name) 子庸
tz'u (compassion, kindly) 慈
tz'u (this) 此
Tz'u Hai 辭海
Tz'u-hu i-shu 慈湖遺書
tz'u-jang 辭讓
Tz'u-lin li-kuan piao 詞林歷官表
tz'u-pei 慈悲
Uriyanqad (Wu-liang-ha) 兀良哈
wai 外
Wan Chang 萬章
wan-ch'üan tzu-tsu 完全自足
Wan-li 萬曆
wan-tuan 輓斷
wang 妄
Wang An-shih 王安石
Wang Chi 王畿
wang-chi 忘己
Wang Chin 王瑾
Wang Ch'un-fu 王純甫
Wang Fu 王浮
Wang Hou-chih 王厚之
wang-hsiang 妄想
Wang Ken 王艮
wang-nien 妄念
Wang Nien-sun 王念孫
Wang Pi (226–249) 王弼
Wang Pi (1511–1587) 王襞
Wang Shih-chen 王世貞
Wang Ssu-ching 王嗣經
Wang Tao 王道
Wang T'ing-hsiang 王廷相
Wang Tsung-mu 王宗沐
Wang T'ung 王通
wang-yeh 王業
Wang Ying-lin 王應麟
Wang Yüan-chen 王元貞

Wang Yüan-jui 王元瑞
wei 僞
wei-chih 謂之
wei-fa 未發
wei-jen 爲仁
Wei-liao Tzu 尉繚子
wei-shih yu-shih 未始有始
wei-yen 微言
Wen (Duke of T'eng) 滕文公
Wen (King) 文王
Wen-chieh (Chiao Hung's father) 文傑
Wen-chung Tzu 文中子
wen-hsüeh 問學
Wen-tuan 文端
Wen T'ung 文通
Wen-yen chuan 文言傳
Weng Cheng-ch'un 翁正春
wo (contamination) 涴
wo (egotism) 我
Wu (King) 武王
wu (matter, thing, thingness) 物
wu (Nothingness) 無
wu-ch'ang 五常
wu-chi 無極
wu-ch'i-p'o 無棲泊
wu-chiao 五教
wu-chien 無見
wu-chih 無知
wu chih ch'u-hsin 吾之初心
wu-ching erh-ching 無靜而靜
Wu-ch'iu-pei chai Lao-tzu chi-ch'eng 無求備齋老子集成
wu ch'iung-chin 無窮盡
wu-chung chih-chin 五種之禁
wu-fang 無方
wu-hsi 無繫
Wu Hsiang-hsiang 吳湘相
wu-hsin 無心
wu-hsing 五行

wu-i-hao t'o-ni tai-shui 無一毫拖泥帶水
Wu-kou chü-shih 無垢居士
wu-kuan 五官
Wu-k'ung 悟空
Wu-lüeh (Chiao Hung's ancestor) 武略
wu-lun 五倫
wu-ming (ignorance) 無明
wu-ming (nameless) 無名
wu-pien 無邊
wu p'ien-i 無偏倚
wu p'ing-chü 無憑據
wu pu-pei 無不備
wu-shih 無事
Wu Tao-nan 吳道南
wu-tsung 吾宗
wu tzu-hsing 無自性
wu-tung 無動
wu-wai 無外
wu-wei 無為
wu-wo 無我
wu-yen 無言
wu-yen ch'i-chih 無言契之
Wu-yen lü-hsi 五言律細
Wu Yü 吳棫
yang 陽
Yang-cheng t'u-chieh 養正圖解
yang-ch'i 養氣
Yang Ch'i-yüan 楊起元
Yang Chien 楊簡
Yang Chu 楊朱
Yang Shen 楊慎
Yang Sheng-an 楊升菴
Yang Shih 楊時
yao (component line) 爻
yao (essentials) 要
Yao (sage-ruler) 堯
Yeh-huo pien 野獲編
Yeh-lü Ch'u-ts'ai 耶律楚材

yeh-shih 野史
Yeh Tsun 葉遵
Yen (Prince) 燕王
Yen Chih-t'ui 顏之推
Yen-chou shih-liao 弇州史料
yeh-erh-yü-chih 厭而飫之
Yen Hui 顏回
yen-tao che 言道者
Yen Tzu (Yen Hui) 顏子
Yen Tzu 晏子
Yen Yen-chih 顏延之
Yen Yüan (1635–1704) 顏元
Yen Yüan (Yen Hui) 顏淵
yin 陰
Yin (Barrier Keeper) 尹
yin (guide) 引
yin-cheng 印證
Yin-fu ching 陰符經
yin-k'o 印可
Yin-wen Tzu 尹文子
yin-yang 陰陽
ying 應
Ying (Prince of Ch'u) 楚王英
Ying-t'ien fu-hsüeh 應天府學
Ying-tsung 英宗
ying-yung 應用
yu (being) 有
yu (fraternal) 友
Yu (King) 幽王
yu (via) 由
yu-erh-jou-chih 優而柔之
yu-hsi fei-hsi yu-nu fei-nu 有喜非喜有怒非怒
yu-shih 有始
Yu Tso 游酢
yu wei-shih fu wei-shih yu-shih 有未始夫未始有始
yu-wu 有無
yü (desire) 欲
Yü (sage-ruler) 禹

yü (subsume) 寓
Yü-an 愚菴
Yü-kung chieh 禹貢解
Yü-t'ang ts'ung-yü 玉堂叢語
yü-te 諭德
Yü Yüeh 俞樾
yüan 元
yüan-ch'i 緣起
yüan-chiao 圓敎
Yüan-chüeh ching 圓覺經
Yüan Chung-tao 袁中道
Yüan-hui (Chu Hsi's courtesy
  name) 元晦
yüan-ju i-ju yü-shih 援儒以入於釋
Yüan-tao lun 原道論

yüan-t'ou 源頭
yüan-tzu hsing-hsing 原自惺惺
yüan-wai-lang 員外郎
yüeh (music) 樂
Yüeh (place name) 越
yüeh (simplicity) 約
Yüeh-ya t'ang ts'ung-shu 粵雅堂
  叢書
yün 蕰
Yün-han 雲漢
Yün Jih-ch'u 惲日初
yün-tung 運動
yung 用
Yung-lo 永樂

Selected Bibliography

Literature in Chinese and Japanese

Araki Kengo 荒木見悟. *Mindai shisō kenkyū* 明代思想研究. Tokyo: Sōbunsha, 1972.

Ashikaga Enjutsu 足利衍述. "Sō igo ni okeru sankyō chōwa no kōgai to sono sankō shomoku" 宋以後に於ける三教調和梗概と其參考書目. *Tōyō tetsugaku* 東洋哲學 (1909), 16(2–3):61–65, 54–58.

Chan Wing-tsit 陳榮捷. "Lun *Ming-ju hsüeh-an chih shih-shuo*" 論明儒學案之師說. *Yu-shih yüeh-k'an* 幼獅月刊 (July 1978), 48(1):6–8.

Chang Hsüeh-ch'eng 章學誠. *Wen-chi* 文集. In *Chang-shih i-shu* 章氏遺書. Chiayeh t'ang edition, 1922.

———. *Wen-shih t'ung-i* 文史通義. In *Chang-shih i-shu*.

Chang Ping-lin 章炳麟. *Ch'ung-ting Ch'i-wu lun shih* 重訂齊物論釋. In *Chang-shih ts'ung-shu* 章氏叢書, 12th *ts'e*. Shanghai: Yu-wen she, 1916.

Chang Tsai 張載. *Chang-tzu ch'üan-shu* 張子全書. Shanghai: Commercial Press, 1935.

Chao Ch'i 趙歧. *Meng Tzu* 孟子. Ssu-pu ts'ung-k'an edition.

Ch'en Hsien-chang 陳獻章. *Pai-sha Tzu ch'üan-chi* 白沙子全集. Taipei: Commercial Press, 1973.

Ch'en Ti 陳第. *Ch'ü-Sung ku-yin i* 屈宋古音義. Ming-pien chai edition, 1863.

——— *Mao-shih ku-yin k'ao* 毛詩古音考. Ming-pien chai edition, 1863.

Ch'en Tso-lin 陳作霖. *Shang-yüan Chiang-ning hsiang-t'u ho-chih* 上元江寧鄉土合志. Nanking: Chiang-Ch'u pien-i shu-chü, 1910.

Ch'eng-ch'ien 承遷. *Chu Chin-shih-tzu chang* 註金師子章. In *Dai Nihon zoku zōkyō* 大日本續藏經, ser. 1, pt. 2, case 8, 1:75b–78b.

Ch'eng Hao 程顥 and Ch'eng I 程頤. *Ho-nan Ch'eng-shih i-shu* 河南程氏遺書. Shanghai: Commercial Press, 1935.

—— *Ho-nan Ch'eng-shih wai-shu* 河南程氏外書. In *Erh-Ch'eng ch'üan-shu* 二程全書, Ssu-pu pei-yao edition.

Chi Wen-fu 嵇文甫. *Tso-p'ai Wang-hsüeh* 左派王學. Shanghai: K'ai-ming shu-tien, 1934.

—— *Wan-Ming ssu-hsiang shih-lun* 晚明思想史論. Chungking: Commercial Press, 1944.

Ch'i-sung 契嵩. *T'an-chin wen-chi* 鐔津文集. In *Taishō shinshū daizōkyō* 大正新修大藏經 52(2115): pp. 646–750.

Chia K'ai 甲凱. *Sung-Ming hsin-hsüeh p'ing-shu* 宋明心學評述. Taipei: Commercial Press, 1967.

Chiang Fan 江藩. *Han-hsüeh shih-ch'eng chi* 漢學師承記. Taipei: Commercial Press, 1964.

Chiang Po-ch'ien 蔣伯潛. *Meng Tzu* 孟子. In Shen Chih-fang 沈知方, ed., *Yü-i kuang-chieh ssu-shu* 語譯廣解四書. Taipei: Ch'i-ming shu-chü, 1952.

Chiang Yung 江永. *Chin-ssu lu chi-chu* 近思錄集注. In a combined volume which also contains *Chou-tzu t'ung-shu* 周子通書 and *Hsiao-hsüeh chi-chu* 小學集注. Taipei: Chung-hua shu-chü, 1966.

Chiao Hsün 焦循. *Lun-yü pu-shu* 論語補疏. In *Chiao-shih ts'ung-shu* 焦氏叢書. Ch'ing, Chia-ch'ing period.

—— *Lun-yü t'ung-shih* 論語通釋. In *Mu-hsi-hsien ts'ung-shu* 木犀軒叢書. 1883–91.

Chiao Hung 焦竑. *Chiao-shih pi-cheng cheng-hsü* 焦氏筆乘正續. Taipei: Commercial Press, 1971.

—— *Chuang-tzu i* 莊子翼. Taipei: Kuang-wen shu-chü, 1970.

—— *Fa-hua ching ching-chieh p'ing-lin* 法華經精解評林. In *Dai Nihon zoku zōkyō*, ser. 1, case 93, 1:29a–77b.

—— *I-ch'üan* 易筌. Xerox copy of the rare Ming edition (Chiao Hung's preface dated 1612) preserved in the Naikaku Bunko, Tokyo.

—— *Kuo-ch'ao hsien-cheng lu* 國朝獻徵錄. Taipei: T'ai-wan hsüeh-sheng shu-chü, 1965.

—— *Kuo-shih ching-chi chih* 國史經籍志. Ch'ang-sha: Commercial Press, 1939.

—— *Lao-tzu i* 老子翼. Taipei: Kuang-wen shu-chü, 1962.

—— *Leng-chia ching ching-chieh p'ing-lin* 楞伽經精解評林. In *Dai Nihon zoku zōkyō*, ser. 1, case 91, 2:194b–224b.

—— *Leng-yen ching ching-chieh p'ing-lin* 楞嚴經精解評林. In *Dai Nihon zoku zōkyō*, ser. 1, case 90, 3:163a–236b.

—— *Tan-yüan chi* 澹園集. Chin-ling ts'ung-shu edition.

—— *Tan-yüan hsü-chi* 澹園續集. Chin-ling ts'ung-shu edition.

—— *Yin-fu ching chieh* 陰符經解. In Ch'en Chi-ju 陳繼儒, ed., *Pao-yen t'ang pi-chi* 寶顏堂秘笈. Reprint, Wen-ming shu-chü, 1922.

—— *Yüan-chüeh ching ching-chieh p'ing-lin* 圓覺經精解評林. In *Dai Nihon zoku zōkyō*, ser. 1, case 94, 1:1a–26b.

Ch'ien Mu 錢穆. *Chu-tzu hsin hsüeh-an* 朱子新學案. Taipei: San-min shu-chü, 1971.

—— *Chung-kuo chin san-pai nien hsüeh-shu shih* 中國近三百年學術史. Taipei: Commercial Press, 1968.

Ch'ien Ta-hsin 錢大昕. *Shih-chia chai yang-hsin lu* 十駕齋養新錄. Shanghai: Commercial Press, 1935.

Chih-i 智顗. *Miao-fa lien-hua ching hsüan-i* 妙法蓮花經玄義. *Taishō shinshū daizōkyō*, 33(1716):681–814.

—— *Miao-fa lien-hua ching wen-chü* 妙法蓮花經文句. *Taishō shinshū daizōkyō*, 34(1718):1–149.

—— *Mo-ho chih-kuan* 摩訶止觀. *Taishō shinshū daizōkyō*, 56(1911):1–140.

Chih-yüan 智圓. *Hsien-chü p'ien* 閑居篇. In *Dai Nihon zoku zōkyō*, ser. 1, pt. 2, case 6, 1:27a–108a.

Chin-kang pan-jo po-lo-mi ching 金剛般若波羅蜜經. *Taishō shinshū daizōkyō*, 8(235):748–52.

Chin Yü-fu 金毓黻. *Chung-kuo shih-hsüeh shih* 中國史學史. Taipei: Commercial Press, 1960.

Chin Yün-ming 金雲銘. *Ch'en Ti nien-p'u* 陳第年譜. Fukien: Hsieh-ho University, 1946.

Ch'ing-ting ssu-ku ch'üan-shu tsung-mu 欽定四庫全書總目. Shanghai: Ta-tung shu-chü, 1930.

Chou I 周易. Ssu-pu pei-yao edition.

Chu Hsi 朱熹. *Chu-tzu ch'üan-shu* 朱子全書. 1714.

—— *Chu-tzu yü-lei* 朱子語類. Ying-yüan shu-yüan edition, 1872.

—— *Chu Wen-kung wen-chi* 朱文公文集. Ssu-pu ts'ung-k'an edition.

—— *Ssu-shu chi-chu* 四書集注. Ssu-pu pei-yao edition.

Chu-hung 袾宏. *Yün-ch'i fa-hui* 雲棲法彙. Nanking: Chin-ling k'o-ching ch'u, 1899.

Ch'ü Ju-chi 瞿汝稷, ed. *Chih-yüeh lu* 指月錄. Taipei: Chen-shan-mei ch'u-pan she, 1968.

Fu-ning fu-chih 福寧府志. Taipei: Ch'eng-wen ch'u-pan she, 1967.

Hou Wai-lu 侯外廬 et al. *Chung-kuo ssu-hsiang t'ung-shih* 中國思想通史. Vols. 4A–B, 5. Peking: Jen-ming ch'u pan she, 1963.

Hsia Hsieh 夏燮. *Ming t'ung-chien* 明通鑑. Peking: Chung-hua shu-chü, 1959.

Hsiu-ning hsien-chih 休寧縣志. Taipei: Ch'eng-wen ch'u-pan she, 1970.

Hsü Fu-kuan 徐復觀. *Chung-kuo ssu-hsiang-shih lun-chi* 中國思想史論集. T'ai-chung: Tung-hai University, 1959.

Hsü Sze-in (Hsü Shih-ying) 許世英. *Chung-kuo mu-lu-hsüeh shih* 中國目錄學史. Taipei: Chung-hua wen-hua ch'u-pan shih-yeh wei-yüan hui, 1954.

Hsü Tzu 徐鼒. *Hsiao-tien chi-chuan* 小腆紀傳. Taipei: Bank of Taiwan, 1963.

—— *Hsiao-tien chi-nien* 小腆紀年. Taipei: Bank of Taiwan, 1962.

Hu Chü-jen 胡居仁. *Chü-yeh lu* 居業錄. Cheng-i t'ang edition.

Huan-ku shu-yüan chih 還古書院志. Xerox copy of the 1741 edition preserved in the

Naikaku Bunko, Tokyo.

Huang Tsung-hsi 黃宗羲. *Ming-ju hsüeh-an* 明儒學案. Taipei: Shih-chieh shu-chü, 1965.

—— and Ch'üan Tsu-wang 全祖望. *Sung-Yüan hsüeh-an* 宋元學案. Taipei: Shih-chieh shu-chü, 1965.

Hui-hai 慧海. *Chu-fang men-jen ts'an-wen yü-lu* 諸方門人參問語錄. In *Dai Nihon zoku zōkyō*, ser. 1, pt. 2, case 15, 5:427–33.

—— *Tun-wu ju-tao yao-men lun* 頓悟入道要門論. In *Dai Nihon zoku zōkyō*, ser. 1, pt. 2, case 15, 5:420–26.

Hui-k'ai 慧開. *Wu-men kuan* 無門關. In *Ch'an-hsüeh ta-ch'eng* 禪學大成. 2:1–23. Taipei: Chung-hua Fo-chiao wen-hua kuan, 1969.

Hui-ming 慧明. *Wu-teng hui-yüan* 五燈會元. N.p. 1906.

Imahama Michitaka 今浜通隆. *Jukyō to "gengo" kan* 儒教と「言語」觀. Tokyo: Ryūkan shoin, 1978.

Jao Tsung-i 饒宗頤. "San-chiao lun yü Sung-Chin hsüeh-shu" 三教論與宋晉學術. *Tung-hsi wen-hua* 東西文化 (May 1968), 9:24–32.

—— *Chung-kuo shih-hsüeh shang chih cheng-t'ung lun* 中國史學上之正統論. Hong Kong: Lung-men shu-tien, 1977.

Juan Chih-sheng 阮芝生. "Hsüeh-an t'i-ts'ai yüan-liu ch'u-t'an" 學案體裁源流初探. In Tu Wei-yün 杜維運 and Huang Chin-hsin 黃進興, eds., *Chung-kuo shih-hsüeh-shih lun-wen hsüan-chi* 中國史學史論文選集, pp. 574–96. Taipei: Hua-shih ch'u-pan she, 1976.

Jung Chao-tsu 容肇祖. "Chiao Hung chi ch'i ssu-hsiang" 焦竑及其思想. *Yen-ching hsüeh-pao* 燕京學報 (1938), 23:1–45.

—— *Li Chih nien-p'u* 李贄年譜. Peking: San-lien shu-tien, 1957.

Kaji Nobuyuki 加地伸行. *Chūgokujin no ronrigaku* 中國人の論理學. Tokyo: Chūō kōron sha, 1977.

Keng Ting-hsiang 耿定向. *Keng T'ien-t'ai hsien-sheng ch'üan-shu* 耿天台先生全書. Wu-ch'ang: Wu-ch'ang cheng-hsin yin-shu kuan, 1925.

—— *Keng T'ien-t'ai hsien-sheng wen-chi* 耿天台先生文集. Taipei: Wen-hai ch'u-pan she, 1970.

Koyanagi Shigeta 小柳司氣太. "Minmatsu no sankyō kankei" 明末の三教關係. In *Takase Hakushi kanreki kinen Shinagaku ronsō* 高瀬博士還曆紀念支那學論叢, pp. 349–70. Tokyo: Kobundō, 1931.

—— "Sankyō sōgo ni kansuru tenseki no nisan" 三教相互に關する典籍の二三. In *Tokiwa Hakushi kanreki kinen Bukkyō ronsō* 常盤博士還曆紀念佛教論叢, pp. 69–76. Tokyo: Kobundō, 1933.

Ku Yen-wu 顧炎武. *Jih-chih lu* 日知錄. 1795.

Kubota Ryōen 久保田量遠. *Shina Judōbutsu sankyō shiron* 支那儒道佛三教史論. Tokyo: Tōhō shoin, 1930.

Kuo T'ing-hsün 過庭訓. *Pen-ch'ao fen-sheng jen-wu k'ao* 本朝分省人物考. Taipei: Ch'eng-wen ch'u-pan she, 1971.

Lao-tzu hua-hu ching 老子化胡經. In *Taishō shinshū daizōkyō*, 54(2139):1266–70.

Li Chih 李贄. *Fen-shu hsü fen-shu* 焚書續焚書. Peking: Chung-hua shu-chü, 1975.

—— *Ts'ang-shu* 藏書. Peking: Chung-hua shu-chü, 1974.

Li Tsung-t'ung 李宗侗. *Chung-kuo shih-hsüeh shih* 中國史學史. Taipei: Chung-hua wen-hua ch'u-pan shih-yeh she, 1964.

Liang Ch'i-ch'ao 梁啟超. *Chung-kuo chin san-pai nien hsüeh-shu shih* 中國近三百年學術史. Taipei: Chung-hua shu-chü, 1962.

Lin K'o-t'ang 林科棠. *Sung-ju yü Fo-chiao* 宋儒與佛教. Taipei: Commercial Press, 1966.

Liu Jo-yü 劉若愚. *Cho-chung chih* 酌中志. Shanghai: Commercial Press, 1935.

Liu Mi 劉謐. *San-chiao p'ing-hsin lun* 三教平心論. In *Taishō shinshū daizōkyō* 52(2117):781–94.

Liu Ts'un-yan 柳存仁. "Ming-ju yü Tao-chiao" 明儒與道教. *Hsin-ya hsüeh-pao* 新亞學報 (1967), 8(1):259–96.

Lo Ch'in-shun 羅欽順. *K'un-chih chi* 困知記. 1622.

Lo Hsiang-lin 羅香林. "T'ang-tai san-chiao chiang-lun k'ao" 唐代三教講論考. *Tung-fang wen-hua* 東方文化 (1954), 1(1):85–97.

Lo Kuang 羅光. *Ju-chia hsing-shang hsüeh* 儒家形上學. Taipei: Chung-hua wen-hua ch'u-pan shih-yeh wei-yüan hui, 1957.

Lu Hsiang-shan 陸象山. *Lu Hsiang-shan ch'üan-chi* 陸象山全集. Hong Kong: Kuang-chih shu-chü, n.d.

Ma Ting-po 馬定波. *Chung-kuo Fo-chiao hsin-hsing shuo chih yen-chiu* 中國佛教心性說之研究. Taipei: Cheng-chung shu-chü, 1978.

Mai Chung-kuei 麥仲貴. *Wang-men chu-tzu chih-liang-chih hsüeh chih fa-chan* 王門諸子致良知學之發展. Hong Kong: Chinese University of Hong Kong, 1973.

Mano Senryū 間野潛龍. "Mindai ni okeru sankyō shishō—toku ni Rin Chōon o chūshin toshite" 明代における三教思想―特に林兆恩を中心として. *Tōyō-shi kenkyū* 東洋史研究 (1952), 12(1):18–34.

—— "Yōmeigaku to Jubutsu ronsō—toku ni Choko shoin o chūshin toshite" 陽明學と儒佛論爭―特に姚江書院を中心として. *Shinagakuhō* 支那學報 (1956), 1:12–22.

—— "Rin Chōon to sono chosaku ni tsuite" 林兆恩とその著作について, *Shimizu Hakushi tsuitō kinen Mindai shi ronsō* 清水博士追悼紀念明代史論叢, pp. 421–56. Tokyo: Daian, 1962.

—— *Shūshi to Ō Yōmei* 朱子と王陽明. Tokyo: Shimizu shoin, 1974.

Ming Shih 明史. Peking: Chung-hua shu-chü, 1974.

Ming shih-lu 明實錄. Nan-kang 南港, Taiwan: Academia Sinica, 1962–66.

Mou Tsung-san 牟宗三. *Chih ti chih-chüeh yü Chung-kuo che-hsüeh* 智的直覺與中國哲學. Taipei: Commercial Press, 1971.

—— *Fo-hsing yü pan-jo* 佛性與般若. Rev. ed. Taipei: T'ai-wan hsüeh-sheng shu-chü, 1979.

—— *Hsin-t'i yü hsing-t'i* 心體與性體. 3 vols. Taipei: Cheng-chung shu-chü, 1970–73.

—— *Ming-chia yü Hsün-tzu* 名家與荀子. Taipei: T'ai-wan hsüeh-sheng shu-chü, 1979.

—— *Ts'ung Lu Hsiang-shan tao Liu Chi-shan* 從陸象山到劉蕺山. Taipei: T'ai-wan hsüeh-sheng shu-chü, 1979.

Naitō Torajirō 內藤虎次郎. *Shina shigaku shi* 支那史學史. Tokyo: Kōbundō, 1950.

Nan Huai-chin 南懷瑾. "Sung-Ming li-hsüeh yü Ch'an-tsung" 宋明理學與禪宗. *K'ung-Meng hsüeh pao* 孔孟學報 (April 1972), 23:23–37.

Ogawa Kan'ichi 小川貫一. "Koji Bukkyō no kinsei teki hatten" 居士佛教の近世的發展. *Ryūkoku Daigaku ronshū* 龍谷大學論集 (1950), no. 333, pp. 46–75.

Ōkubo Eiko 大久保英子. *Min Shin jidai shoin no kenkyū* 明清時代書院の研究. Tokyo: Kokusho kankōkai, 1976.

P'an Tseng-hung 潘曾紘. *Li Wen-ling wai-chi* 李溫陵外紀. Taipei: Wei-wen t'u-shu ch'u-pan she, 1977.

P'eng Shao-sheng 彭紹升. *Chü-shih chuan* 居士傳. 1878.

P'i Hsi-jui 皮錫瑞. *Ching-hsüeh li-shih* 經學歷史. Hong Kong: Chung-hua shu-chü, 1973.

Sakai Tadao 酒井忠夫. *Chūgoku zensho no kenkyū* 中國善書の研究. Tokyo: Kōbundō, 1960.

Seng-chao 僧肇. *Chao Lun* 肇論. In *Taishō shinshū daizōkyō*, 45(1858):150–60.

Seng-yu 僧佑. *Hung-ming chi* 弘明集. In *Taishō shinshū daizōkyō*, 52(2102):1–96.

Shen I-kuan 沈一貫. *Ming chuang-yüan t'u-k'ao* 明狀元圖考. Shuang-feng shu-wu edition, 1875.

Shen Shih-jung 沈士榮. *Hsü yüan-chiao lun* 續原教論. Nanking: Chin-ling k'o-ching ch'u, 1875.

Shigematsu Toshiaya 重松俊章. "Shina sankyōshi jō no jakan no mondai" 支那三教史上の若干の問題. *Shien* 史淵 (1939), 21:125–52.

Shih Huang 施璜, Shih Huan 施潃, and Fang Yün-ch'un 方允淳, eds., *Huan-ku shu-yüan chih* 還古書院志. Xerox copy of an early Ch'ing edition (prefaces by Shih Huan and Fang Yün-ch'un dated 1741) preserved in the Naikaku Bunko, Tokyo.

Shimada Kenji 島田虔次. *Shūshigaku to Yōmeigaku* 朱子學と陽明學. Tokyo: Iwanami shoten, 1967.

Shimizu Taiji 清水泰次. "Mindai ni okeru shūkyō yūgō to kōkakaku" 明代に於る宗教融合と功過格. *Shichō* 史潮 (1936), 6(3):29–55.

Sueki Takehiro 末木剛博. *Tōyō no gōri shisō* 東洋の合理思想. Tokyo: Kōdansha, 1975.

Sun Ch'eng-tse 孫承澤. *Ch'un-ming meng-yü lu* 春明夢餘錄. Ku-hsiang chai edition, 1883.

Sun Ch'i-feng 孫奇逢. *Li-hsüeh tsung-chuan* 理學宗傳. Hangchow: Che-chiang shu-chü, 1880.

Ta-ch'eng ch'i-hsin lun 大乘起信論. In *Taishō shinshū daizōkyō*, 32(1666):575–93.

Ta-fang-kuang yüan-chüeh hsiu-to-lo liao-i ching 大方廣圓覺修多羅了義經. In *Taishō shinshū daizōkyō*, 17(842):913–22.

Ta-fo-ting ju-lai mi-yin hsiu-cheng liao-i chu p'u-sa wan-hsing shou-leng-yen ching 大佛頂如來密因修證了義諸菩薩萬行首楞嚴經. In *Taishō shinshū daizōkyō*,

19(945):105–55.

Ta-pan-jo po-lo-mi-to ching 大般若波羅蜜多經. In *Taishō shinshū daizōkyō*, 5(220): 1–1074; 6(220):1–1073; 7(220):1–1110.

Ta pan-nien-p'an ching 大般涅槃經. In *Taishō shinshū daizōkyō*, 7(374):365–603.

Tai Chen 戴震. *Meng-tzu tzu-i shu-cheng* 孟子字義疏證. Peking: Chung-hua shu-chü, 1961.

—— *Tai Tung-yüan chi* 戴東原集. Shanghai: Commercial Press, 1929.

Takao Giken 高雄義堅. "Unsei Daishi Shukō ni tsuite" 雲棲大師袾宏に就て. *Naitō Hakushi shōju kinen shigaku ronsō* 内藤博士頌壽紀念史學論叢, pp. 215–72. Kyoto: Sōbundō, 1930.

T'ang Chün-i 唐君毅. *Chung-kuo che-hsüeh yüan-lun: yüan-tao p'ien* 中國哲學原論：原道篇. 3 vols. Hong Kong: Hsin-ya shu-yüan yen-chiu so, 1973–74.

—— *Chung-kuo che-hsüeh yüan-lun: tao-lun p'ien* 導論篇. Rev. ed. Hong Kong: Hsin-ya shu-yüan yen-chiu so, 1974.

—— *Chung-kuo che-hsüeh yüan-lun: yüan-hsing p'ien* 原性篇. Rev. ed. Hong Kong: Hsin-ya shu-yüan yen-chiu so, 1974.

—— *Chung-kuo che-hsüeh yüan-lun: yüan-chiao p'ien* 原敎篇. Hong Kong: Hsin-ya shu-yüan yen-chiu so, 1975.

T'ang Yung-t'ung 湯用彤. *Han-Wei liang-Chin Nan-Pei-Ch'ao Fo-chiao shih* 漢魏兩晉南北朝佛敎史. Taipei: Commercial Press, 1965.

—— *Wei-Chin hsüan-hsüeh lun-kao* 魏晉玄學論稿. Peking: Jen-min ch'u-pan she, 1957.

Tao-hsüan 道宣. *Kuang hung-ming chi* 廣弘明集. In *Taishō shinshū daizōkyō*, 52(2103):97–361.

Tao-yüan 道原. *Ching-te ch'uan-teng lu* 景德傳燈錄. Ssu-pu ts'ung-k'an edition.

T'ao Tsung-i 陶宗儀. *Nan-ch'un ch'o-keng lu* 南村輟耕錄. Peking: Chung-hua shu-chü, 1959.

T'ao Wang-ling 陶望齡. "Fang-sheng pien-huo" 放生辨惑. In T'ao Tsung-i and T'ao T'ing 陶珽 eds., *Shuo-fu fu-hsü* 說郛附續, 30:1a–5a. Wei-wan shan-t'ang edition, 1647.

Tokiwa Daijō 常盤大定. *Shina ni okeru Bukkyō to Jukyō Dōkyō* 支那における佛敎と儒教道教. Tokyo: Tōyō bunko, 1930.

Tsa a-han ching 雜阿含經. In *Taishō shinshū daizōkyō*, 2(99):1–273.

Ts'ai Jen-hou 蔡仁厚. *Sung-Ming li-hsüeh: Pei-Sung p'ien* 宋明理學：北宋篇. Rev. ed. Taipei: T'ai-wan hsüeh-sheng shu-chü, 1979.

—— *Sung-Ming li-hsüeh: Nan-Sung p'ien* 南宋篇. Taipei: T'ai-wan hsüeh-sheng shu-chü, 1980.

Tsung-mi 宗密. *Chung-hua ch'uan hsin-ti Ch'an-men shih-tzu ch'eng-hsi t'u* 中華傳心地禪門師資承襲圖. In *Dai Nihon zoku zōkyō*, ser. 1, pt. 2, case 15, 5:433b–38b.

—— *Yüan-jen lun* 原人論. In *Taishō shinshū daizōkyō*, 45(1886):707–10.

Tu Wei-yün 杜維運. *Ch'ing Ch'ien-Chia shih-tai chih shih-hsüeh yü shih-chia* 清乾嘉時代之史學與史家. Taipei: National Taiwan University, 1962.

—— "Ch'ing sheng-shih ti hsüeh-shu kung-tso yü k'ao-chü hsüeh ti fa-chan"

清盛世的學術工作與考據學的發展. In *Shih-hsüeh chi wai-kuo-shih yen-chiu lun-chi* 史學及外國史研究論集, pp. 144–52. Taipei: Ta-lu tsa-chih she, 1967.

Wan Ssu-t'ung 萬斯同. *Shih-yüan wen-chi* 石園文集. 1935.

Wang Hsien-ch'ien 王先謙. *Chuang-tzu chi-chieh* 莊子集解. In a combined volume which also contains *Lieh-tzu chu* 列子注. Taipei: Shih-chieh shu-chü, 1962.

—— *Hsün-tzu chi-chien* 荀子集解. Taipei: Shih-chieh shu-chü, 1968.

Wang Wei-ch'eng 王維誠. "Lao-tzu hua-hu shuo k'ao-cheng" 老子化胡說考證. *Kuo-hsüeh chi-k'an* 國學季刊 (1934), 4(2):147–268.

Wang Yang-ming 王陽明. *Wang Yang-ming ch'üan-chi* 王陽明全集. Hong Kong: Kuang-chih shu-chü, 1959.

Wei-mo-chieh so-shuo Ching 維摩詰所說經. In *Taishō shinshū daizōkyō*, 14(475): 537–57.

Yamashita Ryūji 山下竜二. *Yōmeigaku no kenkyū* 陽明學の研究. 2 vols. Tokyo: Gendai jōhō sha, 1971.

Yanagida Seizan 柳田聖山. *Rinzai roku* 臨濟錄. Tokyo: Daizō shuppan kabushiki kaisha, 1972.

Yang Ch'i-ch'iao 楊啟樵. "Ming-tai chu-ti chih ch'ung-shang fang-shu chi ch'i ying-hsiang" 明代諸帝之崇尚方術及其影响. *Hsin-ya shu-yüan hsüeh-shu nien-k'an* 新亞書院學術年刊 (1962), 4:71–147.

Yang Li-ch'eng 楊立誠 and Chin Pu-ying 金步瀛. *Chung-kuo ts'ang-shu-chia k'ao-lüeh* 中國藏書家考略. Hangchow: Chekiang Provincial Library, 1929.

Yao Ming-ta 姚名達. *Chung-kuo mu-lu-hsüeh shih* 中國目錄學史. Taipei: Commercial Press, 1965.

Yeh Ch'ang-chih 葉昌熾. *Ts'ang-shu chi-shih shih* 藏書紀事詩. Shanghai: Ku-tien wen-hsüeh ch'u-pan she, 1958.

Yeh Shao-chün 葉紹鈞. *Hsün Tzu* 荀子. Shanghai: Commercial Press, 1934.

Yen Ling-feng 嚴靈峯, ed. *Wu-ch'iu-pei chai Lun-yü chi-ch'eng* 無求備齊論語集成. Taipei: I-wen yin-shu kuan, 1966.

Yü Ying-shih 余英時. *Lun Tai Chen yü Chang Hsüeh-ch'eng* 論戴震與章學誠. Hong Kong: Lung-men shu-tien, 1976.

Yüan-wu K'o-ch'in 圓悟克勤. *Pi-yen lu* 碧巖錄. In *Ch'an-hsüeh ta-ch'eng*, 1:1–264. Taipei: Chung-hua Fo-chiao wen-hua kuan, 1969.

Literature in English

Bauer, Walter. *Orthodoxy and Heresy in Earliest Christianity*. 1934. Philadelphia: Fortress Press, 1971.

Beasley, W. G., and E. G. Pulleyblank, eds. *Historians of China and Japan*. London: Oxford University Press, 1961.

Berling, Judith. *The Syncretic Religion of Lin Chao-en*. New York: Columbia University Press, 1980.

Bleicher, Josef. *Contemporary Hermeneutics*. London: Routledge and Kegan Paul, 1980.

Blofeld, John. *The Zen Teaching of Hui Hai.* London: Rider, 1969.

Bloom, Irene. "Notes on Knowledge Painfully Acquired: A Translation and Analysis of the *K'un-chih Chi* by Lo Ch'in-shun (1465–1547)." Ph.D. dissertation, Columbia University, 1976.

Bodde, Derk, trans. *A History of Chinese Philosophy.* 2 vols. Princeton: Princeton University Press, 1952–53.

Chan, Wing-tsit. "Chu Hsi's Appraisal of Lao Tzu." *Philosophy East and West* (April 1975), 25(2):131–44.

—— "Chu Hsi's Completion of Neo-Confucianism." *Etudes Song* (1973), ser. 2, no. 1, pp. 59–90.

—— "The Evolution of the Confucian Concept of *Jen.*" *Philosophy East and West* (January 1955), 4(4):295–319.

—— trans. *Instructions for Practical Living and Other Neo-Confucian Writings by Wang Yang-ming.* New York: Columbia University Press, 1964.

—— "The Neo-Confucian Solution of the Problem of Evil." *Bulletin of the Institute of History and Philology, Academia Sinica* (1959), 28:773–91.

—— trans. *Reflections on Things at Hand.* New York: Columbia University Press, 1967.

—— *A Source Book in Chinese Philosophy.* Princeton: Princeton University Press, 1969.

—— trans. *The Way of Lao Tzu.* Indianapolis: Bobbs-Merrill, 1963.

Ch'en, Kenneth. *Buddhism in China.* Princeton: Princeton University Press, 1964.

—— *The Chinese Transformation of Buddhism.* Princeton: Princeton University Press, 1973.

Cheng, Chung-ying. "Rejoinder to Michael Levin's Comments on the Paradoxicality of the *Kōans.*" *Journal of Chinese Philosophy* (June 1976), 3(3):291–97.

—— *Tai Chen's Inquiry into Goodness.* Honolulu: East-West Center Press, 1971.

—— "On *Yi* as a Universal Principle of Specific Application in Confucian Morality." *Philosophy East and West* (July 1972), 22(3):269–80.

—— "On Zen (Ch'an) Language and Zen Paradoxes." *Journal of Chinese Philosophy* (1973), 1:77–102.

Chien, Edward T. "The Conception of Language and the Use of Paradox in Buddhism and Taoism." *Journal of Chinese Philosophy* (December 1984), 11(4):375–99.

—— "The Neo-Confucian Confrontation with Buddhism: A Structural and Historical Analysis." *Journal of Chinese Philosophy* (September 1982), 9(3): 307–28.

—— "The Transformation of Neo-Confucianism as Transformative Leverage." *Journal of Asian Studies* (February 1980), 34(2):255–58.

Ching, Julia, trans. *The Philosophical Letters of Wang Yang-ming.* Columbia: University of South Carolina Press, 1972.

—— *To Acquire Wisdom: The Way of Wang Yang-ming.* New York: Columbia University Press, 1976.

Cleary, Thomas, and J. C. Cleary, trans. *The Blue Cliff Record.* Boulder: Shambhala, 1977.

Cohen, Paul A. *China and Christianity.* Cambridge: Harvard University Press, 1963.

Conze, Edward, trans. *Buddhist Scriptures.* Baltimore: Penguin, 1971.

——, trans. *Buddhist Wisdom Books, Containing the Diamond Sutra and the Heart Sutra.* New York: Harper, 1972.

Dauenhauer, Bernard P. *Silence: The Phenomenon and its Ontological Significance.* Bloomington: Indiana University Press, 1980.

De Bary, Wm. Theodore. "Buddhism and the Chinese Tradition." *Diogenes* (1964), 47: 102–24.

—— Irene Bloom, eds. *Principle and Practicality.* New York: Columbia University Press, 1979.

—— et al., eds. *The Buddhist Tradition.* New York: Modern Library, 1969.

—— et al., eds. *Sources of Chinese Tradition.* 2 vols. New York: Columbia University Press, paperback ed. 1964.

—— and the Conference on Ming Thought. *Self and Society in Ming Thought.* New York: Columbia University Press, 1970.

—— and the Conference on Seventeenth-Century Chinese Thought. *The Unfolding of Neo-Confucianism,* New York: Columbia University Press, 1975.

Derrida, Jacques. *Of Grammatology,* trans. by Gayatri Chakravorty Spivak. Baltimore: Johns Hopkins University Press, 1976.

—— *Writing and Difference,* trans. by Alan Baas. Chicago: University of Chicago Press, 1978.

Dien, Albert E. "Yen Chih-t'ui (531–591 +): A Buddho-Confucian." In Arthur F. Wright and Denis Twitchett, eds., *Confucian Personalities,* pp. 43–64. Stanford: Stanford University Press, 1962.

Dimberg, Ronald G. *The Sage and Society: The Life and Thought of Ho Hsin-yin.* Honolulu: University Press of Hawaii, 1974.

Dobson, W. A. C. H., trans. *Mencius.* Toronto: University of Toronto Press, 1963.

Dubs, H. H. *The Works of Hsüntze.* London: Arthur Probsthain, 1928.

Dumoulin, Heinrich. *A History of Zen Buddhism.* New York: McGraw-Hill, 1965.

Farlow, John King. "On 'On Zen Language and Zen Paradoxes': Anglo-Saxon Questions for Cheng Chung-ying." *Journal of Chinese Philosophy* (September 1983), 10(3):285–98.

Foucault, Michel. *The Archaeology of Knowledge,* trans. by A. M. Sheridan-Smith. New York: Harper & Row, 1976.

Fu, Charles Wei-hsun. "Morality or Beyond: the Neo-Confucian Confrontation with Mahāyāna Buddhism." *Philosophy East and West* (July 1973), 23(3): 375–96.

Gadamer, Hans-Georg. *Truth and Method,* 2d ed., 1965. Ed. by Garrett Barden and John Cumming. New York: Seabury Press, 1975.

Gedalecia, David. "Excursion into Substance and Function." *Philosophy East and West* (October 1974), 24(4):443–51.

Goodrich, L. Carrington, and Chaoying Fang, eds. *Dictionary of Ming Biography, 1368–1644.* 2 vols. New York: Columbia University Press, 1976.

Graham, A. C. "The Background of Mencius' Theory of Human Nature." *Tsinghua Journal of Chinese Studies* (1967), 6(1–2):215–71.

—— *Two Chinese Philosophers: Ch'eng Ming-tao and Ch'eng Yi-ch'uan.* London: Lund Humphries, 1958.

Hakeda, Yoshito S., trans. *The Awakening of Faith Attributed to Aśvaaghosha.* New York: Columbia University Press, 1967.

Hartman, Sven S., ed. *Syncretism.* Stockholm: Almqvist and Wiksell, 1969.

Ho, Ping-ti. *The Ladder of Success in Imperial China.* New York: Columbia University Press, 1962.

Hu Shih. "The Scientific Spirit and Method in Chinese Philosophy." In Charles A. Moore, ed., *The Chinese Mind*, pp. 104–31. Honolulu: University of Hawaii Press, 1967.

Huang, Siu-chi. *Lu Hsiang-shan: A Twelfth-Century Chinese Idealist Philosopher.* New Haven: American Oriental Society, 1944.

Hummel, Arthur, ed. *Eminent Chinese of the Ch'ing Period.* Taipei: Literature House, 1964.

Hurvitz, Leon. "Chih I." Ph.D. dissertation, Columbia University, 1959.

——, trans. *Scripture of the Lotus Blossom of the Fine Dharma.* New York: Columbia University Press, 1976.

Koseki, Aaron K. "The Concept of Practice in San-lun Thought: Chi-tsang and the 'Concurrent Insight' of the Two Truths." *Philosophy East and West* (October 1981), 31(4):440–66.

Lau, D. C. "The Treatment of Opposites in Lao Tzu." *Bulletin of the School of Oriental and African Studies* (1959), 21:344–60.

——, trans., *Lao Tzu: Tao Te Ching.* Baltimore: Penguin, 1972.

——, trans. *Mencius.* Baltimore: Penguin, 1970.

Legge, James, trans. *The Chinese Classics.* 5 vols. in 4. Taipei: Wen-shih-che ch'u-pan she, 1971.

—— *The I Ching: The Book of Changes.* New York: Dover, 1963.

Levenson, Joseph. *Confucian China and Its Modern Fate: A Trilogy*, Berkeley: University of California Press, 1968.

Levin, Michael. "Comments on the Paradoxicality of Zen *Kōans.*" *Journal of Chinese Philosophy* (June 1976), 3(3):281–90.

Liang, Ch'i-ch'ao. *Intellectual Trends in the Ch'ing Period*, trans. by Immanuel Hsü. Cambridge: Harvard University Press, 1959.

Liebenthal, Walter. *Chao Lun: The Treatises of Seng-chao.* Hong Kong: Hong Kong University Press, 1968.

—— "The Immortality of the Soul in Chinese Thought." *Monumenta Nipponica* (1952), 8:327–97.

Liu, Shu-hsien. "How Idealistic Is Wang Yang-ming?" *Journal of Chinese Philosophy* (June 1983), 10(2):147–68.

Liu, Ts'un-yan. "Lu Hsi-hsing: A Confucian Scholar, Taoist Priest, and Buddhist Devotee of the Sixteenth Century." *Asiatische Studien* (1965), 18–19:115–42.

—— "The Penetration of Taoism into the Ming Neo-Confucian Elite." *T'oung Pao* (1971), 57(1–4):31–102.

Lonegan, Bernard. "The Concept of *Verbum* in the Writings of St. Thomas Acquinas." *Theological Studies* (1946), 7:349–92; (1947), 8:35–39, 406–44; (1949), 10:3–40, 359–93.

Luk, Charles (Lu K'uan-yü), trans. *The Śūraṅgama Sūtra.* London: Rider, 1966.

—— trans. *The Vimalakīrti Nirdeśa Sūtra.* Berkeley and London: Shambala, 1972.

Metzger, Thomas A. *Escape from Predicament.* New York: Columbia University Press, 1977.

Mote, F. W. "Notes on the Life of T'ao Tsung-i." *Kyoto University zimbun-kagaku kenkyūjo, Silver Jubilee Volume*, pp. 279–93. Kyoto: Kyoto University, 1954.

Nakamura, Hajime. *Ways of Thinking of Eastern Peoples.* Honolulu: East-West Center Press, 1964.

Nivison, David. *The Life and Thought of Chang Hsüeh-ch'eng.* Stanford: Stanford University Press, 1966.

Palmer, Richard E. *Hermeneutics.* Evanston: Northwestern University Press, 1969.

Parkes, Graham. "The Wandering Dance: Chuang Tzu and Zarathustra." *Philosophy East and West* (July 1983), 33(3):235–50.

Rachewiltz, Igor de. "Yeh-lü Ch'u-ts'ai (1189–1243): Buddhist Idealist and Confucian Statesman." In Arthur F. Wright & Denis Twitchett, eds., *Confucian Personalities*, pp. 189–216. Stanford: Stanford University Press, 1962.

Robinson, Richard H. *Early Mādhyamika in India and China.* Madison: University of Wisconsin Press, 1967.

Russel, Geffrey B. *Dissent and Reform in the Early Middle Ages.* Berkeley: University of California Press, 1965.

Said, Edward W. *Beginnings.* Baltimore: Johns Hopkins University Press, 1975.

Schloegl, Irmgard, trans. *The Zen Teaching of Rinzai.* Berkeley: Shambala, 1976.

Shih, Vincent Y. C. "Hsün Tzu's Positivism." *Tsing-hua Journal of Chinese Studies* (February 1964), 4(2):162–73.

Takakusu, Junjirō. *The Essentials of Buddhist Philosophy.* Honolulu: Office Appliance Co., 1956.

T'ang, Chün-i. "Chang Tsai's Theory of Mind and Its Metaphysical Basis." *Philosophy East and West* (July 1956), 4(2):113–36.

Taylor, Rodney L. "Proposition and Praxis: The Dilemma of Neo-Confucian Syncretism." *Philosophy East and West* (April 1982), 32(2):187–99.

Tong, Lik Kuen. "The Meaning of Philosophical Silence: Some Reflections on the Use of Language in Chinese Thought." *Journal of Chinese Philosophy* (March 1976), 3(2):169–83.

Tu, Wei-ming. *Humanity and Self-Cultivation: Essays in Confucian Thought.* Berkeley: Asian Humanities Press, 1979.

—— *Neo-Confucian Thought in Action: Wang Yang-ming's Youth (1472–1509).* Berkeley: University of California Press, 1976.

Waley, Arthur, trans. *The Analects of Confucius.* New York: Vintage Books, 1938.

Ware, James, trans. *The Sayings of Confucius.* New York: New American Library, 1955.

Watson, Burton, trans. *The Complete Works of Chuang Tzu.* New York: Columbia University Press, 1968.

—— *Hsün Tzu: Basic Writings.* New York: Columbia University Press (1963).

Wilhelm, Richard, and Cary F., Baynes, trans. *The I Ching.* New York: Pantheon, 1961.

Wright, Dale S. "The Significance of Paradoxical Language in Hua-yen Buddhism." *Philosophy East and West* (July 1982), 32(3): 325–38.

Yampolsky, Philip B., trans. *The Platform Sutra of the Sixth Patriarch.* New York: Columbia University Press, 1967.

Yeh, Michelle. "The Deconstructive Way: a Comparative Study of Derrida and Chuang Tzu." *Journal of Chinese Philosophy* (June 1983), 10(2): 95–126.

Yü, Chün-fang. *The Renewal of Buddhism in China: Chu-hung and the Late Ming Synthesis.* New York: Columbia University Press, 1981.

Yü, Ying-shih. "Some Preliminary Observations on the Rise of Ch'ing Confucian Intellectualism." *Tsing-hua Journal of Chinese Studies* (1975), 11:105–44.

Zürcher, E. *The Buddhist Conquest of China,* Leiden: E. J. Brill, 1959.

Index

Neo-Confucian Studies

Modern Asian Literature Series

Translations from the Oriental Classics

Studies in Oriental Culture

Companions to Asian Studies

Introduction to Oriental Civilizations

Wm. Theodore de Bary, Editor

Sources of Japanese Tradition 1958	Paperback ed., 2 vols., 1964
Sources of Indian Tradition 1958	Paperback ed., 2 vols., 1964
Sources of Chinese Tradition 1960	Paperback ed., 2 vols., 1964